Reactive Messaging Patterns with the Actor Model

Reactive Messaging Patterns with the Actor Model

Applications and Integration in Scala and Akka

Vaughn Vernon

✦Addison-Wesley

New York • Boston • Indianapolis • San Francisco
Toronto • Montreal • London • Munich • Paris • Madrid
Capetown • Sydney • Tokyo • Singapore • Mexico City

Many of the designations used by manufacturers and sellers to distinguish their products are claimed as trademarks. Where those designations appear in this book, and the publisher was aware of a trademark claim, the designations have been printed with initial capital letters or in all capitals.

The author and publisher have taken care in the preparation of this book, but make no expressed or implied warranty of any kind and assume no responsibility for errors or omissions. No liability is assumed for incidental or consequential damages in connection with or arising out of the use of the information or programs contained herein.

For information about buying this title in bulk quantities, or for special sales opportunities (which may include electronic versions; custom cover designs; and content particular to your business, training goals, marketing focus, or branding interests), please contact our corporate sales department at corpsales@pearsoned.com or (800) 382-3419.

For government sales inquiries, please contact governmentsales@pearsoned.com.

For questions about sales outside the U.S., please contact international@pearsoned.com.

Visit us on the Web: informit.com/aw

Library of Congress Cataloging-in-Publication Data
Vernon, Vaughn.
  Reactive messaging patterns with the Actor model : applications and integration in Scala and Akka / Vaughn Vernon.
     pages   cm
  Includes bibliographical references and index.
  ISBN 978-0-13-384683-6 (hardcover : alk. paper)
  1. Scala (Computer program language) 2. Application software—Development. 3. Computer multitasking—Mathematics. 4. Java virtual machine. 5. Business enterprises—Data processing. I. Title.
  QA76.73.S28V47 2016
  005.2'762—dc23

2015016389

ISBN-13: 978-0-13-384683-6
ISBN-10: 0-13-384683-0

Text printed in the United States on recycled paper at RR Donnelley in Crawfordsville, Indiana.
Second printing, November 2015

To my dearest Nicole and Tristan.
Your continued love and support are uplifting.

Contents

Foreword

When Carl Hewitt invented the Actor model in the early 1970s he was way ahead of his time. Through the idea of actors he defined a computational model embracing nondeterminism (assuming all communication being asynchronous), which enabled concurrency and, together with the concept of stable addresses to stateful isolated processes, allowed actors to be decoupled in both time and space, supporting distribution and mobility.

Today the world has caught up with Hewitt's visionary thinking; multicore processors, cloud computing, mobile devices, and the Internet of Things are the norm. This has fundamentally changed our industry, and the need for a solid foundation to model concurrent and distributed processes is greater than ever. I believe that the Actor model can provide the firm ground we so desperately need in order to build complex distributed systems that are up for the job of addressing today's challenge of adhering to the reactive principles of being responsive, resilient, and elastic. This is the reason I created Akka: to put the power of the Actor model into the hands of the regular developer.

I'm really excited about Vaughn's book. It provides a much-needed bridge between actors and traditional enterprise messaging and puts actors into the context of building reactive systems. I like its approach of relying only on the fundamentals in Akka—the Actor model and not its high-level libraries—as the foundation for explaining and implementing high-level messaging and communication patterns. It is fun to see how the Actor model can, even though it is a low-level computation model, be used to implement powerful and rich messaging patterns in a simple and straightforward manner. Once you understand the basic ideas, you can bring in more high-level tools and techniques.

This book also does a great job of formalizing and naming many of the patterns that users in the Akka community have had to discover and reinvent themselves over the years. I remember enjoying reading and learning from the classic *Enterprise Integration Patterns* [EIP] by Hohpe and Woolf a few years ago, and I'm glad that Vaughn builds upon and reuses its pattern catalog, putting it in a fresh context. But I believe that the most important contribution of this book is that it does not stop there but takes the time to define and introduce a unique pattern language for actor messaging, giving us a vocabulary for how to think about, discuss, and communicate the patterns and ideas.

This is an important book—regardless if you are a newbie or a seasoned "hakker"—and I hope that you will enjoy it as much as I did.

— *Jonas Bonér*
   Founder of the Akka Project

Preface

Today, many software projects fail. There are various surveys and reports that show this, some of which report anywhere from 30 to 50 percent failure rates. This number doesn't count those projects that delivered but with distress or that fell short of at least some of the prerequisite success criteria. These failures, of course, include projects for the enterprise. See the *Chaos Report* [Chaos Report], *Dr. Dobb's Journal* [DDJ], and Scott Ambler's survey results [Ambysoft].

At the same time, some notable successes can be found among companies that use Scala and Akka to push the limits of performance and scalability [WhitePages]. So, there is not only success but success in the face of extreme nonfunctional requirements. Certainly it was not Scala and Akka alone that made these endeavors successful, but at the same time it would be difficult to deny that Scala and Akka played a significant role in those successes. I am also confident that those who make use of these tools would stand by their platform decisions as ones that were key to their successes.

For a few years now it has been my vision to introduce the vast number of enterprises to Scala and Akka in the hopes that they will find similar successes. My goal with this book is to make you familiar with the Actor model and how it works with Scala and Akka. Further, I believe that many enterprise architects and developers have been educated by the work of Gregor Hohpe and Bobby Woolf. In their book, *Enterprise Integration Patterns* [EIP], they provide a catalog of some 65 integration patterns that have helped countless teams to successfully integrate disparate systems in the enterprise. I think that leveraging those patterns using the Actor model will give architects and developers the means to tread on familiar turf, besides that the patterns are highly applicable in this space.

When using these patterns with the Actor model, the main difference that I see is with the original motivation for codifying the patterns. When using the Actor model, many of the patterns will be employed in greenfield applications, not just for integration. That is because the patterns are first and foremost *messaging patterns,* not just integration patterns, and the Actor model is messaging through and through. You will also find that when implementing through the use of a Domain-Driven Design [DDD, IDDD] approach that some of the more advanced patterns, such as *Process Manager (292),* will be used to help you model prominent business concepts in an explicit manner.

Who This Book Is For

This book is for software architects and developers working in the enterprise and any software developer interested in the Actor model and looking to improve their skills and results. Although the book is definitely focused on Scala and Akka, Appendix A provides the means for C# developers on the .NET platform to make use of the patterns as well.

What Is Covered in This Book

I start out in Chapter 1, "Discovering the Actor Model and the Enterprise, All Over Again," with an introduction to the Actor model and the tenets of reactive software. Chapter 2, "The Actor Model with Scala and Akka," provides a Scala bootstrap tutorial as well as a detailed introduction to Akka and Akka Cluster. Chapter 3, "Performance Bent," then runs with a slant on performance and scalability with Scala and Akka, and why the Actor model is such an important approach for accomplishing performance and scalability in the enterprise.

This is followed by seven chapters of the pattern catalog. Chapter 4, "Messaging with Actors," provides the foundational messaging patterns and acts as a fan-out for the following five chapters. In Chapter 5, "Messaging Channels," I expand on the basic channel mechanism and explore several kinds of channels, each with a specific advantage when dealing with various application and integration challenges. Chapter 6, "Message Construction," shows you how each message must convey the intent of the sender's reason to communicate with the receiver. Chapter 7, "Message Routing," shows you how to decouple the message source from the message destination and how you might place appropriate business logic in a router. In Chapter 8, "Message Transformation," you'll dig deeper into various kinds of transformations that messages may undergo in your applications and integrations. In Chapter 9, "Message

Endpoints," you will see the diverse kinds of endpoints, including those for persistent actors and idempotent receivers. Finally, I wrap things up with Chapter 10, "System Management and Infrastructure," which provides advanced application, infrastructural, and debugging tools.

Conventions

A major part of the book is a *pattern catalog*. It is not necessary to read every pattern in the catalog at once. Still, you probably should familiarize yourself with Chapters 4 through 10 and, in general, learn where to look for details on the various kinds of patterns. Thus, when you need a given pattern, you will at least know in general where to look to find it. Each pattern in the catalog has a representative icon and will also generally have at least one diagram and source code showing how to implement the pattern using Scala and Akka.

The extensive catalog of patterns actually forms a *pattern language,* which is a set of interconnected expressions that together form a collective method of designing message-based applications and systems. Thus, it is often necessary for one pattern to refer to one or more other patterns in the catalog, as the supporting patterns form a complete language. Thus, when a pattern is referenced in this book, it is done like this: *Pattern Name (#).* That is, the specific pattern is named and then followed by the page number where the referenced pattern begins.

Another convention of this book is how messaging patterns with the Actor model are expressed in diagrams. I worked on formulating these conventions along with Roland Kuhn and Jamie Allen of Typesafe. They are coauthors of an upcoming book on a similar topic: *Reactive Design Patterns*. I wanted our books to use the same, if not similar, ways to express the Actor model in diagrams, so I reached out to Roland and Jamie to discuss. The following shows the conventions that we came up with.

As shown in Figure P.1, actors are represented as circular elements and generally named with text inside the circle. One of the main reasons for this is that

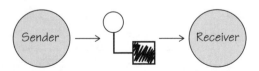

Figure P.1 A Sender actor sends a message to a Receiver actor.

Gul Agha used this notation long ago in his book *Actors: A Model of Concurrent Computation in Distributed Systems* [Agha, Gul].

Further, a message is represented as a component in much the same way that *Enterprise Integration Patterns* [EIP] does, so we reused that as well. The lines with arrows show the source and target of the message. You can actually distinguish a persistent actor (long-lived) from an ephemeral actor (short-lived) using the notations shown in Figures P.2 and P.3. A persistent actor has a solid circular border. Being a persistent actor just means that it is long-lived. It does not necessarily mean that the actor is persisted to disk, but it could also mean that. On the other hand, an ephemeral actor has a dashed circular border. It is one that is short-lived, meaning that it is created to perform some specific tasks and is then stopped.

Figure P.2 A persistent or long-lived actor

Figure P.3 An ephemeral or short-lived actor

One actor can create another actor, as shown in Figure P.4, which forms a parent-child relationship. The act of creation is represented as a small circle surrounded by a large circle and takes the form similar to a message being sent

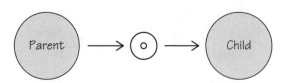

Figure P.4 A parent actor creates a child actor.

from the parent to the child. This is because the process of child actor creation is an asynchronous operation.

Actor self-termination is represented by a special message—a circle with an *X* inside—being sent from the actor to itself, as shown in Figure P.5. Again, this is shown as a message because termination is also an asynchronous operation.

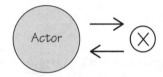

Figure P.5 Actor self-termination

One actor terminating another actor is shown as the same special message directed from one actor to another. The example in Figure P.6 shows a parent terminating one of its children.

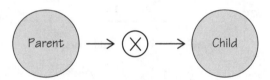

Figure P.6 One actor terminates another actor.

An actor's lifeline can be represented similar to that of a Unified Modeling Language (UML) sequence diagram, as shown in Figure P.7. Messages being received on the lifeline are shown as small circles (like pinheads). You must recognize that each message receipt is asynchronous.

A parent's child hierarchy can be represented as a triangle below the parent with child actors inside the triangle. This is illustrated by Figure P.8.

An actor may learn about other actors using endowment or introduction. Endowment is accomplished by giving the endowed actor a reference to other actors when it is constructed. On the other hand, an actor is introduced to another actor by means of a message.

Introduction, as shown in Figure P.9, is represented as a dotted line where the actor being introduced is placed into a message that is sent to another

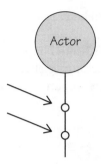

Figure P.7 An actor's lifeline is shown as two asynchronous messages are received.

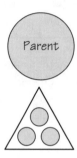

Figure P.8 An actor's child hierarchy

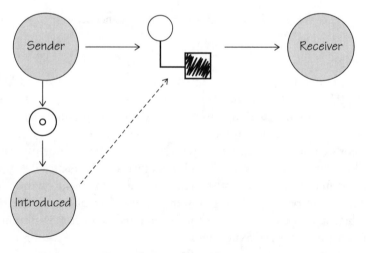

Figure P.9 A child actor is introduced by a sender to the receiver
by means of a message.

actor. In this example, it is a child actor that is being created by a parent that is introduced to the receiver.

Finally, message sequence is shown by sequence numbers in the diagram in Figure P.10. The fact that there are two 2 sequences and two 4 sequences is not an error. This represents an opportunity for concurrency, where each of the repeated sequences show messages that are happening at the same time. In this example, the router is setting a timer and sending a message to receiver concurrently (steps 2). Also, the timer may elapse before a response can be sent by the receiver (steps 3). If the receiver's response is received by the router first, then the client will receive a positive confirmation message as sequence 4. Otherwise, if the timer elapses first, then the client will receive a timeout message as sequence 4.

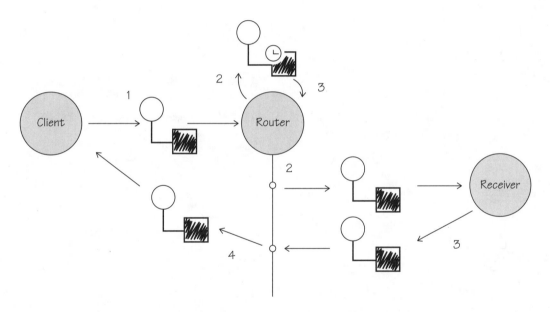

Figure P.10 Message sequence and concurrency are represented by sequence numbers.

Acknowledgments

I'd like to express many thanks to Addison-Wesley for selecting this book to publish under their distinguished label. I once again got to work with Chris Guzikowski and Chris Zahn as my editors. I especially thank Chris Guzikowski for his patience while major sections of the book underwent drastic changes in response to modifications to the Akka toolkit. In the end, I am sure it was worth the wait.

What would a book on the Actor model be without acknowledging Carl Hewitt and the work he did and continues to do? Dr. Hewitt and his colleagues introduced the world to a simple yet most ingenious model of computation that has only become more applicable over time.

I also thank the Akka team for the fine work they have done with the Akka toolkit. In particular, Jonas Bonér reviewed chapters of my book and provided his unique perspective as the original founder of the Akka project. Akka's tech lead, Roland Kuhn, also reviewed particularly delicate parts of the book and gave me invaluable feedback. Also, both Roland Kuhn and Jamie Allen were supportive as we together developed the notation for expressing the Actor model in diagrams. Additionally, Patrik Nordwall of the Akka team reviewed the early chapters.

A special thanks goes to Will Sargent, a consultant at Typesafe, for contributing much of the section on Akka Cluster. Although I wrote a big chunk of that section, it was Will who helped with special insights to take it from ordinary to what I think is quite good.

Two of my early reviewers were Thomas Lockney, himself an Akka book author, and Duncan DeVore, who at the time of writing this was working on his own Akka book. In particular, Thomas Lockney endured through some of the earliest attempts at the first three chapters. Frankly, it surprised me how willing Thomas was to review and re-review and how he consistently saw areas for major improvement.

Other reviewers who contributed to the quality of the book include Idar Borlaug, Brian Dunlap, Tom Janssens, Dan Bergh Johnsson, Tobias Neef, Tom Stockton, and Daniel Westheide. Thanks to all of you for providing the kind of feedback that made a difference in the quality of the book. In particular, Daniel Westheide is like a "human Scala compiler," highlighting even difficult-to-find errors in written code examples.

About the Author

Vaughn Vernon is a veteran software craftsman and thought leader in simplifying software design and implementation. He is the author of the best-selling book *Implementing Domain-Driven Design,* also published by Addison-Wesley, and has taught his *IDDD Workshop* around the globe to hundreds of software developers. Vaughn is a frequent speaker at industry conferences. Vaughn is interested in distributed computing, messaging, and in particular the Actor model. He first used Akka in 2012 on a GIS system and has specialized in applying the Actor model with Domain-Driven Design ever since. You can keep up with Vaughn's latest work by reading his blog at www.VaughnVernon.co and by following him on Twitter: @VaughnVernon.

Chapter 1

Discovering the Actor Model and the Enterprise, All Over Again

Enterprise software development is hard.

Notice that the first sentence of this book that is largely about concurrency didn't say that multithreaded software development that exploits concurrency and parallelism is hard. I just plainly said that enterprise software development is hard. Don't worry. You are going to learn plenty about concurrency and parallelism, along with performance and efficiency, in this book. You may even get tired of all the concurrency and parallelism wisdom that oozes from between the covers before you read all the way to the end. That's why I want to make one up-front point clear. Enterprise software development is hard—much harder than it needs to be.

I am going to show you how much simpler and rewarding software development can be when you employ the reactive approach with the Actor model. Once I have established this important point, then I will move on to the Actor model with Scala and Akka details and being performance bent.

Why Enterprise Software Development Is Hard

Before I can show you how much simpler software development can be when it goes reactive, I am going to remind you why enterprise software development is so hard. Sure, you probably have your own pet peeves about implementing enterprise software systems. Perhaps it's an annoyance with a database you must regularly use, maybe it's a slow application server that makes your software run poorly, or it could even be some bother with your everyday programming language. Yes, there is that.

Yet, I am talking about a lot more than a single irritant. Think for a moment about all the physical tiers, application servers, software layers, frameworks and patterns, toolkits, databases, messaging systems, and third-party applications strutting their obscenely costly stuff all around your data centers. It is truly staggering, as hinted at in the *Ports and Adapters* architecture [IDDD] shown in Figure 1.1. Actually, the 30,000-foot view portrayed in that diagram pays remarkably kind kudos to the real-world enterprise application. Even at 1,000 feet and below, however, it's just plain scary.

Well, of course we senior architects and developers can deal with it. We can even become comfortable enough to say that we like it. That actually adds to the problem, though, because then junior and midlevel developers become stuck with what the seniors admiringly tolerate.

In *Implementing Domain-Driven Design* [IDDD] I explain in fairly extensive detail why you should use the Ports and Adapters (a.k.a. Hexagonal) architecture; it simplifies your way to enterprise solutions. And it does so, at least for typical N-tier applications. Still, to fully implement a complete enterprise application, it means you must embrace the architecture, design, configuration, implementation, and deployment of the detailed components that Figure 1.2 zooms in on.

Quite frankly, it takes months to learn all these pieces and parts, even for the most senior architects and developers. Then there are those not-so-fortunate ones. As you introduce a junior or midlevel developer to your architecture, do you take comfort as you see them repel in fearful intimidation or their eyes glaze over in utter confusion? It is just simply unsafe to turn over the developer reins

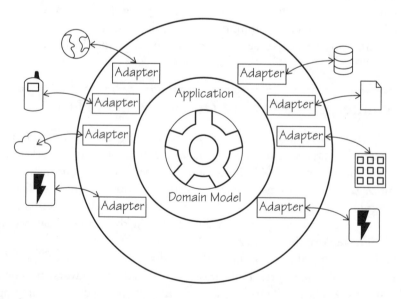

Figure 1.1 A typical Ports and Adapters enterprise application architecture. It could be a round shape as shown here or a hexagon, but all the same are the layers and complex components in between.

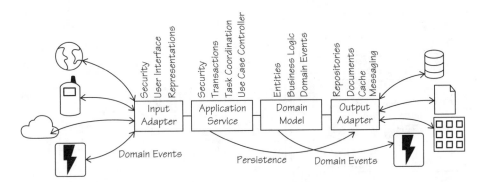

Figure 1.2 The complexity stack. There are a lot of software concerns and responsibilities spread across several layers in a typical enterprise application. It's all there to do something a lot simpler.

to a junior or midlevel staffer with so much accidental complexity at play. The sheer number of things every developer must understand and excel at, from end to end, is astonishing. Even so, I really haven't provided an exhaustive list of everything that makes the enterprise complex, one biggy being integration. For good reason, I call it the *complexity stack*.

Now, let's look at just one small part of the puzzle, *domain events* [IDDD], as shown in Figure 1.2. A persistent store full of domain events represents the happenings within a single business domain. They convey the facts of past occurrences that the domain model has experienced. They are quite informative, and when you get used to working with domain events, they are indispensable.

Yet, domain events are only a result. Each domain event is created as the outcome of some *command* that has been executed in the domain. You know the Command pattern [GoF], where an object in the application expresses the user's or application's intent to carry out some business operation. Once the intent is carried out, the result is a domain event. As Figure 1.3 demonstrates, the bottom line—what you are really trying to achieve in any application—is to submit commands to the domain model and secure domain events as the outcome. It's pretty simple and extremely powerful. It probably even deserves the name *simplicity stack*.

The problem is that some think that the complexity stack and the simplicity stack are one and the same. Nope. The complexity stack sports accidental complexity or, even worse, intentional complexity. It is just unnecessarily complex. The simplicity stack rejects all that extraneous stuff as, well, extraneous. In the end, you have some command input to the system, whether it's a browser, a phone, the cloud, or some other kind or message; you have an *actor*;

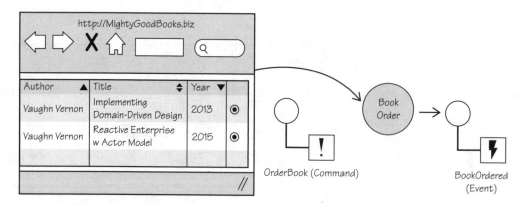

Figure 1.3 The simplicity stack. When you boil away the typical architecture, this is what you want out of a well-designed enterprise application.

and you have a domain event. What you have is a *reactive stack*. You have the *Actor model*.

What Is the Actor Model?

The Actor model promotes actors as the first-class unit of computation and emphasizes communication between actors via message sending. Because message sending is asynchronous, actors operate in a highly concurrent manner, which naturally makes for problem solving in parallel. Each actor generally cares for a single application responsibility. In Figure 1.3, `BookOrder` is an actor.

Because actors are lock-free concurrency agents and because they in general don't block, an application designed with actors makes optimal use of the underlying system's threading resources.

That's only a brief introduction. This entire book provides extensive detail about using the Actor model and the Akka toolkit.

What about security, transactions, persistence, messaging, and all the other things that I so slyly left out of the reactive-simplicity stack? Not to worry. They are all slyly done away with in the real world, or perhaps mildly blended in to the solution in such a subtle way that you may not even notice them much. For example, a single actor makes both a perfect business conceptual entity and a transactional consistency boundary. Another example is that, if using the Play Framework,[1] your user interface is also reactive. As you will discover throughout this book, it's all cared for. Nonetheless, such system-level

---

1. The Play Framework is a reactive user interface toolkit that is a product of Typesafe, the makers of Scala and Akka. The scope of this book does not allow for much to be said about user interfaces, but the literature contains much about Play.

concerns take a noticeable backseat to what's most important: your business domain.

The whole idea behind the reactive-simplicity stack is simplicity at the core, simplicity in the middle, and simplicity at the edges. In fact, you might find that, in the end, the edge, the middle, and the core might even be all the same things. In the end, those working with reactive, Actor model applications must be concerned with only a few important concepts.

- What incoming messages—commands and/or events—do I accept?

- What outgoing messages—commands and/or events—do I emit?

- How can my state be mutated in reaction to incoming messages?

- What is my supervision strategy for supervised actors?

The first two are your contract with the outside world, the other parts of your application, and even the rest of the enterprise. The third is your internal contract and how your actor adheres to the requirements of the business domain.

Now you can feel comfortable with turning over the development reins to junior and midlevel developers because what they need to understand is so greatly reduced. They can focus on the actor's contracts and how to test that the contracts are met. Any developer who works with the Actor model can focus their attention on the smallish, atomic world of the single actor, how it behaves, and how it mutates.

Introducing Reactive Applications

Reactive applications employ an architecture that allows you to build systems that are responsive, resilient, elastic, and message-driven and that are capable of producing a real-time feel. This section follows the definition given by the Reactive Manifesto [Reactive Manifesto].

The manifesto addresses the problem with existing enterprise and Web applications that are generally single-threaded. Regardless of your personal feelings about the value of various computing manifestos, the Reactive Manifesto offers a complete definition of what is both typical of and expected of reactive applications. It is meant to help bridge the gap between current, typical single-threaded thinking, introducing those to the need to scale using a reactive, event-driven approach to software development. Also, even though the Actor model is one of the leading tools used to create reactive applications, the Reactive Manifesto doesn't limit its guidance to using the Actor model.

Reactive applications have a resilient application stack. They execute best when deployed on multicore systems. It is also common for reactive applications to be deployed in multinode clusters, including cloud-based, dynamic provisioning environments. Reactive applications are designed to do the following:

- *React to users and other application components*: Reactive applications meet or exceed application response time to nonfunctional requirements.

- *React to failure*: Software is designed with the ability to recover at every component type by making resilience a central feature.

- *React to load*: Reactive applications tend to avoid shared resource contention by managing discrete resources (for example, system entities) separately. This design constraint allows for system elasticity and high throughput.

- *React to messages*: The principle design philosophy of reactive applications is message-driven through asynchronous messaging at its core.

Consider why each of these areas of reactive applications is vital to the future of the enterprise.

Responsive

Reactive applications must be as responsive as the user interface features demand. This includes real-time user interfaces that allow for overlapping edits by multiple users simultaneously. And, responsiveness must continue in the face of failure. Thus, responsiveness and resiliency go hand-in-glove for reactive applications.

Responsiveness can be achieved through observable models; that is, when changes occur within the system, the system has the ability to inform interested parties of the nature of the change. This calls for the use of event streams and visual models that are tuned for user consumption, versus system models that are tuned to support business operations.

Resilient

Being resilient does not require teams to implement perfect application software, that is, systems that never fail. It means designing in the ability for your applications to recover from errors. I needn't go into a lengthy explanation of why systems must be resilient. You only need to think back to a recent system triage and restoration report offered to customers as an explanation for a major system outage. No matter how forthright they are, such reports are never pleasant to write or to read. No thanks.

A typical application using multithreading on the Java or .NET platform would normally deal with a system failure in a localized way. If an exception is thrown, you will attempt to log the situation and perhaps take some responsible action. The problem is, there is often little, if anything, that can be done to recover from errors at that level. Decidedly, some have concluded that since it's too difficult to be resilient in the face of various complex failure scenarios—ones that can't even be predicted—the best course is to log errors and allow exceptions to trickle up to the user. True, when it's too difficult to anticipate or predetermine, how can you possibly deal with complex failures?

The reactive application anticipates failures by taking a supervisory position over lower-level reactive components. Here an asynchronous boundary and the ability to reify the failure as a message and send it through a dedicated *Message Channel (128)* are essential [Read-Write]. A supervisor will be given the opportunity to react to a failure of a component under its supervision. The corrective reaction may be to stop the failed component altogether, to restart it anew, or to instruct it to resume processing by ignoring the current reason for failure. A supervisor may even choose to fail itself up the chain, allowing its supervisor to take one of these recovery actions.

This approach tends to isolate failures to the area of the application where they occur, which allows them to be dealt with in a way specific to the failure reasons. This can be used to protect other parts of the application from failing as a chain reaction to one or more unrelated areas.

A concluding point about reactive resilience is that reactive systems were for good reason used in artificial intelligence. Artificial intelligence is the field that teaches the software to learn about new and potentially unknown situations. Using both supervision and allowing reactive components to learn from error conditions will strengthen our ever-growing defense against future system failure.

Elastic

Oftentimes when we think of scalability, we think of scaling to a greater degree, either vertically or horizontally. Vertical scalability can be achieved by adding one powerful computer that has more central processing units (CPUs), each with a number of cores (for example, with a combination of Intel Xeon Phi processors), and lots of random access memory (RAM). Horizontal scalability is possible by adding multiple commodity servers, each with an average CPU (for example, with one or two Intel i7 Quad Core 4700HQ processors).

Of course, you can use both of these approaches together to achieve specific scalability requirements.

More practically, though, elasticity is a better term than scalability because *elastic* means scaling to meet current application demands. This might mean scaling to use less computing power during off-peak hours. Regardless of scaling up, out, down, or in, your software must continue to provide the expected responsiveness at all times. This can be supported by elasticity, which is scale on demand, which is reactive at the core.

Because reactive applications are message-driven, where the components do something only when they must, they can be designed to scale in more practical ways. Further, reactive components may be made operational on a given computing node in a manner that is independent of its identity. The node on which any reactive component lives can be determined and changed by various means. In other words, reactive applications enjoy the benefit that their components have location transparency.

Although location transparency is used to overcome network partitioning challenges, it is not a poor attempt to disguise the fact that distributed software runs on a network. Rather, it meets the network head on. You thus need to strike a balance between location transparency and the need to acknowledge and reflect the network as a natural part of the programming model.

Both the message-driven nature of reactive components and their location transparency lend to scaling applications on demand, that is, elasticity.

Message Driven

Because system components react to messages only when they are received, the system can use available threads to run the parts of the application that must presently react to message stimuli. All the while, components that are not currently reacting to messages are not utilizing precious CPU resources. Messages may take the form of *Command Message (202)*, *Document Message (204)*, and *Event Message (207)*.

Since components in a reactive application receive communication from other components through asynchronous message passing, it naturally decouples the various components with regard to both interface and time. Because the reactive components choose how to react to each message-based stimulus individually, they can ready themselves in anticipation for future stimuli. This further decouples the sending component's and receiving component's interfaces because clients don't necessarily need to be aware of the order in which messages must be sent. In fact, reactive components are given no system-level assurance of the order in which any message may be received.

Because the reactive components themselves are smallish, atom-like units and because they react to only a single asynchronous message at a time, it opens the way for the components to reject all locking strategies. Because locking strategies are both unnecessary and rejected by reactive components, it frees the CPU cores to focus on pure throughput and allows all reactive components to constantly move forward during the times that they are consuming a thread. Thus, as components are reacting to messages on an as-needed basis—rather than constantly consuming CPU cycles because of nonreactive polling and blocking mechanisms—it tends to lead to low-latency application responsiveness.

Enterprise Applications

The software applications needed by organizations to run their day-to-day operations are broad and varied. Depending on the kind of business, you can anticipate some of the required application software. Do any of the following application categories overlap with your enterprise?

> Accounting, Accounts (Financial and others), Aerospace Systems Design, Automated Trading, Banking, Budgeting, Business Intelligence, Business Process, Claims, Clinical, Collaboration, Communications, Computer-Aided Design (CAD), Content/Document Management, Customer Relationship Management, Electronic Health Record, Electronic Trading, Engineering, Enterprise Resource Planning, Finance, Healthcare Treatment, Human Resource Management, Identity and Access Management, Invoicing, Inventory, IT and Datacenter Management, Laboratory, Life Sciences, Maintenance, Manufacturing, Medical Diagnosis, Networking, Order Placement, Payroll, Pharmaceuticals, Publishing, Shipping, Project Management, Purchasing Support, Policy Management, Risk Assessment, Risk Management, Sales Forecasting, Scheduling and Appointment Management, Text Processing, Time Management, Transportation, Underwriting

However incomplete the list, much of this software can be acquired as licensed commodities. Oftentimes you will need to integrate with such packaged software, and the patterns in this book can be helpful in those efforts. Yet, what about the specialty application software you'd design and implement within your organization? One of the worst mistakes that a business can make is to try to shoehorn a packaged application into the position of strategic solution. The results will be marginal at best.

Now I am discussing the field of strategic information system (SIS) [SIS], and for good reason. Such systems are specific to each organization, where software development produces business competitive advantage. Software that produces *strategic* results is strictly up to you and your business to achieve. Within each of the general areas across various industries listed earlier, and many others, there will be visions of yet-to-be-realized, company-defining enterprise applications. Such applications may be used to design and manufacture lower-cost yet higher-quality products, deliver new and improved services, and advance the business's ability to react to changing market conditions and more demanding customer expectations.

Perhaps you are at the inception of a *strategic* enterprise project. Compared to what you have previously been able to achieve with "normal" enterprise development tools, your strategic application may have to perform and scale off the charts. You are considering the Actor model to help you attain the inflexible and otherwise unreachable requirements. Beyond performance and scalability demands, you need to produce a software model that reflects the mental model of the business visionaries. Domain-Driven Design [DDD], shortened to DDD, was created to support the development of SIS, your Core Domain [IDDD]. You can benefit from the patterns in this book for application design, which tend to intersect with a DDD-based approach to software modeling. You will find that the Actor model allows you to design responsive, resilient, elastic, message-driven software models that your team can more easily reason about.

Further, as you embark on your new strategic enterprise challenge, you will also no doubt need to integrate with existing systems within your enterprise. As stated previously, this book will also help you with numerous approaches to integration, all while employing the Actor model.

A significant angle to consider in developing strategic enterprise solutions and integrating among various enterprise systems is your choice of tools. Oftentimes it is the role of the enterprise architect to specify job-preserving, no-one-ever-got-fired-for-buying-this product solutions. These are often bloated, slow, not scalable, let alone elastic, and expensive choices. Here those common choices are challenged, and in place of the bloated "enterprisey" solutions, you seek the lightweight, crafted, cost-effective approach.

Actor Model

In a recent interview with *Dr. Dobb's Journal*, Alan Kay, the pioneer of object orientation and co-designer of Smalltalk, said, "The Actor model retained more of what I thought were the good features of the object idea" [Kay-DDJ]. Years before this statement, Alan Kay commented on messaging between components as "the big idea" that should be the focus, rather than the properties of objects and their internal behavior [Kay-Squeak].

In my estimation, with Alan Kay paying a few significant nods to the Actor model approach to software architecture, design, and implementation, as well as the messaging between actors, it's well worth taking a closer look and possibly even employing it yourself. Thus, don't take the Actor model only as a means to squeeze the last drops of power out of a multicore computer. It helps you focus on "the big idea" of software design. It's apparently close to how software would have been implemented in Smalltalk had Alan Kay and the team had the opportunity to mutate the system to another level [Kay-Squeak].

Another thought-provoking comment was made by Gul Agha in his book *Actors: A Model of Concurrent Computation in Distributed Systems:* "Actors are a more powerful computational agent than sequential processes or value transforming functional systems" [Agha, Gul]. What is meant by this? In comparison to other systems' development practices—even those that support concurrency and parallelism—sequential and functional approaches are less powerful. Why? As Gul Agha points out, the Actor model can not only support actor-based systems but can employ both sequential and functional approaches as implementation details. What is more, he further argues the following [Agha, Gul]:

- Actors can create other actors.
- Sequential processes can't create other sequential processes.

This in no way downplays the contribution of sequential programs. It also doesn't mean that sequential processes can't execute other sequential processes because we've had that ability even in the mainstream for several decades. Yet, those newly spawned sequential processes are still static and capable of doing only what their build generated them to do. On the other hand, the Actor model can employ both sequential and functional programming techniques in a highly dynamic environment, where actors come and go as needed, and can even alter their behavior on the fly as the domain or operational environment demands. That is, reactive systems are not only concurrent and distributed but also elastic, dynamic, responsive, and resilient.

As Gul Agha concludes, "In the context of parallel systems, the degree to which a computation can be *distributed* over its lifetime is an important consideration. Creation of new actors provides the ability to abstractly increase the distributivity of the computation as it evolves" [Agha, Gul]. In other words, you can solve any given problem by creating yet another actor.

Origin of Actors

The Actor model is a mathematical model of concurrent computation that treats *actors* as the universal primitives of concurrent digital computation.

Unlike other models of computation, the Actor model was inspired by physics, including general relativity and quantum mechanics [Actor Model].

You can think of the Actor model as one realization of the means to make reactive applications possible. It is a concrete approach to reactive software development that carefully addresses each of the primary areas of reactive applications: responsive, resilient, elastic, and message-driven. Its messaging focus is the reason that all four areas can be achieved.

An interesting fact is while the Reactive Manifesto is only a few months old at the time of this writing, the Actor model is nothing new. As far back as 1973, the Actor model found its place in computing history. If that is so, why haven't we been making extensive use of the Actor model for several decades, and why have many heard of the Actor model only recently?

Dr. Carl Hewitt, the originator of the Actor model approach to software development, was decades ahead of his time. He saw the need to solve computing problems using concurrency and distribution, but his research and development efforts followed the first transistorized computers by only 14 years.[2] Multicore processors didn't exist. In the most powerful Intel processors available around 1973, there were only around 4,000 to 5,000 transistors, and clock speeds were less than 1MHz. See Figure 1.4 for a look at Carl Hewitt's world as he developed the Actor model. There was just not enough power to make Dr. Hewitt's work practical for mainstream computing. Thus, knowledge of distributed and

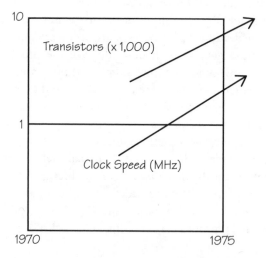

Figure 1.4 Carl Hewitt's world around the year 1973

---

2. See Chapter 3, "Performance Bent."

parallel systems was not advanced enough to adapt this conceptual model to an efficient implementation [Mackay]. Until relatively recently, there were few if any practical examples of applications that use the Actor model.

Fortunately today with the likes of IBM's zEC12 and the Intel Xeon Phi, and even less powerful processors such as the i7, the situation is quite different. Now that we have the kind of computer architecture that can support this 40-something-year-old concept, how does it work?

Understanding Actors

An *actor* is a computational entity that, in response to a message it receives, can do the following:

- Send a finite number of messages to other actors

- Create a finite number of new actors

- Designate the behavior to be used for the next message it receives

There is no assumed sequence to these actions, and they could be carried out in parallel [Actor Model].

In a fully enabled actor system, everything is an actor. This means that even programming elements that we typically consider to be simple or primitive types, such as strings and integers, are actors. Frankly, applying actors at that level could greatly complicate matters, at least until a practical, modern actor language appears.

Yet, it is also acceptable, and most practical, to design an actor system in which an actor is a special kind of system component—larger than a single integer but also not very big either. To give actors a descriptive dimension, think of them as similar to a narrowly focused Application Service, single domain model Entity, or a small domain model Aggregate [IDDD]. That's an oversimplification, but this provides a common point of reference that is understandable to most enterprise software developers. Certainly actors are not limited to such uses, but whatever their use, they should basically adhere to the Single Responsibility Principle (SRP) [SRP]. Figure 1.5 shows examples of various actor types.

Actor systems and actors have the following basic characteristics:

- *Communication via direct asynchronous messaging*: If the actor A1 is to send message M1 to actor A2, the actor A1 must know the address of actor A2. If A1 knows A2's address, it sends M1 directly to A2, but A2 will receive and process M1 on a separate thread. In other words, M1

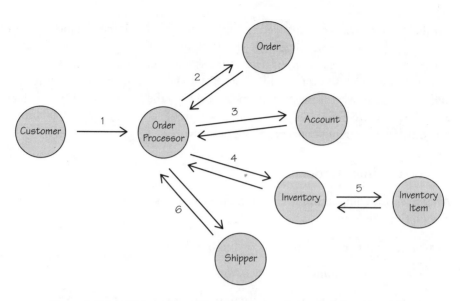

Figure 1.5 Some idea of possible actor size and responsibility based on order processing

is delivered asynchronously to A2. True, there is a layer of indirection between the sending and receiving actor—a mailbox. Even so, the word direct is used because the programming model provides a worthy abstraction that makes it appear that messages are sent directly from one actor to another.

- *State machines*: Actors support finite state machines. When an actor transitions to some expected state, it can modify its behavior in preparation for future messages. By *becoming* another kind of message handler, the actor implements a finite state machine.

- *Share nothing*: Actors do not share their mutable state with any other actor, or any other component for that matter.

- *Lock-free concurrency*: Since actors do not share their mutable state, and because they receive only one message at a time, actors never need to attempt to lock their state before reacting to a message. Because locking strategies are both unnecessary and rejected, it frees the CPU cores to focus on pure throughput and allows all reactive components to constantly move forward when they are consuming a thread.

- *Parallelism*: Concurrency and parallelism are different. Concurrency describes multiple computations occurring simultaneously. Parallelism is concurrency but applied to achieving a single goal. Parallelism is achieved by dividing a single complex process into smaller tasks and executing them concurrently. Parallelism with the Actor model tends to fit well when one higher-level actor can dispatch tasks across several subordinate actors, perhaps even in a complex task processing hierarchy.

- *Actors come in systems*: Carl Hewitt said, "One actor is no actor. Actors come in systems." That is, one actor gives no parallelism. Actors are very lightweight, so creating many actors within a single system is encouraged. *Any problem can be solved by adding yet another actor.*

In addition to these general Actor model characteristics, some others are available as extensions. The following are specifically available with Akka:

- *Location transparency*: Actor addresses are conveyed to actors using an abstract reference. If actor A1 obtains such a reference to actor A2, A1 may send message M1 to A2. The underlying actor system will manage the delivery, whether A2 is on the local actor system or a remote one.

- *Supervision*: Actors form a dependency relationship, where a parent actor supervises child (subordinate) actors. As a supervisor delegates tasks to subordinate actors, it must respond to the failures of those subordinates. A valid response may be to resume, restart, or stop the subordinate. The supervisor may also escalate the failure by electing to fail itself, which would defer failure control to the parent of the supervisor (the supervisor's supervisor). Supervision works well in conjunction with parallelism where the supervisor divides tasks among subordinates, which forms a task-solving hierarchy.

- *Futures/promises:* These provide the means to receive a result from an asynchronous operation, either as successful completion or as failure. To manage receiving the result, the system may use a special actor. The component holding the future may choose to wait/block on the result or to receive it asynchronously.

As a computational entity, an actor is analogous to an atomic unit. Each actor handles one message at a time as the message arrives and when there is an available thread to use for its execution, as depicted in Figure 1.6. An actor's performance is purely based on its own throughput capabilities, so you could say that an actor operates at its own tempo. Still, since an actor shares

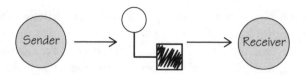

Figure 1.6 Each actor handles one message at a time as the message arrives and when there is an available thread.

none of its mutable state with other actors, there is no need for it to lock system resources when any incoming message is handled through computation or data processing.

Being lock-free, theoretically an actor's throughput should be quite fast. Even though the handling of any given message is a specific case scenario, if computations and processing are kept small, focused, and short-lived, messages should typically be sent, received, and handled in an extremely rapid manner. This assumes you are avoiding the use of blocking mechanisms (locks) and mechanisms that cause blocking (serial devices).[3] All this enables an actor system to support high-performance, high-throughput, and low-latency operations.

Concurrency and parallelism are extremely important for the overall success of reactive, actor-based systems. According to Amdahl's law, the speedup of a program using multiple processors in parallel computing is limited by the time needed for the sequential fraction of the program. For example, if a program needs 20 hours using a single-processor core and a particular portion of the program that takes one hour to execute cannot be parallelized while the remaining 19 hours (95 percent) of execution time can be parallelized, then regardless of how many processors are devoted to a parallelized execution of this program, the minimum execution time cannot be less than that critical one hour. In this particular case then, the speedup is limited to at most 20 times, as illustrated in Figure 1.7 [Amdahl's law].

What constitutes the critical one hour that cannot be parallelized? It could be purely a matter of blocking for input/output (I/O) on various devices.

---

3. Obviously, it is nearly impossible in most enterprise applications to entirely avoid the use of serial devices, such as disk drives. In those cases, I attempt to place required dependencies behind abstractions that allow for nonblocking or at least limited-blocking access. For one possible solution to this challenge, see *Polling Consumer (362)* in this book.

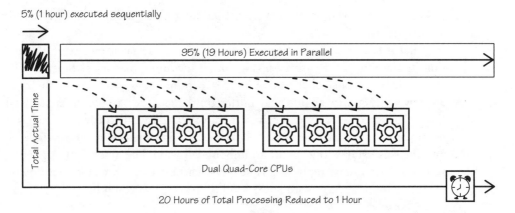

5% (1 hour) executed sequentially

95% (19 Hours) Executed in Parallel

Total Actual Time

Dual Quad-Core CPUs

20 Hours of Total Processing Reduced to 1 Hour

Figure 1.7 Amdahl's law finds the maximum improvement to an overall system's performance based on the parts that can execute in parallel.

However, it could also represent partly the former and some system complexity that could become unmanageable if treated asynchronously.

Amdahl's law emphasizes how important it is to design a system to execute as concurrently as is practical. This calls for making every practical attempt to utilize the maximum number of available cores at all possible times. I use the word *practical* for good reason. There may be a practicality limit to parallelizing certain areas of your specific system, if further parallelization could complicate the system beyond your team's ability to reason on it.

For example, there may actually be a way to parallelize some parts of the 5 percent of the system represented in Figure 1.7 to squeeze out more throughput and performance. As previously indicated, that smaller percentage could be everything that doesn't require blocking for I/O. And yet, it may not be worth the risk to make an attempt to parallelize that small percentage of processing if it could complicate your system beyond your ability to successfully reason about it. At some point it would be far more practical to look at parallelizing parts of other systems than to find ways to turn a 19-hour reduction into 19-hour-and-5-minute reduction.

An actor may receive a message that should cause it to transition to a new state, but the new state is dependent on an intermediate computation or other processing before it can fully transition. Still, the actor must remain responsive during this time. How? By using the *Request-Reply (209)* pattern. When the actor sends an asynchronous message to another actor, it initiates a contract for an eventual reply. Because the initiating actor doesn't block for the reply, it remains available to process subsequent messages until the reply is received.

Request-Reply (209) is a fundamental building block used extensively within actor systems.

What if the actor must receive the reply message that it awaits and transition its state before it can process all other incoming messages? Since it must still remain responsive, the actor with a pending state transition can *stash*[4] all new messages in an internal buffer until the necessary reply is received. Once the expected reply is received, it can then allow all stashed messages to be processed as usual. Yet, what if it takes a long time (seconds) for the reply and the stash starts to grow in an unbounded way? The actor with a pending state transition must reply to any senders whose messages would overflow its pending work capacity with some kind of "sorry, but you'll have to try again later" message.

Further, the actor system itself needn't care about the types of messages that are sent between actors. The receiving actor is the one that must react in a correct way according to its current state. Of course, it is also expected that clients know the actor's message contract and can thus send supported messages.

Considering state transitions, as an actor handles each newly received message, it has the opportunity to prepare its behavior for future messages. In simple terms, an actor does this by exchanging its current receive function for a different one. Internally an actor can completely replace its current receive function for another, or it can keep a stack of previous receive functions, essentially pushing them and then popping them back into context.[5] An actor may have a few or several different receive functions that it swaps among, but it can have only a finite number of them. This capability enables actors to be effective *finite state machines*.

Obviously, there are better situations than others to exchange your actor's receive function. The feature needn't be overused. Assuming that an actor can reach a given state only if it has received a given prerequisite message, when an actor has received a message in a specific receive block, it can assume that the prerequisite message has already been received within its current instance lifetime. It can be helpful to be able to make such assumptions.

In discussing the Actor model, I am not discussing the general use of messaging, as in Publish-Subscribe [POSA1] or message queues, or a remote procedure call (RPC)–based SOAP request for that matter. Of course, ultimately you can argue that these approaches are the Actor model, or at least reminiscent of

---

4. Stashing is not part of the original definition of the actor model but is provided with Akka. Still, there is no reason that you couldn't stash messages using other actor-based toolkits.

5. Akka calls this feature *become*, enabling an actor to become a different kind of message receiver.

it. In fact, even Carl Hewitt explains that you can model e-mail systems and Web service endpoints as Actor systems [Hewitt-ActorComp].

On the other hand, some toolkits bring you much closer to the use of the Actor model as originally specified by Carl Hewitt and his team. This is the use of the Actor model that I am emphasizing, and the specific toolkit I am using—Akka—is one that supports the Actor model in that way.

Managing Nondeterministic Systems

So, what in the world is nondeterminism, and why should you care? In application development, a nondeterministic system is one that, when executed multiple times given the same input, can produce different output. In other words, if you have an application and you tell the application to process A, it is possible that the first time the output will be B and the second time it will be C. That is, if you tell an application to process A and you can't predict whether the output will be B or C, it is nondeterministic. Doesn't that sound like an unreliable system? What is more, event-driven, reactive applications are inherently nondeterministic. Hmm, that doesn't reinforce trust in reactive applications.

Actually, while that sounds scary, in practical terms it needn't be a big concern as long as you understand the conditions of nondeterministic outcomes in your application. Let's consider an example use case that makes a system nondeterministic:

> *Use Case Description*: The `Customer` asks the `OrderProcessor` actor to create an `Order` of a specific book B and, when successful, tells the `Account` actor to `ChargeCreditCard`. Once the `ChargeCreditCard` is processed, the `Order` will hold a reference to the outcome information. There is a time constraint on the `ChargeCreditCard` request. The `Customer`, `Order-Processor`, `Order`, and `Account` must be designed reactive.

1. The `Customer` tells `OrderProcessor` to place an `Order` for book B.

2. The `OrderProcessor` creates `Order` for book B, and as a result an event `OrderPlaced` is created to indicate that fact.

3. Event `OrderPlaced` is delivered from `Order` to `OrderProcessor`.

4. `OrderProcessor` tells the `Account` to `ChargeCreditCard`, which succeeds, and event `AccountCharged` is created to indicate that fact.

5. Event `AccountCharged` is delivered from `Account` to `OrderProcessor`, which in turn tells `Order` to hold a reference to the information conveyed by `AccountCharged`.

6. The use case continues by telling `Inventory` to reserve book B and telling the `Shipper` to ship the `Order`.

That's the happy path because in the end the nondeterministic system responds with the *expected* outcome. Yet, the overall system could encounter any number of possible situations that could cause a different outcome. Sure, OrderProcessor could for some reason fail to create Order, but that failure could occur even in an entirely deterministic system. So, that error condition is not really what we are considering. Where is the main concern then?

One of the requirements that makes the overall system nondeterministic is that there must be a time constraint on the creation of AccountCharged. Since there can be a timeout between the creation of OrderPlaced and AccountCharged, and actually the notification of event AccountCharged, there are two potential outcomes to processing A:

B. AccountCharged is received by OrderProcessor in time, and Order is told to reference the details of AccountCharged.

C. There is some delay in Account when creating AccountCharged, or there is some network latency/failure in delivering AccountCharged, and although Order is created, its reference to AccountCharged information is not set.

If the outcome of process A is the expected outcome B, then everyone is happy. What if, however, the outcome is C? Does it mean that the system is broken, unreliable, and seriously flawed? Not really. It just means that you need to plan for dealing with the possibility that the outcome could be C, even if you really want outcome B. How do you deal with it? You can create a new use case.

Use Case Description: The OrderProcessor tells Order to retry the ChargeCreditCard request.

1. On a periodic basis, OrderProcessor tells Account to request Charge-CreditCard until the request is successful or a retry limit is reached. (If the retry limit is reached, then the OrderProcessor tells the Order to Cancel.)

2. As a result of a successful ChargeCreditCard request (which may have been previously successful but network latency/failure caused delivery failure), Account creates event AccountCharged.

   Event AccountCharged is delivered from Account to OrderProcessor, which in turn tells Order to hold a reference to the information conveyed by AccountCharged.

3. The use case continues by telling Inventory to reserve book B and telling the Shipper to ship the Order.

The fact that the overall system is nondeterministic requires you to think about the complete business process and what ultimately must be accomplished.

As long as you can understand and identify all the conditions of nondeterministic outcomes in your application, you can design for the ultimate successful outcomes that users and the system require. The main focus of the design is to be explicit with your software models, because that's what makes it possible to understand a complex system.

Some have criticized the Actor model for being inherently nondeterministic [Actors-Nondeterministic]. The forgoing article is a weak criticism of the Actor model. In reality, the individual actors themselves make for safe deterministic atomic units. The argument that the whole system is at any given time nondeterministic is true in the sense that any concurrently executing business system is nondeterministic at any given point in time. Unbounded nondeterminism was the source of early controversy around the basic theory of the Actor model [Actors-Controversy]. However, when you boil down the arguments, it is event-driven architecture that is inherently nondeterministic, and the Actor model is an event-driven architecture. Again, the Actor model helps us reason about naturally nondeterministic concurrent business systems by introducing the actor, which itself is an atomic deterministic unit.

Message-driven (a.k.a. event-driven) systems, no matter how they are implemented, are the underlying basis for responsive, resilient, and elastic applications. Also, reactive systems don't have to be highly nondeterministic. Immutable state can make an application deterministic, as well as data flow concurrency (using single-assignment variables).

Thus, the real decision is whether to design using single-threaded architectures that don't scale or to use tools that help make multithreaded, event-driven architectures manageable. Some propose that the Actor model is the best way to deal with nondeterminism in the growing number of event-driven architectures [EDA-Verification]. In fact, designing with actors helps teams successfully reason about complex, nondeterministic systems.

Object-Capability Model

Although the Actor model is different from object models, there is a considerable overlap with the security model known as the *Object-Capability model* [OCM]. Because the conceptual overlap is high, I replace the word *object* with the word *actor* in the following definition.

Actors can interact only by sending messages on references. A reference can be obtained by the following:

1. *Initial conditions*: Actor A may already have a reference to actor B.

2. *Parenthood*: When A creates B, at that moment A obtains the only reference to B.

3. *Endowment*: A creates B, B is born with the subset of references that A chose to endow it with.

4. *Introduction*: If A has references to both B and C, A can send to B a message containing a reference to C. B can retain that reference for subsequent use.

The overlap is obvious. Possibly the strongest form of security is found in the parenthood rule. When a parent actor creates a child actor, at the moment of creation the parent holds the only reference to the child. This fact ensures that the parent can completely isolate all messaging to the child, which makes the child as secure as its tests prove it to be. No other actors may send it messages unless the child is designed to itself create children or to receive messages from or send messages to additional actors, which would lead to the other rules of the Object-Capability model.[6]

Although the Actor model in general serves as an Object-Capability model, there is one obstacle to using Akka as such. Akka supports sending messages to actors via `ActorSelection` (see Chapter 2, "The Actor Model with Scala and Akka"). Using `ActorSelection`, any user-managed actor in the system can be found by path and name, which allows you to bypass encapsulation. If you use the `ActorSelection` feature, know that you are not compatible with the Object-Capability model. Nonetheless, considering the Object-Capability model helps you understand the ways actors can become known to other actors and how they can also potentially be kept unknown.

The Actor Way Is Explicit

Before moving on, one of the main concepts I want you to take away from this chapter is that the Actor model can be leveraged to greatly simplify your enterprise applications. One of the primary goals of Domain-Driven Design is to make the business concepts explicit in a software model [IDDD]. If you glance back at Figure 1.1 and Figure 1.2, all the extra moving parts and static configurations don't help your software models to be explicit. In fact, the best place to look for explicit business knowledge is just at the center of Figure 1.1, the domain model. Yet, there are so many other moving parts in the architecture that sometimes it can muddy your view of what you actually have set out to accomplish in the software model.

---

6. See *Content Filter (321)* for further discussion.

On the other hand, looking back at Figure 1.3, all you have is a user interface and an explicit software model. You might even conclude that the user interface is part of the software model because it reflects and expresses the mental model of the business experts in a way that helps users make important decisions and take significant actions through the software model. This is the goal you should try to achieve with the Actor model: being explicit.

Figure 1.8 further emphasizes being explicit in your software models. There is no wondering who is interested in a given message, whether it be a *Command Message (202)* or an *Event Message (207)*. You only need to view the actors' source code and read their contracts, both external and internal. Don't be distracted by those who might say that the Actor model requires actors to be tightly coupled. It is just not the case, as a reread of the previous "Object-Capability Model" section will reinforce. The actors shown in Figure 1.8 could easily have references to other actors by means of endowment or introduction. If the application process is more complex, you can introduce a *Process Manager (292)* or other kind of *Message Router (140)* between the `BookOrderController`, `BookOrder`, and `OrderFulfillment`. See also Figure 1.5.

Rid your mind of the layers of implicit cognitive dissonance. It's just you and your software model and perhaps a user interface. Go ahead, be explicit. The rest of the book helps you see how you can put much of the other conventional software layers behind you as a thing of the distant past. You are now in the fast lane with the Actor model and its concurrency and parallelism.

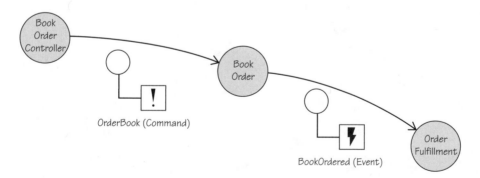

Figure 1.8 Allow the Actor model to rid your mind of the layers of implicit cognitive dissonance. Go ahead, be explicit.

What Next?

With the foregoing foundation laid, you should be ready to experience the use of the Actor model. For you Java developers, you are much closer to embracing Scala and Akka than you might think. Chapter 2 introduces both the Scala programming language and the Akka toolkit. Following that, Chapter 3 addresses the need to perform at scale on single computing nodes and across many such nodes.

For you C# .NET developers, I suggest you look at Appendix A, "Dotsero: An Akka-like Library for .NET," where I discuss the Dotsero Actor Model Toolkit. Dotsero supports C# developers interested in discovering the Actor model on a familiar platform.

Chapter 2

The Actor Model with Scala and Akka

There are a few distinct ways to program with actors. The Actor model can be used through an actor library toolkit, or it can be implemented directly in a language. ActorScript is one example of an actor programming language. Actors were added to Smalltalk. Erlang has actors but is not actor-based through and through. Erlang supports actors/processes as first-class concurrency abstractions. More recently, languages such as Scala and Scratch support actor-based programming.

Scala, a Java virtual machine (JVM) language, also does not implement actors as part of a programming language. Rather, Scala comes with an actor library–based toolkit called Akka. Thus, Scala has significant similarities to Erlang and also significant differences. For example, Erlang is a functional language, where all data is immutable. On the other hand, Scala is a hybrid language that fuses object-oriented with functional. With Scala some concepts can be implemented as mutable, while others are strictly immutable.

> **You Can Use Java with Akka**
>
> There is no absolute need to switch to Scala if you want to use Akka. The Akka toolkit has a Java-compatible application programming interface (API). No matter, using Java with Akka is not nearly as sweet as using Scala with Akka. Many find Scala to be a great language, where a single line of code might replace dozens written in Java. Still, some organizations are slow to move away from Java and embrace Scala. With that in mind, there should be no reason for you to shy away from using Akka with Java. In time, you may be able to also gradually influence Scala adoption in your enterprise. That will be a happy time.

Some libraries bring you much closer to the use of the Actor model as originally specified by Carl Hewitt and his team. Akka lives up to that. Yet, Akka doesn't attempt to implement an actor language. Actually the Akka library/framework is a replacement for the Scala default actor library. Although you can fall back to the Scala default actor library, that would be a very limiting choice. Besides, the scala.actors library was deprecated as of Scala 2.11, so it's unlikely that anyone's feelings were hurt since Akka trumped simple Scala actors.

If you study the Erlang programming language a bit, you can easily identify the parts of Erlang that have greatly influenced Scala and Akka. For example, the pattern-matching features of Erlang are seen clearly in Scala as a language and are also found in Akka's actor features.

Using this brief introduction to Scala and Akka, let's step through how you can start using both.

How to Get Scala and Akka

There are several ways to obtain and use the Scala programming language and the Akka toolkit. This section discusses how you can use the Typesafe Activator or build tools such as sbt, Maven, or Gradle to get what you need by means of repositories. You can also download the tools directly, which you want to do for reasons other than build dependencies.

Using Typesafe Activator

Go to http://typesafe.com/activator/ or anywhere else on the http://typesafe.com Web site and use any one of a number of links to download the Typesafe Activator. This is a developer environment that can be used to kick-start your use of the Typesafe Reactive Platform. Use the wizard-based user interface to generate a wide variety of sample projects. Once a given project is generated, you can safely exit the Typesafe Activator environment and open the sample project in your own development environment.

Using sbt

The Simple Build Tool, or sbt, is more or less a de facto standard for building Scala programs. Lots of Scala developers use sbt, and the same goes for projects using Akka. Here is some basic scripting to place in your **build.sbt** to enable a Scala and Akka project build:

```
name := "RiskRover"

version := "1.0"

scalaVersion := "2.10.4"

resolvers += "Typesafe Repository" at
            "http://repo.typesafe.com/typesafe/releases/"

libraryDependencies += "com.typesafe.akka" %% "akka-actor" % "2.3.4"
```

The Akka dependencies are for a specific version of Akka. You will need to determine which version you will use. If you have never used sbt, you may find it not only interesting but also powerful. You will probably run into some complexities as well, so it will eventually pay to get some additional training on sbt [Westheide]. Also, Josh Suereth's *sbt in Action* [sbt-Suereth] comes highly recommended, even though it was not publicly available at the time of this writing. One thing to remember is that sbt is not just a build tool but actually a powerful REPL[1] programming environment.

Using Maven

Maven has become a de facto standard among Java developers and can be used also with Scala projects. If you are familiar with Maven, you should have no problem putting the following declarations into your build script that will enable you to compile with Scala and use Akka:

```
...
<pluginManagement>
  <plugins>
    <plugin>
      <groupId>net.alchim31.maven</groupId>
      <artifactId>scala-maven-plugin</artifactId>
      <version>3.1.6</version>
      <executions>
        <execution>
          <goals>
            <goal>compile</goal>
            <goal>testCompile</goal>
          </goals>
        </execution>
      </executions>
    </plugin>
  </plugins>
</pluginManagement>
...

<dependency>
  <groupId>com.typesafe.akka</groupId>
  <artifactId>akka-actor_2.10</artifactId>
  <version>2.3.4</version>
</dependency>
```

---

1. REPL is an acronym that means Read, Evaluate, Print, Loop. It is a high-level shell interface that lets you experiment with programming language facilities without taking on the burden of creating a project and performing builds.

Of course, these declarations are for a specific version of Scala and Akka. You will need to determine which versions you are using.

Using Gradle

I like Gradle a lot, mostly because I don't like builds or build tools, and Gradle requires me to understand less and gives me more at the same time. It may be less popular among Scala developers, but I think that could be a mistake. I doubt that Gradle will displace sbt as the popular Scala/Akka build tool, but I think it should displace Maven. Here's a simple script that enables you to build with Scala and Akka:

```
apply plugin: 'scala'

repositories {
  mavenCentral()

  // if using snapshots; otherwise remove;
  // see dependencies, akka
  maven {
    url "http://repo.akka.io/snapshots/"
  }
}

dependencies {
  // replace with specific version
  compile 'org.scala-lang:scala-library:2.10.4'
}

tasks.withType(ScalaCompile) {
  scalaCompileOptions.useAnt = false
}

dependencies {
  // replace with specific versions
  compile group: 'com.typesafe.akka',
           name: 'akka-actor_2.10',
        version: '2.4-SNAPSHOT'
  compile group: 'org.scala-lang',
           name: 'scala-library',
        version: '2.10.4'
}
```

It probably doesn't get much simpler than that, unless you are already using sbt. Gradle is based on Groovy, while sbt is based on Scala. Since you don't get Scala for free with Gradle, you will have to drag in the Scala compiler, which you don't have to do when you use sbt. Still, that's just a few lines of code.

Programming with Scala

If you work in Java and you haven't yet learned Scala, you should. Of all JVM languages other than Java itself, Scala has the greatest uptake. With a mixture of unobtrusive object-oriented and functional programming facilities, it's hard to imagine not finding the tools you want and need to code better and faster.

Back in the early to late 1980s, I was programming in C and C++ and had also spent a bit of time with Smalltalk. I liked Smalltalk a lot, and I kept trying to find ways to make C++ more like Smalltalk. Others made similar efforts. No matter, it seemed that using C++ at that time relegated your coding skills to a snail's pace.[2] Even employing object-oriented techniques with C seemed way faster than development with C++. What I learned is that there was no substitute for Smalltalk. After using Smalltalk to rapidly develop a few applications and tools, I could confirm the claims of those who said you could program 20 to 25 times faster with Smalltalk than with C++. While I can't yet conclude a productivity improvement of 20 to 25 times greater, I find Scala to be a similar *feeling* leap over Java as Smalltalk was over C++. The economy of writing a single line of Scala code that replaces dozens of lines—I am talking 24 to 36 lines—of Java code is difficult to argue against.

I purposely avoid an exhaustive treatment on the Scala programming language. I do provide a simple tutorial on some of the Scala basics, preparing you to read code in this book, and even get started programming in Scala yourself. If you are already familiar with an object-oriented language such as Java or C# and possibly have even studied a bit about functional programming or used a functional language, you should find Scala pretty easy to pick up.

If you want to learn Scala quickly, I recommend getting the book *Atomic Scala* by Bruce Eckel and Dianne Marsh [Atomic-Scala]. Others find *Scala for the Impatient* [Horstmann] to be "the best compact introduction to Scala," including Scala's creator, Martin Odersky. In my estimation, most experienced programmers would be close to ready to use Scala on the job after spending a weekend or two with that book. We all learn differently, and your mileage may vary. There are other books, such as *Scala in Depth* by Joshua D. Suereth [Suereth], that should be open on your desk. You can also check into online classes offered by Coursera [Coursera], and the onsite classes offered by Typesafe Inc. [Typesafe] and their training and consulting partners.

---

2. I won't be too harsh on C++ because I have close friends and colleagues who still think it is the perfect language. We still enjoy wings, pizza, and beer together, as well as some others of life's simple pleasures, and I'd like to keep it that way.

As a parting caveat, I suggest you stay away from the complex libraries, such as scalaz, at least in the beginning. You won't need to solve problems with libraries meant to satisfy a specific programming style. So, if `Functor` and `Monad` sound like viruses you caught as a child, steer clear of scalaz for a while. You will still be productive with the Scala language features you will review in this chapter and throughout the book. After you are grounded in common Scala, it would make sense to venture into scalaz and the "pure functional data structures" it offers, as well as other advanced libraries and language features.

A Condensed Scala Tutorial

Are you ready for the bare essentials needed to read Scala and write a bit of code? This condensed tutorial moves swiftly, but the upside is that it will not waste your time with details that are less important for Scala beginners. Note that here I am primarily treating Scala in comparison to Java or C# object-based development. Although Scala source can be used for scripting, I don't address scripting with Scala. This tutorial is just meant as a jump start to Scala from the standpoint of a Java or C# developer. You can find complete language references and tutorials in the previous discussion.

I also purposely try to avoid references to actors in this Scala tutorial—well, mostly anyway. After you have some background in Scala, you will be ready for the Akka tutorial that follows.

Scala source files end with the `.scala` file extension. The following source file contains the sample for the *Claim Check (325)* pattern:

```
ClaimCheck.scala
```

Every Scala `class` and `object`[3] should be placed in a `package`, and the `package` must be declared and named at the top of the Scala source file. The following declares that the source file for the *Claim Check (325)* sample is found in the `claimcheck` package:

```
package co.vaughnvernon.reactiveenterprise.claimcheck
```

Note that you don't need to use a semicolon to end the package statement as you would if you were coding in Java. As a general rule, you won't have to use semicolons in much, if any, Scala code. Good riddance! And guess what? You C# developers will feel right at home with Scala's ability to scope namespaces as packages.

---

3. Scala object types are explained shortly. For now, think of them as a singleton companion of a given class.

```
package co.vaughnvernon.reactiveenterprise.claimcheck {
  ...
}
```

If you want to use a class, an object, or some other Scala type that is not declared in your own source file or within the same `package` as your source file, you must reference it using an `import` statement. A Scala `import` statement is pretty close to Java's.

```
import akka.actor.Actor
import akka.actor.Props

// or

import akka.actor._
```

In fact, referencing an individual class, such as `akka.actor.Actor`, is done the same way as when using a Java `import`, except you don't need to use a semicolon to end the statement. The second `import` statement example imports all the classes, objects, and so on, found in the `akka.actor` package, which includes `Actor` and `Props`. The `._` in a Scala `import` statement is the same as `.*` in a Java `import` statement.

So, what do you put in a Scala source file? To start, Scala supports classes, just as Java and C# support classes, but with a few nice additions.

```
class ItemChecker {
  ...
}

abstract class ItemContainer {
  ...
}

class ShoppingCart extends ItemContainer {
  ...
}
```

The first defined class, `ItemChecker`, doesn't extend any specific base class. On the other hand, `ShoppingCart` extends `ItemContainer`, which is an abstract base class. The details of these classes are not shown. One feature of both `ItemChecker` and `ShoppingCart` is that both have zero-argument constructors. That means you can currently instantiate a `ShoppingCart` as follows:

```
val shoppingCart = new ShoppingCart()
```

The reference to the `ShoppingCart` instance is held by the `shoppingCart`, which is declared as a `val` but without a type. This introduces a few Scala language concepts. First, instances may be held by references that are either a `val` or a `var`. Once a `val` is assigned to reference an instance, that `val` cannot be reassigned.

```
val shoppingCart = new ShoppingCart

val differentCart = new ShoppingCart

shoppingCart = differentCart // invalid expression; compile-time error
```

On the other hand, if `shoppingCart` were a `var`, it would be perfectly fine to reassign it.

```
var shoppingCart = new ShoppingCart

val differentCart = new ShoppingCart

shoppingCart = differentCart // valid expression
```

Note also that in both `shoppingCart` declarations, the code doesn't provide a type, just a named reference. That's because you can use Scala's type inference as a shorthand. Type inference means that the Scala compiler can analyze the code and detect the type that is implied. It actually works out the same as declaring the type explicitly.

```
val shoppingCart: ShoppingCart = new ShoppingCart
```

Now, let's get back to constructors. Here's how you make the ShoppingCart require one constructor parameter, or what Scala calls a class argument:

```
class ShoppingCart(val maximumItems:Int) extends ItemContainer {
  ...
}
```

Now a client of `ShoppingCart` must pass an `Int` parameter as it creates each instance.

```
val shoppingCart = new ShoppingCart(50)
```

One of the Scala code economy features is demonstrated in the previous constructor. Not only does `maximumItems` serve as a required constructor argument, it also becomes readable outside the instance. That is, all instances of `ShoppingCart` have a read accessor to `maximumItems` of type `Int`.

```
val maximumShoppingCartItems = shoppingCart.maximumItems
```

Further, because `maximumItems` is a `val`, you can never reassign a different `Int` to it. So, when declared as a `val`, `maximumItems` can be read but not modified by clients or inside the class.

```
class ShoppingCart(val maximumItems: Int) extends ItemContainer {
  ...
  maximumItems = 100 // invalid expression; compile-time error
}
```

Actually, if you want to declare `ShoppingCart` with a mutable `maximumItems`, use `var` instead.

```
class ShoppingCart(var maximumItems:Int) extends ItemContainer {
  ...
  maximumItems = if (maximumItems < 10) 10 else maximumItems
}
```

In this case, the `var` declaration makes `maximumItems` both readable and modifiable both inside and outside the class. This code ensures that a customer may buy at least 10 different items, and possibly more. Using `var` here is probably not a realistic requirement, however. A `ShoppingCart` would probably always declare such a `maximumItems` concept as a `val`, never allowing code outside to change it. Actually, you may find that you almost never use `var` as a constructor argument but maybe sometimes you will.

There's a little curious thing about the body of class `ShoppingCart`, and all other classes for that matter. Any expression outside a method is executed when a new instance of the `ShoppingCart` is created. The expressions within the body of the class, whether used to initialize `val` or `var` references or just invocations of methods on this or other objects, are all part of the construction process. As an example, this expression is executed after the `maximumItems` field is set to its initial value:

```
  ...
  maximumItems = if (maximumItems < 10) 10 else maximumItems
```

When you think about this code, it's pretty cool how every expression has some outcome. When the `if` part of the conditional evaluates to `true`, it will yield 10. Otherwise, the `else` part is evaluated and yields whatever value is referenced by `maximumItems`.

You've seen two options for declaring constructor parameters that also serve as instance fields. There are actually three, however.

```
class ShoppingCart(
    catalogSource: CatalogSource,
    val maximumItems: Int)
extends ItemContainer {
  ...
}
```

I've changed `maximumItems` back to be a `val` instead of a `var`, but notice that the `catalogSource` is neither a `val` or a `var`. That means that Scala will not generate a field or any sort of accessor method, neither read nor write. Thus, you'd expect for the `ShoppingCart` to use the `catalogSource` only temporarily.

```
class ShoppingCart(
    catalogSource: CatalogSource,
    val maximumItems: Int)
extends ItemContainer {
  val catalog: Catalog =
    catalogSource.catalog(catalogSource.name) getOrElse↵
  DefaultCatalog()
  ...
}
```

What you really want from the `CatalogSource` is its `Catalog`. The `catalogSource.catalog` returns an `Option`, which means it will have either a `Some` or `None`. An `Option` is a wrapper around a value that eliminates the need for nulls. If it has a `Some`, then the `get` part of the `getOrElse` logic will return the value within the `Some`. Otherwise, the `OrElse` part of the `getOrElse` logic will return the instance of the `DefaultCatalog`.

There might seem to be a bit of magic going on here. For example, where is the dot and the parentheses to invoke the various methods, such as for the `name()` of `CatalogSource`? One convenience of Scala is that you don't need the dot separator, or the `()`, in some cases. This is called *infix notation*.

Sure, but what about the missing `new` for the `DefaultCatalog` constructor? Actually, the following expression is not directly referencing the constructor:

```
val catalog: Catalog = DefaultCatalog()
```

Rather, this `DefaultCatalog` is a special kind of Scala concept called a *companion object*, and it is always a singleton; that is, there is only ever one of them. There is a class named `DefaultCatalog`, and its companion object acts as a factory for getting instances of the `DefaultCatalog`. Of course, a companion object can do other things as well. Here is a simple implementation:

```
object DefaultCatalog {
  ...
  def apply = new DefaultCatalog(catalogConfig)

  def name = catalogConfig.name
}
```

The `apply` method gets invoked when you use the `DefaultCatalog()` expression as shown in the previous examples. The `apply` implementation just returns a new instance of the `DefaultCatalog` class, but without requiring the client to know anything about the `catalogConfig`. You can define any other kind of method inside the companion object, such as `name`. To use that method, the client uses the companion object like this:

```
val catalogName = DefaultCatalog.name
```

That's nice, but what is the motivation behind companion objects? Scala doesn't support static methods, so the companion object provides a means to support various kinds of factories and utility methods needed by the class that the companion object augments.

That brings us to the sort of strange-looking method definitions. Why is there the = following each method definition? In fact, where are the normal curly braces that define the method scope? And where is the return type and the statement?

Every Scala method returns a type, no matter what. Sometimes the type is a meaningful value and sometimes it isn't. In either case, the = means that this method returns a value according to what the following code block evaluates to. It just so happens that if the code block is a single expression, then there is no need for the surrounding curly braces. However, if there are two or more expressions, then you must definitely use curly braces. Still, you could also define the same methods as follows:

```
object DefaultCatalog {
  ...
  def apply: Catalog = {
    new DefaultCatalog(catalogConfig)
  }
```

```
def name: String = {
  catalogConfig.name
}
}
```

Not only are there now curly braces enclosing the code, you also declare the return type of the method by placing a `:type` following the reference. It is a Scala best practice to declare method return types. The code block that `apply` references evaluates to an instance of type `Catalog`, and the code block that `name` references evaluates to an instance of type `String`.

Even so, what about the return statement that provides the outcome of the method to the caller? Actually, you don't need, nor should you use,[4] an explicit return statement because Scala sees to it that the result of the final expression within the method serves as its return value. Thus, the new `DefaultCatalog` is the result of the `apply()` method, and the result of using the `name()` accessor of the `catalogConfig` is the result of the `name()` method. Cool. Less code is, well, better.

Now, inside the `ShoppingCart` you can define any number of methods that are appropriate for electronic shopping carts.

```
class ShoppingCart(
    catalogSource: CatalogSource,
    val maximumItems: Int)
extends ItemContainer {

import scala.collection.immutable.Vector

  val catalog: Catalog =
    catalogSource.catalog(catalogSource name) getOrElse↵
  DefaultCatalog()

  private var itemsContainer = Vector.empty[Item]

  ...
  def add(item: Item): Unit = {
    itemsContainer = itemsContainer :+ item
  }
}
```

First, remember that all expressions in the body of a class are executed during construction. Thus, the `itemsContainer` is initially an empty

---

4. In fact, odd problems can occur if you use return statements in Scala because it changes the meaning of your program. For this reason, return statement usage is discouraged. See http://tpolecat.github.io/2014/05/09/return.html.

`Vector` in which you may hold `Item` instances. Yet, why is it declared as a `private var`? Actually the `Vector` you have imported, as class scoped only, is immutable. You want it to be private so that no outside code may access it directly because the reference itself must be mutable. Why? This question is answered by looking at the implementation of `add(Item)`. To append a newly selected `Item` to the `itemContainer`, you must allow `Vector` to generate a new `Vector` that contains the current contents plus the new `Item`. The `itemContainer` reference must be mutated to now hold a reference to the newly generated `Vector`.

That's interesting, but isn't there a lot of overhead in always creating a new `Vector` just because you want to add a new `Item`? After all, isn't that what mutable collections are so good at handling? Don't worry. In actuality, a completely new `Vector` is not created. As a language that supports functional programming—where things are expected to be immutable—Scala's immutable collections[5] are optimized to eliminate the overhead. Underneath, there is actually a new `Item` element added to the preexisting storing data structure, but it is wired such that those who hold a reference to the previous `Vector` cannot see the newly appended `Item`. Only those who reference the new version of the `Vector` can see the newly appended `Item`.

Take note of one more detail of the `add(Item)`. It is defined as returning type `Unit`, which is Scala's way of saying that the return value is not useful. It's sort of like using `void` with Java or C#. A method that returns `Unit` cannot be used in expression chaining.

Oh, yeah, there's another thing about the class-scoped import of `Vector`. In Java, imports are always added to the top of the file because a `.java` file can contain only one publicly visible class. Yes, you guessed it. Scala allows you to place multiple publicly visible classes, companion objects, and so on, all in a single source file. Booyah! Since there can be multiple classes, objects, and so on, they may each declare imports of their own. Imports can be inside any kind of code blocks enclosed by curly braces, whether those are class bodies, method definitions, or arbitrary other code blocks.

If you've programmed in Java for a while, you've probably been at least a little disappointed that you can't use symbols as method names. Well, Scala changes that, and it's not even a matter of operator overloading as is found in C++. Of course, you shouldn't overuse this facility. Restraint is as important as having the option available. Scala allows you to use, for example, the `!` character as a method name.

---

5. Scala also has mutable collections. The mutable and immutable collections are in two separate library packages.

```
def !(message: Any): Unit = {
  ...
}
```

This is, in fact, one way that Akka messages can be sent:

```
actor ! SomeMessage()
```

Using ! is the same as using the `tell()` method. Also, you don't need to use a dot following the `actor` receiver or parentheses around the parameter `SomeMessage()`, which makes the code much more readable.

That actually isn't the full definition of !, however; this is the complete definition:

```
def tell(message: Any, sender: ActorRef): Unit = this.!(message)↵
  (sender)
...
def !(message: Any)(implicit sender: ActorRef=Actor.noSender): Unit = {
  actorCell.sendMessage(message, sender)
}
```

When you use ! or `tell()` to send a message to the `actor`, you also want to indicate the `sender` of the message. The previous code shows, between the second set of parentheses, the declaration of an implicit parameter, the `sender`. The Scala compiler looks to see whether there is, within the current code context, a declaration of an `implicit val someName: ActorRef`. It doesn't hurt at all that you name the value `sender`, even though any name would work.

```
implicit val sender: ActorRef = sender()
```

The declaration ensures that when ! or `tell()` is used, the `sender` will be passed as an argument. If the code context doesn't have such a reference, the default will be used, which is `Actor.noSender`.

As you can see from the implementation of `tell()`, if you want to provide an explicit value to an implicitly declared method parameter, you must use a second set of parameters.

```
... this.!(message)(sender)
```

It is possible to overuse implicit parameters, making code unreadable. When used conservatively, implicit parameters can greatly add to code readability.

One of the things that can be defined in a Scala source file is a *trait*. A Scala trait is sort of a blend of an interface and an abstract class as you would use in

Java or C#. It's like an interface in that it defines the protocol for objects whose classes use them. It's like an abstract class because at least some part of the interface can have a default implementation. Okay, that actually just sounds like an abstract class, period. That would be true if that's as far as traits could be used. Yet, it's the fact that multiple traits can be implemented or extended by a single class. This is often referred to as *mixing in* multiple traits.

```
class ShoppingCart(
    val catalogSource: CatalogSource,
    val maximumItems: Int)
extends ItemBrowser with ItemContainer {
  ...
}
```

Here both `ItemBrowser` and `ItemContainer` are mixed-in traits. The first trait or superclass is mixed in using the `extends` keyword. Every successive trait is mixed in using the `with` keyword. Each of the two traits declares abstract values. The `ShoppingCart` constructor arguments serve to initialize the variables declared in the traits.

```
trait ItemBrowser {
  val catalogSource: CatalogSource // abstract
  ...
}

trait ItemContainer {
  val maximumItems: Int // abstract
  ...
}
```

I've been discussing the kinds of Scala classes that are similar to kinds of classes you can create in Java or C#. There is, in addition to these familiar classes, another kind called *case classes*.

```
case class ProcessOrder(orderId: String)

val message = ProcessOrder("123")
```

Cool. You don't even have to use the `new` keyword to create a new instance of a case class. But that's not the end of niceties provided by case classes.

As I like to say, case classes are the world's easiest way to create immutable Value Objects [IDDD]. Why? In the `ProcessOrder` case class definition, its class arguments (constructor parameters) are declared just like a normal Scala class. The `orderId` field is automatically declared as a `val` even though you didn't state it explicitly. Beyond this, the Scala compiler automatically generates several methods: `equals()`, `hashCode()`, `toString()`, `copy(...)`, and a public read accessor for each field named as a class argument such as `orderId`. Java and C# programmers familiar with implementing domain objects know what a pain it is to have to create all this boilerplate code time and again. It's Scala to the rescue, once again, with code conservation features. Typically you use case classes to create immutable message types to send between actors. Since they make a perfect Value Object [IDDD], they can be used for much more than message types. Yet, case classes also provide a convenient way to perform pattern matching (discussed below).

If you want to put custom behavior on a case class, it's easy enough to do, just like for regular classes.

```
case class ConfigureProcessor(
    orderProvider: OrderProvider,
    timeOut: Long) {

  def timeOutAsDuration(): Duration = {
    Duration.create(timeOut, TimeUnit.MILLISECONDS)
  }
}
```

By this point you are probably wondering how Scala supports looping and iteration. Actually, it seems like there are a gazillion ways to do so. This condensed tutorial will convey only limited examples. Here is one way to write a `for` loop:

```
for (counter <- 1 to 20) {
  println(counter) // 1 through 20 on new lines
}
```

This `for` expression repeats from 1 to 20, each time placing the current integer range value in the `var` named `counter`. If you change the `to` part of the expression to `until`, the `for` expression will stop short of 20, and `counter` will only ever hold integer values 1 to 19.

```
for (counter <- 1 until 20) {
  println(counter) // 1 through 19 on new lines
}
```

An easy way to iterate over a collection is performed using a for expression.

```
for (element <- Vector(1,2,3,4,5)) {
  println(element) // 1 through 5 on new lines
}
```

Or you can use the collection itself to provide the iteration, and you provide the closure that processes each element.

```
Vector(1,2,3,4,5) map { element => println(element) }
```

This example uses a *for comprehension*:

```
val numbers = Vector(1,2,3,4,5,6,7,8,9,10)

val evenNumbers = for (number <- numbers) {
  if (number % 2 == 0)
} yield number
```

The result of the iteration over the numbers 1 through 10 will filter all except for those that are evenly divisible by 2. The numbers that pass the if (...) filter will be yielded as part of the result. The result is referenced by evenNumbers, which is the Vector of the numbers 2, 4, 6, 8, and 10. Because the source of the iteration is a Vector of Int, the comprehension knows to yield the result into a Vector of Int. Thus, Scala type inference ensures that evenNumbers references a Vector of Int, even though there is no type specified with the declaration of evenNumbers.

Here's a different way to achieve the same result, which is more elegant Scala code:

```
val evenNumbers =
 for {
  number <- numbers
  if number % 2 == 0
 } yield number
```

If you did decide to declare the evenNumbers reference fully, it would look like this:

```
val evenNumbers: Vector[Int] = ...
```

This declares a collection, Vector, of a type, Int. The Scala syntax for generics uses square brackets, [type], rather than the more familiar angle brackets, <type>, used by Java and C#.

One of Scala's most powerful tools performs *pattern matching* in a number of different circumstances, such as each of the numbers in a collection.

```scala
Vector(1,2,3) map {
  case 1 => println("One") // printed first
  case 2 => println("Two") // printed second
  case 3 => println("Three") // printed third
}
```

Matching doesn't have to iterate over a collection. It can work even if the whole value is a single object, which in this case is 10.

```scala
10 match {
  case 1 => println("One")
  case 2 => println("Two")
  case 3 => println("Three")
  case _ => println("Several") // default case is printed
}
```

Take note. You'll be using pattern matching quite a bit as your actors receive messages. It's the way your actors will know which message is being received. When dealing with messages, you will generally need to use types and result parameters in your matching cases. It is strongly encouraged to use case classes, such as **ConfigureProcessor** and **ProcessOrder**, to define message types.

```scala
case class ConfigureProcessor(
    orderProvider: OrderProvider,
    timeOut: Long)

case class ProcessOrder(orderId: String)

val message = ProcessOrder("123")

message match {
  case config: ConfigureProcessor =>
    configureProcessor(init)
  case processOrder: ProcessOrder =>
    val order = orderFor(processOrder.orderId)
    ...
}
```

This shows one way to put match results into parameters so you can use them in the expressions that are associated with each case match. In the previous code, `config` references the `ConfigureProcessor` message instance, and `processOrder` references the `ProcessOrder` message instance. Another way is to name the class arguments.

```
...
message match {
  case ConfigureProcessor(orderProvider, timeOut) =>
    configureProcessor(orderProvider, timeOut)
  case ProcessOrder(orderId) =>
    val order = orderFor(orderId)
    ...
}
```

Although far from exhaustive, this condensed tutorial should provide enough for you to understand the code examples and to even program in Scala yourself.

Programming with Akka

As previously established, using what are considered conventional means for multithreaded programming makes success overly complicated and hard to achieve. Trying to take full advantage of contemporary hardware improvements such as increasing numbers of processors and cores and growing processor cache is seriously impeded by the very tools and patterns that should be helping us. Thus, implementing event-driven, scalable, resilient, and responsive applications is often deemed too difficult and risky and as a result is generally avoided.

The Akka toolkit was created to address the failings of common multithreaded programming approaches, distributed computing, and fault tolerance. It does so by using the Actor model, which provides powerful abstractions that make creating solutions around concurrency and parallelism much easier to reason about and succeed in. This is not to say that Akka removes the need to think about concurrency. It doesn't, and you must still design for parallelism, latency, and eventually consistent application state and think of how you will prevent your application from unnecessary blocking. What Akka and the Actor model do is remove the common concurrency programming problems such as dead-lock, live-lock, inefficient code, and the need to consider threads as a first-class programming model. In a nutshell, it makes concurrent software designs as simple as possible to successfully achieve.

The next subsections discuss the basics of developing reactive applications with the Actor model and Akka. You are introduced to `ActorSystem`, `Actor`, `ActorRef`, `ActorContext`, supervision, remoting, clustering, and testing. With this knowledge you will be ready to start applying the reactive enterprise application and integration patterns.

Actor System

Every Akka application must create a named `ActorSystem`. An actor system collects a hierarchy of actors, which all share the same configuration. This code creates an `ActorSystem` named `ReactiveEnterprise` in the local JVM:

```
import akka.actor._
...
val system = ActorSystem("ReactiveEnterprise")
```

This creates the named `ActorSystem` using default configuration. An actor system configuration includes such things as actor settings, including mailbox types and how remote actors are accessed, declarations of dispatchers that execute actors on threads, and other system and actor properties. The Akka toolkit design prefers that all application values that are expected to change between environments are configured rather than hard-coded inside actors. This can be especially useful for testing.

Grokking Configuration

Here's just a little taste of an Akka configuration. It is typically placed in `application.conf` but can also be defined in several different ways.

```
# application.conf for ActorSystem: RiskRover
akka {

  # default logs to System.out
  loggers = ["akka.event.Logging$DefaultLogger"]

  # Akka configured loggers use this loglevel.
  # Use: OFF, ERROR, WARNING, INFO, DEBUG
  loglevel = "DEBUG"

  # Akka ActorSystem startup uses this loglevel
  # until configs load; output to System.out.
  # Use: OFF, ERROR, WARNING, INFO, DEBUG
  stdout-loglevel = "DEBUG"

  actor {
    # if remoting:    akka.remote.RemoteActorRefProvider
```

```
    # if clustering: akka.cluster.ClusterActorRefProvider

    provider = "akka.actor.LocalActorRefProvider"

    default-dispatcher {
      # Default Dispatcher throughput;
      # set to 1 for as fair as possible,
      # but also poor throughput
      throughput = 1
    }
  }
}
```

The richness with which you can configure a single actor and the overall actor system is too great for the scope of this book. In fact, it's too rich for the scope of the Akka documentation, which also redirects you to the Typesafe Config Library documentation. For full coverage, you should see both the Akka documentation and the Typesafe Config Library documentation. Unless otherwise stated, assume the default configuration for the samples in this book.

You can create multiple `ActorSystem` instances for a single application, but generally speaking, think in terms of creating just one `ActorSystem` per application.[6] If you want one `ActorSystem` to collaborate with another `ActorSystem`, use Akka remoting; see the "Remoting" section later in this chapter. A single `ActorSystem` can span JVMs if you use an Akka cluster; see the "Clustering" section later in this chapter.

When an actor system is created, a few actors are created along with it. These are the *root guardian,* the *user guardian,* and the *system guardian.* These serve as the base supervisory hierarchy for all other actors, and the actors that an application creates are placed under the user guardian, as shown in Figure 2.1.

Recall that supervision was highlighted in the first chapter as an addition to the original Actor model characteristics. Supervision is an important extension provided with Akka that helps you develop highly resilient applications. Basically, any actor that creates a child actor automatically becomes responsible for the supervision of the child. If the child crashes (for example, throws an exception), the parent must determine what should be done: resume, restart, stop, or escalate. The first three actions are parental recovery options, while escalation turns control over to the parent's parent, namely, the crashed child's grandparent. Supervision is covered in detail coming up.

---

6. Note that the Play Framework creates its own `ActorSystem`, so if you use Play, your application will always have two instances of `ActorSystem` because of course you should not use Play's instance.

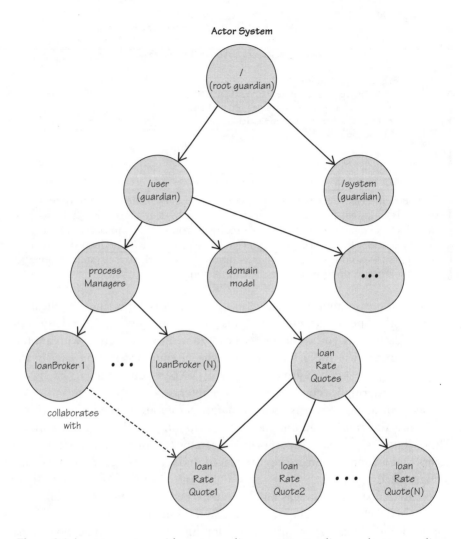

Figure 2.1 An actor system with root guardian, system guardian, and user guardian. All application actors are created under the user guardian.

To create an actor directly under the user guardian, you use your `ActorSystem`, as is shown in the following example with the code `system.actorOf()`:

```
import akka.actor._
...
val system = ActorSystem("ReactiveEnterprise")
```

```
...
// create actor and get its ActorRef
val processManagersRef: ActorRef =
      system.actorOf(Props[ProcessManagers], "processManagers")

// send message to actor using ActorRef
processManagersRef ! BrokerForLoan(banks)
```

Why the ! Symbol?

As discussed in the previous Scala tutorial, the Scala language permits the use of symbols as method names. The ! method is basically the same as the `tell()` method but uses the ! character as the method name. I really like the ! in this case because it is visually appealing, relieving you of the need to visually filter out the otherwise distracting `tell()` noise throughout your code.

Also note that if you were using the `tell()` method, you would pass two parameters, the message instance and the sending `ActorRef`.

```
processManagersRef.tell(BrokerForLoan(banks), self)
```

In the case where you use !, however, the `ActorRef` of the sender is an implicit parameter, which means you don't have to pass it yourself. The Scala compiler looks for an `implicit ActorRef` reference in the code context and, if found, automatically passes the value as a parameter for you. Implicit parameters are also discussed in the Scala tutorial.

The `ActorSystem` method `actorOf()` creates an actor named **process-Managers** of the type **ProcessManagers**. When you ask the `ActorSystem` to create a new actor, it doesn't return the actor instance. Instead, it returns an `ActorRef`, which in this case is held by the value holder, `processManagersRef`. This separation establishes a level of indirection between the actual actor and the client of the actor. When the client uses `processManagersRef` to send a message, such as the `BrokerForLoan` message, to the actor named `processManagers`, the `ActorRef` is responsible only for getting the message enqueued to the actor's mailbox.

Naming the ActorRef Value Holder

There is no need to name the value holder `processManagersRef`. In fact, it is much better to name it `processManagers` instead. The `Ref` was appended to the value holder name to make it stand out as an `ActorRef` just for the sake of the opening example. This was done primarily to avoid causing confusion between the internal actor name and the name of the value holder.

Naming it without the `Ref` postfix makes the name more readable and more adherent to the intended abstraction: `processManagers`. I use this naming convention moving forward.

The parent of the `processManagers` is the actor named `user`, which is the user guardian. The user guardian is a fail-safe component that prevents catastrophic actor system failure when a direct child, such as `processManagers`, crashes.

So, you can just create an actor as a child of the `user` any time you want. Yet, imagine that as you create actor after actor—perhaps thousands or even millions—they are all nested directly under `user`. Actually "nestled" is an inappropriate description of this situation. Although this would work, it wouldn't work well. The huge collection of actors would cause some parts of the system to bog down. Hence, it is much better to create hierarchies of actors. Yet, that's not the only reason you create actor hierarchies. You should also try to prevent the user guardian from ever dealing with application failure situations. What you will do is use your `processManagers` actor as the top level of your own application hierarchy and the top-level supervisor. The `processManagers` actor will be used only to create and supervise specific kinds of *Process Managers (292)*. It will not itself serve as a *Process Manager (292)*. This emphasizes the fact that it's not a good idea to create many actors directly under the user guardian. It is better to create a parent supervisor for a specific category of actors and then possibly another parent supervisor for a given coarse-grained process, task, or domain model entity.

As shown in Figure 2.1, you create both `processManagers` and `domainModel` as top-level supervisors. The `domainModel` actor serves as parent and supervisor for categories of domain model of concepts [IDDD]. For example, under `domainModel` is `loanRateQuotes`, the supervisor for all `LoanRateQuote` entity actors, which the `domainModel` actor creates. There is one `LoanRateQuote` entity actor per `LoanBroker` *Process Manager (292)* actor, as the `LoanBroker` uses a `LoanRateQuote` entity to manage each bank's loan rate quote. All this will help keep your application's actors organized, resilient, and make the overall system perform at its best.

Given the hierarchical structure of an actor system, if you don't already have a reference to an actor, how do you find it? To search from the user guardian downward, use method `actorSelection()` on the `ActorSystem`.

```
val system = ActorSystem("ReactiveEnterprise")
...
val selection = system.actorSelection("/user/processManagers")

selection ! BrokerForLoans(banks)
```

At-Most-Once Delivery Mechanisms

Both `ActorRef` and `ActorSelection` can deliver messages to an actor's mailbox only if the actor exists. There is a chance that both could reference an actor that is in the process of stopping or that has already stopped, in which case the message cannot be delivered. Thus, reloading and retry strategies must be used if you must ensure that a given message is delivered. Much of this will be handled by Akka Persistence, an optional part of the Akka toolkit. These tools are discussed under *Guaranteed Delivery (175)*, *Transactional Actor (354)*, *Idempotent Receiver (382)*, and *Message Store (402)*, and they can be used to support at-least-once delivery of messages.

Table 2.1 `ActorSystem` Methods

Method	Description
`actorOf(...)`	This creates the new actor as a child of this context with the given name, which must not be null, empty, or start with $. Note that not many actors should be created as direct children of the system's user guardian.
`actorSelection(...)`	This answers the `ActorSelection` for the path parameter, which may include wildcards. Since wildcards can resolve to multiple actors, it is possible that `ActorSelection` may resolve to multiple actors.
`awaitTermination(...)`	After using `shutdown()`, you can await the full termination of the system.
`deadLetters`	This answers the `ActorRef` of the *Dead Letter Channel (172)*.
`eventStream`	This answers the system's primary `EventBus`; see *Publish-Subscribe Channel (154)*.
`isTerminated`	This answers `true` if the system is fully stopped after receiving a `shutdown()` request.
`log`	This answers the `LoggingAdapter` for system default logging to the `eventStream`.
`name`	This answers the `String` name of the system.
`scheduler`	This answers the system's scheduler used to create timer events.
`shutdown()`	This stops the user guardian, which recursively stops all user children, then stops the system guardian and all system-level actors, and finally terminates the system.
`stop(actor: ActorRef)`	This asynchronously stops the actor referenced by the `ActorRef`, which involves a message send to the `/user` guardian actor. Although asynchronous, this method internally blocks for a reply.

The method `actorSelection()` returns an `ActorSelection` rather than an `ActorRef`. An `ActorSelection` can be used to send a message to the actor referenced by it. Be aware, however, that using this approach is slower and more resource intensive to resolve than using an `ActorRef`. Yet, `actorSelection()` is a nice facility because it can accept wildcard actor queries, which when resolved allows you to broadcast a message to any number of actors represented by the `ActorSelection`.

```
val system = ActorSystem("ReactiveEnterprise")
...
val selection = system.actorSelection("/user/*")

selection ! FlushAll()
```

The previous code sends the `FlushAll` message to every top-level actor, which includes all actors that are direct children of the user guardian. Table 2.1 (page 49) lists `ActorSystem` methods that you will make use of and some others that may come in handy from time to time. This list is not exhaustive, so be sure to check the Akka documentation for other methods.

Now that you understand what an `ActorSystem` is and how you can interact with it, consider some details about actor implementation and usage.

Implementing Actors

All Akka actors must extend the `akka.actor.Actor` trait. At the minimum, your actor must also support a `receive` block.

```
import akka.actor._

class ShoppingCart extends Actor {

  def receive = {
    case _ =>
  }
}
```

This `ShoppingCart` actor does nothing important. It only receives all messages that are sent to it and returns immediately. The `case _ =>` expression is a pattern matcher for any type of message. Since no code follows the `=>` part of the expression, the case just falls out of the `receive` block and returns.

There are some things that happen behind the scenes, however, which are not yet apparent. There are four default life-cycle methods that are automatically

Table 2.2 The Four Actor Life-Cycle Methods (in Logical Order)

Method	Description
`preStart()`	This is invoked when the actor is started, after it is created. Actors are created asynchronously, and after they are fully created, they are started. The default implementation is empty, which does nothing. Under most circumstances your actor should be able to perform all prestart initialization by overriding this method.
`postStop()`	This is invoked when the actor is stopped. An actor is stopped asynchronously when `stop(ActorRef)` is called on `ActorSystem` or `ActorContext`. (The `Actor` has an `ActorContext`, which is available through its `context` method.) This can give the actor an opportunity to clean up nonchild resources that are not dealt with by `preRestart()`. Under most circumstances your actor should be able to perform all poststop cleanup by overriding this method.
`preRestart(...)`	A supervisor failure strategy can choose to restart the failed child actor. During a restart, this method is invoked just prior to the actor's restart. The default implementation handles the cleanup of resources before the actor is terminated, disposing of all children. After the cleanup, `postStop()` is invoked. Normally your actor should not need to override this method. Due care must be taken if it is overridden.
`postRestart(...)`	This is invoked just following restart on the newly created actor, enabling reinitialization after an actor failure and restart. The default implementation invokes `preStart()`. Normally your actor should not need to override this method. Due care must be taken if it is overridden.

called by the Akka framework when an actor is started, stopped, or restarted. The four methods are defined as part of the `Actor` base class and can be overridden in your concrete actor. Table 2.2 describes the four methods, and sample code follows:

```
import akka.actor._

class ShoppingCart extends Actor {

  override def postRestart(reason: Throwable): Unit {
    ...
  }

  override def postStop(): Unit {
    ...
  }
```

```
override def preRestart(
        reason: Throwable,
        message: Option[Any]): Unit {
  ...
}

override def preStart(): Unit {
  ...
}

def receive = {
  case _ =>
}
}
```

Every actor has an `ActorContext`, which is accessible through method `context()` on the `Actor`. The `ActorContext` gives the owning actor a way to use parts of its underlying implementation but in a safe, nondestructive manner. In this example, the `ActorContext` is used to create a child `Task` actor:

```
import akka.actor._

class TaskManager extends Actor {
  ...
  def nextTaskName(): String = {
    "task-" + ...
  }

  def receive = {
    case RunTask(definition) =>
      val task = context.actorOf(Props[Task], nextTaskName)
      task ! Run(definition)
      ...
    case TaskCompleted =>
      ...
  }
}
```

There is a difference between creating an actor through the `ActorSystem` and one through the `ActorContext`. Assuming that the name of the `TaskManager` is as follows, the individual tasks would be created under their parent and supervisor:

```
"/user/taskManagers/taskManager1"
```

Assuming that `taskManager1` creates three child tasks, their paths and names would be as follows:

```
"/user/taskManagers/taskManager1/task1"
"/user/taskManagers/taskManager1/task2"
"/user/taskManagers/taskManager1/task3"
```

One characteristic that makes the Actor model unique from object models is the actor's ability to dynamically change its behavior. This is discussed in *Design Patterns* [GoF] as the State pattern, which can be achieved in object-based solutions. Compared to an object-based State implementation, however, it's just simple to implement when using Scala and Akka. Again using the `ActorContext`, an actor can switch its behavior from one receive block to another.

```scala
import akka.actor._

class TaskManager extends Actor {
  var statusWatcher: ActorRef = None
  ...
  override def preStart(): Unit = {
    context.become(houseKeeper)
  }

  def houseKeeper: Receive = {
    case StartTaskManagement(externalStatusWatcher) =>
      statusWatcher = Some(externalStatusWatcher)
      context.become(taskDistributor)
    case StartTaskManagementWithoutStatus =>
      context.become(taskDistributor)
  }

  def taskDistributor: Receive = {
    case RunTask(definition) =>
      val task = context.actorOf(Props[Task], nextTaskName)
      task ! Run(definition, statusWatcher)
      ...
    case TaskCompleted =>
      ...
  }
}
```

Here a `TaskManager` can behave as either a `houseKeeper` or a `task-Distributor`. These are two different definitions of `receive`-type partial functions. The `TaskManager` becomes either of these behaviors by using method `become()` on `ActorContext`. Just before the actor is started, its `preStart()` method is invoked. When that happens, the actor *becomes* its `houseKeeper`. This means that only the `StartTaskManagement` message or the `StartTaskManagementWithoutStatus` message can be received and reacted to. After one of the two messages is processed, the actor will next become its `taskDistributor`. The `ActorContext` method `unbecome()` can be used to replace the current behavior with the previous behavior, if there is a previous.

There are several more things you can do with an `ActorContext`, as highlighted in Table 2.3. (This table is not exhaustive; see the Akka documentation.)

Table 2.3 Functions Provided by `ActorContext`

Function	Description
`actorOf(...)`	This creates a child actor. Most actors in your system should be created under an application-level `ActorContext` such as this.
`actorSelection(...)`	This answers the `ActorSelection` for the path parameter, which may include wildcards. Since wildcards can resolve to multiple actors, it is possible that `ActorSelection` may resolve to multiple actors.
`become(...)`	This makes the current actor behavior the given partial function parameter. Of the two parameters, the second is `discardOld`, which defaults to true. When true, the previous behavior is discarded before this one is set. When false, the previous behavior remains on the stack, and the new one is pushed above it.
`children`	This answers an `Iterable` of `ActorRef` for all direct, supervised children.
`parent`	This answers the `ActorRef` of the supervising parent of this actor.
`props`	This answers the `Props` used to create this actor.
`self`	This answers the `ActorRef` of this actor.
`sender()`	This answers the `ActorRef` of the actor that sent the currently received message.
`stop(actor: ActorRef)`	This stops the actor referenced by the given `ActorRef`. Although this is an asynchronous operation, if the actor being stopped is a child of this `ActorContext`, the actor's name is immediately freed for reuse.
`system`	This answers the `ActorSystem` to which this actor belongs.
`unbecome`	This makes the current actor behavior the one prior to the current, if there is a previous.

Be Careful with sender()

Be really careful with your use of `sender()`. It's a function, not an instance `val`, and answers the current sender, which is in context with the current received message. If you close over the method, you will likely experience problems, that is, difficult-to-debug problems.

```
case calculateRisk: CalculateRisk =>
  context.system.scheduleOnce(1 minute) {
    sender ! UnfinishedCalculation()
  }
  ...
```

Since `sender()` is a function, it is not evaluated until the closure is evaluated, which in this case will be one minute later. If other messages have been received since the scheduler was used, and that is likely to have occurred, the `sender()` will at that later time return an `ActorRef` that you were not expecting. The solution? Do this instead:

```
case calculateRisk: CalculateRisk =>
  val requestSender = sender
  context.system.scheduleOnce(1 minute) {
    requestSender ! UnfinishedCalculation()
  }
  ...
```

Now the `requestSender` is a `val` whose evaluation is constant, and it will always reflect the intended `ActorRef`, the one that sent the `CalculateRisk` in context.

Supervision

You've already learned a good deal about actor supervision in the introduction to Akka's `ActorSystem`. What you haven't seen is how to actually implement supervision. First, you must understand who is directly responsible for supervision. As previously stated, a parent actor is responsible for supervising its children. In Figure 2.2, which actor is responsible for dealing with the crashed `loanRateQuote1` and `loanRateQuote2` actors? The `loanBroker1` collaborates with `loanRateQuote1` by sending it messages and receiving messages in return. Does that mean `loanBroker1` is responsible for the supervision of `loanRateQuote1`? No. It is the parent, `loanRateQuotes`, that is responsible for supervising `loanRateQuote1` and all other instances of `LoanRateQuote`, such as `loanRateQuote2`.

What will the `loanRateQuotes` do when `loanRateQuote1` crashes? It depends on how it crashes and how the supervisor's recovery strategy is defined. By default, all parent actors inherit a default `supervisorStrategy`, which has the following policies:

- `ActorInitializationException`: The failed child will be stopped.

- `ActorKilledException`: The child will be stopped.

- **Exception**: The child will be restarted.

- All other **Throwable** types cause an escalation to the parent.

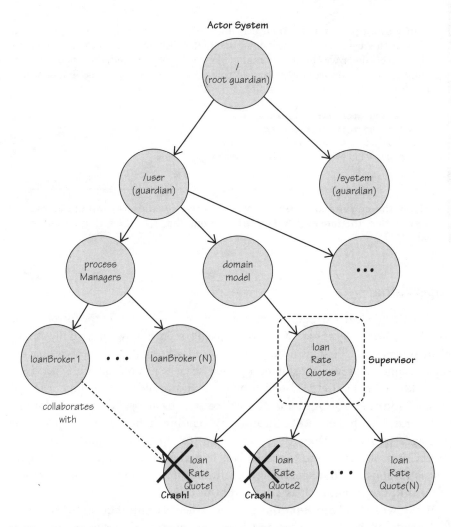

Figure 2.2 Two actors have crashed: **loanRateQuote1** and **loanRateQuote2**. The supervisor is **loanRateQuotes**, not **loanBroker1**.

Let's assume that the default strategy won't work well for your loan quotes application. Yet you will want to keep this as simple as possible. Let's see what problems a **LoanRateQuote** instance can experience and what can be done about it. First, each parent supervisor must override the inherited, default `supervisorStrategy`.

```
class LoanRateQuotes extends Actor {

  override val supervisorStrategy =
      OneForOneStrategy(
          maxNrOfRetries = 5,
          withinTimeRange = 1 minute) {
    case NullPointerException          => Restart
    case ArithmeticException           => Resume
    case IllegalArgumentException      => Stop
    case UnsupportedOperationException => Stop
    case Exception                     => Escalate
  }
  ...
  def receive = {
    case RequestLoanQuotation(definition) =>
      val loadRateQuote =
              context.actorOf(Props[LoanRateQuote], nextName)
      loadRateQuote ! InitializeQuotation(definition)
      ...
    case LoanQuotationCompleted =>
      ...
  }
}
```

There are two parts to the `supervisorStrategy` override.

- You must instantiate a `SupervisorStrategy` subclass, either an `AllForOneStrategy` or a `OneForOneStrategy`. You normally want to declare a `OneForOneStrategy` since it will apply only to the child actor that has crashed. The `AllForOneStrategy` is less often used since it will have the `Decider` effect on all child actors rather than just the one that crashed; it is used when sibling actors logically belong together and are implicitly coupled and when there is a "showstopper" kind of problem where it makes sense to stop the entire hierarchy of actors. The `maxNrOfRetries` and `withinTimeRange` class arguments are used together to determine how many times a given actor is permitted to crash and restart within the given time frame before giving up. The previous sample uses five retries within one minute. Using a negative value for `maxNrOfRetries`, such as –1, and `Duration.Inf` (`infinite`) will make retries unending.

- You must declare a `Decider`, which is the closure surrounded by curly braces. Depending on the kind of exception thrown, the `Decider`matched case determines a directive. The directive can be one of four `akka.actor.`

`SupervisorStrategy.Directive` subclasses: `Escalate`, `Restart`, `Resume`, or `Stop`. When a `Decider` answers any one of these, it tells the Akka recovery mechanism what to do. Most of the directives are self-explanatory. `Escalate` means to fail this supervisor, making it appear that this supervisor failed, and allow its supervisor (the grandparent of the failed child) to deal with the crash. `Resume` is different from `Restart` in that `Resume` leaves current child actor state intact, and the child will process its next available message. `Restart` causes the child to be terminated and completely reconstituted, which means its mailbox is empty; it's not the same actor.

It is easy to imagine the two kinds of failures that would be handled all inclusively or individually. For example, if a single database query fails, it could make sense to address the problem with the single actor that attempted the query, that is, using the `OneForOneStrategy`. On the other hand, if the entire database becomes unreachable for some reason, it may make more sense to stop the entire hierarchy of actors that were created to perform database queries, that is, using the `AllForOneStrategy`.

In the previous example, the following exception types cause a specific kind of recovery:

- `NullPointerException` causes the child actor to `Restart`.

- `ArithmeticException` causes the child actor to `Resume`.

- `IllegalArgumentException` causes the child actor to `Stop`.

- `UnsupportedOperationException` causes the child actor to `Stop`.

All other kinds of `Exception` cause this supervisor to `Escalate` by failing up to its parent supervisor.

You can map any kind of exception to any of the four directives. Your specific exceptions should be carefully designed, semantically explicit application exception classes that will help you achieve resilience. You will want to carefully research and identify the kinds of failures that can occur in your application and create strategies that will allow you to gracefully recover. Be sure to distinguish minor problems from those that are more catastrophic and recover in a manner appropriate for the situation. See the previously discussed actor life-cycle methods to control what happens to the failed actor during `Restart` and `Stop`.

Java and C# developers know all too well that it can be quite difficult to deal with exceptions at the places they may occur. In fact, some developers have altogether abandoned the notion of error recovery because it is too complex. Akka's supervision strategies allow you to gracefully deal with failure, potentially even healing bad data or teaching an actor to adjust to situations that caused a failure before the failed actor is resumed or restarted.

Remoting

Akka supports network-based remote access between separate `ActorSystem` instances, called Akka remoting. Consider some of the characteristics of this feature.

The communication style is peer-to-peer. An actor in one JVM communicates directly[7] with an actor in another JVM by sending it messages. There is no special API that supports remoting between a client of nonactors and a server of actors. Perhaps you consider one JVM to be a "client" because it doesn't contain business logic. Although you can do that, you must have an `ActorSystem` with actors on that "client." Those "client" actors communicate with actors in a remote JVM that you consider to be the "server," and they live in their own `ActorSystem`. What is more, the actors on the "server" can communicate with actors on the "client." Thus, what you think of as "client" and "server" are actually peers and share the ability to communicate bidirectionally. It might work best if you rethink these roles, calling one the "user experience" system and the other a "business capabilities" system. Obviously, you would chose `ActorSystem` names that actually fit your business.

Actually, one `ActorSystem` can span nodes. In other words, you are not required to choose a different `ActorSystem` name for each node just because there is a separation of two or more JVMs. An actor's `ActorPath` includes the hostname and the `ActorSystem` name, so it is easy to avoid actor name collisions. You get name collisions only if you start up an actor with the same name on the same host and `ActorSystem`. Thus, two or more nodes can have the same named `ActorSystem`, which implies that an `ActorSystem` spans a number of nodes. Even so, it might make more sense to name various `ActorSystem` instances according to the role they play in the application.

The foregoing implies that access between actors is location transparent. As far as the actors themselves are concerned, they all live in one large JVM. The

---

7. Again, this is referring to direct asynchronous messaging of the actor model. In reality, it is not direct, especially when the network is involved. It could take considerable time for a message to reach the target actor. Yet, semantically it is direct asynchronous messaging.

following simplistic message-sending protocol holds true for both local and remote actors:

```
val someActor: ActorRef = ...

someActor ! SomeMessage(...)
```

The sender has no idea whether `someActor` references a local actor or a remote actor because the `ActorRef` abstracts the details.

You use a network protocol, such as Transmission Control Protocol (TCP), to enable actors to communicate between separate JVMs, where each JVM has its own `ActorSystem` instance and actors. People generally think of each JVM running on a separate physical server machine, but they could be on the same physical machine, and possibly in a separate virtual server. No matter, all remote communication between actors travels between systems via the network.

Riding on the network is a good thing and gives Akka remoting a big advantage in distributing your system across multiple server nodes. On the other hand, you must keep in mind that any time you involve the network there are all kinds of problems that can occur. Remembering that bandwidth is not infinite and that there is at least some latency—and sometimes a lot of latency—will help you design for the network. Yet, that's not all you have to consider.

Anytime a message is sent from one actor to another actor over the network, the message itself must be serialized. This has its own overhead, which may be considerable depending on the type of serialization you use. Akka defaults to Java serialization, which is one of the worst for both performance and size. Thus, you should choose wisely from among your serialization options when you know your messages will have to cross JVM boundaries. Two notable options are Protocol Buffers [ProtoBuf] and Kryo serialization [Kryo]. You use configuration to specify the serialization you prefer, including disabling Java serialization.

```
# application.conf for ActorSystem: RiskRover
akka {
  actor {
    serializers {
      proto = "akka.remote.serialization.ProtobufSerializer"
      kryo = "com.romix.akka.serialization.kryo.KryoSerializer"
      ...
    }
    serialization-bindings {
```

```
      "java.io.Serializable" = none
      ...
    }
    kryo {
      type = "graph"
      idstrategy = "incremental"
      serializer-pool-size = 16
      buffer-size = 4096
      max-buffer-size = -1
      ...
    }
  }
}
```

To support Akka remoting in any given `ActorSystem` on a single JVM, you must have these minimum configurations in its `application.conf`:

```
# application.conf for ActorSystem: RiskRover
akka {
  ...
  actor {
    # default is: "akka.actor.LocalActorRefProvider"

    provider = "akka.remote.RemoteActorRefProvider"
    ...
  }

  remote {
    # actors at: akka.tcp://RiskRover@hounddog:2552/user

    enabled-transports = ["akka.remote.netty.tcp"]
    netty.tcp {
      hostname = "hounddog"
      port = 2552
    }
  }
}
```

Although the default is to use the `LocalActorRefProvider`, the `RemoteActorRefProvider` is needed to ensure that actors referenced on various JVMs include their remote access information. That seems like a lot of overhead, however, if all local actors are created as if they are remote, and you have to pay a network penalty to send messages to local actors. Gladly, that's not how it works with `RemoteActorRefProvider`. If the actor being created is local, then in fact the remote provider internally uses the `LocalActor-RefProvider`. That is, the `RemoteActorRefProvider` must understand whether an actor is requested on the local system or a remote system and create an appropriate `ActorRef` for each. Thus, internally there is both a `LocalActorRef` and a `RemoteActorRef`, but you only need to know about and use the `ActorRef` abstraction.

With this basic understanding of how remoting works, let's consider two ways to use remoting.

- *Remote creation:* An actor on your local system creates a child actor on a remote system, as illustrated in Figure 2.3. It seems to me that the best mind-set to have with this approach is that of work offloading. On the local system your actor knows what work must be done, but it chooses not to create a child actor locally to do the work. Perhaps it would cause too much overhead to execute the work on the local node. Or perhaps it's just a matter of logical tier roles, and the local node doesn't do a certain kind of work. Instead, the local actor chooses to offload the work to a separate, remote node. So, the local actor creates a child on the remote node and sends a work message to it. Even though the actor is created on a completely different system, it is owned by your local actor, and the local actor is its supervisor. Thus, when the work has completed, your local actor is responsible for stopping any remote child actors. I will cover two ways to perform remote creation.

- *Remote lookup:* An actor on your local system looks up an existing actor on the remote system, as illustrated in Figure 2.4. It exists because some other actor on that remote system created it. You are neither the owner

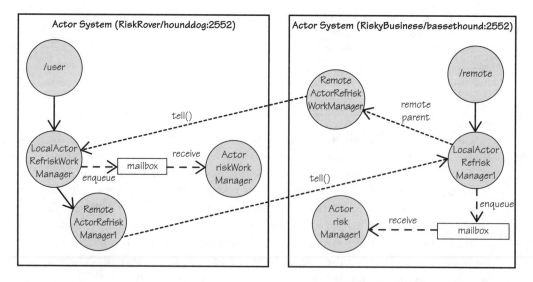

Figure 2.3 Remote actor creation associates `RemoteActorRef` and `LocalActorRef` instances.

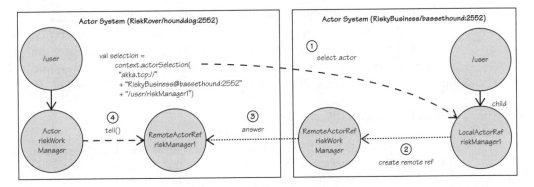

Figure 2.4 Remote actor lookup is an asynchronous action that eventually finds any number of actors on a remote system, if one or more exist that match the query.

nor the supervisor of the remote actor. You can, however, look up one or more such actors and delegate work to them. This may feel a bit more like client-server because you are not in charge of the life cycle or supervision of the remote actor. You are just using the service it provides. However, it isn't a traditional client-server approach because the remote actor can communicate with the local just as easily as the local communicates with the remote.

As you consider these two approaches, try to determine which of the two best suits your needs. It is quite likely that you can find a good use for both.

Remote Creation

Using configuration is the cleanest and most abstract way for a local actor to create a remote actor. In this section, you are going to create a remote actor named `"riskManager1"` on server `bassethound`. To do so, first place the following in your Akka `application.conf`:

```
# application.conf for ActorSystem: RiskRover
akka {
  ...
  actor {
    provider = "akka.remote.RemoteActorRefProvider"
    ...
    deployment {
      /riskManager1 {
        remote = "akka.tcp://RiskyBusiness@bassethound:2552"
      }
    }
  }
}
```

This `deployment` expression says that if I specify `"riskManager1"` as the name of the actor that you create using `ActorSystem` method `actorOf()`, or using `ActorContext` method `actorOf()`, the actor will be created on the system named `RiskyBusiness` at `bassethound:2552`, which is represented in Figure 2.3. This is the first of two ways to use remote actor creation.

Don't You Need a Different Port?

Both the `RiskRover` system and the `RiskyBusiness` system use the same machine port, 2552. Isn't that a problem? It would be if both systems ran on the same physical/logical server. Yet, in this case note that the two different systems run on different servers. One runs on `hounddog` and the other on `bassethound`. If both systems ran on either `hounddog` or `bassethound`, then you would need to use separate ports, such as 2552 and 2553.

The following code creates that specific remote actor from the local actor, `RiskWorkManager`. Again, this is represented in Figure 2.3.

```
// riskWorkManager deployed on hounddog:2552

class RiskWorkManager extends Actor {

  val riskManager =
      context.system.actorOf(Props[RiskManager], "riskManager1")

  def receive = {
      ...
      riskManager ! CalculateRisk(...)
      ...
  }
}
```

Internally the `RemoteActorRefProvider` will tell the `RiskyBusiness` system to create a new actor named `"riskManager1"` on the remote system. The `RemoteActorRef` returned is held by the requester's `riskManager` value. Then when the `CalculateRisk` *Command Message (202)* is sent by way of `RemoteActorRef`, it crosses the network to the remote `RiskyBusiness` system on host `bassethound` at port 2552. When the message reaches that system, it is then delivered to the actor named `"riskManager1"` that lives in the `RiskyBusiness` system.

How Do Remote References Work?

As previously explained, on a local system, your actors are created under the user guardian. This is not where actors live that are created remotely. After creation, remote actors are deployed under a special path (pseudoguardian) named `/remote` on the target system. This is at the top of the hierarchy, just like `/user`.

When you create `riskManager1` on the remote `RiskyBusiness` system, its path becomes as follows:

```
akka.tcp//RiskyBusiness@bassethound:2552/remote/RiskRover@↵
   hounddog:2552/user/riskWorkManager/riskManager1
```

That's a lot of information. After the special `/remote` path, the `riskManager1` path reflects the logical path of the actor, which is as follows:

```
akka.tcp//RiskRover@hounddog:2552/user/riskWorkManager/riskManager1
```

This allows the `RiskyBusiness` host to know how to create a `RemoteActorRef` for `riskManager1`, so messages can be sent to actors that send messages to it. There is no need to store the `akka.tcp` protocol segment twice because it must be the same for both directions of communication.

Since the remote system has the path to `riskManager1`, it can easily deduce the path to its parent.

```
akka.tcp//RiskRover@hounddog:2552/user/riskWorkManager
```

Thus, actors can use the `parent` method of the `riskManager1` `RemoteActorRef` created on `bassethound` to send messages to the parent of `riskManager1`, which is `riskWorkManager`. This is true, even though `riskWorkManager` is not deployed on `bassethound`.

For this creation to work correctly, the Java class generated for the `Actor` type `RiskManager` must be available to both systems. That is, the `RiskRover` system and the `RiskyBusiness` must be able to load class `RiskManager`. This implies that you currently cannot transport the bytes of the class file between systems, such as from `RiskRover` to `RiskyBusiness`.

In addition, your messages, such as `CalculateRisk`, must be serializable so its bytes can cross the network wire. If a message class cannot be serialized, then the message will not be sent to the remote system.

Okay, you've created an actor on a remote system and sent it a message. Part of the remote communication is still missing, however. Recall that each actor that receives a message will also be given an `ActorRef` to the sending actor. Getting that reference allows the request receiving actor to reply to the sender—think *Request-Reply (209)*. In the case of `riskManager1`, when receiving `CalculateRisk`, the `sender` will be encoded as a `RemoteActorRef`. This remote reference will point to the `RiskWorkManager` instance on the remote system `RiskRover` on host `hounddog` at port 2552. When the `riskManager1` replies, its `RiskCalculated` message travels across the network but to the `RiskRover` system.

```
// riskManager1 deployed on bassethound:2552

class RiskManager extends Actor {
  ...
  def receive = {
    ...
      senderFor(riskWorkManagerId) ! RiskCalculated(...)
    ...
  }

  def senderFor(id: String): ActorRef = {
    ...
  }
}
```

Since there is at least some latency to fulfill the previously received CalculateRisk *Command Message (202)*, your RiskManager must react to a later message that indicates completion and, at that time, find the corresponding RiskWorkManager requester by identity. This is done via an internal method named senderFor(), passing the riskWorkManagerId *Correlation Identifier (215)*. This riskWorkManagerId must be held inside the various messages that are sent to actors in the process. Once the ActorRef is looked up, which is a RemoteActorRef, the RiskManager then sends the RiskCalculated *Event Message (207)* back to the RiskWorkManager on the remote system.

You might be wondering if you are limited to creating remote actors on a given ActorSystem just at the top level, directly under /remote (see the earlier "How Do Remote References Work?" sidebar). The answer is yes, remotely created actors are confined to live only under /remote.

This has a few implications. First, you don't want to create many, many actors under /remote. That could cause scalability problems because scanning a lot of collection elements can be costly. Second, perhaps the best kind of actor to remotely create is a kind of work supervisor, such as you have with riskManager1. Design the remote work supervisor, again like riskManager1, to create any number of child actors local to itself. The work supervisor is able to rapidly delegate work to its worker children. Then when the remote parent, as in riskWorkManager, stops its remote child, as in riskManager1, then all the children (grandchildren of riskWorkManager) are also stopped.

On the other hand, there is another way to use remote actor creation; all children of a local creating actor will be remotely created. You again use a deployment expression in the application.conf file to support this.

```
# application.conf for ActorSystem: RiskyBusiness, RiskRover
akka {
  ...
  actor {
    provider = "akka.remote.RemoteActorRefProvider"
    ...
    deployment {
      /riskManager1 {
        remote = "akka.tcp://RiskyBusiness@bassethound:2552"
      }
      /riskManager1/* {
        remote = "akka.tcp://RiskCalculators@bassethound:2553"
      }
    }
  }
}
```

This `application.conf` file demonstrates how one configuration file can be shared among all `ActorSystem` instances employed by an application. No matter from which node `riskManager1` is created, the `/riskManager1` expression (the first) will always cause `riskManager1` to be deployed to `RiskyBusiness@bassethound:2552`. Likewise, the second expression, `/riskManager1/*`, will apply to the actor named `riskManager1` only when it creates children. Thus, when `riskManager1` creates any child actor, it will be deployed to `RiskCalculators@bassethound:2553`. Here is the `riskManager1` instance as it creates one of its children, `riskCalculator1`:

```
// riskManager1 deployed on bassethound:2552

class RiskManager extends Actor {

  val riskCalculator1 =
        context.system.actorOf(Props[RiskCalculator],
                            "riskCalculator1")

  val riskCalculator2 =
        context.system.actorOf(Props[RiskCalculator],
                            "riskCalculator2")

  val riskCalculator3 =
        context.system.actorOf(Props[RiskCalculator],
                            "riskCalculator3")
  ...
}
```

The new child actors, `riskCalculator1`, `riskCalculator2`, and `riskCalculator3`, are all created on the same physical machine, `bassethound`, but on a separate JVM, which is available through port 2553. This further demonstrates that when there are multiple `ActorSystem` instances in two or more separate JVMs on the same physical computer, they must each use a different network port. Figure 2.5 illustrates the full expanse of `RiskRover`, `RiskyBusiness`, and `RiskCalculators` deployments.

Remote Lookup

The second way to use a remote actor is to look it up within a specific system. Akka calls this actor selection since your query for one or more actors results in a selection of actors. There is a lot less detail to this approach than there is with creating remote actors. Assuming that the actors you are looking up are running, it is as simple as this:

```
import akka.actor.ActorSelection
...
val path = "akka.tcp://RiskyBusiness@bassethound:2552/user/↵
riskManager1"

val selection = context.system.actorSelection(path)

selection ! CalculateRisk(...)
```

The returned selection is of type `ActorSelection`. An `ActorSelection` can represent zero, one, or multiple actors, depending on the kind of path you provided to `actorSelection()`.

- *Zero actors found*: The path you provided did not find any matching actors.

- *One actor found*: The path you provided identified a single actor, and it existed at the time the query was run.

- *Multiple actors found*: The path you provided included one or more wild-card characters, which caused the query to find more than a single actor at the time the query was run.

As shown in the previous code, you can use the `ActorSelection` to send a message to all of the actors that were found, assuming there were any. If there is only one actor represented by the `selection`, then the message is sent to it alone. If there are multiple actors represented by the `selection`, then the message is sent to all of them.

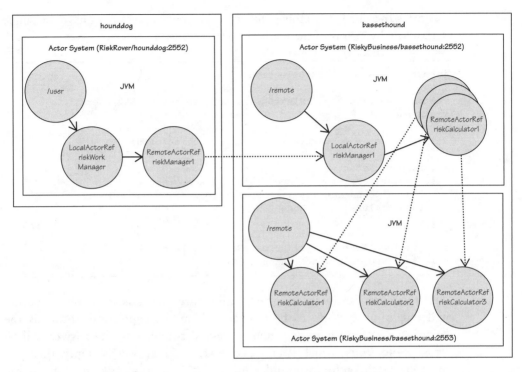

Figure 2.5 There are two physical servers and three JVMs on which actors are deployed.

You are probably wondering whether there is some way to get an `ActorRef` from an `ActorSelection`. After all, you normally send a message to an actor through its reference rather than through an `ActorSelection`. Well, the answer may surprise you. Actually, an `ActorRef` is less reliable than an `ActorSelection`. An `ActorRef` may reference an actor that has been stopped and no longer exists. If you send a message through the `ActorRef` under those conditions, it will not be delivered because there is no actor to which the message can be delivered. On the other hand, an `ActorSelection` is based on an `ActorPath`. Sending by means of a path will cause the Akka internals to look up the actor by its path and, if found, then send the message. So, what's the difference? The difference is that the actor that was stopped may have been restarted and exist by a different `ActorRef` than before, but it will still have the same path as its previous incarnation.

Even so, there is a roundabout way of getting an `ActorRef` from the `ActorSelection` if you prefer a reference over a path. You can ask the

ActorSelection to resolve the internal path representations to a single ActorRef by means of the method resolveOne().

```
import akka.actor.ActorSelection
...
val path = "akka.tcp://RiskyBusiness@bassethound:2552/user/↵
riskManager1"

val selection = context.system.actorSelection(path)

val resolvedActor =
  selection.resolveOne(Timeout(3000)).onComplete {
    case Success(resolved) => Some(resolved)
    case Failure(e) => None
  }

if (resolvedActor isEmpty) createWithCalculateRisk
else resolvedActor.get ! CalculateRisk(...)
```

If the actor cannot be resolved within three seconds, then the operation will fail, causing None to be answered from the expression. (None is the empty Option.) Otherwise, upon successful completion, the answer will be Some(resolved), which is an ActorRef. If the answer is empty, then you must create the actor new and send it a CalculateRisk message. If the answer has an ActorRef, then you will immediately send the Calculate-Risk message.

There is an alternative approach that works in an actor-to-actor collaboration. If one actor uses actorSelection() to look up another actor, it can send a special message to the actor identified by the resulting ActorSelection, asking that actor to identify itself.

```
private var calculatorPath: String = _
private var calculator: ActorRef = _
...
def receive = {
  case CalculateUsing(searchPath) =>
    val selection = context.actorSelection(searchPath)
    selection ! Identify(searchPath)
    calculatorPath = searchPath
  case identity: ActorIdentity =>
    if (identity.correlationId.equals(calculatorPath) {
      calculator = identity.ref.get
      calculator ! CalculateRisk(...)
```

Here a router actor receives the `CalculateUsing` message and calls `actorSelection()` to find the risk calculator actor. With the resulting `ActorSelection`, the router sends an `Identify` message to the selection passing along with it the `searchPath` parameter. The parameter could be anything but should be a unique value that identifies the message being sent and that can be used to correlate the response message. Finally, when the router receives an `ActorIdentity` message, it checks the given `correlationId` with the saved `calculatorPath`. If they are the same, the router knows that the search was resolved and sets the `calculator` to the `ActorRef` provided by the message. This is the `ActorRef` of the searched for calculator actor.

Akka clustering is built on the foundation of Akka remoting. Although Akka clustering is probably all your applications will ever need, it is possible that Akka remoting could come in handy in special circumstances. Yet, your focus will now turn to the more robust Akka clustering feature.

Clustering

*Contributed by **Will Sargent***

Akka clustering has an advantage over Akka remoting in that Akka clustering does not have to know the address of every resource. Instead, with Akka clustering, it's possible to set up machines to join and leave the cluster at runtime. This can be extremely attractive in situations where demands on resources scale up and down—using clustering, extra machines can be provisioned, added, and put to work when there is peak demand and then can be removed when the load does not warrant the additional resources available to the cluster.

To create cluster-capable actors, you will use one or more of the following facilities, each of which is covered more in its own subsection:

- *Cluster singleton*: There will be only one actor of a given type anywhere in the cluster.

- *Cluster sharding*: Actors are distributed evenly across all the nodes in the cluster.

- *Cluster client*: Actors outside the cluster need to send messages to actors inside the cluster, but without knowing their precise location.

- *Cluster-aware routers*: Distribute work across nodes in a cluster by using routers to apportion the work and routees to perform the work.

Akka clustering is useful not only for peak demand but also for failover. Even if you have five machines available, clustering can make more efficient use of resources by assigning extra work to the machines least under load and by rebalancing work between machines if a machine crashes unexpectedly.

Akka clustering is designed to support a multinode, fault-tolerant, distributed system of actors. It does this by creating a cluster of nodes. A node must be an `ActorSystem` that is exposed on a TCP port so that it has a unique identifier. Every node must share the same `ActorSystem` name. Every node member must use a different port number within its host server hardware; no two node members may share a socket port number on the same physical machine. There is no global state shared between `ActorSystem` instances, so within a single machine, you may have several nodes inside a single JVM or several JVMs with one node.

You can feel free to start any number of JVM nodes that work best for your scaling needs. It's not out of the question to start even a few thousand JVM nodes across an appropriate number of physical server computers in order to scale to the extent your application requires [2,400-Node Cluster].

The cluster automatically detects newly joining nodes and failed nodes. A cluster deals with new joining member nodes, as well as existing members leaving the cluster either by choice or even by failing, by maintaining a standard communication protocol between all of the member nodes. This standard communication is known as the Gossip protocol [Gossip Protocol]. This protocol requires all nodes to continually report their availability for the entire cluster to maintain its health. A single node acts as the *leader* of the cluster, and if that node fails for any reason, another node takes its place as the leader.

Each node in the cluster requires a different unique identifier. This unique identifier is made partly from the `hostname` on which the JVM is running, partly the `port` number on that host computer, and partly of an identifier provided by the `ActorSystem`. Altogether, the node's membership to the cluster is made up by the following identifier:

```
hostname:port:uid
```

This tuple combination makes a unique identity for the lifetime of the cluster and cannot be reused. This is one reason why separate JVM nodes are not permitted to share socket ports. (Yet, in actuality it would be inappropriate for two node members to share a socket port even if it didn't represent a portion of its cluster membership unique identity.) Additionally, when a JVM node leaves the cluster, it may not rejoin the cluster using the same `ActorSystem`. Although the same `hostname` and `port` can be reused, the existing `ActorSystem` must be shut down and a new one started, which will provide a new unique `uid` for membership identity. Figure 2.6 shows three different physical servers, each with four JVMs, in a single cluster.

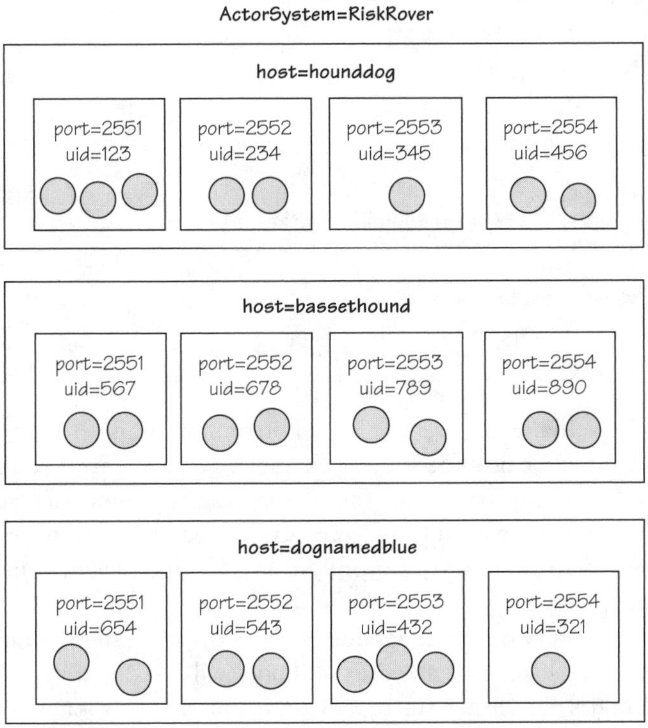

ActorSystem=RiskRover

host=hounddog

| port=2551 uid=123 | port=2552 uid=234 | port=2553 uid=345 | port=2554 uid=456 |

host=bassethound

| port=2551 uid=567 | port=2552 uid=678 | port=2553 uid=789 | port=2554 uid=890 |

host=dognamedblue

| port=2551 uid=654 | port=2552 uid=543 | port=2553 uid=432 | port=2554 uid=321 |

Figure 2.6 An Akka cluster comprised of three different physical servers, each running four JVMs, making a 12-node cluster.

To use Akka clustering, you must at a minimum place the following in your sbt build file:

```
libraryDependencies ++=
            Seq("com.typesafe.akka" %% "akka-cluster" % "2.4")
```

You must also include this kind of configuration in your `application.conf`:

```
akka {
  actor {
    provider = "akka.cluster.ClusterActorRefProvider"
  }
  remote {
    log-remote-lifecycle-events = off
```

```
    netty.tcp {
      hostname = "hounddog"
      port = 0
    }
  }

  cluster {
    seed-nodes = [
      "akka.tcp://RiskRover@hounddog:2551",
      "akka.tcp://RiskRover@bassethound:2551"]

    auto-down-unreachable-after = 10s
  }
}
```

You might actually choose to use different port numbers for the seed-nodes, or a different hostname, for example, but your application.conf must contain these basic parts. (Because the specific hostnames of seed nodes can be different between environments, some users keep cluster settings in an environment-specific cluster-${projenv}.conf file and include it in application.conf.)

The definition of two seed nodes does not limit your cluster to only two nodes total. This just indicates that at least two nodes will exist and that they will act as the seed nodes for cluster startup. A seed node is just a known contact for other nodes that are joining the cluster. Being a seed node does not make the node special in any other way; in other words, a seed node is not necessarily made the leader. Further, newly joining nodes don't have to use the seed nodes to join the cluster. They may contact another preexisting node with their join request instead.

There is one special case to be aware of: When initially starting the cluster, the first node in the seed-nodes list must be started before all others. This case exists to ensure that seed nodes do not form partitions when the cluster is first initialized.

Because clustering relies on the Gossip protocol that sends heartbeats, it is critical to ensure that heartbeat messages are always sent, even when the system is under load. If heartbeat messages are delayed too long, then the cluster will accumulate errors and eventually assume that nodes are down, causing a partition. To ensure that heartbeat messages are given priority, they should be configured with their own dispatcher so that they always have threads available to them.

```
akka.cluster.use-dispatcher = cluster-dispatcher
cluster-dispatcher {
```

```
  type = "Dispatcher"
  executor = "fork-join-executor"
  fork-join-executor {
    parallelism-min = 2
    parallelism-max = 4
  }
}
```

Joining the Cluster   A node joining the cluster can do so in several ways. The first way to join the cluster is to do it through configuration, using the defined seed nodes.

```
val port = 0
val config = ConfigFactory
               .parseString(
                   s"akka.remote.netty.tcp.port=$port")
               .withFallback(
                   ConfigFactory.parseString(
                     "akka.cluster.roles = [frontend]"))
               .withFallback(ConfigFactory.load())

val system = ActorSystem("RiskRover", config)
```

Under this style, the cluster seed nodes that are defined in `akka.cluster.seed-nodes` are used for the initial connection to the cluster. All the required information is contained with the `config` object. The advantage to doing this is simplicity; if the addresses of the seed nodes are known at configuration and at least some of the seed nodes are up, then nothing more need be done.

However, if the configuration is not contained within a file—which may be the case if the cluster exists purely in the cloud or if seed node information is kept in a configuration service such as Zookeeper or Consul—then using configuration may not be appropriate.

The second way to join the cluster is to do it programmatically. If there are no seed nodes available to the configuration system, then the first node to join the cluster has to join itself to kick off the node.

```
val address = Cluster(system).selfAddress
Cluster(system).join(address)
```

If there are seed nodes in the configuration system, then the system can join the seed nodes that are defined from the configuration system.

```
val seeds = configurationSystem
            .getNodeAddresses().map { nodeAddress =>
              AddressFromURIString(s"akka.tcp://${nodeAddress}") }
Cluster(system).joinSeedNodes(seeds)
```

Note that when calling `joinSeedNodes()`, the node that is joining should not be in the list (that is, the list should not contain `selfAddress`).

The final way to join the cluster is manually. You can create a node and join it to a cluster through Java Management Extensions (JMX), using the MBean `akka.Cluster` or the command-line client that wraps JMX. This is useful only in the case where a running cluster is being managed by an external tool, for example in the case of deployment or provisioning. In some cases, operations may have a better understanding of network and machine topology than any hard-coded programming could provide and so is managed outside the system.

In this case, to migrate a particular node from one cluster to another (identified by `$SEEDNODEHOST / $SEEDNODEPORT`), you would specify the following:

```
bin/akka-cluster $NODEHOST $JMXPORT is-available
bin/akka-cluster $NODEHOST $JMXPORT  member-status
bin/akka-cluster $NODEHOST $JMXPORT leave↵
 akka.tcp://RiskRover@$NODEHOST:$NODEPORT
bin/akka-cluster $NODEHOST $JMXPORT join ↵
 akka.tcp://RiskRover@$SEEDNODEHOST:$SEEDNODEPORT
bin/akka-cluster $NODEHOST $JMXPORT cluster-status
```

Cluster Roles and Events   Each cluster member can play a specific application role, where a role represents the kinds of tasks that the actors on the member node perform. It is possible that multiple nodes will play the same roles. In the previous Figure 2.6, you can well imagine that the role played by some nodes is `riskWorkManagers`, another is `riskCalculators`, and yet another is `riskAssessments`. You can assign the role of each node in its `application.conf` using `akka.cluster.roles`.

```
akka {
  ...
  cluster {
    roles = [riskWorkManagers]
    ...
  }
}
```

Alternatively, you can assign the roles of a given node on the command line as a startup parameter.

```
-Dakka.cluster.roles=[riskCalculators]
```

As shown in the earlier "Joining the Cluster" example, the roles that a given node plays are passed along with the `MemberUp` event. Subscribing to the `MemberUp` event and watching for joining nodes with specific roles affords you the opportunity to "dial in" for specific work responsibilities. You can arrange for an actor to subscribe to specific kinds of cluster events in this way:

```
cluster.subscribe(
    self,
    classOf[MemberEvent],
    classOf[UnreachableMember])
```

The first event that your actor will receive as a subscriber is `Current-ClusterState`, which when fully populated contains the full state of the cluster. The event will be followed by incremental changes that occur, such as `MemberUp` when a new member node is fully up and ready for activity. You may receive the following membership events, which are each discussed in Table 2.4:

```
class RiskWorkManager extends Actor {
  ...
  def receive = {
    case state: CurrentClusterState =>
    case MemberUp(member: Member) => ...
    case MemberExited(member: Member) => ...
    case MemberRemoved(member: Member) => ...
    case UnreachableMember(member: Member) => ...
    case ReachableMember(member: Member) => ...
  }
}
```

You can look at all the cluster membership state as a single snapshot by calling the following:

```
val system = ActorSystem("RiskRover")
...
val state = Cluster(system).state
```

Table 2.4 The Common Membership Events Provided by Akka Clustering

Event Name	Description
`CurrentClusterState`	This is the first event to be received after your node subscribes to cluster events. The event will contain no member information if you subscribe before any member has completed joining the cluster. Otherwise, this event will contain a `members` collection with one `Member` element for each member node. Each `Member` element, which is the same passed with individual member events, may be used to ask what role or roles the member node supports. Other potentially useful methods are `allRoles(): Set[String]`; `leader(): Option[Address]`; `roleLeader(): Option[Address]`; `unreachable(): Set[Member]`.
`MemberUp`	A newly joined member node is now ready for use. The `Member` parameter can be used to determine the role or roles played by the node. You can use these methods: `hasRole("roleName")`, which returns a `Boolean`; `roles`, to get a collection of all the named roles played by the member node; and `status`, which returns one of `Joining`, `Up`, `Leaving`, `Exiting`, or `Down`. There are a few other methods, but you may not find them useful at the application level.
`MemberExited`	A member has chosen to exit the cluster and may have already exited by the time this event is received. This member can be used again only if its `ActorSystem` is shut down and then restarted, producing a new `uid` for the cluster membership.
`MemberRemoved`	The cluster has proactively removed this member. This member can be used again only if its `ActorSystem` is shut down and then restarted, producing a new `uid` for the cluster membership.
`UnreachableMember`	The cluster has detected a failure and marked this member node unreachable. This may be only a temporary situation, or it may escalate to `MemberRemoved`. One reason that a member may appear unreachable is because of network traffic, where member heartbeat messages are not received by peers on an expected periodic basis.
`ReachableMember`	The cluster has again recognized this member as reachable. One reason why a member may have been temporarily unreachable is because of network traffic slowing regular heartbeat messages. Yet, the network may have again delivered heartbeats on a timely basis, and the member node is once again considered reachable.

The `state` references an instance of `CurrentClusterState`, the same found in Table 2.4. You must recognize that this state may be stale by the time you are reading it. Active members of the cluster can change apart from the snapshot that was considered current at the time it was read.

Cluster Singleton   There are times when you want precisely one actor functioning through the entire cluster. This is usually the case for an actor that has a responsibility to the entire cluster—it monitors or aggregates information from the cluster, or it functions as a centralized node to route messages through the cluster. An example might be an actor that aggregates metrics from each node in the cluster and broadcasts the overall cluster health. Another example is a work router that requires all work tasks to pass through the single router so it can control how tasks are run and monitored for completion.

Creating a cluster singleton is done through specifying an actor with specialized `ClusterSingletonManager` properties.

```
import akka.contrib.pattern.ClusterSingletonManager
...
val clusterSingletonProperties =
    ClusterSingletonManager.props(
      singletonProps = Props(classOf[SingletonActor]),
      singletonName = "SingletonActor",
      terminationMessage = PoisonPill,
      role = None)
system.actorOf(clusterSingletonProperties, "clusterSingleton")
```

The `ActorSystem` will create the cluster singleton on the oldest node in the cluster, which is not necessarily on the same node where the create request is made. If the node that the cluster singleton is on goes down, messages are buffered on the local proxy using a stash until a new cluster singleton is created.

There is a caveat to using cluster singletons: They assume that the cluster has not undergone partition, and so if a partition occurs and a new leader is elected, it is possible that a second cluster singletons will be created. This condition is commonly called *split-brain* [Split-Brain]. To avoid this, specify the `min-nr-of-members` property to prevent a leadership election until there is an established quorum of nodes.

Cluster Sharding   Sharding is a common practice where data is horizontally partitioned across multiple nodes. Cluster sharding allows actors to be distributed evenly across all the nodes in the cluster, with each node acting as a shard. This is important because while actors take up little memory by themselves, a large number of stateful actors can still take up more memory than can exist on any one JVM. Another reason to shard is to create node-actor affinity, where you design a scheme to keep related actors on the same node so they use local message dispatching. Still another reason to shard is to collect certain kinds of actors into a region or cache that is predictably stored in a consistent location on the cluster. Using cluster sharding, actors will be transparently distributed across several nodes in the cluster and can be referenced by identifier.

An actor in a shard is called an *entry*. A shard contains a number of entries. There is a cluster singleton called `ShardCoordinator`. It knows the location of each shard and maps each shard to a region. A `ShardRegion` actor runs on each participating node in the cluster and contains a number of shards. The `ShardCoordinator` keeps track of which regions have the most shards and by default will allocate new shards to the shard region with the fewest shards. See Figure 2.7 for an example.

How Are Entries Placed in a Shard?

Initially there are no entries in any shard anywhere in the cluster. Then when you send a message to an entry, even if it doesn't exist in memory, the entry is looked up. This means that the message is directed to the shard in which the entry should be located, even if it isn't there yet. If the entry does not yet exist, it is automatically created before the message is delivered to it. If the entry has preexisting state by extending `PersistentActor`, its state is first restored after creation before the message is delivered. Finally, the message is delivered to the newly created or the preexisting entry in the resolved shard.

How will you know the identity of an entry to which you will send a message when the entry doesn't exist in memory? If the entry already existed at one time, you can find its identity by querying a data store for it. You will have at least some user-provided data to match to the entry's searchable properties. When you've resolved the identity, you just send a message by way of the `ShardRegion`, and the rest happens automatically.

All of this allows entries to come and go (a.k.a. passivated) and be rebalanced across various nodes, all without your needing to worry about how it all works.

When there are newly participating nodes available in the cluster, then the `ShardCoordinator` can rebalance shards so that existing actors in a shard can be migrated from one node to another. The state in the actors is not transferred with the migration, so typically Akka Persistence is used to ensure that an actor's state can be recovered, although it is not a requirement. The `ShardCoordinator` itself is a `PersistentActor` because it must know the location of all the shards at all times. This means that cluster sharding must be configured with an Akka Persistence journal plugin, such as the one for Cassandra.

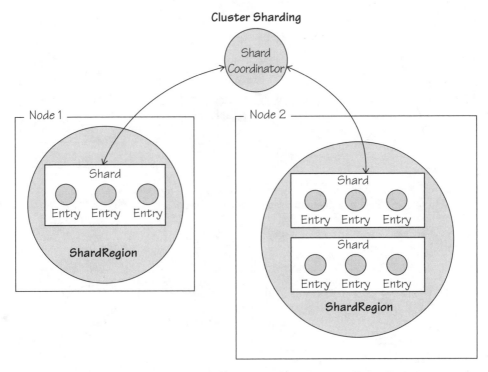

Figure 2.7 Cluster sharding with a `ShardCoordinator`, `ShardRegion` instances, shards, and entries

Sharding Caution

It is important to note that cluster sharding only ensures that shared actors are spread out evenly among the shared nodes. Out of the box, sharding does not do anything if one particular shard or node is under heavy load. This is because determining performance and load on sharded data has to happen at an application level. Only you know which data is likely to become mysteriously popular and why.

When a message is sent, it first goes to the relevant `ShardRegion` on the node. The `ShardRegion` then extracts the identity for the entry and forwards the message to the matching actor (see Figure 2.8).

Messages are delivered on a best-effort basis. Cluster sharding does not guarantee delivery of messages, and messages must often be delivered across a distributed network. This means that it is quite possible for messages to an entry to be lost because the default is at-most-once delivery, as depicted in Figure 2.9. `AtLeastOnceDelivery`, a feature available in Akka Persistence, can be used to ensure that the message is delivered successfully.

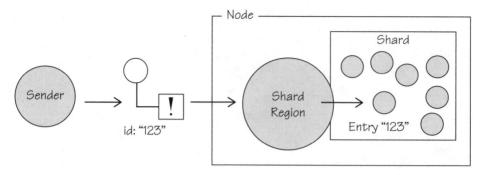

Figure 2.8 A `ShardRegion` performs ID extraction on messages so it can dispatch a given message to the relevant actor.

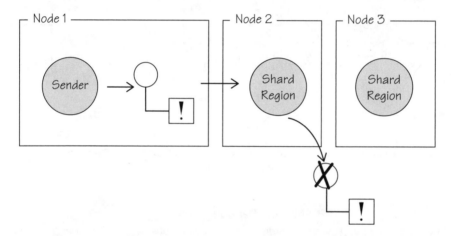

Figure 2.9 With at-most-once delivery, messages can be lost between sending and receiving actors.

Cluster sharding can be useful in situations where stateful objects map cleanly to actors. As an example, the users of an application can be modeled as actors using cluster sharding.

```scala
object UserEntry {
  def props(): Props = Props(new UserEntry())
  case class GetData(username:String)
  case class UserDataAdded(firstName:Option[String],
                           lastName:Option[String])

  val idExtractor: ShardRegion.IdExtractor = {
    case gd: GetData => (gd.username, gd)
  }
```

```
  val shardResolver: ShardRegion.ShardResolver = { msg =>
    msg match {
      case GetData(username) =>
        (math.abs(username.hashCode) % 100).toString
    }
  }
  val shardName: String = "UserEntry"
}

class UserEntry
  extends PersistentActor
  with AtLeastOnceDelivery {
  import UserEntry._

  private var firstName: Option[String] = None
  private var lastName: Option[String] = None

  override def receiveRecover = {
    case UserDataAdded(f, l) =>
      firstName = Option(f)
      lastName = Option(l)
  }

  override def receiveCommand = {
    case AddUserData(f, l) =>
      persist(UserDataAdded(f, l)) { evt =>
        firstName = f
        lastName = l
      }
    case GetData(_) =>
      sender() ! UserData(firstName, lastName)
  }
}
```

Starting the cluster system is done through the `ClusterSharding` extension.

```
ClusterSharding(system)
    .start(
      typeName = UserEntry.shardName,
      entryProps = Some(UserEntry.props()),
      idExtractor = UserEntry.idExtractor,
      shardResolver = UserEntry.shardResolver)
```

When the system is sent a `GetData(username)` message, the `Shard-Coordinator` will determine on which shard the entry with `username` exists and then forward the `GetData` message. When a message is sent to a shard entry that is currently not in memory, the entry will first be autocreated and reconstituted from any previous persistent state, and then the message will be delivered to it. In the previous source block, the `entryProps` are the properties needed to autocreate each `UserEntry` actor. An entry can be automatically reconstituted from persistent state only if it extends `PersistentActor`.

`UserEntry` extends `PersistentActor`, and uses trait `AtLeastOnce-Delivery`, to recover from node failure and lost messages; see *Guaranteed Delivery (175)* and *Transactional Client/Actor (351)* for examples.

Cluster Client   Once a cluster is defined, then actors outside the cluster may need to send messages to an actor inside the cluster without knowing the precise location of the actor. This is particularly important in the case where the actor in the cluster is not a cluster singleton and is not managed through cluster sharding. The way to talk to actors inside a cluster is by using a cluster client.

Setting up the cluster client involves some scaffolding that manages communication between a client actor and actors inside the cluster. This is done by a special `ClusterReceptionist`, which is used inside the cluster to register actors that will provide services to clients outside the cluster. A `ClusterReceptionist` is an ordinary actor, but it must exist on every participating node in the cluster (see Figure 2.10). It can be started automatically on every node by setting the `ClusterReceptionistExtension` in `application.conf`.

```
akka.extensions =
  ["akka.contrib.pattern.ClusterReceptionistExtension"]
```

Once the cluster receptionist is up, the actors that should be available for use by clients outside the cluster are registered on whichever nodes they are running. Actors can be started on as many nodes as you like. The only limiting factor is that they have to register themselves with the local cluster receptionist. In this case, you have a node monitor that lives on every node, which can monitor or disable services:

```
// For every actor that wants to be accessible
// through the client, register it as a service.
val requestLimiter: ActorRef =
    system.actorOf(
        Props[RequestLimiter],
        "requestLimiter")

ClusterReceptionistExtension(system)
    .registerService(requestLimiter)
```

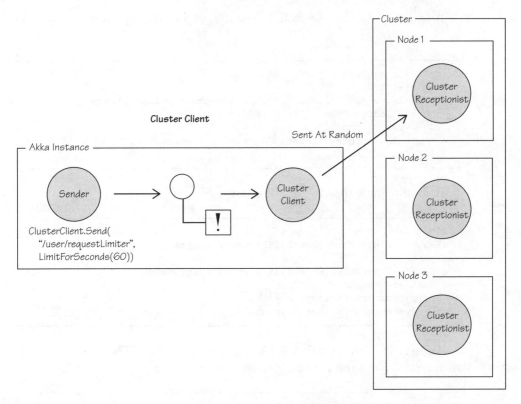

Figure 2.10 The `Sender` sends a message through the `ClusterClient`, which is randomly delivered to one of three `ClusterReceptionist` instances.

By the way, the basic idea behind this sample `RequestLimiter` actor is that it receives incoming requests but also has the capability to deny processing of any number of requests that arrive during a period of time. Among other messages, the `RequestLimiter` can accept a message of type `LimitForSeconds(nrOfSeconds)` to deny message processing on the node where it is deployed for that given time period.

Now you need to access the service from the client. This entails setting up contact points and initializing the cluster client. Setting contact points for the initial cluster receptionist can be done in a similar way that seed nodes are configured. First, configure the `contact-points` property in `application.conf`.

```
contact-points = [
  "akka.tcp://RiskRover@host1:2551",
  "akka.tcp://RiskRover@host2:2552"]
```

And then read in the initial contacts to the cluster receptionist from configuration.

```
// Set up the cluster receptionist nodes
val initialContacts =
   immutable.Seq(config.getStringList("contact-points")).map {
      case AddressFromURIString(addr) =>
         system.actorSelection(
            RootActorPath(addr) / "user" / "receptionist")
   }.toSet
```

Logically this is the same as the following:

```
val path1 =
 "akka.tcp://RiskRover@host1:2551/user/receptionist"
val path2 =
 "akka.tcp://RiskRover@host1:2552/user/receptionist"
val initialContacts =
   Set(system.actorSelection(path1),
       system.actorSelection(path2))
```

And yet the configuration is likely the better choice. The cluster client is then created using the `initialContacts`.

```
// Create the cluster client to talk to
// the service through the receptionist.
val clusterClient =
      system.actorOf(ClusterClient.props(initialContacts))
```

The cluster client can send messages to a given service by path without specifying a specific node. The cluster receptionist behaves much like a real receptionist. When the client sends a message, the receptionist on each node determines whether the actor exists on that particular node. For example, if you want one of the nodes to stop taking requests for 60 seconds but you don't care which one, you can do that as follows:

```
clusterClient ! ClusterClient.Send(
                  "/user/requestLimiter",
                  LimitForSeconds(60))
```

Note that the message is passed to a node at random, using consistent hashing to load balance the client connections among the nodes in the cluster. If the client wants to send a message to every instance of that actor, on every node, then it can broadcast by using the `SendToAll()` method. In this example, you can disable every node from taking requests for 60 seconds:

```
clusterClient ! ClusterClient.SendToAll(
                "/user/requestLimiter",
                LimitForSeconds(60))
```

The cluster client also has another mode, which does not register services by a named path but by a topic. In this case, the client does not send messages to a path but uses an agreed-on string to serve as a topic. All the actors subscribe with the receptionist to be notified of messages sent to this topic by the client. To register the cluster actor with the receptionist, use `registerSubscriber()`.

```
ClusterReceptionistExtension(system)
    .registerSubscriber(
        "requestLimit",
        requestLimiter)
```

Once the subscribers have been registered with the receptionist, then the cluster client can publish a message to every subscriber by using the `Publish()` method. In this example, every actor registered to the topic `"requestLimit"` is sent a `LimitForSeconds` message.

```
clusterClient ! ClusterClient.Publish(
                "requestLimit",
                LimitForSeconds(60))
```

Cluster-Aware Routers   Routers exist in two forms in Akka: as *groups* and as *pools*. In the case of a group, the router is talking to a set of preexisting actors already, running on different nodes in the cluster. For a pool, the router owns the life cycle of the actors and can create new actors on different nodes. You will look more closely at groups first and then pools.

At first glance, cluster-aware groups don't seem all that useful. The router doesn't control the life cycle of the actors it is routing to (a.k.a. routes). So while the router can send a message to the least loaded node, it can't add more actors or more nodes directly.

However, groups become more useful when you know that you can have many routers all pointing to the same group. When configured with cluster roles, this means that a number of nodes in the cluster can act as a group of actors all doing the same work—typically "back-end" services. In such a case a number of front-end handlers would each have a cluster-aware router pointing to the "back-end" services group. Inherently a router that connects to a group can exist in a many-to-many relationship with its routes (see Figure 2.11).

The cluster-aware group router can be configured through `application.conf`. Defining a cluster-aware router with a group is much like defining a regular router. The main difference is that the router is defined with a `cluster` section.

```
akka.actor.deployment {
  /groupRouter {
    router = consistent-hashing-group
    nr-of-instances = 100
    routees.paths = ["/user/backendService"]
    cluster {
      enabled = on
      allow-local-routees = on
    }
  }
}
```

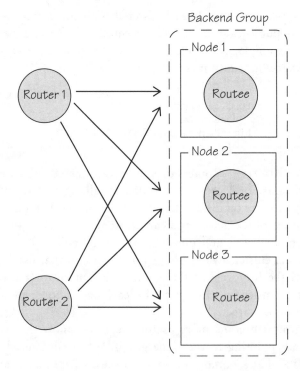

Figure 2.11 Multiple cluster-aware routers route messages to a group of back-end service routees.

The router here is defined with `consistent-hashing-group`. This is a useful default for cluster-aware routers because it attempts to spread the load evenly even when new nodes are added or removed from the cluster by creating a virtual "circle" of nodes and then assigning "intervals" (sections of the circle) to nodes. Other routers, such as `random-group`, can be used according to the specific use case.

In this example, the routees' path is to the external service, defined as `"/user/backendService"` (see `routees.paths` in the configuration), which must be started independently of the router:

```
val backendService =
      system.actorOf(
          Props[BackendService],
          name = "backendService")
```

After the `backendService` actor is started, then the group router can be started, and messages can be sent to the back-end service. Note that if you are sending messages through the router, then you should use an *Envelope Wrapper (314)* named `ConsistentHashableEnvelope` to wrap the message. This envelope provides the key to the router's hash function, used to evenly distribute messages across routees. By default Akka uses `MurmurHash`, although it is possible to implement your own custom hashing logic.

A `ConsistentHashableEnvelope` may sound intimidating, but the only work that must be done is to determine an appropriate logical ID for the message. You do not have to use a UUID or a cryptographic hash like SHA-1 and are encouraged not to. If you have a `QueryForUser(userId)` message, then the following will work fine as a key:

```
val key = s"QueryForUser-${userId}-${System.currentTimeMillis}"
```

Now you can create the group router and send messages through it. Refer to the earlier `/groupRouter` configuration since the actor name refers to it.

```
val groupRouter =
      system.actorOf(
          FromConfig.props(Props.empty),
          name = "groupRouter")

groupRouter ! ConsistentHashableEnvelope(
              message,
              hashKey = message.id)
```

Once the router is started and the cluster is up, messages sent to the router will be routed to routees in the cluster. As new routees are made available, they will be added to the router, up to the value set by `nr-of-instances`. If a node goes down or is otherwise unavailable, the routees will be automatically unregistered from the router. If only one instance of the service is required, it is perfectly acceptable to set `nr-of-instances=1` and have the group router act as a cluster-aware proxy to other actors in the cluster looking for the service. For actors outside of the cluster, it is more appropriate to use a cluster client.

Next you will turn your attention to pools. A cluster-aware router that manages a pool is different from one that uses a group. In a pool the router is responsible for the life cycle of the routees underneath it (see Figure 2.12). This is because it is inherently a one-to-many relationship, which implies that there is precisely one router in the entire cluster that is responsible for the routees. Thus, the router is defined as a cluster singleton.

Pools are most useful in situations where the routees are workers that run resource-intensive tasks, typically on hardware that is assigned specifically to this task. As an example, consider a cluster that takes audio files (each 50MB in uncompressed WAV format) and transcodes those files to a variety of formats.

Defining a router to manage a pool of actors is ideal in this case. The router will take `TranscodeJob` messages that tell the routees how to transcode individual audio files and distribute them across actors in different nodes on the cluster. A number of high-end machines are assigned as nodes. Each machine

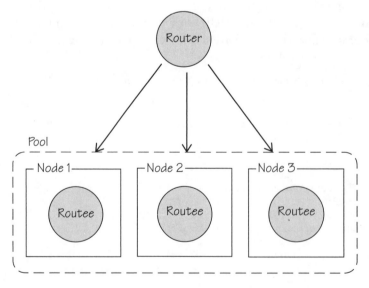

Figure 2.12 This cluster-aware router is responsible for its pool of routees.

used for transcoding will have two CPUs, each with four cores that support hyperthreading.[8]

```
akka.actor.deployment {
  /singleton/transcodingService/poolRouter {
    router = consistent-hashing-pool
    nr-of-instances = 100
    cluster {
      enabled = on
      max-nr-of-instances-per-node = 16
      allow-local-routees = off
      use-role = transcode
    }
  }
}
```

The router here is defined with `consistent-hashing-pool` and has a `max-nr-of-instances-per-node` of 16, which will result in two actors per hyperthreading core. Also note that `allow-local-routees` is off since the processing should be done on remote cores.

There is some additional housekeeping that should happen for transcoding. You tell the `TranscodeJob` that it can use a unique ID as a consistent hash key, which avoids the hassle of using a `ConsistentHashableEnvelope` when sending messages to the router.

```
import akka.routing.ConsistentHashingRouter.↵
ConsistentHashable
...
case class TranscodeJob(
    id: String,
    transcodeOptions: TranscodeOptions)
  extends ConsistentHashable {
  override def consistentHashKey = id.toString
}
```

You define a `TranscodingService` class, which functions as an intermediary between the workers and the router and ensures that duplicate jobs are not dispatched and that failed jobs are logged and restarted. The `TranscodingService` defines the router internally.

---

8. Each hyperthreaded core supports two simultaneous threads of execution. Thus, this specific hardware architecture can have 16 simultaneous threads of execution.

```scala
class TranscodingService extends Actor {
  // The configured pool router
  val poolRouter =
        context.actorOf(
          FromConfig.props(Props[TranscodeWorker]),
          name = "poolRouter")

  def receive = {
    case job:TranscodeJob =>
      // Verify job has not already been seen,
      // restart failed jobs etc.
      val originalSender = sender()
      poolRouter ! job
      // start a scheduled timeout for jobs
      // which were sent to router which
      // timed out without a result...
    case result:TranscodeResult =>
      // Additional logic for processing result
      // messages from workers, etc.
  }
}

object TranscodingService {
  def props = Props[TranscodingService]
}
```

Then you create the cluster singleton manager on each node in the proxy. The singleton manager will be limited to nodes tagged with the `"transcode"` role.

```scala
system.actorOf(
  ClusterSingletonManager.props(
    singletonProps = TranscodingService.props,
    singletonName = "transcodingService",
    terminationMessage = PoisonPill,
    role = Some("transcode")),
  name = "singleton")
```

To send messages to the `TranscodingService`, create a singleton proxy and send messages to it.

```scala
val path = "/user/singleton/transcodingService"
val transcodingService =
    system.actorOf(
      ClusterSingletonProxy.props(
        singletonPath = path,
        role = Some("transcode")),
      name = "transcodingServiceProxy")
```

```
val transcodeJob = createTranscodeJob()
transcodingService ! transcodeJob
```

Using a pool router, all the routees will receive the same number of transcoding jobs. If a node goes down, the router will evenly distribute work to the available routees in the pool. If a new node is added, the router will automatically start new routees in the pool and start sending work to them.

Scaling with Load   You've seen that clustering allows actors to transparently communicate with each other across nodes and that nodes can be dynamically added and removed from the cluster. You've seen how using a cluster-aware router will allow you to evenly distribute messages across nodes, using consistent hashing.

Consistent works well when each message takes roughly the same number of resources to process. When similar messages result in large differences in the processing required, then it's not enough to evenly distribute messages. Instead, the router must ensure that the load across the cluster is evenly distributed.

Going back to the transcoding example, you've made the assumption that all transcoding jobs are the same and take up the same amount of resources. However, if the input parameters vary—the size of the file, the input format, and the transcoding operation—then a randomly unfortunate node may be loaded with difficult transcoding jobs even if it was sent exactly the same number of messages as its peers.

Load-balancing routers address this problem. In the same way that there are consistently hashing routers for pools and groups, there are adaptive load-balancing routers for pools and groups. These routers look at the collected metrics from each node and use that to assign probabilities so that a heavily stressed node is less likely to have a message sent to it. A number of different metrics can be used to determine load.

- "heap": A metric that uses JVM available heap

- "load": A metric that uses Unix system load average (in turn based on CPU run queue length)

- "cpu": A metric that uses CPU utilization

- "mix": A metric that combines heap, cpu, and load

The metrics are gathered from JMX by default, but this is not nearly as accurate as using a native operating system (OS) system monitor. Akka clustering uses Hyperic Sigar if available, and it is highly recommended to use Sigar in production for more accurate metrics. Sigar is a native package library. To download the native binary packages, add the following to your `build.sbt`:

```
libraryDependencies += "org.fusesource" % "sigar" % "1.6.4" %
classifier("native") classifier("")
```

Converting a cluster-aware router from consistent hashing to adaptive load balancing is relatively easy.

```
akka.actor.deployment {
  /singleton/transcodingService/poolRouter {
    router = adaptive-pool
    metrics-selector = load
    nr-of-instances = 100
    cluster {
      enabled = on
      max-nr-of-instances-per-node = 16
      allow-local-routees = off
      use-role = transcode
    }
  }
}
```

The only change needed here is to set the `router` option to `adaptive-pool` and to set a `metrics-selector` of `load`. The choice of metrics selector is subtle. Since transcoding is primarily a CPU-bound process, the first instinct might be to look at CPU utilization. However, an effectively used machine in an Akka cluster should be close to 100 percent, so weighting load based on the CPU run queue length (`metrics-selector = load`) is a better indication of how many processes are waiting for CPU time.

Next let's take a look at metrics events. The metrics information used by the routers for load balancing can also be used directly. To listen for metrics events, subscribe an actor to the `ClusterMetricsChanged` class. Running a cluster singleton as a metrics listener can be useful because it gives you an immediate understanding of metrics through messages, as opposed to querying JMX beans or deciphering Unix command-line utilities.

An example metrics listener class is provided here for reference:

```
import akka.actor.{Actor, ActorLogging, Address}
import akka.cluster._
import akka.cluster.ClusterEvent._
import akka.cluster.StandardMetrics.{Cpu, HeapMemory}
import akka.cluster.routing._

class CentralMetricsListener
  extends Actor with ActorLogging {
```

```scala
val cluster = Cluster(context.system)
var nodes = Set.empty[Address]
var nodeCpu = Map[Address, Cpu]()
var nodeHeap = Map[Address, HeapMemory]()
var cpuCapacity = Map[Address, Double]()
var heapCapacity = Map[Address, Double]()
var loadCapacity = Map[Address, Double]()
var mixCapacity = Map[Address, Double]()

override def preStart(): Unit = {
  cluster.subscribe(self, classOf[MemberEvent])
  cluster.subscribe(self, classOf[ClusterMetricsChanged])
}

override def postStop(): Unit =
  cluster.unsubscribe(self)

def receive = {
  case ClusterMetricsChanged(clusterMetrics) =>
    clusterMetrics.foreach { nodeMetrics =>
      val address = nodeMetrics.address
      extractHeap(nodeMetrics).map(
        heap => nodeHeap = nodeHeap + (address -> heap))
      extractCpu(nodeMetrics).map(
        cpu => nodeCpu = nodeCpu + (address -> cpu))
    }
    extractCapacity(clusterMetrics)
    logMetrics()

  case state: CurrentClusterState =>
    nodes = state.members.collect {
      case m if m.status == MemberStatus.Up => m.address
    }
    filterMetrics()

  case MemberUp(member) =>
    nodes += member.address

  case MemberRemoved(member, _) =>
    nodes -= member.address
    filterMetrics()

  case _: MemberEvent => // ignore
}

def filterMetrics(): Unit = {
  nodeHeap = nodeHeap.filterKeys(
          address => nodes.contains(address))
  nodeCpu = nodeCpu.filterKeys(
          address => nodes.contains(address))
}
```

```scala
def extractHeap(
  nodeMetrics: NodeMetrics):
Option[HeapMemory] =
nodeMetrics match {
  case HeapMemory(address, timestamp, used,
                  committed, max) =>
    Some(HeapMemory(address, timestamp, used,
                    committed, max))
  case _ =>
    None
}

def extractCpu(nodeMetrics: NodeMetrics): Option[Cpu] =
nodeMetrics match {
  case Cpu(address, timestamp,
           systemLoadAverage, cpuCombined,
           processors) =>
    Some(Cpu(address, timestamp,
             systemLoadAverage, cpuCombined,
             processors))
  case _ =>
    None
}

def extractCapacity(
    nodeMetricsSet: Set[NodeMetrics]):
Unit = {
  loadCapacity =
    SystemLoadAverageMetricsSelector.capacity(
      nodeMetricsSet)
  heapCapacity = HeapMetricsSelector.capacity(
      nodeMetricsSet)
  cpuCapacity = CpuMetricsSelector.capacity(
      nodeMetricsSet)
  mixCapacity = MixMetricsSelector.capacity(
      nodeMetricsSet)
}

def logMetrics() = {
  nodes.foreach { node =>
    val heap = nodeHeap(node)
    val cpu = nodeCpu(node)
    log.info(s"port = ${node.port}, committed =↵
${heap.committed}, max = ${heap.max}, used = ${heap.used}")
    log.info(s"port = ${node.port}, cpuCombined =↵
${cpu.cpuCombined},systemLoadAverage =↵
${cpu.systemLoadAverage}, processors = ${cpu.processors}")
    log.info(s"port = ${node.port}, loadCapacity =↵
${loadCapacity(node)}")
    log.info(s"port = ${node.port}, heapCapacity =↵
${heapCapacity(node)}")
```

```
    log.info(s"port = ${node.port}, cpuCapacity =↵
${cpuCapacity(node)}")
    log.info(s"port = ${node.port}, mixCapacity =↵
${mixCapacity(node)}")
    }
  }
}
```

On a four-core Macbook Pro, running the `CentralMetricsListener` on the cluster logs the following for a single node:

```
port = Some(52038), committed = 487587840, max =↵
 Some(954728448), used = 317080792
port = Some(52038), cpuCombined =↵
 Some(0.9891756869275603),systemLoadAverage =↵
 Some(3.84326171875), processors = 4
port = Some(52038), loadCapacity = 0.0391845703125
port = Some(52038), heapCapacity = 0.6678837918109255
port = Some(52038), cpuCapacity = 0.010824313072439695
port = Some(52038), mixCapacity = 0.23929755839862174
```

You can see that each metrics selector returns a capacity as a `Double`, which is 1 for "completely unloaded," to 0, meaning that the node is at full capacity. You can also see that the node has a fair amount of JVM heap available (0.66), while having little CPU capacity (0.01) and only a little more load capacity (0.03). Finally, the `mix` selector aggregates the `load`, `mix`, and `heap` capacities to show 0.23, which is better but doesn't show where the system is bottlenecked.

Since a metrics listener can look at all the nodes and keep a record of the capacity associated with it, it can be used in far more flexible ways than a simple router to modify behavior across the entire cluster.

When you see that the load is too high across the entire cluster and there is simply no more capability, you have two options to preserve behavior: push back on clients to reduce the demand on the application or provision additional supply.

Reducing demand is always unpalatable because it comes down to telling clients that they can't get what they want. There are several ways to reduce demand, listed here in rough order of severity:

- Provide a channel to clients of available capacity and rely on them to be polite and back off.

- Send explicit messages to clients to scale back their requests.

- Institute rate limiting or throttling of incoming requests and deny clients that behave badly.

- Flat out deny some incoming requests, especially low-priority requests such as repeated polling for data.

In addition, there is an architectural pattern known as Backpressure that can automatically manage load by managing work through an internal bounded queue. Work is pulled off the queue by multiple workers and backs up as more work comes into the queue. When the work in the queue reaches a highwater mark, further requests (which would result in work being placed on the queue) are automatically rejected (see Figure 2.13). Note that this internal queue is *not* the same as an actor mailbox, which intentionally does not reveal its internals to an actor. The queue should be explicitly defined in the actor itself.[9]

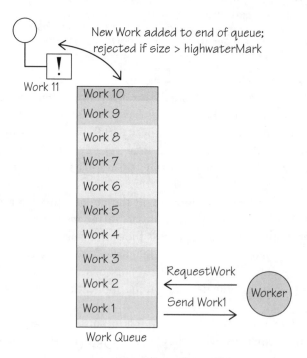

Figure 2.13 Backpressure can be applied by setting up a work queue that fills up until the work items reach a "highwater mark," or threshold, at which time new work items are rejected.

---

9. Chapter 3 describes a similar kind of work queue that is used by individual threads.

The second option is much better: When high load is detected across the entire cluster, send a message to a resource provisioner such as Apache Mesos asking to provision additional resources. When load goes down, the metrics listener can send messages to individual nodes telling them to shut themselves down and avoid wasting unused resources. The details are out of scope for this book, but at the time of writing there was a ferocious rush among vendors to provide this functionality.

Testing Actors

As you've been reading thus far about Actor model, you've also probably been contemplating how you would test actors. You probably imagined that it could be difficult since there are so many things that could happen on the outside of the actor and how the inside would have to be flexible enough to react to all those happenings.

For one thing, an actor can't determine whether messages are received out of order since the system outside is asynchronous and won't generally react in exact, predetermined, serialized ways. Well, that's all part of dealing with non-determinism as discussed in Chapter 1. Remember, however, that an actor that holds and manages state may be designed as a finite state machine. This allows you to design your actor to understand a given state, which messages can be handled in that state, how the current state will be transitioned, and what to do about messages that can't be handled while in that state. Yet, that's design, not test.

Gladly, the Akka team understands the ins and outs since they have to test actors themselves to ensure Akka's robustness. When you have to eat your own dog food, you usually try to make it tasty; you know, simple and as usable as possible. You would expect, then, that the Akka TestKit would taste great.

The Akka team has provided two ways to test an actor. The first way addresses the fitness of the actor's state machine. The second way treats how an actor reacts to the outside world through its message processing.

Unit Testing Actors

If you are familiar with unit testing with Java or C#, you are going to find unit testing with Akka familiar and easy. To get started, all you have to do is import the TestKit, create an actor, get a test-based `ActorRef` for it, and get a reference to the underlying actor.

```
import akka.testkit.TestActorRef

val riskManagerRef = TestActorRef[RiskManager]
val riskManager = actorRef.underlyingActor
```

Don't bother trying to directly instantiate an actor. It won't do you any good. Akka prevents you from using the actor directly, even if its methods are publicly accessible. If you try to construct a new instance, you will see a runtime error like this:

```
Exception in thread "main" akka.actor.↵
ActorInitializationException: You cannot create an↵
  instance of [ActorClassname] explicitly using the↵
  constructor (new).
```

The `TestActorRef` gives you the ability to sidestep that normal limitation, and you can even get a reference to the `Actor` instance. Testability is one good reason for not making internal actor methods private, unless one must be called from a higher-level operation only. There is no reason to hide any high-level operations since under normal runtime conditions you won't be able to call them directly. In other words, sending a message is the only way for anything outside to get an actor to function under normal conditions.

The other benefit of the `TestActorRef` is that messages you send through it will be delivered directly to the `receive` partial function rather than being sent asynchronously and delivered through the actor's mailbox. As far as the actor is concerned, it still just handles one message at a time, so there is no need to do anything special to the actor to make it testable.

With that understanding, you can now use any conventional Scala- or Java-based unit test framework that you like. For example, you might want to use ScalaTest [ScalaTest]. Place the following in your sbt build project:

```
libraryDependencies += "org.scalatest" % "scalatest_2.11"↵
  % "2.2.0" % "test"
```

If you are using Maven instead, add this:

```
<dependency>
  <groupId>org.scalatest</groupId>
  <artifactId>scalatest_2.10</artifactId>
  <version>2.2.0</version>
  <scope>test</scope>
</dependency>
```

Or perhaps you are using Gradle; use this:

```
buildscript {
    repositories {
```

```
        mavenCentral()
    }
    dependencies {
        classpath 'com.github.maiflai:gradle-scalatest:0.4'
    }
}

apply plugin: 'scalatest'

dependencies {
    compile 'org.scala-lang:scala-library:2.10.1'
    testCompile 'org.scalatest:scalatest_2.10:2.0'
    testRuntime 'org.pegdown:pegdown:1.1.0'
}
```

Here let's use ScalaTest and its FunSuite tool that makes those familiar JUnit and the like comfortable:

```
import org.scalatest.FunSuite
import akka.testkit.TestActorRef

class RiskManagerTestSuite extends FunSuite {
  val riskManagerRef = TestActorRef[RiskManager]
  val riskManager = actorRef.underlyingActor

  test("Must have risks when told to calculate.") {
    riskManagerRef ! CalculateRisk(Risk(...))
    assert(!riskManager.risksToCalculate.isEmpty)
  }
  ...
}
```

See ScalaTest [ScalaTest] for all kinds of wonderful testing facilities, including xUnit, Behavior-Driven Development, and even some in between. You may find it necessary to mock some components, such as **ActorRef** instances, that actors are endowed with or introduced to.

Behavioral Testing Message Processing

Behavior-Driven Development (BDD) and Specification By Example (SBE) are names given to a form of testing that places emphasis on business requirements. The tests are meant to reflect actual business scenarios and serve as requirements for the software. With BDD/SBE, the goal is to get agreement from all appropriate stakeholders on what the requirements are and to code those into a set of tests that serve as *the* canonical documentation. This is purposely the opposite of having lots of different requirements documents and one-off or lots-off tests and software models found in a typical project. The effort is intended to lead to the creation of a carefully crafted software model with behavior that is verified by the assertions made in the specification-based tests.

Akka TestKit provides a class named `TestKit` that you use in BDD-style testing.[10] You also must mix in a number of Scala classes/traits that help you to write robust tests. Here is one such requirements/test specification:

```
import org.scalatest.BeforeAndAfterAll
import org.scalatest.WordSpecLike
import org.scalatest.matchers.Matchers
import akka.testkit.ImplicitSender
import akka.testkit.TestKit
class RiskCalculatorSpec(testSystem: ActorSystem)
      extends TestKit(testSystem)
      with ImplicitSender
      with WordSpecLike
      with Matchers
      with BeforeAndAfterAll {

  // there is an implicit class argument
  def this() = this(ActorSystem("RiskCalculatorSpec"))

  override def afterAll {
    TestKit.shutdownActorSystem(system)
  }

  "A RiskCalculator" must {
    "confirm that a risk calculation request is in progress" in {
      val riskCalculator = system.actorOf(Props[RiskCalculator])
      riskCalculator ! CalculateRisk(Risk(...))
      expectMsg(CalculatingRisk(...))
    }
  }
}
```

This is only a brush with specification-based tests and TestKit. See the samples provided by Ray Rostenburg [Roestenburg] that demonstrate a spectrum of specification-based test tools available with Akka TestKit.

The CompletableApp

Throughout the code samples you will see what may at first appear to be a mysterious object, the `CompletableApp`. The `CompletableApp` extends the standard Scala `App` trait but adds a little bit of extra behavior. As a

---

10. The Akka team refers to these as integration tests because you use them to test how well your actor integrates with the many actors running in the system that surrounds it. By any other name, they are BDD/SBE tests.

convenience, it creates an instance of the `ActorSystem`. Scala objects that extend it, such as `RequestReplyDriver`, set themselves up for step completion counting. When you see an `Int` value given to the `CompletableApp` constructor, that value is the number of completable steps that the overall process will perform. Once all steps have completed, the `CompletableApp` will finish and shut down the `ActorSystem`. This makes it possible for the main thread of the code examples to wait until the various actors have completed all expected steps.

> **Don't Use CompletableApp in Your Reactive Applications**
>
> Awaiting a number of steps to complete, or awaiting at all, is not the way to write a high-throughput reactive application. The waiting for steps to complete in the main driver `CompletableApp` is just an easy way to demonstrate the implementation of the pattern being discussed. Yet, you should not do the same in your reactive applications.
>
> A much better way to deal with the completion of a number of steps is to send an *Event Message (207)* to some actor that will react in the proper way to the outcome. Which actor? Introduce the completion actor to actors involved in the main processing through messages. The message-based introductions may be controlled by a *Process Manager (292)*, a *Message Bus (192)*, a *Pipes and Filters (135)* chain, or some other processing pattern. When using a *Process Manager (292)*, for example, it would be the *Process Manager (292)* itself that tells a known completion actor an *Event Message (207)* when the process has completed its final step.

Here's the `CompletableApp` source code:

```
package co.vaughnvernon.reactiveenterprise

import akka.actor._

class CompletableApp(val steps:Int) extends App {
  val canComplete =
      new java.util.concurrent.CountDownLatch(1);
  val canStart =
      new java.util.concurrent.CountDownLatch(1);
  val completion =
      new java.util.concurrent.CountDownLatch(steps);

  val system = ActorSystem("ReactiveEnterprise")

  def awaitCanCompleteNow() = canComplete.await()

  def awaitCanStartNow() = canStart.await()

  def awaitCompletion() = {
    completion.await()
    system.shutdown()
```

```
  }

  def canCompleteNow() = canComplete.countDown()

  def canStartNow() = canStart.countDown()

  def completeAll() = {
    while (completion.getCount > 0) {
      completion.countDown()
    }
  }

  def completedStep() = completion.countDown()
}
```

In the case of the `RequestReplyDriver`, there are a number of steps configured on the `CompletableApp` base object, but the rest of the actors in the example must help the driver count down. That's done at specific points as follows:

```
...
RequestReplyDriver.completedStep()
...
```

The other `CompletableApp` methods can be used under special circumstances. For example, `awaitCanStartNow()` will be used by the driver when it must pause for some setup processing to be accomplished among a number of actors before the main processing can begin. Once the actors are ready for action, one of the actors will call `canStartNow()`.

Thus, this special case of the standard `App` manages the final completion of the steps of each example. The `CompletableApp` will be used liberally throughout the book's code examples. Still, you should also filter out its use or take it with a grain of salt. The `CompletableApp` should not be considered a normal part of Akka development. It's just some scaffolding to help make the example code more readable and understandable.

Summary

That was a healthy dose of Scala and Akka guidance. To recap, here's what was covered in this chapter:

• You were given a number of different ways to obtain Scala and Akka, which primarily focused on using one of a few build interfaces. I then stepped you through an abbreviated Scala programming tutorial. You learned everything from naming your packages and importing Scala tools to using conditionals, looping, and various iteration constructs.

- Then you took a deep dive into programming with Akka. This included the basics such as creating an `ActorSystem`, creating actors, sending them messages, and supervising actor hierarchies.

- You also looked at advanced topics such as remoting and clustering.

- Finally the chapter wrapped up with essential information on testing actors.

Next you will look at why the Actor model is important for developing performance-oriented applications and the tools it provides to achieve your concurrent processing goals.

Chapter 3

Performance Bent

Transistors. Transistors and clock speed. Yes, transistors and clock speed. What indulgences we have enjoyed.

Do you give much consideration to these qualities of microprocessors while you are programming? For about half a century, transistors and clock speed played an exponentially increasing role on our software systems. Our addiction to accelerating numbers of transistors and increasing clock speeds went unchecked. To keep our ever-more complex programs running at the accelerating speeds, we craved greater numbers, and the semiconductor pros delivered.

Take transistors. Early transistorized computers were developed by those who struggled to keep a few thousand brittle transistors operational. Today there are many millions—hundreds of millions—of transistors clustered in microprocessors, and those microprocessors are in computers, large and tiny, just about everywhere on Earth. Without most of us giving much thought at all to transistors, it seems as if they have just taken care of our craving for processing power and speed all along. Yet, take notice. Our future with transistors could be quite different than our sumptuous past.

Make no mistake. Transistors matter and clock speeds matter—in ever-changing ways.

Transistors Matter

On October 22, 1925, in Canada, Julius Edgar Lilienfeld, an Austrian-Hungarian physicist, filed a patent for the first transistor. Unfortunately, his work was not widely known, and it would require more than 20 years before the transistor would take a significant step out of obscurity. Previously in 1906, vacuum tubes were invented as the sole means of electronic amplification, and these ushered in the electronic age. With Lilienfeld's discovery remaining largely unknown, vacuum tubes would experience an enduring run as the means to power electronics [Triode].

It wasn't until the year 1947 that scientists achieved successful use of transistors. The first workable use of transistors took even longer, until 1953. And the first real practical use occurred in 1954. With computers? Well, yes and no. The first transistorized computer was in fact developed in 1953 by

Dick Grimsdale at Sussex University. However, at that time the unreliability of the transistors themselves hindered the ongoing development of his computer. Computers would have to wait their turn. Transistors had to go through several refinements before they could experience broad commercial use [Transistor].

In the same year that Grimsdale had limited success with his transistorized computer, transistors were used successfully to produce the first commercial radio of its kind. The TR-1 used a total of four transistors and cost $49.95. Considering inflationary rates, buying a TR-1 could be likened to today buying an iPod for about $449.95. Although relatively expensive to own, transistor radios had a great advantage over contemporary vacuum tube radios. Transistors were smaller, used less power, and didn't require nearly as much time to warm up as was required by vacuum tubes. Luxury items indeed, transistor radios sported an "instant-on" feature [Transistor].

Most importantly for advances with computers, all the research and development that led to the mass production of transistor radios—the TR-1 sold roughly 150,000 units—helped refine transistors for even broader commercial application.

One of the first successes among commercial transistorized computers is attributed to Control Data Corporation and the team led by Seymour Cray, which delivered the CDC 1604 in 1960 [Cray-CDC]. Still, apparently the second-generation IBM 7090 [IBM-History], now based on transistors, was first installed in November 1959, preceding the CDC 1604 by a number of months. The newer IBM 7090 packed a sixfold increase in speed over its vacuum-tube predecessor. Way back then, one of those IBM 7090s housing around 50,000 transistors would set you back approximately $2.9 million. Radios weren't the only transistor-based luxury items.

Shortly following these innovations, the cofounder of Intel Corporation recognized a trend regarding the effect that transistors would have on computing power over a long period of time. By 1965, Gordon E. Moore had observed that *the number of transistors* on integrated circuits had doubled rapidly. He thus predicted that this trend would continue, and the industry could count on a *doubling number of transistors* approximately every two years (see Figure 3.1). Moore's observation—known as Moore's law—has proved true for more than 50 years. In actuality, Moore's law has been not just a prediction or a trend. Moore's law has proved true, at least in part, because it has been established as the standard cadence for the semiconductor industry to keep pace with [Moore's Law].

Thus, from 1959 until 2014, the industry has basically held this pace, even exceeding it. And yet we must ask, how long can this blistering pace be maintained? By the year 2005, some were estimating that it could continue only until 2015 or 2020. Yet, by 2010 a semiconductor industry road map indicated

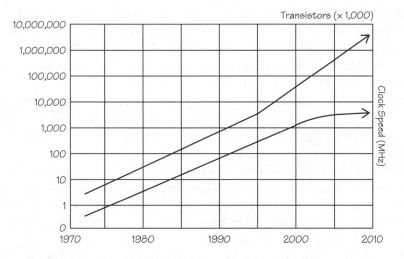

Figure 3.1 Moore's law since approximately 1973 through 2010

that growth would slow by the end of 2013. It was suggested that, at that point, transistor counts and densities would double only every three years. In 2005, Moore stated that his "law"—perhaps more accurately described as *Moore's prediction*—"can't continue forever." Moore indicated that by the time transistors are miniaturized to the size of atoms, they will have reached a physical barrier.

Others have a more positive outlook based on other potential breakthroughs, such as increased processor size, quantum computing, or future concepts that could completely replace integrated circuits. Although Moore, in 2005, stated that transistors may eventually number in the billions, today at least one processor has reached beyond that level. While not a central processing unit (CPU), the Nvidia GPU contains 7.08 billion transistors. That's nearly three times the transistors available on one of the fastest CPUs to date, IBM's zEC12 [IBM-zEC12], at 2.75 billion transistors [Transistor Count].

While still an uncertainty, the future of exponential gains in numbers of transistors seems to have a horizon.

Clock Speed Matters

There's another factor. Even beyond Moore's law, Intel executive David House predicted, *chip performance* will double every 18 months. His daring upstaging of Moore's law was based on not only a *doubling number of transistors* but also on *increasing processor speeds*.

While the increasing numbers of transistors have kept up with the break-neck pace predicted some 50 years ago, processor clock speeds have already fallen off a cliff. As Herb Sutter [Herb Sutter] stated and Figure 3.2 shows, although House's statement held true for several processor generations, by the beginning of 2003 CPU clock speed increases began to fall off sharply. In other words, even if transistors were to continue on the path of Moore's law, CPU speeds have not continued on the path of House's prediction for more than a decade—since 2003. If they had, by 2005 CPUs would have been running at roughly 10GHz.

Wasn't it great while it lasted? You must admit, over the past 35 years, if you've been developing software anywhere in that time frame, you've been spared many times. The increasing microprocessor speeds saved your other-wise slowing software every 18 months. But, no more. The luxury of exponen-tially increasing CPU speeds has ended. Why?

Even in 2014 I am using a notebook computer with an Intel i7 Quad Core 4700HQ, which runs at a mere 2.4GHz. There are faster Intel processors, but not that much faster (perhaps 3.9GHz). Go ahead, pile on more transistors. It's not going to push CPU speeds from the stratosphere to the mesosphere. The fact is, the linearly increasing performance of CPU clock speeds reached its exponential growth limits around 2003. These are the primary factors for the limitations:

- CPUs having clock speeds greater than those available today run too hot to cool using conventional methods.

- CPU power consumption is too high to support higher clock rates.

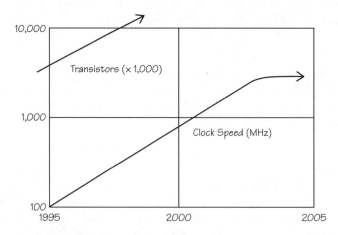

Figure 3.2 Intel's David House's prediction falls off by 2003.

So then, how will contemporary computing meet increasing performance demands?

Cores and Cache Matter

The major difference between microprocessors that were available a decade ago, and the ones we can commonly obtain today—on notebook computers—are as follows:

- 64-bit instruction set (versus 32-bit processor in 2005)

- Four cores, with the capability to run eight threads simultaneously (versus one core, and possibly hyperthreading in 2005)

- 6MB CPU cache (versus perhaps 2MB in 2005)

It's not always an automatic performance boost to go from a 32-bit processor to a 64-bit processor. Although a 64-bit CPU has more registers, a superior instruction set, and other optimizations, the increase in pointer size can have a negative impact. For example, if your software makes extensive use of pointers, your CPU cache can fill up more quickly. When the CPU cache fills, the processor will have to make the much slower trip to main memory to fetch program data on a more frequent basis. Thus, a 2MB CPU cache from 2005 that has been replaced with 6MB CPU cache today makes it three times more likely for the CPU to have a successful cache hit when it is executing your code. The fact is, the large CPU cache is the primary means of performance boost to software that does not take specific advantage of multiple cores [Herb Sutter].

Yet, beyond the raw throughput of a 64-bit processor and the speed benefits of accessing on-CPU cache, what's left to squeeze out additional precious computing cycles? In a word, *cores*. Unless the ever-increasing numbers of CPU cores are put to full use, software performance will have hit an impenetrable wall. It is only by means of concurrent programming techniques—assigning threads to processor cores—that makes the software run faster. Using Intel's Many Integrated Core (MIC) architecture, which is a set of top-end multi-core processors (Ivy Bridge Xeon and Xeon Phi together), a computer can now achieve 33.86 PetaFLOPS.

Interestingly, each of the 72 cores in the "Knights Landing" Xeon Phi processor execute four threads per core. That's a total of 288 simultaneous threads on a single CPU. Compared to the IBM 7090 of 1960, at approximately $4,000 per chip, this top-end Intel Xeon Phi is a bargain. Of course, those

72 cores will run 288 simultaneous threads if we as programmers know what we are doing. Otherwise, we are talking about 71 ¾ cores sitting idle much of the time. Why? Note this significant quote about the experience report from researchers of the Intel Xeon Phi:

> An empirical performance and programmability study has been performed by researchers. The authors claim that to achieve high performance [the] Xeon Phi still needs help from programmers and that merely relying on compilers with traditional programming models is still far from reality. See: Fang, Jianbin; Sips, Henk; Zhang, Lilun; Xu, Chuanfu; Yonggang, Che; Varbanescu, Ana Lucia (2014). "Test-Driving Intel Xeon Phi." 2014 ACM/SPEC International Conference on Performance Engineering. Retrieved December 30, 2013 [http://en.wikipedia.org/wiki/Xeon_Phi].

Ah, now the weight of the future of computing performance rests not on the microprocessors alone but on our shoulders. It's almost like it's 1981 again; we just got a job offer to work as a semiconductor engineer at Intel, and it's our job to make the next generation of software run faster...except it's our software that will make our software faster, not the hardware alone.

Scale Matters

In the mid to late 1990s, a popular solution to software performance challenges was to throw big hardware at the problems. During one project I consulted on, it became clear that the Java-based e-commerce system would not perform on the existing Sun Enterprise 450 servers. The answer? Buy a Sun Enterprise 10,000. The prospect of starting off with several UltraSPARC II processors and adding more as needed—up to a total of 64—seemed to be a desirable scalability path. If you didn't agree, all you had to do is ask the Sun sales force.

If you were working on large-scale Java server projects like that in the day, you'll likely recall that it was strictly forbidden to create and manage your own threads on a Java 2 Platform Enterprise Edition (J2EE) container. The container owned the threads, not you and your application. If you didn't adhere, the planets in our solar system would for certain spin off their axes. Of course, creating threads without care could potentially cause problems for a J2EE container, or just a Java virtual machine (JVM) for that matter. Still, my experience proved that some application thread usage did not cause disaster. Yet, multithreading was still not an option for broad application in problem solving. It is possible that selling more Sun Enterprise 10,000 servers had more to do with the then-contemporary guidance more than the potential for negative impact on containers.

At roughly the same time that the "scale up" message was being sent throughout the industry, a few innovators were proving that scale-out was a much more powerful, practical, and versatile choice. Some forerunners were the researchers and developers of the Inktomi search engine. As described by Inktomi's Dr. Eric Brewer, the goal was to create a "supercomputer" from many commodity *workstation* nodes. Why? Inktomi was addressing a pair of challenges. First, even though at the time processor speeds were still increasing, the Web's document and user growth was outpacing those hardware increases, and there was no way to accurately predict future hardware needs. Second, Inktomi needed to scale out to place its crawler and search engine near the data and its users, both of which were experiencing rapid global growth. Otherwise, Inktomi's solution would only add to the congestion being experienced across continents. Deploying high-end servers globally would have prohibitive cost implications, even in the days of the dot-com bubble [Brewer-Inktomi].

One key driver to Inktomi's architectural direction was that commodity hardware could be purchased and deployed within days, compared to the lengthy time needed to acquire high-end servers. As commodity hardware moved up the power curve, which at the time seemed to be an unceasing reality, newer hardware could be deployed alongside older, slower nodes. Configuration could be used to put more processing responsibility on newer nodes. The clustered workstations architecture collaborating on high-speed network connections was designed to scale without limit and without significant deterioration in performance as additional workstations were added to the cluster. Furthermore, the architecture supported adding workstations incrementally, without any negative impact on concurrent cluster operations [Inktomi-Architecture].

Another competitor in the search engine space would take a similar approach to scalability. Google uses commodity-class x86 server computers. In recent years Google's hardware consisted of custom-made systems containing two dual-core processors, a considerable amount of random access memory (RAM), and two SATA hard disk drives [Google-Platform]. Figure 3.3 provides a Google reference architecture [Google-Architecture].

As was the case with Inktomi, Google's search engine requires a fast network to support the distribution shown in Figure 3.3. Although the details of its network is top secret, based on some information disclosed by Google, we can guess at a few details about its private network topology and capabilities. Google's private network is thought to use custom-built, high-radix switch-routers, each of which may have a capacity of 128×10 Gigabit Ethernet port. For redundancy, there are at least two such routers per data center. Based on what is known, it is possible that the Google private network scales in the terabit per second range. Yes, that's a fast network [Google-Platform].

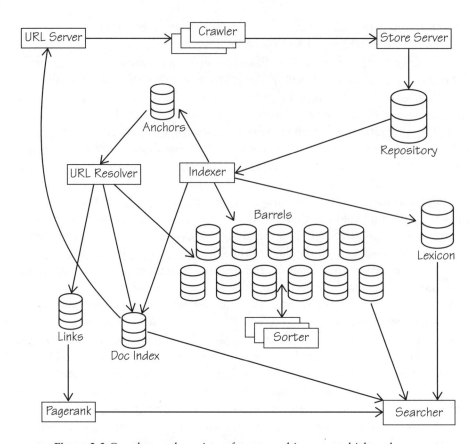

Figure 3.3 Google search engine reference architecture, which scales out using many commodity x86 computers

Regardless of how fast your network is—and there may not be any faster than Google's—there are still very real challenges to distributed computing. For example, Google has tracked at least some of the reasons for its network outages and network partitions[1] [Google-Owies]. Assuming that network partition recovery is never instantaneous, what are the consequences to Google's software systems and applications? We don't have details, but evidently there is significant concern over the following:

Developing easy-to-use abstractions for resolving conflicting updates to multiple versions of some state. In other words, reconciling replicated state in different

---

1. A network partition refers to the failure of a network device that causes a split network [Network-Partition].

data centers after repairing a network partition is a difficult problem to avoid and to solve.

Although there are many possible rewards from employing distributed architectures, the network can also have a negative impact on such solutions. Remembering that distributed computing is inherently unreliable [IDDD], it's understandable why the first rule of distributed computing is "don't distribute" [Fowler EAA].

Even so, scaling out is going to be necessary for now and the future. Consider the architectural principles used by Amazon.com [ACM-Amazon], one of the largest global computing systems. Amazon.com CTO Werner Vogels states it clearly that "scalability cannot be an afterthought" [Vogels-Scalability]. At the core of its architectural principles, Amazon.com applies Eric Brewer's[2] CAP theorem first, as shown in Table 3.1, and designs services from that point forward [CAP]. Your architecture may use only two of the three.

The CAP theorem says that it's impossible to have all three of the system properties, so you have to choose only two. Not surprisingly, Amazon.com makes a single first assumption regarding its systems: that partitioning is the only way to scale, and Amazon.com must scale. Thus, it always assumes Partition Tolerance. Partitioning involves the network, which means dealing with inconsistency for various reasons. Nevertheless, Amazon.com must scale. It's one down and one to go.

From there, you have to understand how Amazon.com builds software. Its teams are small, and each team is responsible for a single service [Vogels-Scalability]. To give you an idea of the size of a service, there are more than 100 services used to render a single Web page. Based on the kind of service being designed, Amazon.com allows the team to determine whether Consistency or

Table 3.1 CAP Theorem and the Three Properties of Distributed Systems

Property	Description
Consistency	All nodes see the same data at the same time.
Availability	A guarantee that every request receives a response about whether it was successful or failed.
Partition Tolerance	The system continues to operate despite arbitrary message loss or failure of part of the system.

---

2. Remember Dr. Eric Brewer? You just read about his Inktomi architecture.

Availability is more important. Yet, the following basic guidelines apply when choosing one or the other [Vogels-AsyncArch]:

- *Example 1, shopping cart input*: Always accept and store shopping cart input from a customer and deal with minor problems in the data later. It means revenue. You never want to tell the customer you can't accept their input. Choose Availability.

- *Example 2, order submitted*: When an order is finally placed, various order fulfillment services are doing all kinds of things with the data, and you are not interacting directly with the customer. Choose Consistency. If you can't obtain consistency for one data item, you can move on to process a different data item and come back later. Also take advantage of the fact that part of this task's services required at this stage of processing will just need read-only data access. You can plan for consistency around databases that support high-performance reads.

Since CAP properties are determined by the kind of service being built, you can implement by choosing the best two on a case-by-case basis. You should never build systems with a one-size-fits-all mentality toward CAP and scalability.

> **Amazon.com Designs with Actor Model Principles**
> In an interview with Association for Computing Machinery (ACM), Amazon.com CTO Werner Vogels comments on service orientation in Amazon's architecture [ACM-Amazon]:
>
> > This was way before service-oriented was a buzzword. For us service orientation means encapsulating the data with the business logic that operates on the data, with the only access through a published service interface. No direct database access is allowed from outside the service, and there's no data sharing among the services.
>
> As you will see in the "How the Actor Model Helps" section, these very principles of "encapsulating the data with the business logic...and there's no data sharing among the services" are central to the Actor model.

Since scalability is necessary and must never be an afterthought, there had better be some way to deal with the network's impact on distributed systems. The network is not the only challenge found among scalable systems.

Multithreading Is Hard

You realize, of course, that the experience report by the researchers of the Intel Xeon Phi is alluding to your ability to write multithreaded software. Yet, that's never been an easy thing to do, nor something that many programmers succeed at. Sure, just about everyone has learned to use threads and perhaps experimented with them—you know, by typing in some code that they've found on a programming how-to Web site. But, have you really used multithreading in an actual production system? Believe me, when you have to lean on shared mutable state and mutexes to protect it, it's hard to get it right, and I've been doing it since the mid-1980s.

Probably one of the most difficult things about designing a multithreaded application is not necessarily the initial design. Sometimes the design seems to just fall into place. I've experienced it. It's possible. You keep things simple and understandable. You test. It works. You test more. It works more. Hurray.

And then comes the user acceptance tests and impending change requests. With entirely unanticipated requirements, your once-understandable multithreaded code starts to take on unexpected twists and turns. You never could have anticipated this. Right in the middle of an asynchronous operation, the user will now, under some exceptional condition, need to provide corrective input. If only you had known that from the beginning. That new requirement would have influenced your design from the start. You face a fast-approaching release date, and there's no time to redesign your now brittle multithreaded code.

The other thing that goes wrong with multithreaded software is the production environment. Although you test and test and test and test some more, there is no way to predict everything that could possibly happen in the production environment. That's because you probably don't program using the production environment. Even a great test lab is no true reflection of the production environment. Users can do things or not do things, the network can do things or not do things, other software will do things or not do things, and machines can break in ways that you could never have imagined. Still, imagination can't undo the problems caused.

So far I haven't even mentioned thread deadlocks, livelocks, and the likely possibility of just writing really bad multithreaded code. Compare these lurking problems:

- *Deadlock*: Two or more competing threads are each waiting for another to finish with a given resource, and none can continue because desired locks can never be obtained. It's like a deadly embrace.

- *Livelock*: This is similar to a deadlock, except that the states of the threads involved in the livelock constantly change with regard to one another, none progressing. It's like a dance that never ends.

- *Starvation*: Some threads run tasks regularly, but others don't and thus "starve" for CPU cycles. This can happen when tasks are allocated to certain threads but not others, which is generally the result of writing inefficient code (the next problem).

- *Inefficient code*: Although locks are working, the code design doesn't allow threads to run smoothly. The constant acquiring and releasing of locks can cause CPU cores to burn cycles that could otherwise be used for processing. The multithreaded solution is so synchronized that it executes in many scenarios only as effectively as a single-threaded program.

- *False sharing*: This is similar to inefficient code, except for reasons that far too many programmers are completely unaware of and unprepared to deal with. As indicated earlier in the "Cores and Cache Matter" section, modern CPU designs cache application data close to the cores. This has resulted in a few levels of cache, typically L1, L2, and L3 for quad-core processors, with L1 and L2 owned by a core. Caches are filled with cache lines,[3] each of which is taken from main memory. When threads execute, they can too easily use bytes from the same cache line. As thread X needs to perform an operation on one variable in the cache line, thread Y may need to perform an operation on a different variable in the same cache line.[4] Say that thread X invalidates the cache line by one means. Thread Y, using the same cache line, has an invalidated L2 cache line. The L2 cache line used by thread Y must be refreshed from main memory based on modifications of thread X. The more cache has to be refreshed from main memory, the slower multithreading software becomes. Yet, threads X and Y are not modifying the same bytes of the cache line. Although you could design your threading code well, cores will commonly thrash because of false sharing [False-Sharing].

All of these problems are because multithreaded software is difficult to reason about and because modern processors can work against the best of intentions. Although we can understand the design challenges we face when each task is considered individually as a discrete operation and with respect to a given state in the system, it is difficult to predict how each task, when run simultaneously with all the others, will affect all the others. That's because we cannot predict when the processor will schedule the tasks. It's also why

---

3. A typical cache line is 64 bytes. Some hardware may support other 32-byte or 128-byte cache lines.

4. Think of a single `CircularQueue` object where one thread is writing to its buffer and another is reading from its buffer. There are three ways for the two threads to compete for one or more cache lines: (1) the buffer modification, (2) the write index modification, and (3) the read index modification.

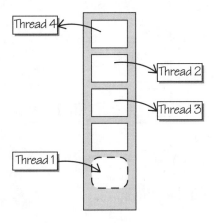

Figure 3.4 One thread enqueues new work items
while worker threads dequeue work items.

multithreaded code is considered nondeterministic. This is all pointing to the
fact that multithreading inherently causes temporal coupling and dependencies
among the threads. We've been trained to work hard to loosely couple our
software objects, and yet the very nature of common multithreading programming models and practices forces us to couple in a manner that our brains
can't comprehend very well.

What we need is an easier way to be multithreaded. If temporal coupling
is a problem, then we should attempt to decouple temporally. Oftentimes it is
suggested to use a queue to manage work items for threads to perform. One
thread enqueues new work items while worker threads dequeue work items, as
shown in Figure 3.4. As each worker thread goes to the work queue to get its
next task, this can ease the tension between threads. Each thread is now more
loosely coupled from the others.

One potential problem with this approach is that it creates a natural competi-
tion between consuming threads. If one thread tends to get the tasks that can be
completed more quickly, it will constantly be locking the shared queue ahead of
the other worker threads, causing the starvation of the others. Even the thread
responsible for keeping the queue full of work items may find that the queue is
often locked out of its reach. Then there is the possibility that work items will
specify the use of the same system entities, causing overlap in resource dependencies between threads, which reintroduce deadlock and livelock scenarios. Even if
deadlock and livelock can be avoided, the shared resources themselves will cause
competing threads to block, leading to suboptimal access implications. This is
illustrated in Figure 3.5.

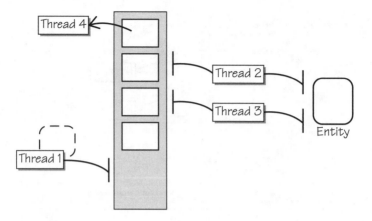

Figure 3.5 Even work item queues can lead to contention between the enqueuing thread and workers. Workers may also obtain overlapping work items that cause blocking on shared resources, such as model entities.

There are lock-free queue implementations, such as Java's `Concurrent-LinkedQueue`, and others. Yet, even with a lock-free queue, if the queue is not designed to prevent false sharing, the design can work against optimal concurrency. Obviously, there are more than a few problems to solve, even when using standard Java and C# threading mechanisms. Unfortunately, neither compilers nor multithreading toolkits save us from the unseen overhead caused by false sharing. Even though analyzing a single object, such as a queue, may prevent false sharing on that one set of contiguous bytes, it is often difficult to determine what separate objects may reside in a single cache line.

How do you design each thread such that it is good at doing all the things the system needs to do? Sure, it's possible, but is it straightforward? Further, currently each worker thread is responsible for retrieving its next work item, using poll-based queue access. Could we possibly do better by handing work items to worker threads when it is known that they are available to perform their next task?

Although the work item queue is often a much better approach to multi-threaded designs and chances are much more in favor of the success, it still is not ideal. Thinking about the Intel Xeon Phi for a moment, would you be able to design a queue-based work item multithreaded application that could keep 288 cores busy all the time, or 287 if you are leaving one free for the operating system?

The problem here is that we keep working toward designs that force threads to share system resources. One big sharing bottleneck is the single work item queue. The other potential sharing bottleneck, or deadlock/livelock disaster zone, is the shared use of model entities.

Often the problem is what to do when a problem occurs. What exactly do you do when multiple concurrent processes running in your system suddenly receive data that they can't deal with, misbehave in terms of what they are expected to do, or just outright crash?

With all the potential for concurrency and parallelism going sideways on us, it is understandable why mainstream business enterprise solutions have largely avoided such designs. That's why, for the most part, multithreaded designs have been used by bleeding-edge projects that must squeeze every bit of computational processing and scale out of multiple cores and networked nodes. Actually, though, what about the enterprise?

We should be able to design better multithreaded applications more easily. The following assertions challenge our assumptions about typical multithreading approaches that must justifiably be avoided by mainstream enterprises that could otherwise benefit from concurrency and parallelism:

- If sharing causes problems, and even more so when network partitions occur, then don't share. Stop sharing queues, stop sharing domain model entities, and stop sharing the processes that operate on them.

- If production environments make for unwelcome surprises, then make our development and production environments work as similarly as possible.

- If it's difficult to design threads to do all the things your system needs to do, assign threads to perform only discrete tasks that they are specially capable of performing and only when the tasks need to be performed.

- If work polling is inefficient, then don't poll for work items. Design your system such that threads receive work when they can handle their next task. Rather than proactively polling for the next thing to do, components should react to the next task they are told to perform, but only if the component is good at doing that task and only when a thread is available to run it.

- If scheduling tasks is difficult and error prone, leave the task scheduling to software that is best at that job, and focus on your system's use cases instead.

- If errors happen—and errors do happen—design your system to expect errors and react to errors by being fault tolerant.

These are powerful assertions. Yet, is there a way to realize these sound concurrency design principles? Or have we just identified a panacea of wishful thinking? Can we actually use multithreaded software development techniques that enable us to reason about our systems, that react to changing conditions, that are scalable and fault tolerant, and that really work?

How the Actor Model Helps

A system of actors helps you leverage the simultaneous use of multiple processor cores. Each core can be kept busy executing a given actor's reaction to its current incoming message. A scheduler is generally employed to divvy up its pool of threads among actors that have messages waiting in their mailboxes. With a busy system where messages are continually being queued for many actors, the scheduler will distribute work across threads without letup. Making constant use of threads without blocking is the most efficient concurrent processing system we can hope to have.

This does not mean that sending a message from one actor to another is anywhere near as fast as one object invoking a method on another object within the same process. These are two completely different uses of a processor core, where the latter represents a few extremely optimized processor instructions, and the former requires a multitude of processor instructions in comparison. Even so, the Actor model isn't trying to compete at the single invocation level. As Gul Agha shows, sequential systems are not good at supporting concurrency and parallelism because they tend to deadlock in concurrent situations [Agha, Gul]. So, we use the Actor model for what it does best.

Yet, to make efficient use of processors and processor cache and deal with a very high throughput application, does it mean we must scale our server clusters to the moon? You can still design your applications after the Inktomi, Google, and Amazon.com distribution models without utilizing thousands upon thousands of servers. It might surprise you that an Akka cluster can actually reduce the number of servers your solution needs when compared to typical application servers and third-party business process solutions.

Consider one case study of the WhitePages [WhitePages], which is the leading provider of contact information for people and businesses in the United States. It has 50 million unique users each month and processes 2 billion searches. It needed to replace a system implemented in Perl- and Ruby-based solutions. According to the WhitePages, the hardware costs alone had grown to a "ridiculous" degree, with one service needing 80+ servers to process just 400 queries per second [WhitePages]. Yet another service required 60 servers. It seems that the Perl and Ruby programs spent 70 percent of the processor power serializing and deserializing data.

The results of redesigning and reimplementing with Scala and Akka were astonishing. The results of the one service that required 60 servers, after going reactive, radically reduced server count to 5. In fact, the WhitePages has realized an overall *15x reduction* in servers [WhitePages].

Don't worry. If your application needs to scale to 1,000 servers or more in a single cluster, Akka can accommodate your needs. Another experience report shows how Akka scaled to a 2,400-node cluster on Google Compute Engine [Akka-Google]. Just think of what you could accomplish with a 1,000-server cluster compared to what the WhitePages could do with 5. The main takeaway here is that however many servers you have, their cores and processor cache will be fully utilized to the benefit of the business, rather than dealing with programming language and technology inefficiencies.

Let's address each of the six previously stated assertions and see how the Actor model answers. Some of the answers are blended with others:

1. *Share nothing:* The Actor model emphasizes that actors must not share any mutable state with other actors. Actors may provide snapshots of data with other actors, but that data must be immutable to the receiving actor. Further, actors don't share queues. As point #3 reinforces, actors have individual mailboxes. Essentially, actors that operate as intended have no chance to deadlock or livelock. One of the few ways to write inefficient actor code is to block on some resource, such as a disk. Thus, all but a few actors should always avoid blocking.

2. *Think reactively:* Many production errors are caused by sequential implementations that can't adapt to changing and unexpected environmental issues. Since you are designing reactive systems when you use the Actor model, try to anticipate the unexpected. It's not that you can think of every possible situation up front, because you can't. However, you can plan for the unexpected by building in resiliency through supervision that gracefully deals with what you can't know beforehand; see #6.

3. *Model with actors:* Create a different actor type to represent each of your application's major concepts. Delegate tasks specific to each business function to the type of actor that represents that area of the business. Carefully divide actor systems by major business function. See "Aggregate" and "Bounded Context" in [IDDD].

4. *Tell actors what to do:* In addition to point #3, actors have mailboxes that temporarily store messages that they need to process. When the actor is ready to process its next message, the next message in its mailbox is received and processed. The actor will only react to messages that it

understands and that are applicable to its current state and when there is a thread available with the scheduler.

5. *Actor systems provide scheduling:* The Akka toolkit comes with a set of schedulers that can be configured to support various message delivery options. If you need a specialty scheduler, you can create your own. However, if a given out-of-the-box scheduler requires some optimizations, you can count on the Akka team eventually providing those. Just focus on your application and allow Akka to do what it does best.

6. *Design for resilience:* Design your actors to model as closely as possible to the production environment, but also design actors to be adaptable. If your system encounters an unanticipated production condition that causes failure, adapt your actor to the new condition. If you can't process under the unanticipated circumstances without new design and implementation efforts, your actor supervision can probably still recover to the point where it can continue by safely logging and avoiding consumption of incompatible kinds of messages in future scenarios.

To thoroughly carry through with a performance bent, you may need to revisit Chapter 1 for some of the very basic characteristics of actors and the Actor model. There is so much power available in such a simple set of tools. Employing the Actor model, you can design with the reactive-simplicity stack and keep every processor core pegged on your clusters of servers. You get efficiency of design and efficiency of concurrency.

Dealing with False Sharing

It is fair to say that many who use the Actor model and Akka will never have to worry about false sharing. Yet, for those who do need to worry about designing highly performing systems, false sharing is a significant concern.

As previously stated, false sharing can cause significant unseen performance hits on multithreaded code. Intel says that the best way to avoid false sharing is currently through "code inspection" [Intel-FalseSharing]. Once detected, you can use byte-padding techniques to place hot data on cache line boundaries (for example, the read and write indexes used by the CircularQueue). Although this can protect against false sharing in a single object, it can be difficult to determine which separate objects reside in the same cache line.

The good news is that the Actor model helps. Each actor will be accessed by a single thread at a time. There will never be two threads sharing the same actor instance, with its internal data, simultaneously. At any given time, every state transition to a single actor will occur because of a single thread of execution. Thus, you don't have to be concerned with using byte padding to place individual fields on cache line boundaries. That's one of the greatest potentials for false sharing eliminated.

This leaves us with the situation where multiple actors, or an actor and some other objects, reside in the same cache line. Unfortunately, there is a high potential for this to occur because Akka's `Actor` trait has only two object reference fields. Most of the time that's great news because the default overhead of an `Actor` is only 16 bytes of storage on a 64-bit architecture. Still, with 64-byte cache lines you can store four times more bytes in a single cache line. Of course, you still must figure in the number and types of fields declared in your `Actor` subclass to find out the actual size of each concrete actor. Let's say you add four reference fields to some concrete actor. That's only 32 bytes. Add the 16 bytes from the base `Actor`, and you've still used only 48 bytes of a 64-byte cache line. From this brief exercise, you can see that it is easy to have two `Actor` instances on the same cache line, or one actor and some other object.

So, what to do? It doesn't seem to make sense to go through every actor and force it to align on a 64-byte boundary. That would unnecessarily bloat your application's memory heap, greatly limiting the number of actors you can have in a single JVM.

Even so, many times you can identify and tune at least the *hottest* data in an application on a case-by-case basis. How so? If you know which actors or related objects (for example, `CircularQueue`) are involved in very performance-intensive operations, make sure that they occupy one or more entire cache lines. To do so, you can use padding techniques [Nitsan Wakart]. This approach will produce good results, perhaps with some trial and error. Yet, given that our actors will be accessed by only a single thread at a time, you have fewer problems to solve than when using typical multithreading approaches. Perhaps in some cases the randomness of how actors and other data are allocated in the heap will help keep same-cache-line data from false sharing. However, don't count too heavily on this notion.

Unfortunately, the advice you've received here is currently the only way to solve the problems of false sharing, at least until compilers provide intrinsics to help with this [Mechanical-Sympathy].

The Patterns

Next up is a series of chapters about patterns. The patterns can be used for both application design and integration.

- Chapter 4: Messaging with Actors
- Chapter 5: Messaging Channels
- Chapter 6: Message Construction
- Chapter 7: Message Routing
- Chapter 8: Message Transformation
- Chapter 9: Message Endpoints
- Chapter 10: System Management and Infrastructure

The final element of the book is Appendix A, "Dotsero: An Akka-like Toolkit for .NET," that presents Dotsero, an Actor model toolkit for C# developers on the .NET platform. This is meant to give C# developers the means to experiment with the Actor model and try the patterns found in the patterns chapters.

Chapter 4

Messaging with Actors

The patterns in this chapter provide you with a basic understanding of messaging with the Actor model and Akka. You gain not only a foundational vocabulary but also primary knowledge of how to design parts of a single actor system and how they can be integrated.

- *Message Channel*: This is the means by which a message producer and a message consumer communicate, but both the producer and consumer remain decoupled from one another. Using the Actor model, logically speaking a *Message Channel (128)* is the actor's mailbox, a first-in, first-out (FIFO) queue for all incoming messages.

- *Message*: A fundamental building block when using message-based systems, here the contrast is made between a *Message (130)* on a traditional middleware system and the Actor model. You will see how to design *Messages (130)* and how to package them for practical use in your own actor system and how they can be used for integration.

- *Pipes and Filters*: Learn how simple and elegant the use of *Pipes and Filters (135)* can be when using the Actor model. The example uses *Message (130)* decryption, authentication, and de-duplication to demonstrate how the chain messages processors together.

- *Message Router*: In your actor systems, you will make use of all kinds of message routers, including both stateful and stateless routers, environment-based or context-based routers, lookback routers, and *Content-Based Routers (228)*. This pattern gives you a foundation on which to build a basic understanding of how to employ *Message Routers (140)* and how routers will determine the receiver of any given *Message (130)*.

- *Message Translator*: There are various kinds of transformations that *Messages (130)* may go through when they enter or exit your system. When integrating with other systems, you will likely use some form of *Message Translator (143)*. The informational data accepted by any given system must be compatible in order to be properly consumed, which likely means that a data format transformation or data translation must take place.

- *Message Endpoints*: There is nothing mysterious about endpoints in an actor-based system. They are the individual actors, and you can have many millions of them hard at work. See how actor endpoints are put to use in a single local actor system as well as when integrating with other systems.

Use this chapter to learn not only the basics of actor-based messaging but also as a preview of future chapters that contain much deeper discussions of the basic techniques found here.

Message Channel

Message Channel is the means by which a message producer and a message consumer communicate, but both the producer and consumer remain decoupled from one another. Using a typical messaging mechanism, a producer creates a channel with an identity/name that is made known to the one who wants to consume the producer's messages. The consumer opens the receiver end of the channel, prepared to consume messages. Once the producer sends a message, the consumer receives it.

It works a little differently when using the Actor model. Although there is no actual Message Channel, you can still think of it logically existing. In a way, each actor provides its own Message Channel by means of which it will receive messages. This channel is most simply represented by the actor's mailbox (see Figure 4.1), although there are other components that make the overall channel usable. Still, the mailbox basically functions as a FIFO queue for all incoming messages. In the case of the Actor model, it's not the producer that creates this mailbox channel. Rather, it's the creation of the actor that causes the underlying conceptual Message Channel to be created.

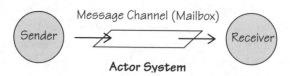

Figure 4.1 The actor's mailbox is its logical FIFO Message Channel.

```
val processor = system.actorOf(Props[Processor], "processor")
// message ProcessJob delivered to actor named "processor"
processor ! ProcessJob(1, 3, 5)
```

According to the rules of the Actor model, a message producer must know the address of the actor—in essence its Message Channel—to which it wants to send messages. This means that all actor-based Message Channels are *Point-to-Point Channels (151)*. Even when using *Publish-Subscribe Channel (154)* semantics, each subscribing actor still has a *Point-to-Point Channel (151)* through which the publisher must communicate messages to.

By definition, when using the Actor model, messages are delivered to an actor *at most once*. For many uses this all works out just fine, especially when considering that any given message is almost always successfully delivered. As well, when a given message is not actually delivered, there are ways to make sure that it is eventually. For example, the sending actor can listen for a response to its sent message and also set a timeout. If the timeout fires before the response is received, the client actor will simply resend the message. In the case of a crash, possibly restart the receiving actor before it sends the repeat message.[1]

This seems more than a little risky in the age of widespread use of trans-actions. After all, in business enterprises it's unacceptable to allow a message communicating, for example, financial transactions, to go completely undeliv-ered, especially when the messaging style of design emphasizes *fire and forget*. Who wants to take responsibility for using fire and forget in an at-most-once delivery environment? With those characteristics, how could the Actor model be suitable for use in business enterprises?

Not to worry. There are a few ways to ensure that a given actor eventually receives a message that must be delivered to ensure business success. I take up a complete discussion of Akka persistence when discussing *Guaranteed Delivery (175)*, *Transactional Client/Actor (351)*, and *Message Journal/Store (402)*.

---

1. A supervisor can watch for a crash and restart a crashed actor. It is also possible to set up a routing scheme where the supervisor first receives a message, ensures that the target actor is running, and then dispatches to it. See the "Supervision" section in Chapter 2.

Message

A Message is a fundamental building block when using message-based systems, one within which you package the information necessary to communicate actions and related data between systems. Since *Enterprise Integration Patterns* [EIP] discusses messaging systems often labeled *middleware* (implemented as a message server) rather than the Actor model, a message holds part system-level information and part application-level information. For *Enterprise Integration Patterns* [EIP], a message consists of two basic parts.

- *Header*: Information used by the messaging system
- *Body*: The data being transmitted

Further, using the middleware messaging system, the class of object used to carry messages between processes is generally provided by the messaging system. For example, on both Java and .NET systems, the type `Message` is provided by most middleware systems and holds both header and body parts (see Figure 4.2).

On the other hand, when using the Actor model, a message consists only of the second part, the body. In other words, the message is just the application-level data being transmitted between actors (see Figure 4.3). If there is any header information used by the underlying system, it is unseen by the actors in the applications.

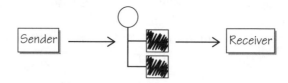

Figure 4.2 A Message using a middleware tool has a header and a body.

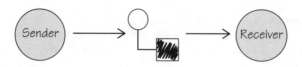

Figure 4.3 A Message within the Actor model has only application data.

Thus, there is a lot of versatility in the basic types of messages that can be sent from actor to actor, even including scalar values. That being so, you can design any given actor to accept messages of the following Scala types:

`String`

`Int`

`Long`

`Float`

`Double`

`BigDecimal`

`Byte`

`Char`

`...`

`Any` (represents specific types of case classes defined by the application)

So, an Akka actor may receive messages as follows:

```scala
class ScalarValuePrinter extends Actor {
  def receive = {
    case value: String =>
      println(s"ScalarValuePrinter: received String $value")
    case value: Int =>
      println(s"ScalarValuePrinter: received Int $value")
    ...
  }
}
```

Even though you can send scalar values as messages, it doesn't necessarily mean that they are the best choice. Under some circumstances, they may be just the thing you need to convey simple data between actors. Yet, when designing full-fledged actor-based systems and integrating among them and legacy systems, it generally works out to your advantage to define a *Canonical Message Model (333)*. Using Scala, the message types of a *Canonical Message Model (333)* can be efficiently created using case classes. Here's a sample *Command Message (202)*:

```scala
case class ExecuteBuyOrder(portfolioId: String,
    symbol: Symbol, quantity: Int, price: Money)
```

Case classes have two big advantages. First, they exist specifically to be efficiently used with Scala pattern matching. Second, they are one of the easiest ways to create immutable value types. Even though there is a stated rule to never mutate messages across actors, proper use of case classes for message types ensures that each message instance will remain immutable.

There are a few primary conventions for declaring message types in Scala source modules. The first is to place all messages supported by a given actor type in the source module along with the definition of the receiving actor. This may work best when your actor system uses primarily local actors and every actor in the system has package-level access to all public types. That source-level association makes it clear which message types any given actor will need to send so that a specific receiving actor will understand the individual messages.

The second convention is to place all common message types into one Scala source file. This may work out best when the actors of a given set of actor systems integrate and together define a *Canonical Message Model (333)*, which is an approach suggested in *Message Bus (192)*. The following are a set of *Command Messages (202)* and *Event Messages (207)* used in the sample Trading Bus:

```
case class ExecuteBuyOrder(portfolioId: String,
    symbol: Symbol, quantity: Int, price: Money)
case class ExecuteSellOrder(portfolioId: String,
    symbol: Symbol, quantity: Int, price: Money)
case class BuyOrderExecuted(portfolioId: String,
    symbol: Symbol, quantity: Int, price: Money)
case class SellOrderExecuted(portfolioId: String,
    symbol: Symbol, quantity: Int, price: Money)
...
```

This is especially useful if the types will be used across remote actor systems and the message types must be deployed and used for either sending or receiving on the multiple systems. Now you need only to go to one source module, or a few, to find the messages supported across systems. This has the downside that it may be a bit more difficult to understand which actors support which message types. However, some documentation or programming techniques can help to distinguish them.

```
// OrderProcessor messages
object OrderProcessorMessages {
  case class ExecuteBuyOrder(portfolioId: String,
    symbol: Symbol, quantity: Int, price: Money)
```

```
   case class ExecuteSellOrder(portfolioId: String,
      symbol: Symbol, quantity: Int, price: Money)
}
```

This places message case classes inside the scope of the object `OrderPro-cessorMessages`. This serves not only as documentation but as a name scoping technique. Now, to use the messages associated with order processing, you must import the specific object and all its scoped case classes.

```
import orders.processor.OrderProcessorMessages._
```

Additionally, you can extend all Messages from a sealed trait, which supports a special protection when matching.

```
// OrderProcessor messages
object OrderProcessorMessages {
  sealed trait OrderProcessorMessage
  case class ExecuteBuyOrder(portfolioId: String,
      symbol: Symbol, quantity: Int, price: Money)
      extends OrderProcessorMessage
  case class ExecuteSellOrder(portfolioId: String,
      symbol: Symbol, quantity: Int, price: Money)
      extends OrderProcessorMessage
}
```

Now you can enforce that attempts to match any one of the case classes will require the programmer to match on all of them. Yet, it does require you to use a nested match construct.

```
class OrderProcessor extends Actor {
  import OrderProcessorMessages._
  def receive = {
    case message: OrderProcessorMessage => message match {
      case buy: ExecuteBuyOrder =>
        ...
        sender ! BuyOrderExecuted(...)

      // warning will be given:
      // "match may not be exhaustive... ExecuteSellOrder(_)"
    }
  }
}
```

This is a way to prevent developers from forgetting to consider some cases, such as when there is a design change and new messages are added to a messaging contract. The Scala compiler will flag any omissions as a specific matching warning.

Using this approach of course means that a *Canonical Message Model (333)* based on case classes will need to be redeployed on every system as the types change. This will also tend to work against contemporary enterprise integration guidance to make integrating systems dependent on schema rather than class and dependent on weak schema rather than strong schema.[2] However, it is also the style generally used when developing with Scala and Akka, and you'd have the same challenges to contend with when message types change using typical messaging middleware.

I offer a different approach in *Implementing Domain-Driven Design* [IDDD] in the "Integrating Bounded Contexts" section, which in some integration cases may work best. In *Implementing Domain-Driven Design* [IDDD] the messages are called *notifications*. That approach emphasizes the use of text-based messages formed as JavaScript Object Notation (JSON) weak schema and on-the-fly typesafe parsing when received. The message contract is conveyed using a Published Language [IDDD] that is designed as a REST custom media type. By both sides of the messaging integration adhering to the Published Language, messages can be exchanged in this way without the need to distribute or generate message type classes on the receiver side. You may, thus, find it helpful to use message type versions distinguished by *Format Indicator (222)* so you can support multiple dependent actor systems at the same time. This will be especially helpful when messages are exchanged between actors and nonactor systems using a *Message Bridge (185)*, *Message Translator (143)*, *Normalizer (332)*, and the like.

When using *Message Bus (192)*, another design consideration is to include a set of bus-level messages that carry application-level messages around the bus.

```
case class TradingCommand(
    commandId: String, command: Any)
case class TradingNotification(
    notificationId: String, notification: Any)
```

Thus, the specific trading *Command Messages (202)* such as Execute-BuyOrder and *Event Messages (207)* such as BuyOrderExecuted will be toted around the Trading Bus by means of either a TradingCommand in the

---

2. An example of a strong schema is when using strict XML schemas. An example of a weak schema is JSON.

command field or a `TradingNotification` in the `notification` field, respectively. A *Channel Adapter (183)* is responsible for packing and unpacking each individual `TradingCommand` and `TradingNotification`. The bus-level messages may remind you a little of a header in a middleware messaging system. While they are similar, they are usually a bit different as well. After all, it's the bus, not Akka, that requires the wrapper messages. See *Message Bus (192)*.

As *Enterprise Integration Patterns* [EIP] indicates, besides *Command Message (202)* and *Event Message (207)*, the *Document Message (204)*, *Request-Reply (209)*, *Message Sequence (217)*, and *Message Expiration (218)* can all be useful add-ons to the use of the basic Message.

Pipes and Filters

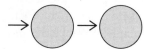

When using the Pipes and Filters architecture, you compose a process by chaining together any number of processing steps. Each of the steps is decoupled from the others. Thus, each of the steps could be rearranged or replaced as the need arises.

Composing a Pipes and Filters process using the Actor model can be quite simple, even pleasant. Take, for example, the pipeline illustrated in Figure 4.4. An order message enters the system, but before it can be processed to fulfill the purchase, you must handle some preliminary processing. First you must decrypt the order message, then you ensure that the external entity placing the order is authenticate, and finally you make sure that this order is not a duplicate of one that has been previously placed. Each of these steps is managed by an actor-based filter: `Decrypter`, `Authenticator`, and `Deduplicator`.

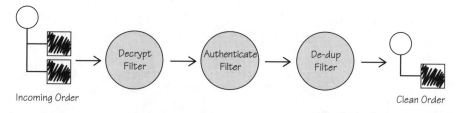

Figure 4.4 Actors serve as filters in a composed Pipes and Filters process.

There are also a few additional filter actors, including one *Message End-point (145)* actor that accepts incoming orders from external systems and one actor that processes the order once it has been fully prepared. In all, these are the filters in their composed sequence:

- OrderAcceptanceEndpoint

- Decrypter

- Authenticator

- Deduplicator

- OrderManagementSystem

In the sample, all of the filter actors in the pipeline, other than the first, receive the same standard message, `ProcessIncomingOrder`. Further, each filter actor, other than the last, is given the next filter in the pipeline as a constructor argument. Both of these design decisions allow for any of the filers other than the last to be rearranged in the pipeline, or completely replaced, and for new filters to be added as needed.

First let's look at the driver application, which is where the pipeline is composed:

```
object PipesAndFiltersDriver extends CompletableApp(9) {
  val orderText = "(encryption)(certificate)<order id='123'>...</↵
order>"
  val rawOrderBytes = orderText.toCharArray.map(_.toByte)

  val filter5 = system.actorOf(
                  Props[OrderManagementSystem],
                  "orderManagementSystem")
  val filter4 = system.actorOf(
                  Props(classOf[Deduplicator], filter5),
                  "deduplicator")
  val filter3 = system.actorOf(
                  Props(classOf[Authenticator], filter4),
                  "authenticator")
  val filter2 = system.actorOf(
                  Props(classOf[Decrypter], filter3),
                  "decrypter")
  val filter1 = system.actorOf(
                  Props(classOf[OrderAcceptanceEndpoint], filter2),
                  "orderAcceptanceEndpoint")

  filter1 ! rawOrderBytes
  filter1 ! rawOrderBytes

  awaitCompletion()
```

```
      println("PipesAndFiltersDriver: is completed.")
}
```

The filter actors are created in the reverse order that they are composed in the pipeline so that the previously created actor becomes the next filter for the subsequently created actor. For example, `OrderManagementSystem` becomes the next filter for the `Deduplicator`, and so forth. The driver scenario sends the same `rawOrderBytes` twice to the pipeline, forcing the `Deduplicator` to detect and ignore a duplicate order.

Here now are the filter actors in the order in which they are composed in the pipeline process, starting with `OrderAcceptanceEndpoint`:

```
class OrderAcceptanceEndpoint(nextFilter: ActorRef) extends Actor {
  def receive = {
    case rawOrder: Array[Byte] =>
      val text = new String(rawOrder)
      println(s"OrderAcceptanceEndpoint: processing $text")
      nextFilter ! ProcessIncomingOrder(rawOrder)
      PipesAndFiltersDriver.completedStep()
  }
}
```

As previously noted, the `OrderAcceptanceEndpoint` is a boundary actor and does not receive the message `ProcessIncomingOrder`. Rather, this actor creates that message from the `rawOrderBytes` for each newly received order that enters the system. Recall that the order is encrypted and contains a binary security certificate and thus is best accepted as an array of bytes. As each new raw order is received, `OrderAcceptanceEndpoint` sends the bytes to its `nextFilter` actor, wrapping the bytes in a `ProcessIncomingOrder` message.

The next filter in the pipeline is the `Decrypter`, which receives a `ProcessIncomingOrder`.

```
class Decrypter(nextFilter: ActorRef) extends Actor {
  def receive = {
    case message: ProcessIncomingOrder =>
      val text = new String(message.orderInfo)
      println(s"Decrypter: processing $text")
      val orderText = text.replace("(encryption)", "")
      nextFilter ! ProcessIncomingOrder(
                    orderText.toCharArray.map(_.toByte))
      PipesAndFiltersDriver.completedStep()
  }
}
```

In this trivial implementation, the decryption is only simulated by removing the text "(encryption)" from the order bytes after converting it to text. The Decrypter then sends a new ProcessIncomingOrder message, now without the "(encryption)" text, to the subsequent filter in the process, the Authenticator.

```scala
class Authenticator(nextFilter: ActorRef) extends Actor {
  def receive = {
    case message: ProcessIncomingOrder =>
      val text = new String(message.orderInfo)
      println(s"Authenticator: processing $text")
      val orderText = text.replace("(certificate)", "")
      nextFilter !
          ProcessIncomingOrder(orderText.toCharArray.map(_.toByte))
      PipesAndFiltersDriver.completedStep()
  }
}
```

As with the Decrypter, the Authenticator doesn't really do any authentication. It simulates authentication and removing the certificate from the message. After this step, it sends the order along the pipeline to its next-Filter, the Deduplicator.

```scala
class Deduplicator(nextFilter: ActorRef) extends Actor {
  val processedOrderIds = scala.collection.mutable.Set[String]()

  def orderIdFrom(orderText: String): String = {
    val orderIdIndex = orderText.indexOf("id='") + 4
    val orderIdLastIndex = orderText.indexOf("'", orderIdIndex)
    orderText.substring(orderIdIndex, orderIdLastIndex)
  }

  def receive = {
    case message: ProcessIncomingOrder =>
      val text = new String(message.orderInfo)
      println(s"Deduplicator: processing $text")
      val orderId = orderIdFrom(text)
      if (processedOrderIds.add(orderId)) {
        nextFilter ! message
      } else {

        println(s"Deduplicator: found duplicate order $orderId")
      }
      PipesAndFiltersDriver.completedStep()
  }
}
```

This `Deduplicator` actually does track duplicate orders. In a crude manner it extracts the ID of each order from the Extensible Markup Language (XML) text. It then attempts to add the order ID to a set of unique identities. (Of course, this would normally be handled using reliable persistent storage.) If the order is in fact unique, then it is sent along the pipeline. Otherwise, if it is a duplicate, as indicated by the set not accepting the order ID value, then the order is ignored.

Finally, the `OrderManagementSystem` is the final filter in the pipeline.

```
class OrderManagementSystem extends Actor {
  def receive = {
    case message: ProcessIncomingOrder =>
      val text = new String(message.orderInfo)
      println(s"OrderManagementSystem: processing unique order: $text")
      PipesAndFiltersDriver.completedStep()
  }
}
```

In this trivial example, the `OrderManagementSystem` indicates only that it has received a unique order and is processing it.

Here is the output from the sample:

```
OrderAcceptanceEndpoint: processing (encryption)(certificate)↵
<order id='123'>...</order>
OrderAcceptanceEndpoint: processing (encryption)(certificate)↵
<order id='123'>...</order>
Decrypter: processing (encryption)(certificate)↵
<order id='123'>...</order>
Decrypter: processing (encryption)(certificate)↵
<order id='123'>...</order>
Authenticator: processing (certificate)<order id='123'>...</order>
Authenticator: processing (certificate)<order id='123'>...</order>
Deduplicator: processing <order id='123'>...</order>
Deduplicator: processing <order id='123'>...</order>
Deduplicator: found duplicate order 123
OrderManagementSystem: processing unique order: ↵
<order id='123'>...</order>
PipesAndFiltersDriver: is completed.
```

As stated in *Enterprise Integration Patterns* [EIP], although each of the process filters in the Pipes and Filters architecture is called a *filter*, these are not of necessity filters in the same sense as those described by *Content Filter (321)* and *Message Filter (232)*. The filters described herein as components in a Pipes and Filters architecture do not need to filter data out of a *Message (130)* but instead may serve only as a processing step in a pipeline. That said, it so happens that the `Decrypter`, `Authenticator`, and `Deduplicator` are filters in the actual sense of the word.

Message Router

Often Message Routers are used in a *Pipes and Filters (135)* environment. Yet, Message Routers need not be limited to use with that style. There is a possibility of using all kinds of Message Routers, including both stateful and stateless routers, environment-based or context-based routers, lookback routers, and *Content-Based Routers (228)*.

The common characteristic of routers is that when a message is received, the router checks some property of the message (perhaps its own state), some property of the environment, or any and all of these, and dispatches the current message over the *Message Channel (128)* that satisfies the technical or business condition. In other words, the Message Router serves as a branching mechanism, much like an if-else block or a switch statement, with the conditional path chosen being a separate Message Channel (see Figure 4.5).

When thinking about the Actor model, the Message Router itself can be an actor. The router actor is placed somewhere appropriate in the processing pipeline. When the router receives a message, it checks the conditions specified by its contract and dispatches the message to the appropriate actor based on those conditions. It really doesn't matter how many potential actors there are

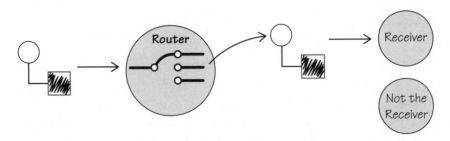

Figure 4.5 The Message Router selects the ultimate receiver of the *Message (130)*.

to which the router may route the message, just that there is one actor to fulfill each possible routing condition.

Let's look at a sample router, one that alternates sending messages between two processors. First, here's the driver application:

```
object MessageRouterDriver extends CompletableApp(20) {
  val processor1 = system.actorOf(Props[Processor], "processor1")
  val processor2 = system.actorOf(Props[Processor], "processor2")

  val alternatingRouter = system.actorOf(
        Props(classOf[AlternatingRouter], processor1, processor2),
            "alternatingRouter")

  for (count <- 1 to 10) {
    alternatingRouter ! "Message #" + count
  }

  awaitCompletion()

  println("MessageRouter: is completed.")
}
```

The two instances of the `Processor` actor are created as `processor1` and `processor2`, and then the `AlternatingRouter` is created. The driver then sends a total of ten messages to the `AlternatingRouter`, each uniquely identified by the current message count. Finally, the driver blocks until 20 total steps are completed. There's one step completed each time the router receives a message, as well as one step completed each time either of the two processors receives a message.

The `AlternatingRouter` is really simple.

```
class AlternatingRouter(
      processor1: ActorRef, processor2: ActorRef)
  extends Actor {
  var alternate = 1;

  def alternateProcessor() = {
    if (alternate == 1) {
      alternate = 2
      processor1
    } else {
      alternate = 1
      processor2
    }
  }
```

```
   def receive = {
     case message: Any =>
       val processor = alternateProcessor
       println(s"AlternatingRouter: routing $message to ↵
${processor.path.name}")
       processor ! message
       MessageRouter.completedStep()
   }
}
```

As the router receives each message, it asks for its current `alternate-Processor()`. It will receive either `processor1` or `processor2`. The router then routes the current message to the current `Processor` actor, after which it informs the driver that a step has completed.

The `Processor` actor is also quite simple. As an actor instance receives a message, it prints it and informs the driver that another step has completed.

```
class Processor extends Actor {
  def receive = {
    case message: Any =>
      println(s"Processor: ${self.path.name} received $message")
      MessageRouter.completedStep()
  }
}
```

Here's the output of the router and the alternating processes:

```
AlternatingRouter: routing Message #1 to processor1
AlternatingRouter: routing Message #2 to processor2
Processor: processor1 received Message #1
Processor: processor2 received Message #2
AlternatingRouter: routing Message #3 to processor1
AlternatingRouter: routing Message #4 to processor2
Processor: processor1 received Message #3
AlternatingRouter: routing Message #5 to processor1
Processor: processor2 received Message #4
Processor: processor1 received Message #5
AlternatingRouter: routing Message #6 to processor2
Processor: processor2 received Message #6
AlternatingRouter: routing Message #7 to processor1
AlternatingRouter: routing Message #8 to processor2
Processor: processor1 received Message #7
AlternatingRouter: routing Message #9 to processor1
Processor: processor2 received Message #8
AlternatingRouter: routing Message #10 to processor2
Processor: processor1 received Message #9
Processor: processor2 received Message #10
MessageRouter: is completed.
```

It's easy to imagine the `AlternatingRouter`, or some other kind of Message Router, being plugged in to a *Pipes and Filters (135)* process. This `AlternatingRouter` provides just one example of how routing can be used. See *Content-Based Router (228)* and *Dynamic Router (237)* for more specialized kinds of routing.

Message Translator

Use a Message Translator to transform the data from an incoming *Message (130)* to data that is compatible with the local, receiving application (see Figure 4.6). As *Implementing Domain-Driven Design* [IDDD] shows, when using a Domain-Driven Design approach, this translation could be handled in a couple of ways.

- When using the Ports and Adapters architecture style [IDDD] (a.k.a. Hexagonal), the Adapter [GoF] at the application boundary can be used to translate less challenging message payload to parameters that are compatible with the central Application Services. Perhaps the translation is mostly from text-based messages to scalar data, which the API accepts as valid parameters. In this case the port's adapter is a *Channel Adapter (183)* and is itself a suitable translator.

- For more complex translations, the *Channel Adapter (183)* should use an Anti-Corruption Layer [IDDD]. Some incoming data may be complex and require a more aggressive form of translation. This may require multiple Adapters and special translators that transform clusters of raw scalar data into concepts modeled in the local domain.

You could think of the first and second approaches as the same but just with less or more required translation components. It is true that you could consider a port's adapter as a simple Anti-Corruption Layer. Yet, the difference could be explained as follows. When using a Ports and Adapters architecture, you will always have a port's adapter at the system boundary, even when the translation is complex. It is the port's adapter at the system boundary that would of necessity delegate to one or more other adapters specifically suited for complex translation.

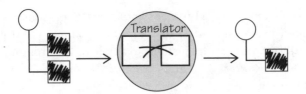

Figure 4.6 A Message Translator transforms an incoming Message to one that is suited for consumption by the receiving system.

As demonstrated in *Enterprise Integration Patterns* [EIP], the transformation process itself may be accomplished using a variety of tools. For example, XML may be effectively translated using Extensible Stylesheet Language (XSL). You can also use a visual translation tool that allows you to visually map fields from one data format to another. If you are using a weak schema such as with JSON, you can also use on-the-fly parser-based translation as demonstrated in *Implementing Domain-Driven Design* [IDDD] in "Integrating Bounded Contexts." It may also work out at times to deserialize a given message payload directly into a local object or record type.[3]

The type of message received, either *Command Message (202)*, *Document Message (204)*, or *Event Message (207)*, will often determine the amount of necessary translation. For example, a Command Message carries a payload that is specified by the receiving system. The incoming message must fulfill the client's contract for the specific application command being requested. Further, the outcome of a Command Message may well be an *Event Message (207)*.

An incoming *Event Message (207)* may require more translation than a *Command Message (202)*, but likely little more. Events are meant to convey a limited amount of information but enough to clearly inform other systems what has previously happened in the originating system. The message type/name itself conveys much of the intent of the event, usually including a verb in past tense indicating what happened. In addition, many times Event Messages are limited to identifiers and scalar data. When translated by the receiving system, the event becomes a command and is dispatched to the local Application Services.

On the other hand, a *Document Message (204)* could very well carry a large(r) payload of data with a complex and detailed structure. Thus, specifically accept a Document Message when you know that the message must pack

---

3. A record can mean something quite versatile, such as a dictionary or map, or a specific record type in a functional language.

in more information than is required to merely execute a command or process an event.

As far as using a Message Translator within the Actor model, the integrated receiver of the *Message (130)* will be a *Message Endpoint (145)* actor. The endpoint may use another actor as the primary translating adapter, with the understanding that the transformation will be completed asynchronously. This may be especially to your advantage when a data format is large and complex and requires a user-perceivable time frame to perform the translation.

Message Endpoint

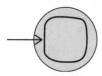

In a messaging system, a Message Endpoint is the sender and receiver of *Messages (130)* that are sent over a *Message Channel (128)*. When considering the Actor model, since actors are both the senders and receivers of messages, in a general sense actors are Message Endpoints (see Figure 4.7). That being so, it's possible to have many—thousands, millions, or even billions—Message Endpoints in an actor-based system.

Yet, when integrating, you may choose to think of Message Endpoints in a less general sense and more specifically as they are applied to integration. In the more specific sense, you may have one or more actor endpoints at a system boundary that provide specialized interfaces for integration. That is, the actor

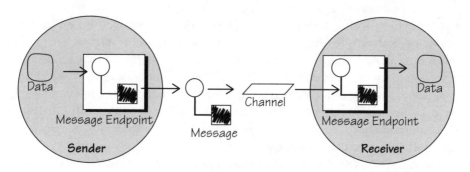

Figure 4.7 Every actor that receives and processes *Messages (130)* is a Message Endpoint.

endpoints allow for integration from application to application. This could be the case whether or not there are other actors in the system that play application-specific roles. If there are application-specific actors that receive messages from the specialized integration endpoint actors, then you may choose to think of the application-specific actors not as endpoints but rather as domain-specific concepts.

For example, you may have a number of high-volume online retailers that want to integrate with your discounting system to get price quotes for various products you sell. You can create the actor type `HighSierraPriceQuotes` and deploy it on your system boundary as an integration endpoint. This boundary actor provides an integration interface that supplies price quotes for the high-volume retailers.

```scala
case class CalculateDiscountPriceFor(requester: ActorRef, ...)
...
class HighSierraPriceQuotes(discounter: ActorRef) extends Actor {
  val quoterId = self.path.name
  def receive = {
    case rpq: RequestPriceQuote =>
      discounter ! CalculateDiscountPriceFor(sender, rpq.retailerId,
                                 rpq.rfqId, rpq.itemId)
    case pricing: DiscountPriceCalculated =>
      pricing.requestedBy ! PriceQuote(quoterId, pricing.retailerId,
                            pricing.rfqId, pricing.itemId,
                            pricing.retailPrice,
                            pricing.discountPrice)
    ...
  }
}
```

The `HighSierraPriceQuotes` actor is the integration endpoint. It receives `RequestPriceQuote` messages from the external, high-volume online retailer. To fulfill this request, the `HighSierraPriceQuotes` boundary actor delegates to the `discounter` actor that it receives a reference to when instantiated. `HighSierraPriceQuotes` knows that the `discounter` actor—actually an `ItemDiscountCalculator`—understands messages of type `CalculateDiscountPriceFor`. When the `discounter` has completed its calculations for the specific retailer, it replies with a `DiscountPrice-Calculated` message to the sender of `CalculateDiscountPriceFor`, that is, the `HighSierraPriceQuotes` actor.

Finally, when the `DiscountPriceCalculated` message is received by your boundary endpoint, the `HighSierraPriceQuotes` replies with a `PriceQuote` to the original sender—now referenced by the `ActorRef` held in the `pricing.requestedBy`. So, while the `HighSierraPriceQuotes` is the boundary endpoint, the `ItemDiscountCalculator` is a domain-specific actor. Even so, when reasoning in a general sense, you could also say that the `ItemDiscountCalculator` is an endpoint. Still, it seems to say far more about the `ItemDiscountCalculator` when you refer to it as an actor.

Summary

You have just been introduced to the basic of the Actor model programming and patterns for application design and enterprise integration. You now have a functional vocabulary for the primary patterns you will use.

The patterns in this chapter also serve as a preview of the subsequent chapters that will deal with each of these topics in greater detail. For example, there is a large chapter that covers the various kinds of *Message Routers (140)*.

Chapter 5

Messaging Channels

In the previous chapter, you looked at *Message Channels (128)* as a basic communications mechanism that supports actor-to-actor messaging. In this chapter, I will expand on the basic channel mechanism and explore several kinds of channels, each with a specific advantage when dealing with various application and integration challenges.

- *Point-to-Point Channel*: This is the "bread and butter" of the Actor model because it replaces the normal method invocations found in object-oriented systems. Actor communication forms a natural *Point-to-Point Channel (151)* because the actor sending the *Message (130)* must know the address of the receiving actor. This pattern will demonstrate message ordering and show why actors must be prepared to accept and reject messages based on their current state.

- *Publish-Subscribe Channel*: An actor can publish a single message that will fan out and be delivered to multiple actors using a built in *Publish-Subscribe Channel (154)*. Actually, there are Akka facilities for both local and remote Pub-Sub.

- *Datatype Channel*: You create a separate actor as a *Datatype Channel (167)* when a receiving application anticipates and must be assured of the data type of the incoming message without examining the message content.

- *Invalid Message Channel*: Sometimes clients can send messages to actors that the actor does not understand or that in its current state cannot be consumed. In such cases, the receiving actor can reroute those messages to a channel meant to deal with them in some application-specific way.

- *Dead Letter Channel*: When the actor system cannot deliver a message to the intended receiver, it will send it through the *Dead Letter Channel (172)* instead. This can happen when latent messages are sent to an actor that has already been stopped and can no longer receive them.

- *Guaranteed Delivery*: The Actor model does not naturally guarantee message delivery. Its deliveries are said to be "at most once." This often works out well for various reasons because a message will just be delivered in

149

almost all cases and you don't want to incur the overhead of reliable messaging. However, sometimes actor-to-actor communication must be reliable; that is, messages must be delivered despite any impedance. This pattern shows how Akka actors can reliably send messages to other actors that will just about always be delivered.

- *Channel Adapter*: When actors at the outside edge of the application must forward messages to the interior, the *Messages (130)* may need to be made to conform to internal contracts. In such cases, the message receiving actor can adapt the messages to the contract of actors before it sends them onward.

- *Message Bridge*: When two applications need to integrate with each other but their messaging systems are not interoperable, you need a *Message Bridge (185)* between the two. An example of such a situation is between a system that supports Java Message System (JMS) or RabbitMQ and an Akka-based actor system.

- *Message Bus*: This is one of the more complex kinds of channels but is possibly useful in a diverse enterprise. You have a number of disparate business systems, from purchased commodity applications to custom-developed applications that help achieve competitive advantage to those of integrating business partners. You can use a *Message Bus (192)* to get all of these systems to work together, although they run on different platforms and have various service interfaces.

As *Enterprise Integration Patterns* [EIP] points out, you can think of these patterns as fitting into various messaging themes, including the following:

- *One-to-one*: *Point-to-Point Channel (151)*

- *One-to-many*: *Publish-Subscribe Channel (154)*

- *What type of data*: *Datatype Channel (167)*

- *Invalid and dead messages*: *Invalid Message Channel (170)* and *Dead Letter Channel (172)*

- *Crash Proof*: *Guaranteed Delivery (175)*. That is, delivery of a message stands up to any system failures that may prevent it, which is different from the general resiliency of supervised actors with Akka.

- *Non-messaging clients and adaptive messaging channels*: *Channel Adapter (183)* and *Message Bridge (185)*

- *Communications backbone*: *Message Bus (192)*

This list of messaging themes shows that it requires considerable thought and design effort when putting together an actor system. You must understand each of these types of channels regardless of how basic any one of them may seem. Proper use of these channel types for various application and integration scenarios is essential.

Point-to-Point Channel

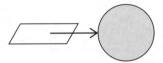

When using the Actor model, all actor-specific *Message Channels (128)* are Point-to-Point Channels. This is not to say that *Publish-Subscribe Channels (154)* cannot be supported within the Actor model. They can be. Yet, each actor that subscribes to a given topic/exchange has a Point-to-Point Channel through which the publisher of the topic/exchange will ultimately send messages. You can conclude that Point-to-Point Channel defines the basic semantics of the Actor model, as shown in Figure 5.1. Similarly, when an actor receives a message, it also is an *Event-Driven Consumer (371)*.

Figure 5.1 Actors form natural Point-to-Point Channels.

One of the guarantees of the Actor model is sequential message delivery. That is, by default actor mailboxes are first-in, first-out (FIFO) channels. When a message arrives through the actor's channel, it will be received in the order in which it was sent. Thus, if actor A sends a message to actor B and then actor A sends a second message to actor B, the message that was sent first will be the first message received by actor B.

```
// inside actor A
actorB ! "Hello, from actor A!"
actorB ! "Hello again, from actor A!"
```

```
// inside actor B
class ActorB extends Actor {
  var hello = 0
  var helloAgain = 0

  def receive = {
    case message: String =>
      hello = hello +
        (if (message.contains("Hello")) 1 else 0)
      helloAgain = helloAgain +
        (if (message.startsWith("Hello again")) 1 else 0)
      assert(hello > helloAgain)
  }
}
```

What if you introduce a third actor, C? Now actor A and actor C both send one or more messages to actor B. There is no guarantee which message actor B will receive first, either the first from actor A or the first from actor C. Nevertheless, the first message from actor A will always be received by actor B before the second message that actor A sends, and the first message from actor C will always be received by actor B before the second message that actor C sends.

```
// inside actor A
actorB ! "Hello, from actor A!"
actorB ! "Hello again, from actor A!"

// inside actor C
actorB ! "Goodbye, from actor C!"
actorB ! "Goodbye again, from actor C!"

// inside actor B
class ActorB extends Actor {
  var goodbye = 0
  var goodbyeAgain = 0
  var hello = 0
  var helloAgain = 0

  def receive = {
    case message: String =>
      hello = hello +
        (if (message.contains("Hello")) 1 else 0)
      helloAgain = helloAgain +
        (if (message.startsWith("Hello again")) 1 else 0)
      assert(hello == 0 || hello > helloAgain)

      goodbye = goodbye +
        (if (message.contains("Goodbye")) 1 else 0)
      goodbyeAgain = goodbyeAgain +
```

```
        (if (message.startsWith("Goodbye again")) 1 else 0)
      assert(goodbye == 0 || goodbye > goodbyeAgain)
  }
}
```

Note that in this implementation of `ActorB`, there is no practical way to correctly assert that `hello` and `goodbye` will ever be equal or that one will be greater than the other.[1] It is only practical to assert that `hello` must be 0 or greater than `helloAgain` and that `goodbye` must be 0 or greater than `goodbyeAgain`.

What is implied? Actors must be prepared to accept and reject messages based on their current state, which is reflected by the order in which previous messages were received. Sometimes a latent message could be accepted even if it is not perfect timing, but the actor's reaction to the latent message may have to carefully take into account its current state beforehand. This may be dealt with more gracefully by using the actors `become()` capabilities.

There is a potential message ordering caveat to be aware of when using Akka Remoting. When a local actor uses the `actorOf()` through the `ActorSystem` to create an actor on a remote node, the creation is requested via a message sent to the remote node. The local actor receives an `ActorRef`, which abstracts away the `RemoteActorRef`. Yet, actor creations are always handled asynchronously, which means that the `RemoteActorRef` exists before the actual remote actor that it represents. Now, if the local actor that used `actorOf()` sends a message to the remote actor identified by the `RemoteActorRef`, the message is guaranteed to be delivered after the remote actor has been created. However, if any other actor on the local `ActorSystem`, or an actor on a third node, sends a message via the `RemoteActorRef`, there is no guarantee that the remote actor's creation will have completed by that point in time. If the actor does not yet exist, any message sent to it will be lost.

The lesson here? The creator of the remote actor may endow other actors with the `RemoteActorRef` only after it knows that the remote actor is fully created. The local actor could set up a *Request-Reply (209)* contract where the remote actor must confirm its existence to its parent/creator. Or, the first message sent to the remote actor from its parent could endow the newly created actor with the `ActorRef` instances that it will collaborate with. That would allow the newly created actor to inform its collaborator of its existence, with

---

1. This assumes that there could be any number of messages sent, not just four. Even if you concluded that `ActorB` received only four total messages ever, you would have to wait until after the fourth message is received to assert that `hello` and `goodbye` are equal to `helloAgain` and `goodbyeAgain`.

the downside being that it must know for whom it provides services. While the first approach is more practical for most design situations, there may be good reason to sometimes take the second approach.

Publish-Subscribe Channel

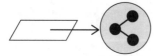

You may have first been introduced to the Publish-Subscribe pattern [POSA1] when you read about the Observer pattern [GoF]. The fundamental design principals of both Observer and Publish-Subscribe is the decoupling of those interested in being informed about *Event Messages (207)* from the one who is doing the informing. Observer [GoF] calls these two roles the *observers* and the *subject*, respectively. Publish-Subscribe [POSA1] names the same roles the *subscribers* and the *publisher*.

Frankly, when you evaluate a typical messaging middleware system, you assume that both durable and nondurable Publish-Subscribe Channels are supported out of the box. The Actor model is not a typical messaging system, nor is the supported messaging focused on Publish-Subscribe. The focus is *Point-to-Point Channels (151)*. Still, nothing stands in the way of implementing Publish-Subscribe on top of the basic tools that the Actor model provides. In fact, that's exactly what Akka does by supplying a few built-in Publish-Subscribe Channels. Figure 5.2 illustrates how this works using the Akka `EventBus`.

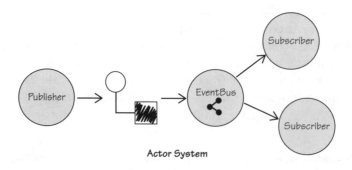

Figure 5.2 An actor can publish a message through the `EventBus` to multiple subscribers.

Local Event Stream

One of the built-in Publish-Subscribe Channels uses the `EventBus` trait. A standard instance of the `EventBus`, called the *event stream*, is available as the `eventStream` property on your local `ActorSystem`. This standard `Event-Bus` can be used in a local JVM and allows you to quite easily register subscribers and allow publishers to publish events.

Tapping in to some of Akka's standard system messages supported by the `EventBus` is a good way to see how easy it is to create a subscriber. This example borrows from *Dead Letter Channel (172)*:

```
val system = ActorSystem("TradingSystem")
val sysListener =
        system.actorOf(
                Props[SystemListener],
                "sysListener")
system.eventStream.subscribe(
                sysListener,
                classOf[akka.actor.DeadLetter])
```

Using the same Event Stream, you could also subscribe to standard logging events. Even so, standard events are not application events, and you may want a local Publish-Subscribe Channel that is capable of supporting application-specific needs. One approach is to piggyback on the standard Event Stream by registering subscribers with an application-specific classifier.

```
case class Money(amount: BigDecimal) { ... }
case class Market(name: String)
case class PriceQuoted(
        market: Market,
        ticker: Symbol,
        price: Money)
...
val system = ActorSystem("TradingSystem")
val quoteListener =
        system.actorOf(
                Props[QuoteListener],
                "quoteListener")
system.eventStream.subscribe(
                quoteListener,
                classOf[quotes.PriceQuoted])
```

The second half of the solution is to publish `PriceQuoted` events to the channel.

```
system.eventStream.publish(PriceQuoted(ticker, price))
```

In this example, the simple case class `PriceQuoted` is the classifier that determines the one type of event that a specific set of subscribers can listen for. Thus, it may be unnecessary to create your own `EventBus` implementation.

Yet, why might you still want to implement your own `EventBus`? One reason could be to support registering subscribers to specific event types, in essence enabling the implementation of topics. Your custom `EventBus` must extend an `EventBus` trait, such as `ActorEventBus`, and also mix in a classification trait. Table 5.1 presents some with practical classification uses.

Let's examine the design of the `SubchannelClassification` as described in Table 5.1 to create a `QuotesEventBus`. You need some supporting case classes and then the custom `EventBus` that mixes in `SubchannelClassification`.

Table 5.1 Classification Traits

Classification	Description
akka.event. LookupClassification	Supports simple lookup by matching on a specific event type. For example, you could have channels `quotes` and `priortityQuotes` both supported by the same `EventBus`. If you subscribe to `quotes`, you receive only events published to that channel. If you subscribe to `priortityQuotes`, you receive only events published to that channel.
akka.event. SubchannelClassification	Supports subchannel hierarchies by matching on event types and subtypes. For example, you could have channel `quotes` with subtypes `quotes/NYSE` and `quotes/NASDAQ` all supported by the same `EventBus`. Publishers can publish to `quotes`, `quotes/NYSE`, and `quotes/NASDAQ`, and subscribers subscribe to those specific subtypes. Subscribers to `quotes` will receive events for `quotes`, `quotes/NYSE`, and `quotes/NASDAQ`. Subscribers to `quotes/NYSE` will receive events only for that channel. Subscribers to `quotes/NASDAQ` will receive events only for that channel.
akka.event. ScanningClassification	Mix in this trait when you need your `EventBus`'s entire set of classifications to be scanned in case a given event falls within two or more channels and must be published to all of the subscribers within each of the qualifying channels. Although you would never have a quote that qualifies both as `quotes/NYSE` and as `quotes/NASDAQ`, every trading day you will have quotes that qualify both as `quotes/NASDAQ` and as `quotes/NASDAQ-CLOSING_BELL`.

```scala
case class Money(amount: BigDecimal) {
  def this(amount: String) =
          this(new java.math.BigDecimal(amount))

  amount.setScale(4, BigDecimal.RoundingMode.HALF_UP)
}

case class Market(name: String)

case class PriceQuoted(
          market: Market,
          ticker: Symbol,
          price: Money)

class QuotesEventBus
          extends EventBus
          with SubchannelClassification {
  type Classifier = Market
  type Event = PriceQuoted
  type Subscriber = ActorRef

  protected def classify(event: Event): Classifier = {
    event.market
  }

  protected def publish(
          event: Event,
          subscriber: Subscriber): Unit = {
    subscriber ! event
  }

  protected def subclassification =
          new Subclassification[Classifier] {
    def isEqual(
        subscribedToClassifier: Classifier,
        eventClassifier: Classifier): Boolean = {

      eventClassifier.equals(subscribedToClassifier)
    }

    def isSubclass(
        subscribedToClassifier: Classifier,
        eventClassifier: Classifier): Boolean = {

      subscribedToClassifier.name.startsWith(eventClassifier.name)
    }
  }
}
```

Three case classes support the `QuotesEventBus` implementation: `Money`, `Market`, and `PriceQuoted`. Creating a custom `EventBus` requires the declaration of a few types: `Classifier`, `Event`, and `Subscriber`. In this `SubchannelClassification`, these are each set to `Market`, `PriceQuoted`, and `ActorRef`, respectively.

```
class QuotesEventBus
        extends EventBus
        with SubchannelClassification {
  type Classifier = Market
  type Event = PriceQuoted
  type Subscriber = ActorRef
  ...
```

The `classify()` function answers/returns the `Classifier` of the `Event`, which in this case is the `PriceQuoted` event's `market` attribute. This is the means by which a specific `Market`, or a subclassification, may be matched with the `Market` that each subscriber has specified.

The `subclassification`, an instance of `Subclassification[Classifier]`, provides two means to match a given `Market`, using `isEqual()` and `isSubclass()`. If function `isEqual()` determines an exact `Market` match, the subscriber will receive the `PriceQuoted` event.

Alternatively, function `isSubclass()` is used to match subclassifications. The first parameter is the `subscribedToClassifier`, that is, the `Market` to which a given subscriber is subscribed. The second parameter is the `eventClassifier`, that is, the `Market` associated with the `PriceQuoted` event that is being published. The rather simple design of this `isSubclass()` allows for the `name` of the `subscribedToClassifier` to match some first part of the `name` of the `eventClassifier`, including a complete `name` match, to determine successful subclassification. Thus, having two fully equal classifications is considered a valid subclassification.

```
  ...
  def isSubclass(
     subscribedToClassifier: Classifier,
     eventClassifier: Classifier): Boolean = {

   subscribedToClassifier
        .name
        .startsWith(eventClassifier.name)
  }
  ...
```

To test the `QuotesEventBus`, I have created a simple `CompletableApp` named `SubClassificationDriver`.

```
object SubClassificationDriver extends CompletableApp(6) {
  val allSubscriber =
        system.actorOf(
              Props[AllMarketsSubscriber],
              "AllMarketsSubscriber")
  val nasdaqSubscriber =
        system.actorOf(
              Props[NASDAQSubscriber],
              "NASDAQSubscriber")
  val nyseSubscriber =
        system.actorOf(
              Props[NYSESubscriber],
              "NYSESubscriber")

  val quotesBus = new QuotesEventBus

  quotesBus.subscribe(allSubscriber, Market("quotes"))
  quotesBus.subscribe(nasdaqSubscriber, Market("quotes/NASDAQ"))
  quotesBus.subscribe(nyseSubscriber, Market("quotes/NYSE"))

  quotesBus.publish(PriceQuoted(Market("quotes/NYSE"),
                    Symbol("ORCL"), new Money("37.84")))
  quotesBus.publish(PriceQuoted(Market("quotes/NASDAQ"),
                    Symbol("MSFT"), new Money("37.16")))
  quotesBus.publish(PriceQuoted(Market("quotes/DAX"),
                    Symbol("SAP:GR"), new Money("61.95")))
  quotesBus.publish(PriceQuoted(Market("quotes/NKY"),
                    Symbol("6701:JP"), new Money("237")))

  awaitCompletion
}
```

The first step is to create three actors. One subscribes to all quotes by specifying `Market("quotes")`. One subscribes only to the NASDAQ by specifying `Market("quotes/NASDAQ")`. One subscribes only to the NYSE by specifying `Market("quotes/NYSE")`. Here are the simple implementations of the three actor types:

```
class AllMarketsSubscriber extends Actor {
  def receive = {
    case quote: PriceQuoted =>
      println(s"AllMarketsSubscriber received: $quote")
      SubClassificationDriver.completedStep
  }
}
```

```
class NASDAQSubscriber extends Actor {
  def receive = {
    case quote: PriceQuoted =>
      println(s"NASDAQSubscriber received: $quote")
      SubClassificationDriver.completedStep
  }
}

class NYSESubscriber extends Actor {
  def receive = {
    case quote: PriceQuoted =>
      println(s"NASDAQSubscriber received: $quote")
      SubClassificationDriver.completedStep
  }
}
```

Following the creation of the three actors, the `SubClassification-Driver` application publishes events. Given the four total `PriceQuoted` events that are published to the `QuotesEventBus`, the following is a sample of the output produced by the three actors:

```
AllMarketsSubscriber received:↵
 PriceQuoted(Market(quotes/NYSE),'ORCL,Money(37.84))
NYSESubscriber received:↵
 PriceQuoted(Market(quotes/NYSE),'ORCL,Money(37.84))
AllMarketsSubscriber received:↵
 PriceQuoted(Market(quotes/NASDAQ),'MSFT,Money(37.16))
NASDAQSubscriber received:↵
 PriceQuoted(Market(quotes/NASDAQ),'MSFT,Money(37.16))
AllMarketsSubscriber received:↵
 PriceQuoted(Market(quotes/DAX),'SAP:GR,Money(61.95))
AllMarketsSubscriber received:↵
 PriceQuoted(Market(quotes/NKY),'6701:JP,Money(237))
```

The `AllMarketsSubscriber` receives all four events, while the `NYSE-Subscriber` and the `NASDAQSubscriber` each received just one event.

Distributed Publish-Subscribe

A second built-in Publish-Subscribe Channel is available when using an Akka cluster. This kind of Publish-Subscribe Channel provides the means to publish a topic-based message to subscribers across the nodes of a cluster. This channel also supports sending a message to a single actor somewhere in the cluster and to one actor on each of multiple nodes, but without the need for the sender to

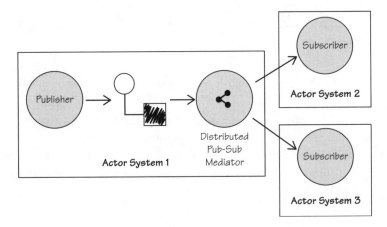

Figure 5.3 Use the `DistributedPubSubMediator` to publish Messages to subscribers in remote actor systems.

know on which node any receiving actors are running. It's Publish-Subscribe but with a twist, supporting a message sent directly, yet in a decoupled manner.

Akka provides an actor that supports these clustered Publish-Subscribe capabilities, the `DistributedPubSubMediator`, as shown in Figure 5.3. This mediator actor must be started on all nodes that will participate in a given Publish-Subscribe topic or sender-receiver collaborations. Although this mediator actor may support any number of topics, with separate logical groups of publisher and subscribers using just one mediator, you may also choose to start a separate `DistributedPubSubMediator` for each of the logical Publish-Subscribe groups. For example, you may choose to start a mediator actor for the `"bids"` topic and start a different mediator actor for the `"sold"` topic, each with its own group of subscribers.

It is possible to start the `DistributedPubSubMediator` as you would any actor or to manage it using the `DistributedPubSubExtension`. Using the extension will limit you to using just one `DistributedPubSubMediator` throughout the cluster. Should you decide to use the extension, it must be configured to your needs. Here are sample external configuration properties, which reflect the standard defaults, followed by the line that instructs Akka to autorun the `DistributedPubSubExtension`:

```
akka.contrib.cluster.pub-sub {
  name = distributedPubSubMediator
  role = ""
  routing-logic = random
```

```
      gossip-interval = 1s
      removed-time-to-live = 120s
      max-delta-elements = 3000
  }

  akka.extensions = ["akka.contrib.pattern.DistributedPubSubExtension"]
```

The final entry tells Akka to run the `DistributedPubSubExtension`, which causes a single instance of the actor to be created with the name `"distributedPubSubMediator"`. Table 5.2 describes each configuration property. The description provides some important details about how the mediator works.

Table 5.2 `DistributedPubSubExtension` Properties

Property	Description
name	The name given to the actor when it is created by the `ActorSystem`. Using the name `distributedPubSub-Mediator`, the actual name, once created, would be `/user/distributedPubSubMediator`.
role	When a role name is given, start the mediator actor only on cluster nodes that have the same role name. If the role name is not given (""), start the mediator actor on all cluster nodes.
routing-logic	The name of the routing strategy to use when one cluster node has multiple actors to which a message is sent using `Send` (not `Publish`). Possible routing-logic types are `random`, `round-robin`, `consistent-hashing`, and `broadcast`.
gossip-interval	Each mediator actor maintains a registry of subscribers. Subscribers registered with the mediator on a given node must become known to mediators running on other nodes. Mediators use the gossip protocol to communicate changes, which eventually become known to mediators on other nodes. The `gossip-interval` is the time interval between updates that are sent by each mediator to other nodes.
removed-time-to-live	Any subscribers in the mediator's registry that have terminated or by other means marked for removal are actually pruned from the registry at specific intervals. This property specifies the time between full pruning removal of previously subscribed actors.
max-delta-elements	At each gossip interval, deltas of changes to each mediator's registry are sent to mediators on other nodes. This property specifies the maximum number of elements that can be transferred in a single gossip chunk. Any remaining or new delta elements will be sent on subsequent intervals.

Actually, the properties are not used to configure the `DistributedPub-SubExtension`. Rather, the `DistributedPubSubExtension` just loads the properties and uses them to create the instance of the mediator.

```scala
class DistributedPubSubExtension(system: ExtendedActorSystem)
    extends Extension {
  private val config =
        system.settings.config.getConfig(
                    "akka.contrib.cluster.pub-sub")
  private val role: Option[String] =
        config.getString("role") match {
    case "" => None
    case r => Some(r)
  }

  def isTerminated: Boolean =
        Cluster(system).isTerminated ||
        !role.forall(Cluster(system).selfRoles.contains)

  val mediator: ActorRef = {
    if (isTerminated)
      system.deadLetters
    else {
      val routingLogic =
        config.getString("routing-logic") match {
        case "random" =>
            RandomRoutingLogic()
        case "round-robin" =>
            RoundRobinRoutingLogic()
        case "consistent-hashing" =>
            ConsistentHashingRoutingLogic(system)
        case "broadcast" =>
            BroadcastRoutingLogic()
        case other =>
            throw new IllegalArgumentException(s"...")
      }
      val gossipInterval =
            Duration(config.getMilliseconds(
                        "gossip-interval"),
                    MILLISECONDS)
      val removedTimeToLive =
            Duration(config.getMilliseconds(
                        "removed-time-to-live"),
                    MILLISECONDS)
      val maxDeltaElements =
            config.getInt("max-delta-elements")
      val name = config.getString("name")
      system.actorOf(DistributedPubSubMediator.props(
                        role, routingLogic,
                        gossipInterval, removedTimeToLive,
```

```
                        maxDeltaElements),
                    name)
        }
      }
}
```

The `DistributedPubSubExtension` uses the `ActorSystem` function `actorOf()` to create the `DistributedPubSubMediator`. Note that you would use the same approach to create a mediator instance if you chose not to manage it through the extension. However, in the second case, you will need to provide a valid `Props` instance to pass in to the `ActorSystem` function `actorOf()`. The `DistributedPubSubMediator` companion object provides a handy helper method just for that purpose.

```
object DistributedPubSubMediator {

  def props(
    role: Option[String],
    routingLogic: RoutingLogic = RandomRoutingLogic(),
    gossipInterval: FiniteDuration = 1.second,
    removedTimeToLive: FiniteDuration = 2.minutes,
    maxDeltaElements: Int = 3000): Props =
    Props(classOf[DistributedPubSubMediator],
          role, routingLogic, gossipInterval,
          removedTimeToLive, maxDeltaElements)
  ...
}
```

Comparing these default parameter values to those in the previous configuration properties file, you can see that the same standard values are used by the companion object. Using all possible default parameters, you can create a mediator just like this:

```
val mediator = system.actorOf(
                DistributedPubSubMediator.props(None),
                "bidsPubSubMediator")
```

This code creates a new mediator with no `role` and the `name` "bidsPubSubMediator", while the `routingLogic`, `gossipInterval`, `removedTimeToLive`, and `maxDeltaElements` will each have their standard default value. The fact that there is no role means that the mediator can be started on any node in the cluster, and support one or more Publish-Subscribe Channels on whatever node where it is running.

Next let's see what operations can be performed on the `Distributed-PubSubMediator`. There are three primary operations of interest, each of which is supported by a specific message type that is sent to the mediator actor. Table 5.3 describes these operations.

There are two ways to register actors with and remove actors from their local mediator so that they can participate as receivers of *Messages (130)* from the `DistributedPubSubMediator`.

- When *Messages (130)* are sent using `Send` or `SendToAll` as described in Table 5.3, intended receivers must register with their local mediator by sending it a `DistributedPubSubMediator.Put` message. The single parameter to the `Put` message is the `ActorRef` of the intended receiver. It's important that each intended receiver be local to the mediator, that is, in the same local `ActorSystem`. To remove the registered actor from its local mediator, use the `DistributedPubSubMediator.Remove` message. This takes a single parameter, which is the `String` path of the actor to be removed.

- When *Messages (130)* are sent using `Publish` as described in Table 5.3, intended receivers must register with their local mediator by sending it a `DistributedPubSubMediator.Subscribe` message. There are two parameters to `Subscribe`. The first is the `String`-based topic name to which you are subscribing, and the second parameter is the `ActorRef` of the subscribing actor. A successful subscription is acknowledged by sending the subscriber a `DistributedPubSubMediator.SubscribeAck`. Here again it's important that each subscriber be local to the mediator, that is, in the same local `ActorSystem`. To remove the registered actor from its local mediator, use the `DistributedPubSubMediator.Unsubscribe` message. This takes two parameters, which are the `String` topic of the subscription and the `ActorRef` that is being unsubscribed. A successfully unsubscribed actor will receive the `DistributedPubSubMediator.UnsubscribeAck` reply message.

In addition, when an actor is terminated, it will be automatically unregistered or unsubscribed from its local `DistributedPubSubMediator`.

Armed with this knowledge, you are ready to use Publish-Subscribe on distributed nodes within an Akka cluster.

Table 5.3 `DistributedPubSubMediator` Operations

Message	Description
`DistributedPubSubMediator` `.Send`	Use `Send` if you need to route a message to one of possibly several routees in the cluster.
	Message case class `Send` takes three initializers: `path`, `message`, and `localAffinity`. The `message` initializer is the ultimate message to be sent and will be sent to one and only one actor in the cluster that matches `path`. If the name used to create the actor that the `message` will be sent to is `"bidProcessor"`, then the `path` that identifies the receiver actor must be `"/user/bidProcessor"` and must not be prepended with the address or the name of the `ActorSystem`. Thus, if there are multiple actors in the cluster whose `path` matches (at most one running within each live `ActorSystem`), the `message` will be sent to just one actor within one `ActorSystem` somewhere in the cluster according to the `routingLogic` parameter with which the mediator was initialized.
	When `localAffinity` is `true`, the mediator will attempt to send (actually forward) the `message` to an actor on its local system, if one exists locally that matches the given `path`. If there is no matching actor path on the local system, then the `message` will be sent to just one actor within one `ActorSystem` somewhere in the cluster according to the `routingLogic` parameter with which the mediator was initialized.
`DistributedPubSubMediator` `.SendToAll`	Use `SendToAll` if you need to broadcast a message to all possible recipients in the cluster that match the given `path`.
	Message case class `SendToAll` takes up to three initializers: `path`, `message`, and `allButSelf`. The `message` initializer is the ultimate message to be sent and will be sent to all actors in the cluster that match `path`. Because there can be only one actor within an `ActorSystem` with a given matching path, the message will be delivered to, at most, one actor per `ActorSystem`. If the name used to create the actor that the `message` will be sent to is `"bidRelay"`, then the `path` that identifies the receiver actor must be `"/user/bidRelay"` and must not be prepended with the address or the name of the `ActorSystem`.
	When `allButSelf` is `false` (the default), the mediator will attempt to send (actually forward) the `message` to an actor on its local system, if one exists locally that matches the given `path`. If `allButSelf` is `true` or if there is no such actor on the local system matching `path`, the `message` will be sent only to actors on other systems.

Table 5.3 `DistributedPubSubMediator` Operations

Message	Description
`DistributedPubSubMediator .Publish`	Use `Publish` if you need to broadcast a message to all recipients in the cluster that are subscribed to a given topic.
	Message case class `Publish` takes two initializers: `topic` and `message`. The `message` initializer is the ultimate message to be broadcast and will be sent to all actors in the cluster that have subscribed to `topic`. A `topic` is different from a `path` that identifies a given actor, and the `topic` name should reflect that fact. Rather than using the path `"/user/bidProcessor"`, as shown previously, to identify the actor receiver, a suitable topic name might be `"bids"`.
	A subscriber registers itself with a mediator using the `Subscribe` message, which takes two initialization parameters: `topic` and `actorRef`. The `topic` is the string name to which messages may be published, and the `actorRef` is the reference to the subscriber actor. The subscriber is informed of successful subscription when it receives a `SubscribeAck` message. The `SubscribeAck` message contains the original `Subscribe` message. When a `Publish` message is sent to the mediator, all actors subscribed to the matching `topic` will be sent the `message`.
	Subscribers may be removed by sending the mediator an `Unsubscribe` message. The subscriber is informed when it is successfully unsubscribed upon receiving an `UnsubscribeAck` message. The `UnsubscribeAck` message contains the original `Unsubscribe` message.

Datatype Channel

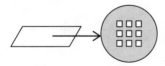

Use Datatype Channels when a receiver application must know the datatype of the incoming message without examining the message content. Create a different actor type corresponding to each separate datatype. A Datatype Channel is both a *Message Channel (128)* and a *Message Endpoint (145)*. Figure 5.4 illustrates how a Datatype Channel works.

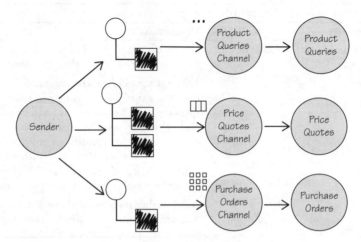

Figure 5.4 Using a Datatype Channel, a sender is required to send each message to an actor that can react to messages of specific datatypes.

When employing the Actor model, you normally define a typesafe message for each message accepted by a given actor type. Each message type is a unique datatype. Even though an actor can receive a few to perhaps several message types, you could still conclude that the actor's *Message Channel (128)* is a Datatype Channel because there is a clear contract for acceptable messages by type.

Even so, sometimes it may not be possible to create different message types to represent each datatype. One such case is when the actors are receiving messages from a middleware message server. For example, you might define an actor that receives messages from RabbitMQ or an implementation of JMS that is composed of binary byte arrays.[2]

In the following sample code, each of the actors extends a specialty abstract actor type, which in this sample is the `RabbitMQReceiver`. This implies that each actor is backed by a RabbitMQ Java client that listens to a named channel.

```
// listens to the product_queries_channel
class ProductQueriesChannel extends RabbitMQReceiver {
  def receive = {
    case message: Array[Byte] =>
```

---

2. The message format could also be text rather than binary, such as XML that would need to adhere to a schema. Or the message could be JSON and need to meet the requirements of a weak schema. As stated, a binary format is just one example among other possibilities.

```
      val productQuery = translateToProductQuery(message)
      ...
  }

  def translateToProductQuery(
        message: Array[Byte]): ProductQuery = {
    ...
  }
}

// listens to the price_quote_channel
class PriceQuoteChannel extends RabbitMQReceiver {
  def receive = {
    case message: Array[Byte] =>
      val priceQuote = translateToPriceQuote(message)
      ...
  }

  def translateToPriceQuote(
        message: Array[Byte]): PriceQuote = {
    ...
  }
}

// listens to the purchase_order_channel
class PurchaseOrderChannel extends RabbitMQReceiver {
  def receive = {
    case message: Array[Byte] =>
      val purchaseOrder = translateToPurchaseOrder(message)
      ...
  }

  def translateToPurchaseOrder(
        message: Array[Byte]): PurchaseOrder = {
    ...
  }
}
```

Because RabbitMQ doesn't support the exchange of typesafe messages, each of these actor types—`ProductQueriesChannel`, `PriceQuoteChannel`, and `PurchaseOrderChannel`—receives messages consisting entirely of byte arrays. It is the *Message Channel (128)* that determines the message datatype. Each of these actors uses a *Message Translator (143)* to convert the received byte array to an instance of the specific datatype needed to successfully process the message.

It is possible that the `RabbitMQReceiver` abstract base class could be implemented to perform translations in order to deliver typesafe messages to each actor. That may be a worthy design decision. Yet, the examples make it clear which mandatory steps are needed to process each message received on a type-specific channel.

There is still a possibility that a message sender could place a byte array for the wrong message type onto a given Datatype Channel. If that happens, consider employing an Invalid *Message Channel (128)*.

Invalid Message Channel

Messages sent on a *Message Channel (128)* should be only those compatible with the types of messages accepted by the receiver. In other words, the channel should be a *Datatype Channel (167)*. When using the Actor model, the *Datatype Channel (167)* of a specific actor type may receive a few or perhaps several different message types. All messages sent to an actor must adhere to the actor's contract. You can use an Invalid Message Channel, as shown in Figure 5.5, to deal with messages that do not adhere to the contract.

A *Dead Letter Channel (172)* is generally used by the messaging system as a way to route messages that cannot be delivered to the intended receiver, whereas an Invalid Message Channel is used to route messages that are not understood by the receiver. Even so, when using Akka, it could be worthwhile to also send invalid messages to the *Dead Letter Channel (172)*.

Should you choose to design a separate Invalid Message Channel, you can easily create one using Akka.

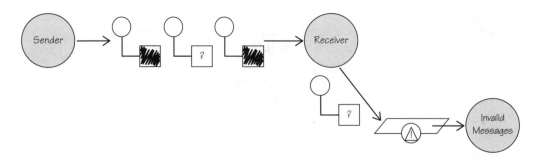

Figure 5.5 A Message that is not understood by the intended receiver
should be sent to an Invalid Message Channel.

```
case class InvalidMessage(
        sender: ActorRef,
        receiver: ActorRef,
        message: Any)

class InvalidMessageChannel extends Actor {
  def receive = {
    case invalid: InvalidMessage =>
      ...
  }
}
```

Now consider part of the example from *Pipes and Filters (135)* and what the `Authenticator` could do if it receives anything other than a `ProcessIncomingOrder` message.

```
class Authenticator(
        nextFilter: ActorRef,
        invalidMessageChannel: ActorRef)
     extends Actor {
  def receive = {
    case message: ProcessIncomingOrder =>
      val text = new String(message.orderInfo)
      ...
      nextFilter ! ProcessIncomingOrder(
                     orderText.toCharArray.map(_.toByte))
    case invalid: Any =>
      invalidMessageChannel ! InvalidMessage(
                                 sender, self, invalid)
  }
}
```

The question is, what should the `InvalidMessageChannel` do about the `InvalidMessage` once it is received? Should the `message` be output to an application error log? Should the original sender be notified? Does the message get saved to some persistent store to be dealt with later and perhaps redelivered once the intended receiver is redeployed to now understand the previously invalid message? The `InvalidMessage` is capable of supporting any of those possibilities.

Yet, if the application has no goal beyond logging the invalid message information, the original receiver (the `Authenticator` in this example) can do that on its own.

```
import akka.actor._
import akka.event.Logging
```

```
import akka.event.LoggingAdapter

class Authenticator(nextFilter: ActorRef) extends Actor {
  private val log: LoggingAdapter =
              Logging.getLogger(context.system, self)
  def receive = {
    case message: ProcessIncomingOrder =>
      val text = new String(message.orderInfo)
      ...
      nextFilter ! ProcessIncomingOrder(
                    orderText.toCharArray.map(_.toByte))
    case invalid: Any =>
      log.error(s"Unknown: ${invalid.getClass.getName}")
  }
}
```

Here the `LoggingAdapter` is the Invalid Message Channel. Although the `LoggingAdapter` is not itself an actor, it is backed by the `EventBus` of the `ActorSystem` and operates asynchronously. The `EventBus` implements a general-purpose *Publish-Subscribe Channel (154)* for both system- and application-level interests.

Dead Letter Channel

When a messaging system cannot deliver a message to the intended receiver, it may have the option to send it through the Dead Letter Channel instead. This, in fact, is the way that Akka works, as shown in Figure 5.6.

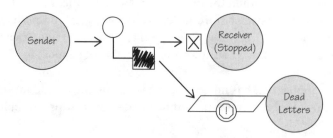

Figure 5.6 When a message cannot be delivered to the intended receiver, the Message can be redirected through a Dead Letter Channel.

Using the Actor model, and Akka specifically, there is an actor-based Dead Letter Channel named `/deadLetters`. Each `ActorSystem` creates this special actor, and when Akka determines that a message cannot be delivered to the actor it was sent to, the message is instead sent to the synthetic actor named `/deadLetters`.

There are a few reasons for Akka to use its Dead Letter Channel.

- When a message is sent by a local actor to another local actor that is the receiver, it is possible that the receiver actor no longer exists by the time the message is to be delivered. At that point, Akka will send the message to the local `deadLetters` actor. Yet, you wonder, how could a sender send a message to a nonexistent receiver? The simple answer is, because of the decoupling between the `ActorRef` and the actual `Actor` implementor. Since a sender has only a reference to the actor via an `ActorRef`, the `Actor` itself could be in the process of terminating for some reason just as the sender sends a message to it. When Akka detects that situation, it sends the message to `deadLetters` on the local system.

- When a message is sent by an actor on one node to an intended actor receiver on another node, the network connection between the two nodes may be lost. When Akka detects this situation on the sender's node, the message will be sent to `deadLetters` on the sender's side.

- When a message is sent by an actor on one node to an intended actor receiver on another node, the network connection may be fine, but the receiver actor on the remote node may no longer exist by the time the message is to be delivered. When Akka detects that situation, it sends the message to `deadLetters` on the remote system, that is, on the system where the receiver actor previously existed.

So, how does an Akka-based application know that messages have been delivered to `deadLetters`? You can simply register an actor as a listener by way of the `EventStream` of the local `ActorSystem`.

```
val system = ActorSystem("TradingSystem")
val sysListener = system.actorOf(Props[SystemListener], "sysListener")
system.eventStream.subscribe(
        sysListener, classOf[akka.actor.DeadLetter])
```

After subscribing, the actor referenced by the `sysListener` will receive messages of type `akka.actor.DeadLetter` from the `EventStream` of the `ActorSystem`.

```
class SystemListener extends Actor {
  def receive = {
    case deadLetter: DeadLetter =>
      ...
  }
}
```

You might have gotten the idea by now that a `DeadLetter` listener could be used as a means to implement *Guaranteed Delivery (175)*. Since a `DeadLetter` message contains the `ActorRef` for both the original sender and receiver, you might conclude that the `SystemListener` could simply dynamically reload the actor to which the message was to be delivered and then send it again. You could use a similar approach to attempt to reconnect to a remote node when you lose the network connection. Yet, before drawing that conclusion, consider a couple of caveats with routing undeliverable messages through `/deadLetters`.

- It is possible that Akka will be unable to detect that the intended receiver of a message is in the process of termination. Under that condition, Akka could attempt to deliver the message to the receiver and consider it delivered, and yet the message may never actually be received by the terminating/terminated actor. This is typically caused by a race condition that may occur between the sender and receiver threads, and given the current Akka implementation, it is impossible to detect. In such cases, the undeliverable message will be completely lost.

- A local Akka system may send a message over the network to an actor on a remote node, but the network connection could fail during the message transport across the wire. The local Akka system could think that the network transport succeeded, and yet the connection failed before the message was successfully delivered to the remote node. Because of the way Akka is implemented, neither end of the TCP network connection may know that the message was undeliverable, and thus the message will not be sent to `deadLetters` on either side of the network.

Neither of these caveats is considered to be a failure on the part of Akka. Rather, these are the consequences of the design choice that adheres to the basic premise of the Actor model: *Messages are delivered at most once.* For many applications, at-most-once delivery is perfectly acceptable where increased throughput outweighs the unnecessary overhead that *Guaranteed Delivery (175)* would introduce for systems that don't require it.

These consequences also do not mean that Akka cannot support a higher service level agreement for guaranteed message delivery. See *Message Channel*

(128) and *Guaranteed Delivery (175)* for details. Still, given the previous potential caveats, you cannot assume that the Akka Dead Letter Channel can be used to support *Guaranteed Delivery (175)* since it is not an entirely dependable approach. Akka's `deadLetters` is not meant to be used in that way. Rather, it is intended more as a debugging tool, giving developers the ability to watch for the arrival of Dead Letter messages that would indicate a problem with the implementation of some messaging design strategy being used by an application.You have already considered the fact that a message sent to an actor on a remote node could be routed through the `EventStream` of either the local or remote node, depending on the reason for failed delivery. Thus, you may have to look at two or more `EventStream` feeds to understand the reason for a single undelivered message. Isn't there a way to combine the `EventStream` feeds from multiple nodes? Akka does not support this out of the box, but it can be done as a homegrown solution. Implementing such a centralized `EventStream` would require the implementation of an *Aggregator (257)* on one of the application's nodes. If using an Akka cluster, the *Aggregator (257)* would likely be deployed as a cluster singleton. (See Akka `ClusterSingletonManager`.) This would be much more difficult or impossible, however, if you are integrating with third parties whose systems will not participate in the aggregation.

Guaranteed Delivery

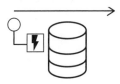

Use Guaranteed Delivery when you need to ensure that any given *Message (130)* will be received by the actor to which it is sent. Using this pattern with Akka ensures that *Messages (130)* sent to an actor will be delivered at least once. To accomplish this, sent *Messages (130)* will be journaled in a *Message Store (402)*, and then delivery will be attempted periodically until there is a confirmation of receipt, which is also saved in the *Message Store (402)*. Unless special effort is made to delete any one message, all *Messages (130)* are journaled permanently.

Typically a confirmation *Message (130)* is received by the sender after the first attempt to deliver. Once delivery confirmation is received, Akka will prevent the same *Message (130)* from being delivered again. However, if the first attempt to deliver is not confirmed before an interval period, then there will be at least one attempt to deliver the *Message (130)* again. Because of various latency factors and primarily a lost confirmation, this redelivery attempt could cause the actor, to which the *Message (130)* is targeted, to receive it two or more times. Figure 5.7 shows Akka's Guaranteed Delivery contract.

To facilitate this, Akka provides a persistence add-on, namely, Akka Persistence. To use Akka Persistence in your project, include the following JAR files in your build:

- *akka-persistence_x.y.z.jar*: Akka Persistence add-on. At the time of writing, this was still in experimental stage, with the JAR file named akka-persistence-experimental_2.10-2.3.6.jar.

- *leveldb-x.y.jar*: LevelDB functionality

- *leveldb-api-x.y.jar*: LevelDB application programming interface (API)

- *leveldbjni-all-x.y.jar*: LevelDB Java Native Interface (JNI) links

- *protobuf-java-x.y.z.jar*: Google's ProtoBuf library for Java

The previous filenames each have an *x.y.z* notation, which is a placeholder for its release version. Although LevelDB is the default journal, there is no need to use it as your production *Message Store (402)*. There are also various third-party replacements that support other data stores. Still, the previous JAR files will get you up and running quickly as you try Akka Persistence.

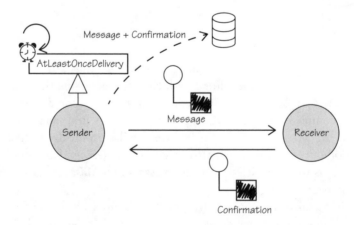

Figure 5.7 A Message sent via Akka's `AtLeastOnceDelivery` fulfills the Guaranteed Delivery contract.

When you have your environment set up to build and run your code, you can create your first actor that supports sending *Messages (130)* with Guaranteed Delivery.

```
class LoanBroker
    extends PersistentActor
    with AtLeastOnceDelivery {

  override def receiveCommand: Receive = {
    ...
  }

  override def receiveRecover: Receive = {
    ...
  }
}
```

To send messages with Guaranteed Delivery, you must mix in both the `PersistentActor` and the `AtLeastOnceDelivery` Akka traits to your actor class. Your actor must be a `PersistentActor` to support `AtLeastOnceDelivery`. Being a `PersistentActor`, your actor overrides both `receiveCommand` and `receiveRecover` partial functions, providing the core of the solution inside these. Your actor will receive new incoming messages through `receiveCommand`. During `PersistentActor` recovery, your actor will process all previously persisted *Event Messages (207)* and confirmations through `receiveRecover`. See *Transactional Client/Actor (351)* for more about the `PersistentActor` trait. Here I will focus more on the implementation of your actor with regard to `AtLeastOnceDelivery`.

Next let's look at the steps needed to send a message with Guaranteed Delivery and to confirm that it was received. You start by looking inside the `receiveCommand` of the `LoanBroker`.

```
class LoanBroker
    extends PersistentActor
    with AtLeastOnceDelivery {

  private var processes =
      Map[String, LoanRateQuoteRequested]()
  ...
  def checkCredit(
      loanRateQuoteId: String,
      taxId: String) = {
    ...
  }

  def duplicate(command: QuoteBestLoanRate): Boolean = {
```

```
    ...
    if (duplicateFound) {
      sender ! loanRateQuoteRequested
    }
  }
  ...
  def receiveCommand: Receive = {
    case command: QuoteBestLoanRate =>
      if (!duplicate(command)) {
        val loanRateQuoteId =
            LoanRateQuote.id(command.id)

        val loanRateQuote = loanRateQuoteFrom(command)

        startProcess(
            command.id,
            loanRateQuoteId,
            loanRateQuote)
      }

    case started: LoanRateQuoteStarted =>
      persist(started) { ack =>
        confirmDelivery(ack.id)
      }
      checkCredit(started.loanRateQuoteId, started.taxId)
    ...
  }

  override def receiveRecover: Receive = {
    ...
  }

  def startProcess(
        quoteRequestId: Int,
        loanRateQuoteId: String,
        loanRateQuote: ActorRef) = {

    val loanRateQuotePath = loanRateQuote.path

    val loanRateQuoteRequested =
            LoanRateQuoteRequested(
                    quoteRequestId,
                    loanRateQuoteId,
                    loanRateQuotePath)

    persist(loanRateQuoteRequested) { event =>
      updateWith(event)

      deliver(
          loanRateQuotePath,
          id => StartLoanRateQuote(totalBanks, id))
```

```
      sender ! event
    }
  }

  def totalBanks(): Int = {
    ...
  }
  ...
  def updateWith(event: LoanRateQuoteRequested) = {
    if (!processes.contains(event.processId)) {
      processes = processes +
                  (event.processId -> event)
    }
  }
}
```

Inside `receiveCommand`, you first handle the incoming *Command Message (202)* `QuoteBestLoanRate`. When it's received, you first ensure that the command is not a duplicate request. You see, the contract is for the client to also be an `AtLeastOnceDelivery` actor. If it is a duplicate, you have preserved the *Event Message (207)* originally sent to the client as a confirmation, and the best thing you can do now is resend that confirmation so the client will stop resending. You can see the origin of the `LoanRateQuoteRequested` *Event Message (207)* in `startProcess()` and how it is saved as the operational state by `updateWith()`. If it is not a duplicate, you then create a new `loanRate-QuoteId` and the associated `loanRateQuote`; then you call `startProcess()`.[3]

Inside `startProcess()`, you reference the `ActorPath` of the `LoanRate-Quote` actor with `loanRateQuotePath`. At this point, you create the new *Event Message (207)* of type `LoanRateQuoteRequested` and persist it to the *Message Store (402)*. (It's possible that you might want to validate something about the incoming command or the current state before creating and persisting `LoanRateQuoteRequested`, but in this case you do not.)

The outcome of `persist()` will cause the associated handler block to execute. As a first step inside the handler you update the `LoanBroker` operational state using `updateWith()` and passing the `event` as a parameter. To be clear, the `event` parameter is the same `LoanRateQuoteRequested` instance that was just persisted and is saved as state to handle request de-duplication. This state can be safely removed once the loan quotation process has completed.

Key to this Guaranteed Delivery pattern, you now use the specialized `AtLeastOnceDelivery` behavior to send a related *Command Message*

---

3. For more details on how this overall process works, see the *Process Manager (292)* implementation example.

(202), `StartLoanRateQuote`, to the `LoanRateQuote` actor. To accomplish this, you use `deliver()`, passing the `ActorPath` of the `LoanRateQuote` actor and the `StartLoanRateQuote` *Command Message (202)*. Recall that using the `ActorPath` and `actorSelection()` makes sending the message more reliable because you will resolve the most recent incarnation of the related actor.

The syntax of the second `deliver()` parameter may look a bit strange. This code is passing a function parameter to `deliver()`. The function parameter has the code to create an instance of `StartLoanRateQuote` but needs `deliver()` to provide the function an `id` parameter to fully create the instance. Internally `deliver()` generates a new identity by way of its own, private `nextDeliverySequenceNr()` method and then passes it to the function parameter. This identity, called the `deliveryId`, must be used by the `LoanRateQuote` actor when it replies with its `LoanRateQuoteStarted` confirmation message (discussed later in this section).

The last statement of the `persist()` handler code block replies to the sender of the `QuoteBestLoanRate` *Command Message (202)* with the `LoanRateQuoteRequested` *Event Message (207)*. Assume here that the client, the sender of `QuoteBestLoanRate` received in the `receiveCommand`, is itself a `PersistentActor` with `AtLeastOnceDelivery` mixed in. Thus, the `LoanRateQuoteRequested`, initialized with the `deliveryId` of the incoming `QuoteBestLoanRate`, serves as the `LoanBroker` confirmation message to the client requester. When received by the client, `LoanRateQuoteRequested` will prevent the `LoanBroker` from receiving the same `QuoteBestLoanRate` again.

Finally, looking back at the `receiveCommand`, note the match for the `LoanRateQuoteStarted` message. This *Event Message (207)* is sent by the `LoanRateQuote` actor after it has processed the `LoanBroker` *Command Message (202)* `StartLoanRateQuote`. The `LoanBroker` must both persist the `LoanRateQuoteStarted` and use it to `confirmDelivery()`. Here again, you use the `deliveryId` of the `LoanRateQuoteStarted`, which is the same `deliveryId` generated inside `startProcess()` when the `StartLoanRateQuote` was first created by `deliver()`. (The `started` and `ack` values reference the same `LoanRateQuoteStarted` message object.) Following this `confirmDelivery()`, the `LoanRateQuote` actor will never again receive the `StartLoanRateQuote` associated with this `deliveryId`. You still haven't looked at the `receiveRecover` partial function, which shows you how the `LoanBroker` is reconstituted from persisted events. Yet, as shown here, the `receiveRecover` also has a role to play for `AtLeastOnceDelivery`:

```
class LoanBroker
    extends PersistentActor
    with AtLeastOnceDelivery {
  ...
  override def receiveRecover: Receive = {
    case event: LoanRateQuoteRequested =>
      updateWith(event)

      deliver(
          event.loanRateQuotePath,
          id => StartLoanRateQuote(totalBanks, id))

    case started: LoanRateQuoteStarted =>
      confirmDelivery(started.id)
    ...
  }
  ...
}
```

Because you are reconstituting the state of a given `LoanBroker`, you process any persisted `LoanRateQuoteRequested` events. As you did in the `persist()` handler block, you here also update the state of the `LoanBroker` using `updateWith()` and passing the `LoanRateQuoteRequested` instance. Directly following this, you also attempt delivery of the related `StartLoanRateQuote` *Command Message (202)*. This ensures that any messages still undelivered when the `LoanBroker` was previously stopped will once again be placed into the at-least-once delivery process.

But, wait! What if a particular `StartLoanRateQuote` associated with a given `LoanRateQuoteRequested` was already delivered? Won't this repeated `deliver()` request cause unnecessary, and thus never-ending, redelivery? Actually, this is where being in recovery mode and the second case match comes in to play.

Recall that you previously persisted `LoanRateQuoteStarted` messages that you received from a given `LoadRateQuote` actor. As you process the persisted messages, you will replay any `LoanRateQuoteStarted` messages. As you do so, you then use `confirmDelivery()` and pass that message's `deliveryId`. While you are in recovery mode, no messages passed to `deliver()` will actually be sent. Instead, `AtLeastOnceDelivery` waits until recovery has been fully completed to check for any messages that were not also confirmed by `confirmDelivery()`. Only those unconfirmed messages—the ones passed to `deliver()` but whose matching `deliveryId` was not also given to `confirmDelivery()`—will be processed for redelivery.

The sequence diagram in Figure 5.8 shows this entire process of `AtLeastOnceDelivery` for `LoanBroker` and `LoanRateQuote`.

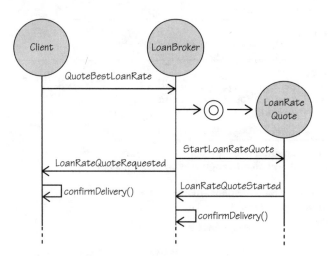

Figure 5.8 The interactions between the `Client`, the `LoanBroker`, and the `LoanRateQuote` are shown as message sequences and method invocations in the order that they occur.

You can control configurations such as how often `AtLeastOnceDelivery` attempts to redeliver unconfirmed messages. These configurations and overrides are listed here:

- `akka.persistence.at-least-once-delivery.redeliver-interval`: The interval between redelivery attempts. This can be over-ridden by individual actors using `redeliverInterval()`, which should return the actor's custom interval.

- `akka.persistence.at-least-once-delivery.max-unconfirmed-messages`: The limit to the number of messages held in memory until they are confirmed as delivered. This can be overridden by individual actors using `maxUnconfirmedMessages()`, which should return the actor's custom maximum.

- `akka.persistence.at-least-once-delivery.warn-after-number-of-unconfirmed-attempts`: After a number of unsuccessful delivery attempts, you will have the opportunity to cancel a particular message send when your `AtLeastOnceDelivery` actor receives the message `AtLeastOnceDelivery.UnconfirmedWarning`. If you receive this warning, you can call `confirmDelivery()` to cancel resending. Note that there is no distinction between successful and cancellation types of confirmations, only that resending will terminate. This can be overridden by individual actors using `warnAfterNumberOfUnconfirmedAttempts()`, which should return the actor's custom number.

- `akka.persistence.at-least-once-delivery.redelivery-burst-limit`: The maximum number of messages that will be sent during each redelivery burst, which may be used to prevent a large number of unconfirmed messages from being sent at one time. This can be overridden by individual actors using `redeliveryBurstLimit()`, which should return the actor's custom limit.

Note that `receiveCommand` always receives both *Command Messages (202)* and *Event Messages (207)*. This is because to the `PersistentActor` the perspective is that even *Event Messages (207)* are treated as *Command Messages (202)* when they are received by `receiveCommand`. For example, the `LoanRateQuoteStarted` was generated as an *Event Message (207)* by the `LoanRateQuote` actor, but to the `LoanBroker` it can be seen as representing an implicit *Command Message (202)* with the intent to stop redelivery. Even if you don't agree with this perspective, just consider `receiveCommand` as the replacement for the normal `Actor receive` partial function, and it is the means for a `PersistentActor` to react to all kinds of *Messages (130)*.

Channel Adapter

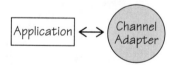

A Channel Adapter is a *Message Endpoint (145)*. When an application provides a messaging interface at the system boundary with centralized Application Services in the interior, use a Channel Adapter between the messaging and the Application Services. This is exemplified in Figure 5.9. Your Channel Adapters may be entirely comprised of actors, or you may have both actors and message listeners, if you support both the Actor model and a middleware messaging server at your system's boundary.

When using the Ports and Adapters architecture style [IDDD] (a.k.a. Hexagonal), the Channel Adapter is the messaging client at the application boundary. The Channel Adapters receive messages and translate the payload to parameters that are compatible with the central API. In its simplest form, message translation is from text to scalar data that adhere to the API's contract for valid parameters. Yet, if there are more challenging translations to perform, your Channel Adapter should use a full-fledged *Message Translator (143)*, possibly in the style of an Anti-Corruption Layer [IDDD].

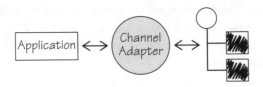

Figure 5.9 A Channel Adapter implemented as an actor sits between the Application Services and the actual processing components.

Besides adapting incoming messages to the API's contract and invoking the services, a Channel Adapter can also be used to adapt application results to outgoing messages. In this case, messages may be sent both to remote actors and through a middleware messaging server.

Since you are focused on the Actor model, let's consider a typical actor-based Channel Adapter. The *Message Bus (192)* example has a `StockTrader` actor that attaches to the bus to receive and send messages.

```
class StockTrader(tradingBus: ActorRef) extends Actor {
  val applicationId = self.path.name

  tradingBus ! RegisterCommandHandler(
                  applicationId,
                  "ExecuteBuyOrder",
                  self)
  tradingBus ! RegisterCommandHandler(
                  applicationId,
                  "ExecuteSellOrder",
                  self)

  def receive = {
    case buy: ExecuteBuyOrder =>
      val result = buyerService.placeBuyOrder(
                      buy.portfolioId,
                      buy.symbol,
                      buy.quantity,
                      buy.price)
      tradingBus ! TradingNotification(
                      "BuyOrderExecuted",
                      BuyOrderExecuted(
                          result.portfolioId,
```

```
                        result.orderId,
                        result.symbol,
                        result.quantity,
                        result.totalCost))

    case sell: ExecuteSellOrder =>
      val result = sellerService.placeSellOrder(
                        buy.portfolioId,
                        buy.symbol,
                        buy.quantity,
                        buy.price)
      tradingBus ! TradingNotification(
                        "SellOrderExecuted",
                        SellOrderExecuted(
                            result.portfolioId,
                            result.orderId,
                            result.symbol,
                            result.quantity,
                            result.totalCost))
    }
}
```

The `StockTrader` accepts two messages from the *Message Bus (192)*, `ExecuteBuyOrder` and `ExecuteSellOrder`. As a Channel Adapter, the `StockTrader` adapts the incoming messages to API invocations. The `ExecuteBuyOrder` message is adapted to parameters that the `BuyerService` accepts, and the `ExecuteSellOrder` message is adapted to parameters that the `SellerService` accepts.

This sample doesn't introduce the possibility that the stock trading system's application implementation uses actors, but that would miss the point of Channel Adapters. Here an actor adapts both incoming and outgoing messages, which is the main thrust of a Channel Adapter, no matter what kind of components comprise the application's internal design.

Message Bridge

In a typical enterprise, there will be loads of different architectural mechanisms in use, including various databases, and probably at least a few different messaging systems. What if two applications need to integrate with each other but their message systems are not interoperable? Should the two systems find another way to integrate, such as with files or by using a database? Assuming that *Enterprise Integration Patterns* [EIP] removed any curiosity about that approach, how can you possibly enable the two applications to use their own, familiar messaging mechanisms and still allow the two to integrate using messaging? The answer is found in the use of a Message Bridge.

As shown in Figure 5.10, a Message Bridge supports the interoperability between two disparate messaging systems, enabling two or more different kinds of messaging middleware to operate together.

Assume that one of the two applications uses RabbitMQ and the other Akka. You could try to influence the team that uses RabbitMQ to implement some Akka-based actors in their application. That effort assumes a few things, including that the team using RabbitMQ is also running their application on a JVM. What if, on the other hand, that team is using C# on .NET and the RabbitMQ .NET client? The least common denominator in this case is RabbitMQ because you can get clients for lots of different platforms, including Java as well as .NET. So, you are probably looking at using a RabbitMQ-Akka Message Bridge.

The other variable that could influence the decision is, for what reasons do the two applications need to integrate with each other? For this project, your Scala and Akka application is an inventory system. The .NET application is an order management system. The .NET order management system will need to collaborate with the Scala and Akka inventory system to get product inventory information, and when an order is placed, it must allocate at least one product unit to the fulfillment chain. If the Scala and Akka team could create/download an actor-based RabbitMQ-Akka Message Bridge, that would enable the .NET order management system to place inventory requests onto a RabbitMQ Message Channel and have those requests delivered through RabbitMQ to an Akka actor in the inventory application. This seems like an accommodating approach since the inventory application is the supplier side in a Customer-Supplier Development [IDDD] relationship.

Assuming that is the way that the decision goes, and it likely is, in the inventory application you would create a Message Bridge actor.

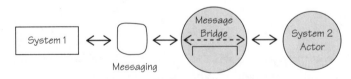

Figure 5.10 A Message Bridge supports the interoperability
between two disparate messaging systems.

```
class InventoryProductAllocationBridge(
            config: RabbitMQBridgeConfig)
        extends RabbitMQBridgeActor(config) {

  private val log: LoggingAdapter =
                Logging.getLogger(context.system, self)

  def receive = {
    case message: RabbitMQBinaryMessage =>
      log.error("Binary messages not supported.")
      ...
    case message: RabbitMQTextMessage =>
      log.error(s"Received text: ${message.textMessage}")
      ...
    case invalid: Any =>
      log.error(s"Don't understand message: $invalid")
      ...
  }
}
```

The `InventoryProductAllocationBridge` extends the `Rabbit-MQBridgeActor`, an actor base class that does the heavy lifting for Rabbit-MQ-Akka Message Bridges. Behind the implementation of `RabbitMQBridge-Actor`, there is a connection, a queue channel, and a queue consumer that interface as a RabbitMQ client and, when a message is received through the RabbitMQ queue channel, sends the message to the concrete implementor.

Here's the `RabbitMQBridgeActor`:

```
abstract class RabbitMQBridgeActor(
            config: RabbitMQBridgeConfig)
        extends Actor {
  private val queueChannel = new QueueChannel(self, config)

/*-----------------------------------------------
  def receive = {
    case message: RabbitMQBinaryMessage =>
      ...
    case message: RabbitMQTextMessage =>
      ...
    case invalid: Any =>
      ...
  }
  -----------------------------------------------*/

}
```

Apparently the bulk of the work is behind the `QueueChannel`, and indeed it is. The abstract base class, `RabbitMQBridgeActor`, doesn't even have a receive block. The block is commented out only to show how concrete extenders should implement their blocks. The underlying `QueueChannel` creates a `DispatchingConsumer`, which is the RabbitMQ message consumer/listener. When the `DispatchingConsumer`, which is a `com.rabbitmq.client .DefaultConsumer`, receives a `handleDelivery()` invocation, it repackages the message and sends it to the Akka actor.

```
private class DispatchingConsumer(
    queueChannel: QueueChannel,
    bridge: ActorRef)
  extends DefaultConsumer(queueChannel.channel) {

  override def handleDelivery(
      consumerTag: String,
      envelope: Envelope,
      properties: BasicProperties,
      body: Array[Byte]): Unit = {

    if (!queueChannel.closed) {
      handle(bridge, new Delivery(envelope, properties, body));
    }
  }

  override def handleShutdownSignal(
      consumerTag: String,
      signal: ShutdownSignalException): Unit = {
    queueChannel.close
  }

  private def handle(
      bridge: ActorRef,
      delivery: Delivery): Unit = {
    try {
      if (this.filteredMessageType(delivery)) {
        ;
      } else if (queueChannel.config.messageType == Binary) {
        bridge !
          RabbitMQBinaryMessage(
              delivery.getProperties.getType,
              delivery.getProperties.getMessageId,
              delivery.getProperties.getTimestamp,
              delivery.getBody,
              delivery.getEnvelope.getDeliveryTag,
              delivery.getEnvelope.isRedeliver)
      } else if (queueChannel.config.messageType == Text) {
        bridge !
          RabbitMQTextMessage(
              delivery.getProperties.getType,
              delivery.getProperties.getMessageId,
              delivery.getProperties.getTimestamp,
```

```
                new String(delivery.getBody),
                delivery.getEnvelope.getDeliveryTag,
                delivery.getEnvelope.isRedeliver)
        }
        ...
```

The concrete Message Bridge actor may choose to receive binary (`Rabbit-MQBinaryMessage`) or text (`RabbitMQTextMessage`) messages. There are these message types and a few other supporting objects:

```scala
object RabbitMQMessageType extends Enumeration {
    type RabbitMQMessageType = Value
    val Binary, Text = Value
}

import RabbitMQMessageType._

case class RabbitMQBridgeConfig(
    messageTypes: Array[String],
    settings: RabbitMQConnectionSettings,
    name: String,
    messageType: RabbitMQMessageType,
    durable: Boolean,
    exclusive: Boolean,
    autoAcknowledged: Boolean,
    autoDeleted: Boolean) {

  if (messageTypes == null)
    throw new IllegalArgumentException(
              "Must provide empty messageTypes.")
  if (settings == null)
    throw new IllegalArgumentException(
              "Must provide settings.")
  if (name == null || name.isEmpty)
    throw new IllegalArgumentException(
              "Must provide name.")
}

case class RabbitMQConnectionSettings(
    hostName: String,
    port: Int,
    virtualHost: String,
    username: String,
    password: String) {

  def this() =
    this("localhost", -1, "/", null, null)

  def this(hostName: String, virtualHost: String) =
    this(hostName, -1, virtualHost, null, null)
```

```
    def hasPort(): Boolean =
      port > 0

    def hasUserCredentials(): Boolean =
      username != null && password != null
}

case class RabbitMQBinaryMessage(
    messageType: String,
    messageId: String,
    timestamp: Date,
    binaryMessage: Array[Byte],
    deliveryTag: Long,
    redelivery: Boolean)

case class RabbitMQTextMessage(
    messageType: String,
    messageId: String,
    timestamp: Date,
    textMessage: String,
    deliveryTag: Long,
    redelivery: Boolean)
```

There is the `RabbitMQMessageType`, which is an `Enumeration` used to determine the message type—either `Binary` or `Text`—for a given bridge. The `RabbitMQBridgeConfig` is used to declare the full configuration of the Message Bridge actor. Table 5.4 describes each of the configurations.

The `InventoryProductAllocationBridge` is configured to accept `Text` messages, not `Binary`. Thus, both customer and supplier [IDDD] must agree on the text format. Oftentimes integrations are best supported using JavaScript Object Notation (JSON), a weak schema, rather than a rigid, even brittle, Extensible Markup Language (XML) scheme. Assuming that the `InventoryProductAllocationBridge` accepts JSON messages, its receive block will use a *Message Translator (143)* to transform the JSON text payload into a type that the local application accepts.

```
class InventoryProductAllocationBridge(
            config: RabbitMQBridgeConfig)
        extends RabbitMQBridgeActor(config) {

  private val log: LoggingAdapter =
            Logging.getLogger(context.system, self)

  def receive = {
    case message: RabbitMQTextMessage =>
      val inventoryProductAllocation =
```

```
        translateToInventoryProductAllocation(
            message.textMessage)
    ...
        acknowledgeDelivery(message)
  }
}
```

Once the `RabbitMQTextMessage` has been handled to completion, using `acknowledgeDelivery()`, the Message Bridge actor acknowledges that the message has been handled successfully. If `InventoryProductAllocation-Bridge` asynchronously dispatches the translated `InventoryProductAllocation` for another actor to process, it will need to use `acknowledgeDelivery()` only after the secondary actor responds with a success reply.

Table 5.4 `RabbitMQBridgeConfig` Configurations for the Message Bridge Actor

Parameter Name	Type and Description
messageTypes	An `Array[String]` that contains the full name of all message types that are accepted by the bridge. If all message types are accepted, the `Array` will be empty (but it must not be null).
settings	A `RabbitMQConnectionSettings` that determines how a connection to RabbitMQ will be made.
name	The `String` name of the queue to listen to.
messageType	The `RabbitMQMessageType`, either `Binary` or `Text`.
durable	The `Boolean` that determines whether the queue is durable.
exclusive	The `Boolean` that determines whether the queue is exclusive.
autoAcknowledged	The `Boolean` that determines whether received messages are auto-acknowledged.
autoDeleted	The `Boolean` that determines whether the queue is automatically deleted when closed.

Message Bus

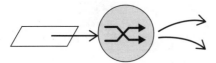

You have a number of disparate business systems, from purchased commodity applications to custom-developed applications that help achieve competitive advantage to those of integrating business partners. You need all of these systems to work together, although they run on different platforms and have various service interfaces, and each set of service interfaces specifies a unique data model. Sometimes it can work best to create a Message Bus that implements a simple Service-Oriented Architecture, which is illustrated in Figure 5.11. Such a Message Bus must unify the service interface across all integrated applications, and they must all share a common *Canonical Message Model (333)*.

This example presents a stock trading system with three subsystems: Stock Trader, Portfolio Manager, and Market Analysis Tools. I create a single actor that implements the Message Bus, the `TradingBus`. Each of the subsystems is given an actor that serves as its connector: `StockTrader`, `PortfolioManager`, and `MarketAnalysisTools`.

It is quite likely that each of these systems could require a *Channel Adapter (183)* and possibly a *Message Bridge (185)* to complete the integration with the `TradingBus`. The Channel Adapter would take the specific message delivered to one of the bus participating actors (for example, `StockTrader`) and adapt it to the data model and service interface of the underlying subsystem (for example, the Stock Trader system). If the underlying subsystem employs a messaging mechanism of some kind—such as Microsoft Message Queuing

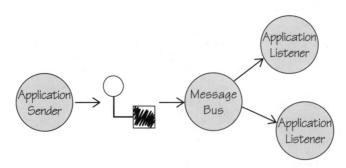

Figure 5.11 A Message Bus unifies the service interface across all integrated applications.

(MSMQ), a JMS implementation, RabbitMQ, and so on—the Message Bridge would create and send a message to the application-native messaging mechanism. Of course, the Channel Adapter and Message Bridge would also be responsible for receiving and adapting outgoing messages/responses compatible with the Message Bus and its *Canonical Message Model* (333).

Here is the driver application for the sample:

```scala
import scala.collection.mutable.Map
import akka.actor._
import co.vaughnvernon.reactiveenterprise._

object MessageBus extends CompletableApp(9) {
  val tradingBus =
              system.actorOf(
                    Props(classOf[TradingBus], 6),
                    "tradingBus")
  val marketAnalysisTools =
              system.actorOf(
                    Props(classOf[MarketAnalysisTools],
                      tradingBus),
                    "marketAnalysisTools")
  val portfolioManager = system.actorOf(
                    Props(
                      classOf[PortfolioManager],
                      tradingBus),
                    "portfolioManager")
  val stockTrader = system.actorOf(
          Props(classOf[StockTrader],tradingBus), "stockTrader")

  awaitCanStartNow()

  tradingBus ! Status()

  tradingBus ! TradingCommand(
                "ExecuteBuyOrder",
                ExecuteBuyOrder(
                  "p123", "MSFT", 100, 31.85))
  tradingBus ! TradingCommand(
                "ExecuteSellOrder",
                ExecuteSellOrder(
                  "p456", "MSFT", 200, 31.80))
  tradingBus ! TradingCommand(
                "ExecuteBuyOrder",
                ExecuteBuyOrder(
                  "p789", "MSFT", 100, 31.83))

  awaitCompletion
  println("MessageBus: is completed.")
}
```

The `TradingBus` is first created, and then the subsystem actors, which are endowed with a reference to the `TradingBus` actor, are created. The Trading-Bus is responsible for the following:

- Managing registrations for command handlers and notification interests

- Dispatching specific commands to registered command handlers

- Dispatching specific notifications to registered notification interested parties

It is essential that all `TradingBus` participants use the same *Canonical Message Model (333).* A minimal one is presented here along with the Trading-Bus actor:

```
case class CommandHandler(
            applicationId: String,
            handler: ActorRef)
case class ExecuteBuyOrder(
            portfolioId: String, symbol: String,
            quantity: Int, price: Money)
case class BuyOrderExecuted(
            portfolioId: String, symbol: String,
            quantity: Int, price: Money)
case class ExecuteSellOrder(
            portfolioId: String, symbol: String,
            quantity: Int, price: Money)
case class SellOrderExecuted(
            portfolioId: String, symbol: String,
            quantity: Int, price: Money)
case class NotificationInterest(
            applicationId: String,
            interested: ActorRef)
case class RegisterCommandHandler(
            applicationId: String,
            commandId: String, handler: ActorRef)
case class RegisterNotificationInterest(
            applicationId: String,
            notificationId: String,
            interested: ActorRef)
case class TradingCommand(
            commandId: String, command: Any)
case class TradingNotification(
            notificationId: String, notification: Any)

case class Status()

class TradingBus(canStartAfterRegistered: Int)
        extends Actor {
  val commandHandlers =
```

```scala
            Map[String, Vector[CommandHandler]]()
val notificationInterests =
            Map[String, Vector[NotificationInterest]]()

var totalRegistered = 0

def dispatchCommand(command: TradingCommand) = {
  if (commandHandlers.contains(command.commandId)) {
    commandHandlers(command.commandId) map {
          commandHandler =>
      commandHandler.handler ! command.command
    }
  }
}

def dispatchNotification(
      notification: TradingNotification) = {
  if (notificationInterests.contains(
        notification.notificationId)) {
    notificationInterests(
        notification.notificationId) map {
            notificationInterest =>
      notificationInterest.interested !
              notification.notification
    }
  }
}

def notifyStartWhenReady() = {
  totalRegistered += 1

  if (totalRegistered == this.canStartAfterRegistered) {
    println(s"TradingBus: is ready: $totalRegistered")
    MessageBus.canStartNow()
  }
}

def receive = {
  case register: RegisterCommandHandler =>
    println(s"TradingBus: registering: $register")
    registerCommandHandler(register.commandId,
                           register.applicationId,
                           register.handler)
    notifyStartWhenReady()

  case register: RegisterNotificationInterest =>
    println(s"TradingBus: registering: $register")
    registerNotificationInterest(register.notificationId,
                                 register.applicationId,
                                 register.interested)
    notifyStartWhenReady()

  case command: TradingCommand =>
```

```
          println(s"TradingBus: dispatching: $command")
          dispatchCommand(command)

      case notification: TradingNotification =>
          println(s"TradingBus: dispatching: $notification")
          dispatchNotification(notification)

      case status: Status =>
          println(s"TradingBus: STATUS: $commandHandlers")
          println(s"TradingBus: STATUS: $notificationInterests")

      case message: Any =>
          println(s"TradingBus: received unexpected: $message")
    }

    def registerCommandHandler(
        commandId: String,
        applicationId: String,
        handler: ActorRef) = {

      if (!commandHandlers.contains(commandId)) {
        commandHandlers(commandId) = Vector[CommandHandler]()
      }

      commandHandlers(commandId) =
          commandHandlers(commandId) :+
              CommandHandler(applicationId, handler)
    }

    def registerNotificationInterest(
        notificationId: String,
        applicationId: String,
        interested: ActorRef) = {

      if (!notificationInterests.contains(notificationId)) {
        notificationInterests(notificationId) =
              Vector[NotificationInterest]()
      }

      notificationInterests(notificationId) =
          notificationInterests(notificationId) :+
            NotificationInterest(applicationId, interested)
    }
}
```

By convention, every concrete command and notification that enters the
TradingBus must be wrapped by a corresponding TradingCommand or
TradingNotification object. These are the two fundamental elements of
the *Canonical Message Model (333)*. If any subsystem actor attempts to send a
raw command or notification, it will be rejected. However, when a command
is sent to a registrant, it is unwrapped by the TradingBus and sent as the

underlying, raw/concrete message type. The same goes for delivering a notification to each registrant.

In this example, there are only a few concrete commands and notifications that may be sent through the `TradingBus`. The commands are `ExecuteBuyOrder` and `ExecuteSellOrder`. The notifications are `BuyOrderExecuted` and `SellOrderExecuted`. The `StockTrader` actor registers itself as a command handler of `ExecuteBuyOrder` and `ExecuteSellOrder`, and it is the sole sender of `BuyOrderExecuted` and `SellOrderExecuted`. Two subsystem actors, `PortfolioManager` and `MarketAnalysisTools`, register themselves as interested in `BuyOrderExecuted` and `SellOrderExecuted` notifications.

Here is the source code for the three subsystem actors:

```
class MarketAnalysisTools(tradingBus: ActorRef) extends Actor {
  val applicationId = self.path.name

  tradingBus ! RegisterNotificationInterest(applicationId,
                "BuyOrderExecuted", self)
  tradingBus ! RegisterNotificationInterest(applicationId,
                "SellOrderExecuted", self)

  def receive = {
    case executed: BuyOrderExecuted =>
      println(s"MarketAnalysisTools: adding: $executed")
      MessageBus.completedStep()

    case executed: SellOrderExecuted =>
      println(s"MarketAnalysisTools: adjusting: $executed")
      MessageBus.completedStep()

    case message: Any =>
      println(s"MarketAnalysisTools: unexpected: $message")
  }
}

class PortfolioManager(tradingBus: ActorRef)
        extends Actor {
  val applicationId = self.path.name

  tradingBus ! RegisterNotificationInterest(
                applicationId,
                "BuyOrderExecuted", self)
  tradingBus ! RegisterNotificationInterest(
                applicationId,
                "SellOrderExecuted", self)

  def receive = {
    case executed: BuyOrderExecuted =>
      println(s"PortfolioManager: adding holding:
```

```scala
                          $executed")
      MessageBus.completedStep()

    case executed: SellOrderExecuted =>
      println(s"PortfolioManager: adjusting holding:
                          $executed")
      MessageBus.completedStep()

    case message: Any =>
      println(s"PortfolioManager: unexpected: $message")
  }
}

class StockTrader(tradingBus: ActorRef) extends Actor {
  val applicationId = self.path.name

  tradingBus ! RegisterCommandHandler(
                  applicationId,
                  "ExecuteBuyOrder",
                  self)
  tradingBus ! RegisterCommandHandler(
                  applicationId,
                  "ExecuteSellOrder",
                  self)

  def receive = {
    case buy: ExecuteBuyOrder =>
      println(s"StockTrader: buying for: $buy")
      tradingBus ! TradingNotification(
                  "BuyOrderExecuted",
                  BuyOrderExecuted(
                      buy.portfolioId,
                      buy.symbol,
                      buy.quantity,
                      buy.price))
      MessageBus.completedStep()

    case sell: ExecuteSellOrder =>
      println(s"StockTrader: selling for: $sell")
      tradingBus ! TradingNotification(
                  "SellOrderExecuted",
                  SellOrderExecuted(
                      sell.portfolioId,
                      sell.symbol,
                      sell.quantity,
                      sell.price))
      MessageBus.completedStep()

    case message: Any =>
      println(s"StockTrader: received unexpected: $message")
  }
}
```

When running the driver application, the following partial output is produced:

```
TradingBus: dispatching:↵
 TradingCommand(ExecuteSellOrder,ExecuteSellOrder(↵
p456,MSFT,200,31.8))
StockTrader: buying for: ExecuteBuyOrder(↵
p123,MSFT,100,31.85)
TradingBus: dispatching:↵
 TradingCommand(ExecuteBuyOrder,ExecuteBuyOrder(↵
p789,MSFT,100,31.83))
StockTrader: selling for: ExecuteSellOrder(↵
p456,MSFT,200,31.8)
TradingBus: dispatching:↵
 TradingNotification(BuyOrderExecuted,BuyOrderExecuted(↵
p123,MSFT,100,31.85))
StockTrader: buying for: ExecuteBuyOrder(↵
p789,MSFT,100,31.83)
TradingBus: dispatching:↵
 TradingNotification(SellOrderExecuted,SellOrderExecuted(↵
p456,MSFT,200,31.8))
PortfolioManager: adding holding: BuyOrderExecuted(↵
p123,MSFT,100,31.85)
MarketAnalysisTools: adding: BuyOrderExecuted(↵
p123,MSFT,100,31.85)
TradingBus: dispatching:↵
 TradingNotification(BuyOrderExecuted,BuyOrderExecuted(↵
p789,MSFT,100,31.83))
PortfolioManager: adjusting holding: SellOrderExecuted(↵
p456,MSFT,200,31.8)
MarketAnalysisTools: adjusting: SellOrderExecuted(↵
p456,MSFT,200,31.8)
PortfolioManager: adding: BuyOrderExecuted(↵
p789,MSFT,100,31.83)
MarketAnalysisTools: adding: BuyOrderExecuted(↵
p789,MSFT,100,31.83)
MessageBus: is completed.
```

You probably figured out by now that the Message Bus is a kind of *Content-Based Router (228)*. Depending on the message that the `TradingBus` receives, it looks up the registrants of that specific message type and routes it to each. (The `TradingBus` is also a Service Directory or Service Registry.) Additionally, each of the three subsystem actors is a *Service Activator (390)*, allowing the Application Services of each to be reached via messaging whether or not the individual application natively supports synchronous or asynchronous access.

Summary

In this chapter, you looked at the details of several messaging channel themes: one-to-one or *Point-to-Point Channel (151)*, one-to-many or *Publish-Subscribe Channels (154)*, data-specific channels or *Datatype Channel (167)*, invalid and dead messages using *Invalid Message Channel (170)* and *Dead Letter Channel (172)*, crash-proofing channels using *Guaranteed Delivery (175)*, nonmessaging and adaptive messaging channels with *Channel Adapter (183)* and *Message Bridge (185)*, and communications backbones using *Message Bus (192)*.

This has taken you beyond the basic messaging that actors provide and produced a strong foundation for more advanced reactive application designs and enterprise integrations.

Chapter 6

Message Construction

In Chapter 4, "Messaging with Actors," I discussed messaging with actors, but I didn't cover much about the kinds of messages that should be created and sent. Each message must convey the intent of the sender's reason to communicate with the receiver. As *Enterprise Integration Patterns* [EIP] shows, there may be any number of motivations based on the following:

- *Message intent*: Why are you sending a message? Are you requesting another actor to perform an operation? If so, use a *Command Message (202)*. Are you informing one or more other actors that you have performed some operation? In that case, use an *Event Message (207)*. Have you been asked for some large body of information that you must convey to the requester via a *Message (130)*? The request can be fulfilled using a *Document Message (204)*.

- *Returning a response*: When there is a contract between two actors that follows *Request-Reply (209)*, the actor receiving the request needs to provide a reply, or *response*. The request is a *Command Message (202)* and the reply is generally a *Document Message (204)*. Since you are using the Actor model, the actor receiving the request knows the *Return Address (211)* of the sender and can easily reply. If there are multiple incoming requests that are related to one another or multiple outgoing replies that are logically bundled, use a *Correlation Identifier (215)* to associate separate messages into one logical package.

- *Huge amounts of data*: Sometimes you need more than a *Correlation Identifier (215)* to bundle related messages. What happens if you can correlate a set of messages but you also need to ensure that they are ordered according to some application-specific sequence? That's the job of a *Message Sequence (217)*.

- *Slow messages*: As I have taken the opportunity to repeat in several places through the text, the network is unreliable. When a *Message (130)* of whatever type must travel over the network, there is always a change that network latency will affect its delivery. Even so, there are also latencies in actors when, for example, they have a lot of work to do before they

201

can handle your requests. Although this can point to the need to redesign some portion of the application to deal with workload in a more acceptable time frame, you also need to do something about it when encountered. You can use a *Message Expiration (218)* and perhaps the *Dead Letter Channel (172)* to signal to the system that something needs to be done about the latency situation, if in fact it is deemed unacceptable.

- *Message version*: Oftentimes a *Document Message (204)*, or actually an *Event Message (207)* or even a *Command Message (202)*, can have a number of versions throughout its lifetime. You can identify the version of the message using a *Format Indicator (222)*.

In much the same way that you must think about the kind of *Message Channel (128)* you will use for various application and integration circumstances, you must also think about and design your messages specifically to deal with the reaction and concurrency scenarios at hand.

Command Message

When a message-sending actor needs to cause an action to be performed on the receiving actor, the sender uses a Command Message.

If you are familiar with the Command-Query Separation principle [CQS], you probably think of a Command Message as one that, when handled by the receiver, will cause a side effect on the receiver (see Figure 6.1). After all, that's what the C in CQS stands for: a request that causes a state transition. Yet, a Command Message as described by *Enterprise Integration Patterns* [EIP] may also be used to represent the request for a query—the Q in CQS. Because of the overlap in intended uses by *Enterprise Integration Patterns* [EIP], when designing with the CQS principle in mind and discussing a message that causes a query to be performed, it is best to instead use the explicit term *query message*. Even so, this is not to say that a message-based actor system must be designed with CQS in mind. Depending on the system, it may work best for a given Command Message to both alter state and elicit a response message, as discussed in *Request-Reply (209)*.

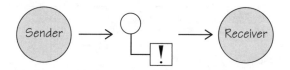

Figure 6.1 The `Sender`, by means of a Command Message,
tells the `Receiver` to do something.

Each Command Message, although sent by a requestor, is defined by the receiver actor as part of its public contract. Should the sent Command Message not match one defined as part of the receiver's contract, it could be redirected to the *Invalid Message Channel (170)*.

Command Messages are designed as imperative exhortations of actions to be performed; that is, the exhortation for an actor to perform some behavior. The Command Message will contain any data parameters and collaborating actor parameters necessary to perform the action. For example, besides passing any data that is required to perform the command, a Command Message may also contain a *Return Address (211)* to indicate which actor should be informed about possible side effects or outcomes.

In essence you can think of a Command Message as a representation of an operation invocation. In other words, a Command Message captures the intention to invoke an operation, but in a way that allows the operation to be performed at a time following the message declaration.

The following case classes implement Command Messages for an equities trading domain:

```
case class ExecuteBuyOrder(
    portfolioId: String,
    symbol: String,
    quantity: Int,
    price: Money)

case class ExecuteSellOrder(
    portfolioId: String,
    symbol: String,
    quantity: Int,
    price: Money)
```

Here a `StockTrader` receives the two Command Messages but rejects any other message type by sending them to the *Dead Letter Channel (172)*, which doubles as an *Invalid Message Channel (170)*:

```
class StockTrader(tradingBus: ActorRef) extends Actor {
  ...
  def receive = {
    case buy: ExecuteBuyOrder =>
      ...
    case sell: ExecuteSellOrder =>
      ...
    case message: Any =>
      context.system.deadLetters ! message
  }
}
```

Normally a Command Message is sent over a *Point-to-Point Channel (151)* because the command is intended to be performed once by a specific receiving actor. To send a broadcast type of message, likely you will want to use an *Event Message (207)* along with *Publish-Subscribe Channel (154)*.

Document Message

Use a Document Message to convey information to a receiver, but without indicating how the data should be used (see Figure 6.2). This is different from a *Command Message (202)* in that while the command likely passes data parameters, it also specifies the intended use. A Document Message also differs from an *Event Message (207)* in that while the event conveys information without specifying its intended use, an event associates the data it carries with a past occurrence in the business domain. Although a Document Message communicates information about the domain, it does so without indicating that the concept is a fact that expresses a specific past occurrence in the business domain. See also Domain Events, as discussed in *Implementing Domain-Driven Design* [IDDD].

Oftentimes a Document Message serves as the reply in the *Request-Reply (209)* pattern. In the implementation diagram the `Receiver` may have previously sent a *Command Message (202)* to the `Sender` to request to data, as in *Request-Reply (209)*, or the `Sender` may send the Document Message to the `Receiver` without the `Receiver` previously requesting the information of the `Sender`.

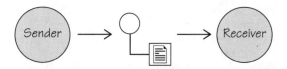

Figure 6.2 The `Sender`, by means of a Document Message, provides the `Receiver` with information but without indicating how it should be used.

The following is a Document Message that conveys data about a quotation fulfillment:

```
case class QuotationFulfillment(
    rfqId: String,
    quotesRequested: Int,
    priceQuotes: Seq[PriceQuote],
    requester: ActorRef)
```

The information provided by the `QuoteFulfillment` document includes the unique identity of the request for quotation, the number of quotations that were requested, the number of `PriceQuote` instances that were actually obtained, and a reference to the actor that originally requested the quotations. The `PriceQuote` itself could be considered a full Document Message but in this example is just part of the composed `QuoteFulfillment` Document Message:

```
case class PriceQuote(
    quoterId: String,
    rfqId: String,
    itemId: String,
    retailPrice: Double,
    discountPrice: Double)
```

As the `PriceQuote` structure indicates, it is not the size or complexity of the message type that determines whether it is a Document Message. Rather, it is the fact that information is conveyed without indicating intended usage (command) or that it is conveyed as part of an application outcome (event). To reinforce this, consider the following *Command Message (202)* and *Event Message (207)*, respectively, that are used in conjunction with obtaining the `QuoteFulfillment` Document Message:

```
case class RequestPriceQuote(
    rfqId: String,
```

```
        itemId: String,
        retailPrice: Money,
        orderTotalRetailPrice: Money)

case class PriceQuoteFulfilled(priceQuote: PriceQuote)
```

The first case class, which is a *Command Message (202)*, is used to request a set of quotations for a specific item. The second case class, that being an *Event Message (207)*, is published when a price quotation has been fulfilled. These are both quite different from the `QuoteFulfillment` Document Message, which merely carries information about the results of the previously requested price quotation.

Managing Flow and Process

You can use a Document Message to assist in managing workflow or long-running processes [IDDD]. Send a Document Message on a *Point-to-Point Channel (151)* to one actor at a time, each implementing a step in the process. As each step completes, it appends to the document that it received, applying the changes for the processing step as it is completed. The actor for the current step then dispatches the appended Document Message on to the actor of the next processing step. This dispatch-receive-append-dispatch recurrence continues until the process has completed.

It is the final step that determines what to do with the now fully composed Document Message. Since long-running processes may be composed from a few to many different smaller processes, it's possible that the final step in a given process merely completes one branch of a larger process. In all of this, no Document Message is actually mutated to an altered state. Instead, each step composes a new Document Message as a combination of the current document and any new information to be appended. The merging of the current Document Message with new data might be performed as a simple concatenation. Assuming a linear process where each step is responsible for gathering a `PriceQuote` from a given vendor, this example shows how a `QuotationFulfillment` can be appended:

```
case class QuotationFulfillment(
    rfqId: String,
    quotesRequested: Int,
    priceQuotes: Seq[PriceQuote],
    requester: ActorRef) {

  def appendWith(
      fulfilledPriceQuote: PriceQuote):
  QuotationFulfillment {
    QuotationFulfillment(
```

```
            rfqId,
            quotesRequested,
            priceQuotes :+ fulfilledPriceQuote,
            requester)
    }
}
```

The Document Message itself may contain some data describing how each processing step actor is to dispatch to the next step. This might be handled by placing the actor address+name of each step inside the original document in the order in which the steps should occur. As each step completes, it simply looks up the next actor and dispatches, sending it the appended document.

```
val quotationFulfillment =
        quotationFulfillment.appendWith(newPriceQuote)
quotationFulfillment.stepFollowing(name) ! quotationFulfillment
```

As an alternative to this document-based lookup approach, you may instead choose to use the Akka `DistributedPubSubMediator`, as discussed in *Publish-Subscribe Channel (154)*, to dispatch to a single actor in the cluster without the need to actually look up the actor. This approach uses the `DistributedPubSubMediator.Send` router message. If using `Send`, you would simply place the name of each processing step actor in the document, leaving off the address. The contract of the `DistributedPubSubMediator` ensures that a matching actor somewhere in the cluster will receive the next Document Message per a specified routing policy.

When a long-running process has a complex routing specification, it would be best to use a *Process Manager (292)* to coordinate dispatching to each step. Generally, you would need such a *Process Manager (292)* when the dispatching rules include conditional branching based on values appended to the Document Message by one or more steps.

Event Message

Use an Event Message, as illustrated in Figure 6.3, when other actors need to be notified about something that has just occurred in the actor that produces the event. Generally, a *Publish-Subscribe Channel (154)* is used to inform

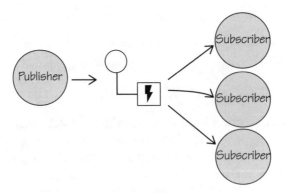

Figure 6.3 Using an Event Message, a `Publisher` may notify multiple `Subscriber` actors about something that happened in the domain model.

interested parties about a given event. Yet, sometimes it may be appropriate to tell a specific actor about an event or tell the specific actor and also publish to an abstract set of subscribers. See also Domain Events as discussed in *Implementing Domain-Driven Design* [IDDD].

For example, when an `OrderProcessor` receives a `RequestForQuotation` message, it dispatches a request to fulfill the quotations to any number of product discounters. As each discounter that chooses to participate responds with a `PriceQuote` *Document Message (204)* describing the discount offer, the `OrderProcessor` sends a `PriceQuoteFulfilled` Event Message to an *Aggregator (257)*.

```
case class PriceQuote(
    quoterId: String,
    rfqId: String,
    itemId: String,
    retailPrice: Double,
    discountPrice: Double) // Document Message

case class PriceQuoteFulfilled(
    priceQuote: PriceQuote) // Event Message
```

In this specific case, it is unnecessary to broadcast the event using a *Publish-Subscribe Channel (154)* because it is specifically the *Aggregator (257)* that needs to know about the price quote fulfillment. You could have designed the *Aggregator (257)* to accept a *Command Message (202)* or a *Document Message (204)* rather than an Event Message. Yet, the `OrderProcessor` need not be concerned with how the *Aggregator (257)* works, only that it will satisfy

its contract once it has received some required number of `PriceQuoteFul-`
`filled` events. Also note that the `PriceQuoteFulfilled` is a *Document
Message (204)* in that the Event Message packs the small `PriceQuote` *Document Message (204)* as the `PriceQuoteFulfilled` event information.

Request-Reply

When a message is sent from one actor to another, it is considered a request.
When the receiver of the request message needs to send a message back to the
request sender, the message is a reply. As shown in Figure 6.4, a common usage
pattern of Request-Reply has the requestor sending a *Command Message (202)*
and the receiver replying with a *Document Message (204)*. In such a case, and
as described in *Command Message (202)*, the command is probably a *Query
Message* [IDDD].

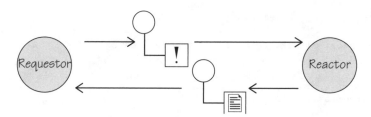

Figure 6.4 A `Requestor` and a `Reactor` collaborate with
each other using Request-Reply.

 While the requestor will normally send a *Command Message (202)*, replying with a *Message Document Message (204)* is not a strict requirement. Still,
if you consider the document payload of the reply to be any simple structure,
not necessarily a complex one, then it is often appropriate to refer to the reply
as a *Document Message (204)*. The point is that the document carries data but
does not indicate what the consumer should do with it.
 Request-Reply is quite simple and straightforward to implement using
the Actor model. In fact, Request-Reply is considered part of the basic actor
semantics. Here is how it works:

```
package co.vaughnvernon.reactiveenterprise.requestreply

import akka.actor._
import co.vaughnvernon.reactiveenterprise._

case class Request(what: String)
case class Reply(what: String)
case class StartWith(server: ActorRef)

object RequestReply extends CompletableApp(1) {
  val client = system.actorOf(Props[Client], "client")
  val server = system.actorOf(Props[Server], "server")
  client ! StartWith(server)

  awaitCompletion
  println("RequestReply: is completed.")
}

class Client extends Actor {
  def receive = {
    case StartWith(server) =>
      println("Client: is starting...")
      server ! Request("REQ-1")
    case Reply(what) =>
      println("Client: received response: " + what)
      RequestReply.completedStep()
    case _ =>
      println("Client: received unexpected message")
  }
}

class Server extends Actor {
  def receive = {
    case Request(what) =>
      println("Server: received request value: " + what)
      sender ! Reply("RESP-1 for " + what)
    case _ =>
      println("Server: received unexpected message")
  }
}
```

The following output is produced by the `Client` and `Server`:

```
Client: is starting...
Server: received request value: REQ-1
Client: received response: RESP-1 for REQ-1
Client: is completing...
```

The three classes at the top of the file are the messages that can be sent. Following the message types there is the application (App) object, and then the Client and Server actors. Note that the use of awaitCompletion() in the App bootstrap object makes the application stick around until the two actors complete.

The first message, StartWith, is sent to the Client to tell it to start the Request-Reply scenario. Although StartWith is a *Command Message (202)* request, note that the Client does not produce a reply to the App. The StartWith message takes one parameter, which is the instance of the Server actor (actually an ActorRef). The Client makes a request to the Server, and the Server makes a reply to the Client. The Request and Reply are the other two different message types.

Specifically, a Client knows how to StartWith and how to react to Reply messages, while a Server knows how to react to Request messages. If the Client receives anything but StartWith and Reply, it simply reports that it doesn't understand. The Server does the same if it receives anything but a Request.

These details notwithstanding, the main point of this simple Scala/Akka example is to show how Request-Reply is accomplished using the Actor model. It's pretty simple. Wouldn't you agree? Request-Reply is a natural form of programming using the Actor model. As you can see, the Server doesn't need to know it is replying to the Client actor. It only needs to know it is replying to the sender of the Request, and the sender of the Request needs to know that it will receive a Reply to its Request.

All of this happens asynchronously. The Client and the Server share nothing; that is, their states are completely encapsulated and protected. That, and the fact that each actor will handle only one message at a time, allows the asynchronous message handling to be completely lock free.

Return Address

When reasoning on *Request-Reply (209)*, what if you want your request receiver to reply to an actor at an address other than the direct message sender? Well, that's the idea behind Return Address, as shown in Figure 6.5, and one that you can implement in a few different ways.

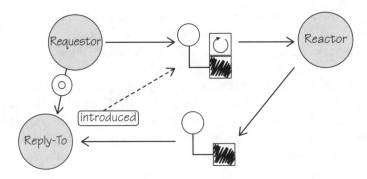

Figure 6.5 A `Requestor` uses a Return Address to tell the `Reactor`
to reply to a third party.

It's interesting that the Actor model actually uses addresses to identify how to send messages to actors. You see, each actor has an address, and to send a given actor a message, you must know its address. One actor can know the address of another actor by a few different means.

- An actor creates another actor and thus knows the address of the actors it has created.

- An actor receives a message that has the address of one or more other actors that it will send messages to.

- In some cases, an actor may be able to look up the address of another actor by name, but this may create an unseemly binding to the definition and implementation of a given actor.

The *Enterprise Integration Patterns* [EIP] Return Address fits really well with the fundamental ideas behind the Actor model.

One obvious way to provide a Return Address in a given message is to put the address of the actor that you want to receive the reply right in the message that you send. Recall that you did something similar in the *Request-Reply (209)* example.

```
case class StartWith(server: ActorRef)
```

The first message that the client receives is `StartWith`, and that message must contain the `ActorRef` of the server that the client is to use. That way, the client will know how to make requests of some server. Okay, so that's not really a Return Address, but you could send a Return Address as part of a message in the same way.

If the client chose to, it could also send messages to the server and provide the Return Address of the actor that should receive the reply. Of course, the request message itself would have to support that protocol and allow the `ActorRef` to be included in the message.

```
case class Request(what: String, replyTo: ActorRef)
```

That way, when the server is ready to send its reply to the request, it could send the reply to the `replyTo` actor, like so:

```
class Server extends Actor {
  def receive = {
    case Request(what, replyTo) =>
      println("Server: received request value: " + what)
      replyTo ! Reply("RESP-1 for " + what)
    case _ =>
      println("Server: received unexpected message")
  }
}
```

That works, but it does require you to design the message protocol in a certain way. What if you have an existing message protocol and you later decide to redesign the existing receiving actor to delegate some message handling to one of its child actors? This might be the case if there is some complex processing to do for certain messages and you don't want to heap too much responsibility on your original actor, for example the server. It would be nice if the server could create a child worker to handle a specific kind of complex message but design the worker to reply to the original client sender, not to the parent server. That would free the parent server to simply delegate to the child worker and allow the worker to react as if the server had done the work itself.

```
package co.vaughnvernon.reactiveenterprise.returnaddress

import akka.actor._
import co.vaughnvernon.reactiveenterprise._

case class Request(what: String)
case class RequestComplex(what: String)
case class Reply(what: String)
case class ReplyToComplex(what: String)
case class StartWith(server: ActorRef)

object ReturnAddress extends CompletableApp(2) {
  val client = system.actorOf(Props[Client], "client")
  val server = system.actorOf(Props[Server], "server")
```

```
    client ! StartWith(server)

    awaitCompletion
    println("ReturnAddress: is completed.")
}

class Client extends Actor {
  def receive = {
    case StartWith(server) =>
      println("Client: is starting...")
      server ! Request("REQ-1")
      server ! RequestComplex("REQ-20")
    case Reply(what) =>
      println("Client: received reply: " + what)
      ReturnAddress.completedStep()
    case ReplyToComplex(what) =>
      println("Client: received reply to complex: "
              + what)
      ReturnAddress.completedStep()
    case _ =>
      println("Client: received unexpected message")
  }
}

class Server extends Actor {
  val worker = context.actorOf(Props[Worker], "worker")

  def receive = {
    case request: Request =>
      println("Server: received request value: "
              + request.what)
      sender ! Reply("RESP-1 for " + request.what)
    case request: RequestComplex =>
      println("Server: received request value: "
              + request.what)
      worker forward request
    case _ =>
      println("Server: received unexpected message")
  }
}

class Worker extends Actor {
  def receive = {
    case RequestComplex(what) =>
      println("Worker: received complex request value: "
              + what)
      sender ! ReplyToComplex("RESP-2000 for " + what)
    case _ =>
      println("Worker: received unexpected message")
  }
}
```

This is the output produced by the Return Address example:

```
Client: is starting...
Server: received request value: REQ-1
Server: received request value: REQ-20
Client: received reply: RESP-1 for REQ-1
Worker: received complex request value: REQ-20
Client: received reply to complex: RESP-2000 for REQ-20
```

Note that when the `Server` is created, it uses its context to create a single child `Worker` actor. This `Worker` is used by the `Server` only when it receives a `RequestComplex` message. Also note that there is no reason to design the `RequestComplex` message with a `replyTo ActorRef`. Thus, as far as the `Client` is concerned, it is the `Server` that handles the `RequestComplex` message.

Now notice that the `Server` doesn't just tell the `Worker` what to do by sending it the `RequestComplex` message. Rather, the `Server` *forwards* the `RequestComplex` message to the `Worker`. By forwarding, the `Worker` receives the message as if it had been sent directly by the `Client`, which means that the special sender `ActorRef` has the address of the `Client`, not of the `Server`. Therefore, the `Worker` is able to act on behalf of the `Server`, as if the `Server` itself had done the work. Yet, the `Server` is freed from acting as a mediator between the `Client` and the `Worker`, not to mention that the `Server` is ready to process other messages while the `Worker` does its thing.

Correlation Identifier

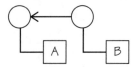

Establish a Correlation Identifier to allow requestor and replier actors to associate a reply message with a specific, originating request message. The unique identifier must be associated with both the message sent by the requestor and the message sent by the replier, as shown in Figure 6.6.

In its discussion of Correlation Identifier, *Enterprise Integration Patterns* [EIP] suggests creating an independent, unique message identifier on the request message and then using that message identifier as the Correlation Identifier in the reply message. The unique message identifier would generally be

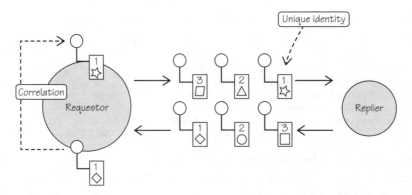

Figure 6.6 A `Requestor` attaches a Correlation Identifier to outgoing *Messages (130)* in order for the `Replier` to associate its replies with the originating Message.

generated by the messaging system and would be attached only to the message header. Additionally, *Enterprise Integration Patterns* [EIP] suggests setting the identifier as the *request ID* on the request message but to be named *correlation ID* on the reply message.

In principle this is also what is done with the Actor model. Yet, modeling messages for use with the Actor model works a bit differently as well. For example, there is no separate message header, unless one is created as part of the message's type. Thus, it makes more sense to design message types to contain unique *business identities*. In this case, you would not need to name the identifier using different names on each message type. In fact, it would most often be best to name the identifier the same on all message types that contain it. That way, it's just a unique identity that is business specific.

Each of the following message types are correlated using the `rfqId` (request for quotation ID):

```
case class RequestPriceQuote(
    rfqId: String,
    itemId: String,
    retailPrice: Double,
    orderTotalRetailPrice: Double)

case class PriceQuote(
    quoterId: String,
    rfqId: String,
    itemId: String,
    retailPrice: Double,
    discountPrice: Double)

case class PriceQuoteTimedOut(rfqId: String)
```

```
case class RequiredPriceQuotesForFulfillment(
    rfqId: String,
    quotesRequested: Int)

case class QuotationFulfillment(
    rfqId: String,
    quotesRequested: Int,
    priceQuotes: Seq[PriceQuote],
    requester: ActorRef)

case class BestPriceQuotation(
    rfqId: String,
    priceQuotes: Seq[PriceQuote])
```

Although *Enterprise Integration Patterns* [EIP] focuses on the use of Correlation Identifier with *Request-Reply (209)*, there is no reason to limit its use to that pattern. For example, you should associate a Correlation Identifier as a unique business identity with all messages involved in a long-running process [IDDD], whether using ad hock process management or a formal *Process Manager (292)*.

Message Sequence

Use a Message Sequence when you need to send one logical *Message (130)* that must be delivered as multiple physical *Messages (130)*. Together all the messages in the sequence form a batch, but the batch is delivered as separate elements. Each *Message (130)* will have the following:

- A unique Message Sequence identity, such as a *Correlation Identifier (215)*.

- A sequence number indicating the sequence of the particular message in the separated batch. The sequence could run from 1 to N or from 0 to N-1, where N is the total number of messages in the batch.

- Some flag or other indicator of the last message in the batch. This could also be achieved by placing a total on the first message to be sent.

On first considering the way the Actor model messages are sent and received, it may seem unnecessary to use a Message Sequence. Also discussed in *Resequencer (264)*, Akka direct asynchronous messaging has the following characteristics, as applicable in a discussion of *Message Sequence (217)*:

- Actor Batch-Sender sends messages M1, M2, M3 to Batch-Receiver.

Based on this scenario, you arrive at these facts:

1. If M1 is delivered, it must be delivered before M2 and M3.

2. If M2 is delivered, it must be delivered before M3.

3. Since there is no (default) guaranteed delivery, any of the messages M1, M2, and/or M3, may be dropped, in other words, not arrive at Batch-Receiver.

Although sequencing is not a problem in itself, note that the problem arises if any one message sent from Batch-Sender does not reach Batch-Receiver. Thus, when multiple messages comprising a batch must be delivered to Batch-Receiver for the use case to complete properly, you must assume that Batch-Receiver will be required to interact with Batch-Sender if Batch-Receiver detects missing messages from the batch.

When designing the interactions between Batch-Sender and Batch-Receiver, it may work best to design Batch-Receiver as a *Polling Consumer (362)*. In this case, the Batch-Sender tells the Batch-Receiver that a new batch is available, communicating the specifications of the batch. Then the Batch-Receiver asks for each messages in the batch in order. The Batch-Receiver moves to the next sequence in the batch only once the current message in the sequence is confirmed. The Batch-Receiver can perform retries as needed using schedulers, which is also discussed with regard to *Polling Consumer (362)*.

Otherwise, if the Batch-Sender drives the process by sending the message batch in an enumerated blast, the Batch-Receiver must be prepared to request redelivery for any sequence that it doesn't receive.

Message Expiration

If it is possible for a given message to become obsolete or in some way invalid because of a time lapse, use a *Message Expiration (218)* to control the timeout

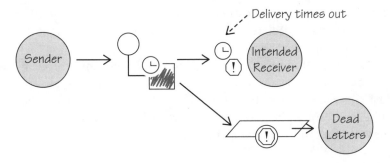

Figure 6.7 A Message Expiration is attached to a Message that may become stale.

(see Figure 6.7). While you have already dealt with the process timeouts in the *Scatter-Gather (272)* implementation, this is different. A Message Expiration is used to determine when a single message has expired, rather than setting a limit on the completion of a larger process.

When using message-based middleware, it is possible to ask the messaging system to expire a message before it is ever delivered. Currently Akka does not support a mailbox that automatically detects expired messages. No worries, you can accomplish that on your own quite easily. You could create a custom mailbox type or just place the expiration behavior on the message itself. There are advantages to both. Here I explain how to do this using a trait for messages. Whether or not the mailbox supports expiring messages, the message itself must supply some parts of the solution.

It is the message sender that should determine the possibility of message expiration. After all, the sender is in the best position to set the message time-to-live based on some user or system specification for the type of operation being executed. Here is how it can be done. First design a trait that allows an extending message to specify the `timeToLive` value.

```
trait ExpiringMessage {
  val occurredOn = System.currentTimeMillis()
  val timeToLive: Long

  def isExpired(): Boolean = {
    val elapsed = System.currentTimeMillis() - occurredOn

    elapsed > timeToLive
  }
}
```

The trait initializes its `occurredOn` with the timestamp of when it was created. The trait also declares an abstract `timeToLive`, which must be set by the extending concrete class.

The `ExpiringMessage` trait also provides behavior, through method `isExpired()`, that indicates whether the message has expired. This operation first gets the system's current time in milliseconds, subtracts the number of milliseconds since the message was created (`occurredOn`) to calculate the elapsed time, and then compares the elapsed time to the client-specified `timeToLive`.

Note that this basic algorithm does not consider differences in time zones, which may need to be given consideration depending on the system's network topology. At a minimum, this approach assumes that different computing nodes that host various actors will have their system clocks synchronized closely enough to make this sort of calculation successful.

This trait is used in the implementation sample, which defines a `Place-Order` *Command Message (202)*:

```
package co.vaughnvernon.reactiveenterprise.messageexpiration

import java.util.concurrent.TimeUnit
import java.util.Date
import scala.concurrent._
import scala.concurrent.duration._
import scala.util._
import ExecutionContext.Implicits.global
import akka.actor._
import co.vaughnvernon.reactiveenterprise._

case class PlaceOrder(
    id: String,
    itemId: String,
    price: Money,
    timeToLive: Long)
  extends ExpiringMessage

object MessageExpiration extends CompletableApp(3) {
  val purchaseAgent =
        system.actorOf(
            Props[PurchaseAgent],
            "purchaseAgent")

  val purchaseRouter =
        system.actorOf(
            Props(classOf[PurchaseRouter],
                    purchaseAgent),
            "purchaseRouter")
```

```
    purchaseRouter ! PlaceOrder("1", "11", 50.00, 1000)
    purchaseRouter ! PlaceOrder("2", "22", 250.00, 100)
    purchaseRouter ! PlaceOrder("3", "33", 32.95, 10)

    awaitCompletion
    println("MessageExpiration: is completed.")
}
```

In the `MessageExpiration` sample runner, you create two actors, a `Pur-chaseAgent` and a `PurchaseRouter`. In a real application, the `Purchase-Router` could be a *Content-Based Router (228)* and route to any number of different purchase agents based on the kind of purchase message. Here you aren't really concerned about that kind of routing but use the `Purchase-Router` to simulate delays in message delivery from various causes.

```
class PurchaseRouter(purchaseAgent: ActorRef) extends Actor {
  val random = new Random((new Date()).getTime)

  def receive = {
    case message: Any =>
      val millis = random.nextInt(100) + 1
      println(s"PurchaseRouter: delaying delivery of↵
$message for $millis milliseconds")
      val duration =
            Duration.create(millis, TimeUnit.MILLISECONDS)
      context
        .system
        .scheduler
        .scheduleOnce(duration, purchaseAgent, message)
  }
}
```

To familiarize yourself even more with the Akka `Scheduler`, you can see another example in *Resequencer (264)*.

Now, more to the point, this is how the actual `PurchaseAgent` checks for Message Expiration and branches accordingly:

```
class PurchaseAgent extends Actor {
  def receive = {
    case placeOrder: PlaceOrder =>
      if (placeOrder.isExpired()) {
        context.system.deadLetters ! placeOrder
        println(s"PurchaseAgent: delivered expired↵
$placeOrder to dead letters")
      } else {
        println(s"PurchaseAgent: placing order for↵
```

```
$placeOrder")
    }

  MessageExpiration.completedStep()

  case message: Any =>
    println(s"PurchaseAgent: received unexpected:↵
$message")
 }
}
```

If the `PlaceOrder` message is expired, the `PurchaseAgent` sends the message to the Akka `ActorSystem`'s special `deadLetters` actor, which implements the *Dead Letter Channel (172)*. Note that *Enterprise Integration Patterns* [EIP] discusses the possibility of expired messages being delivered to a different *Message Channel (128)* for one reason or another, but the motivation is the same. You also have the option to ignore the message altogether.

Here's the output from running the process:

```
PurchaseRouter: delaying delivery of PlaceOrder(↵
1,11,50.0,1000) for 87 milliseconds
PurchaseRouter: delaying delivery of PlaceOrder(↵
2,22,250.0,100) for 63 milliseconds
PurchaseRouter: delaying delivery of PlaceOrder(↵
3,33,32.95,10) for 97 milliseconds
PurchaseAgent: placing order for PlaceOrder(↵
2,22,250.0,100)
PurchaseAgent: placing order for PlaceOrder(↵
1,11,50.0,1000)
PurchaseAgent: delivered expired PlaceOrder(↵
3,33,32.95,10) to dead letters
MessageExpiration: is completed.
```

Format Indicator

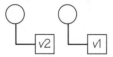

Use a Format Indicator to specify the current compositional definition of a given *Message (130)* type. This technique is discussed in the "Integrating Bounded Contexts" chapter in *Implementing Domain-Driven Design* [IDDD] by using a Format Indicator as part of a *Published Language* [IDDD].

When a *Command Message (202)*, a *Document Message (204)*, or an *Event Message (207)* is first defined, it contains all the information necessary to support all consumers. Otherwise, the systems depending on the given message—in fact, depending on the many messages needed for a complete implementation—would not work. Yet, within even a short period of time any given message type could fail to pack all of the current information for the changing requirements. I'm not limiting this discussion to just one system but possibly many that are integrated.

Over time, there is simply no way that the original definition of all solutionwide messages will remain unchanged. As requirements change, at least some messages must also change. As new integrating systems are added to the overall solution, new messages must be added, and existing messages must be refined. The use of a Format Indicator, as shown in Figure 6.8, can ease the tension between systems that can continue to use the original or earlier format and those that force changes and thus must consume the very latest definition.

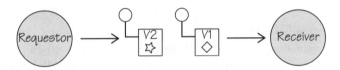

Figure 6.8 Use a Format Indicator to specify the current compositional definition of a given *Message (130)* type.

As *Enterprise Integration Patterns* [EIP] asserts, some systems can continue to support the original format of any given message. Even so, newer integrators or subsystems with more demanding refinement goals will force existing message types to be enhanced. Quite possibly no two teams involved in the overall solution development will be able to agree on synchronized release dates, let alone merging the schedules of every team involved.

So, how does a Format Indicator work? *Enterprise Integration Patterns* [EIP] defines three possibilities, and I add a fourth, shown here:

- *Version Number*: This approach is discussed in *Implementing Domain-Driven Design* [IDDD]. Each message type embeds a version number as an integer or a text string. The version allows consuming systems to branch on deserialization or parsing[1] logic based on the indicated mes-

---

1. While parsing may sound evil, *Implementing Domain-Driven Design* [IDDD] discusses a very simple and type-safe approach that is easy to maintain.

sage format. Generally, at least some, if not most, of the consuming systems may be able to ignore the version number as long as all message changes are additive rather than subtractive. In other words, don't take current correct information properties away from working subsystems; only add on newly required properties.

- *Foreign Key*: This could be the filename of a schema, a document definition, or other kind of format, such as `"messagetype.xsd"`. It could be a URI/URL or some other kind of identity, such as a key that allows for a database lookup. Retrieving the contents of what the foreign key points to would provide the format's definition. This may be less effective since it requires all message consumers to have access to the location that the foreign key points to.

- *Format Document*: Use this to embed the full format definition, such as a schema, into the message itself. This has the obvious size and transport disadvantages when the containing message must be passed between systems.

- *New Extended Message Type*: This approach actually doesn't modify the older message format at all but instead creates a new message that is a superset of the previous message format. Thus, all subsystems that depend only on the original/current version of a message will continue to work, while all subsystems that require the new message can recognize it by its new and distinct type. The new message type name may be closely associated with the one that it extends. For example, if an original *Event Message (207)* is named `OrderPlaced`, the newer extending message could be named `OrderPlacedExt2`. Adding an increasing digit at the end of the message name will allow it to be enhanced multiple times.

Beware When Defining a New Extended Message Type

Defining a New Extended Message Type (the fourth approach in the previous list) may require subsystem actors that happily consume the older message type and that don't understand the new message type to safely ignore the new ones. This may mean logging any newer message types only as a warning rather than interrupting normal system operations with a fatal error. This approach also assumes that both the older and newer types will continue to be sent, at least until all systems can support the extended message type. Otherwise, all systems that were content with the older message type will have to be enhanced to recognize and consume the newest message type, which defeats the purpose of Format Indicator.

The following uses the Version Number approach to enhance the Execute-BuyOrder *Command Message (202)*:

```scala
// version 1
case class ExecuteBuyOrder(
    portfolioId: String,
    symbol: String,
    quantity: Int,
    price: Money,
    version: Int) {
  def this(portfolioId: String, symbol: String,
               quantity: Int, price: Money)
    = this(portfolioId, symbol, quantity, price , 1)
}

// version 2
case class ExecuteBuyOrder(
    portfolioId: String,
    symbol: String,
    quantity: Int,
    price: Money,
    dateTimeOrdered: Date,
    version: Int) {
  def this(portfolioId: String, symbol: String,
          quantity: Int, price: Money)
    = this(portfolioId, symbol, quantity,
          price, new Date(), 2)
}
```

Version 1 of the ExecuteBuyOrder message specifies a total of four business properties: portfolioId, symbol, quantity, and price. On the other hand, version 2 requires a total of five business properties: portfolioId, symbol, quantity, price, and dateTimeOrdered. The design of both versions of ExecuteBuyOrder allows clients to construct both versions passing only four parameters.

```scala
val executeBuyOrder = ExecuteBuyOrder(portfolioId, symbol,
                                  quantity, price)
```

In version 2, the dateTimeOrdered is automatically provided by the constructor override. The Format Indicator version adds an additional property to each of the message types. An overridden constructor on each version allows for the instantiation of ExecuteBuyOrder with the version indicator defaulted to the correct value, either 1 or 2.

Since this is a *Command Message (202)*, you can assume that it is the defining and consuming subsystem (one and the same) that requires the new `dateTimeOrdered` property to be provided. Yet, it can still support both versions of the message by providing a reasonable default for all version 1 clients.

```
class StockTrader(tradingBus: ActorRef) extends Actor {
  ...
  def receive = {
    case buy: ExecuteBuyOrder =>
      val orderExecutionStartedOn =
        if (buy.version == 1)
          new Date()
        else
          buy.dateTimeOrdered
      ...
  }
}
```

Although all version 1 clients will have their buy orders executed based on a slightly inaccurate `orderExecutionStartedOn` date and time value, they can continue to function with the enhanced `StockTrader` actor. It is likely, however, that version 1 of `ExecuteBuyOrder` will be deprecated and all clients will have to update to version 2 by some near-term cutoff.

Summary

In this chapter, you surveyed the kinds of *Messages (130)* your actors can sent and receive and how the intent of each operation determines the kind of *Message (130)* you will use. You will use *Command Message (202)* to request an operation to be performed, a *Document Message (204)* to reply to a query request, and an *Event Message (207)* to convey that something has happened in your actor system's domain model. A *Command Message (202)* and a *Document Message (204)* will be used together to form a *Request-Reply (209)*. The Actor model always provides the *Return Address (211)* of the actor to which the reply part of *Request-Reply (209)* should be sent. You also saw how to leverage a *Correlation Identifier (215)* to associate a reply with a given request and how you can use *Message Sequence (217)* when the order of messages to be handled is important. When messages can become stale, use a *Message Expiration (218)* to indicate the "shelf life." You also saw how versions of messages can be set by using *Format Indicator (222)*.

Chapter 7

Message Routing

In Chapter 4, "Messaging with Actors," you were introduced to the basic idea of *Message Routers (140)* and why they should be used, both in your local actor system and beyond, for integration purposes. Routers allow you to decouple the message source from the message destination, and you can place business logic in any given *Message Router (140)* to determine how the routing should take place. There's nothing inherently wrong with a *Message Router (140)* being responsible for the business logic, but depending on the type of router used, you can limit the amount of business logic needed.

Since routing can be used both within an Akka cluster and across clusters for integration, remember that routing to remote routees is at your disposal. Otherwise, it would be impossible to use Akka-based routers for integration purposes, other than for implementing *Message Bridges (185)*. You can divide routers into three categories.

- *Simple routers*: A *Content-Based Router (228)* is one that inspects the content of received messages and routes them to specific business components. In an actor-only system, the *Content-Based Router (228)* would route only to other actors. A *Message Filter (232)* is a Content-Based Router that may choose to discard certain messages without routing them onward. When the routing logic is not static but based on dynamic properties of the application, you can employ a *Dynamic Router (237)*. You can use a *Recipient List (245)* router to send messages to multiple recipients, each of which performs a different operation based on a single message. A *Splitter (254)* can be used to divide up a single message so that discrete functions can be performed based on different parts of one message. Because a *Splitter (254)* divides work, it may also need to employ an *Aggregator (257)* to bring diverse results back into a single form. And because a *Splitter (254)* and *Aggregator (257)* must regather messages in the proper order, you can make use of a *Resequencer (264)*.

- *Composed routers*: A composed router is one that takes any number of simple routers and composes them into a single kind of router to perform a specific job. For example, a *Composed Message Processor (270)* is such a router, as is *Scatter-Gather (272)*, and both can use a *Routing Slip (285)* to help out with routing to various routees.

- *Architectural routers*: When you think about various kinds of routers, they may certainly be joined to make a coarse-grained *Pipes and Filters (135)* architecture. Another type is a *Message Broker (308)*, which can form a large network of subnetworks of message routers, altogether comprising a hub-and-spoke architectural style. The *Message Broker (308)* can be used to solve a specific class of problem, which may be comparable to a *Message Bus (192)*.

At the introduction of Chapter 7 of *Enterprise Integration Patterns* [EIP], there is a useful diagram that helps you decide which patterns can be used under various circumstances. Of course, each of the pattern problem solvers are described herein, but you may find the *Enterprise Integration Patterns* [EIP] diagram a useful reference.

Content-Based Router

As noted in *Splitter (254)*, a Content-Based Router has a different motivation. While both of these router types are designed to route a message based on message content, the Content-Based Router doesn't break up the composite parts of one message into multiple messages as does a *Splitter (254)*. Rather, it routes the whole message based on some message content analysis.

Further, in contrast to *Message Filter (232)*, which removes unwanted messages from the receiving *Message Channel (128)*, a Content-Based Router ensures that unwanted messages never reach a system that cannot consume them. At the same time, a Content-Based Router must route all messages to the systems with which they are compatible.

The Content-Based Router example used by *Enterprise Integration Patterns* [EIP] is an order system that must route each order to the inventory system to check on order item availability (see Figure 7.1). This assumes that a given order has only those order items that are kept by one of two or more inventory systems. If, on the other hand, a single order can have multiple order items each potentially kept by a different Inventory System, you'd need to use a *Splitter (254)* to check on availability.

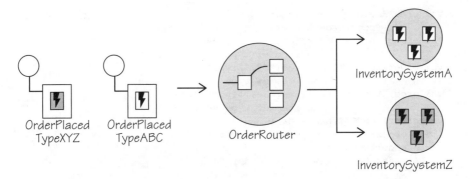

Figure 7.1 A Content-Based Router distinguishes order *Messages (130)* meant for two different inventory systems.

Here's an example of using a Content-Based Router to check on inventory availability:

```
package co.vaughnvernon.reactiveenterprise.contentbasedrouter

import scala.collection.Map
import akka.actor._
import co.vaughnvernon.reactiveenterprise._

case class Order(id: String, orderType: String,
                 orderItems: Map[String, OrderItem]) {
  val grandTotal: Double =
        orderItems.values.map(orderItem =>
          orderItem.price).sum

  override def toString = {
    s"Order($id, $orderType, $orderItems,↵
 Totaling: $grandTotal)"
  }
}

case class OrderItem(
     id: String, itemType: String,
     description: String, price: Double) {
  override def toString = {
    s"OrderItem($id, $itemType, '$description', $price)"
  }
}

case class OrderPlaced(order: Order)

object ContentBasedRouter extends CompletableApp(3) {
```

```
    val orderRouter = system.actorOf(
            Props[OrderRouter], "orderRouter")
    val orderItem1 = OrderItem("1", "TypeABC.4",
                    "An item of type ABC.4.", 29.95)
    val orderItem2 = OrderItem("2", "TypeABC.1",
                    "An item of type ABC.1.", 99.95)
    val orderItem3 = OrderItem("3", "TypeABC.9",
                    "An item of type ABC.9.", 14.95)
    val orderItemsOfTypeA = Map(
        orderItem1.itemType -> orderItem1,
        orderItem2.itemType -> orderItem2,
        orderItem3.itemType -> orderItem3)

    orderRouter ! OrderPlaced(Order(
                "123", "TypeABC", orderItemsOfTypeA))

    val orderItem4 = OrderItem("4", "TypeXYZ.2",
                    "An item of type XYZ.2.", 74.95)
    val orderItem5 = OrderItem("5", "TypeXYZ.1",
                    "An item of type XYZ.1.", 59.95)
    val orderItem6 = OrderItem("6", "TypeXYZ.7",
                    "An item of type XYZ.7.", 29.95)
    val orderItem7 = OrderItem("7", "TypeXYZ.5",
                    "An item of type XYZ.5.", 9.95)
    val orderItemsOfTypeX = Map(
        orderItem4.itemType -> orderItem4,
        orderItem5.itemType -> orderItem5,
        orderItem6.itemType -> orderItem6,
        orderItem7.itemType -> orderItem7)

    orderRouter ! OrderPlaced(Order("124", "TypeXYZ",
                    orderItemsOfTypeB))

    awaitCompletion
    println("ContentBasedRouter: is completed.")
}

class OrderRouter extends Actor {
  val inventorySystemA =
            context.actorOf(Props[InventorySystemA],
                            "inventorySystemA")
  val inventorySystemX =
            context.actorOf(Props[InventorySystemX],
                            "inventorySystemX")

  def receive = {
    case orderPlaced: OrderPlaced =>
      orderPlaced.order.orderType match {
        case "TypeABC" =>
          println(s"OrderRouter: routing $orderPlaced")
          inventorySystemA ! orderPlaced
```

```
        case "TypeXYZ" =>
          println(s"OrderRouter: routing $orderPlaced")
          inventorySystemX ! orderPlaced
      }

      ContentBasedRouter.completedStep()
    case _ =>
      println("OrderRouter: received unexpected message")
  }
}

class InventorySystemA extends Actor {
  def receive = {
    case OrderPlaced(order) =>
      println(s"InventorySystemA: handling $order")
      ContentBasedRouter.completedStep()
    case _ =>
      println("InventorySystemA: unexpected message")
  }
}

class InventorySystemX extends Actor {
  def receive = {
    case OrderPlaced(order) =>
      println(s"InventorySystemX: handling $order")
      ContentBasedRouter.completedStep()
    case _ =>
      println("InventorySystemX: unexpected message")
  }
}
```

This process produces the following (partial) output:

```
OrderRouter: routing OrderPlaced(Order(123, TypeABC,↵
 Map(TypeABC.4 -> OrderItem(1, TypeABC.4, 'An item of↵
 type ABC.4.', 29.95), TypeABC.1 -> OrderItem(2, ↵
TypeABC.1, 'An item of type ABC.1.', 99.95), TypeABC.9↵
 -> OrderItem(3, TypeABC.9, 'An item of type ABC.9.',↵
 14.95)), Totaling: 144.85))
...
ContentBasedRouter: is completed.
InventorySystemX: handling Order(124, TypeXYZ, Map(↵
TypeXYZ.2 -> OrderItem(4, TypeXYZ.2, 'An item of type↵
 XYZ.2.', 74.95), TypeXYZ.1 -> OrderItem(5, TypeXYZ.1,↵
 'An item of type XYZ.1.', 59.95), TypeXYZ.7 -> ↵
OrderItem(6, TypeXYZ.7, 'An item of type XYZ.7.',↵
 29.95), TypeXYZ.5 -> OrderItem(7, TypeXYZ.5, 'An item↵
 of type XYZ.5.', 9.95)), Totaling: 174.80)
```

The Content-Based Router—in this example the `OrderRouter`—checks every `Order` for some specific content to determine how to route each one. Under some conditions `OrderRouter` determines that available inventory must be checked by inventory system A, while others must be determined by inventory system X.

In this example, the `OrderRouter` uses only the `orderType` content to route `OrderPlaced` messages to a specific inventory system. Even so, there is no reason why the `OrderRouter` could not use other or additional content to make a careful examination of routing requirements. You may also consider whether the `OrderPlaced` message itself could supply some behavior to help with this, shielding the `OrderRouter` from having deep knowledge of `OrderPlaced` content. Yet, depending on team structure and who is responsible for designing the `OrderPlaced` message versus the `OrderRouter`, you may not be able to depend on another team to supply special behavior for the router's needs. However, if `OrderPlaced` is not an exact copy of a domain object—and ideally it is not—but produced by a *Content Filter (321)* or *Content Enricher (317)*, the message may indeed contribute to ease of routing.

Message Filter

Use a Message Filter when the possibility exists that your system could receive messages that are not of interest or otherwise incompatible and you need to discard those unwanted messages. Figure 7.2 illustrates this pattern.

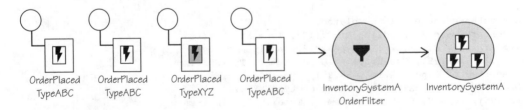

Figure 7.2 A Message Filter is used to discard unwanted *Messages (130)* sent to the inventory system.

The *Content-Based Router (228)* demonstrates how messages of various types can be routed to specific systems based on message type compatibility. In other words, if a specific system supports a specific message type, messages of that type are routed to that specific system by a *Content-Based Router (228)*. This likely means that the router is deployed as part of the sending system, or exists as a kind of hub that acts as a proxy to the actual destination system. Hence, when employing a *Content-Based Router (228)*, a target system will never be sent a message that is incompatible with its processing goals.

A Message Filter is different in that the system receiving messages may encounter those that are incompatible with its processing goals because the sending system has no knowledge—or has out-of-date knowledge—of the kinds of messages that can and cannot be handled by the target. Thus, the target system must filter out incompatible messages prior to executing the core business process. At the same time, the Message Filter on the target system must forward messages to the actor that manages the core processing. In this case, the Message Filter appears to be the target system but in reality is only a proxy.

As discussed in *Content-Based Router (228)*, consider the `OrderPlaced` events that are sent to `InventorySystemA` and `InventorySystemX`. To introduce the Message Filter example, rather than routing specific message types to specific inventory systems, you will send orders of `"TypeABC"` and of `"TypeXYZ"` to both `InventorySystemA` and `InventorySystemX`. Here is the driver application:

```
object MessageFilter extends CompletableApp (4) {
  val inventorySystemA =
        system.actorOf(
          Props[InventorySystemA],
          "inventorySystemA")
  val actualInventorySystemX =
        system.actorOf(
          Props[InventorySystemX],
          "inventorySystemX")
  val inventorySystemX =
        system.actorOf(
          Props(classOf[InventorySystemXMessageFilter],
            actualInventorySystemX),
        "inventorySystemXMessageFilter")

  val orderItem1 = OrderItem("1", "TypeABC.4",
                    "An item of type ABC.4.", 29.95)
  val orderItem2 = OrderItem("2", "TypeABC.1",
                    "An item of type ABC.1.", 99.95)
  val orderItem3 = OrderItem("3", "TypeABC.9",
                    "An item of type ABC.9.", 14.95)
  val orderItemsOfTypeA = Map(
```

```
                    orderItem1.itemType -> orderItem1,
                    orderItem2.itemType -> orderItem2,
                     orderItem3.itemType -> orderItem3)
    inventorySystemA ! OrderPlaced(Order("123", "TypeABC",
                               orderItemsOfTypeA))
    inventorySystemX ! OrderPlaced(Order("123", "TypeABC",
                               orderItemsOfTypeA))

    val orderItem4 = OrderItem("4", "TypeXYZ.2",
                            "An item of type XYZ.2.", 74.95)
    val orderItem5 = OrderItem("5", "TypeXYZ.1",
                            "An item of type XYZ.1.", 59.95)
    val orderItem6 = OrderItem("6", "TypeXYZ.7",
                            "An item of type XYZ.7.", 29.95)
    val orderItem7 = OrderItem("7", "TypeXYZ.5",
                            "An item of type XYZ.5.", 9.95)
    val orderItemsOfTypeX = Map(
                    orderItem4.itemType -> orderItem4,
                    orderItem5.itemType -> orderItem5,
                    orderItem6.itemType -> orderItem6,
                    orderItem7.itemType -> orderItem7)
    inventorySystemA ! OrderPlaced(Order("124", "TypeXYZ",
                orderItemsOfTypeX))
    inventorySystemX ! OrderPlaced(Order("124", "TypeXYZ",
                orderItemsOfTypeX))

    awaitCompletion
    println("MessageFilter: is completed.")
}
```

Since each of the two inventory systems receive messages of both types, it is the responsibility of the individual systems to filter out message types that they do not support. Each of the inventory systems will take a different approach.

First let's consider how `InventorySystemA` filters. Because of the way an actor's receive block can be implemented, the Message Filter could be designed on the `InventorySystemA` actor, for example.

```
class InventorySystemA extends Actor {
  def receive = {
    case OrderPlaced(order) if (order.isType("TypeABC")) =>
      println(s"InventorySystemA: handling $order")
      MessageFilter.completedStep()
    case incompatibleOrder =>
      println(s"InventorySystemA: filtering out:↵
 $incompatibleOrder")
      MessageFilter.completedStep()
  }
}
```

This simple Message Filter implementation rejects all `OrderPlaced` events that don't contain an `Order` of `"TypeABC"`. However, it may be advantageous to implement the Message Filter as a separate actor, as is the case in `InventorySystemX`.

```
class InventorySystemX extends Actor {
  def receive = {
    case OrderPlaced(order) =>
      println(s"InventorySystemX: handling $order")
      MessageFilter.completedStep()
    case _ =>
      println("InventorySystemX: unexpected message")
      MessageFilter.completedStep()
  }
}

class InventorySystemXMessageFilter(
        actualInventorySystemX: ActorRef)
    extends Actor {
  def receive = {
    case orderPlaced: OrderPlaced
          if (orderPlaced.order.isType("TypeXYZ")) =>
      actualInventorySystemX forward orderPlaced
      MessageFilter.completedStep()
    case incompatibleOrder =>
      println(s"InventorySystemXMessageFilter: filtering:↵
$incompatibleOrder")
      MessageFilter.completedStep()
  }
}
```

As far as the driver application is concerned, `InventorySystemXMessageFilter` is the `InventorySystemX` because it references that actor as `InventorySystemX`.

```
object MessageFilter extends CompletableApp (4) {
  ...
  val actualInventorySystemX =
        system.actorOf(
              Props[InventorySystemX],
              "inventorySystemX")
  val inventorySystemX =
        system.actorOf(
              Props(classOf[InventorySystemXMessageFilter],
                    actualInventorySystemX),
              "inventorySystemXMessageFilter")
```

In reality, however, the Message Filter held by the driver's `Inventory-SystemX` actor reference is concerned only with forwarding system-compatible messages and filtering out all others. The Message Filter is passed a constructor argument, `actualInventorySystemX`, which is a reference to the actor that serves as the entry point to the actual inventory system. When an `OrderPlaced` event is received that contains an `Order` of `"TypeXYZ"`, the Message Filter forwards the event to the actor referenced by `actualInventorySystemX`.

Here is the output produced when the driver application is run:

```
InventorySystemA: handling Order(123, TypeABC,↵
Map(TypeABC.4 -> OrderItem(1, TypeABC.4, 'An item↵
of type ABC.4.', 29.95), TypeABC.1 -> OrderItem(2,↵
TypeABC.1, 'An item of type ABC.1.', 99.95),↵
TypeABC.9 -> OrderItem(3, TypeABC.9, 'An item of↵
type ABC.9.', 14.95)), Totaling: 144.85)
InventorySystemXMessageFilter: filtering: OrderPlaced(↵
Order(123, TypeABC, Map(TypeABC.4 -> OrderItem(1,↵
TypeABC.4, 'An item of type ABC.4.', 29.95), TypeABC.1↵
-> OrderItem(2, TypeABC.1, 'An item of type ABC.1.',↵
99.95), TypeABC.9 -> OrderItem(3, TypeABC.9, 'An item↵
of type ABC.9.', 14.95)), Totaling: 144.85))
InventorySystemA: filtering: OrderPlaced(Order(124,↵
TypeXYZ, Map(TypeXYZ.2 -> OrderItem(4, TypeXYZ.2,↵
'An item of type XYZ.2.', 74.95), TypeXYZ.1 ->↵
OrderItem(5, TypeXYZ.1, 'An item of type XYZ.1.',↵
59.95), TypeXYZ.7 -> OrderItem(6, TypeXYZ.7, 'An↵
item of type XYZ.7.', 29.95), TypeXYZ.5 -> OrderItem(↵
7, TypeXYZ.5, 'An item of type XYZ.5.', 9.95)), Totaling:↵
174.79999999999998))
InventorySystemX: handling Order(124, TypeXYZ,↵
Map(TypeXYZ.2 -> OrderItem(4, TypeXYZ.2, 'An item↵
of type XYZ.2.', 74.95), TypeXYZ.1 -> OrderItem(5,↵
TypeXYZ.1, 'An item of type XYZ.1.', 59.95), TypeXYZ.7↵
-> OrderItem(6, TypeXYZ.7, 'An item of type XYZ.7.',↵
29.95), TypeXYZ.5 -> OrderItem(7, TypeXYZ.5, 'An item↵
of type XYZ.5.', 9.95)), Totaling: 174.79999999999998)
MessageFilter: is completed.
```

One major advantage to implementing a separate `InventorySystemX-MessageFilter` is that it can be maintained separate from the `Inventory-SystemX` itself. In contrast, the `InventorySystemA` actor must be changed each time the new message type is supported or a previously supported message type is no longer compatible. One disadvantage of the `InventorySys-temX` design could be the slight overhead of introducing another actor to filter, but any overhead is minimal. You would likely choose in favor of the strength of the *Pipes and Filters (135)* architecture demonstrated by `InventorySys-temX` and its Message Filter.

Dynamic Router

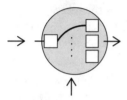

If some of the other routing patterns such as *Splitter (254)* and *Content-Based Router (228)* seem a bit commonplace, the Dynamic Router offers a more challenging design. With this router there are several moving parts, and anything that's *dynamic* is always more fun to code and discuss. Besides, it uses rules, and rules have a sort of intrigue about them. The rules aren't that complex, but it's an improvement over those observed in *Splitter (254)* and *Content-Based Router (228)*.

To receive messages from a Dynamic Router, an actor must register interest in a given message, as depicted in Figure 7.3. With the most basic of registration processes, an actor would tell a Dynamic Router that it is interested in a specific type of message. Or there could be more elaborate rules that require

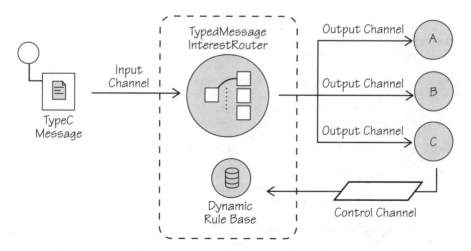

Figure 7.3 This Dynamic Router routes *Messages (130)* only to actors that register interest in specific kinds.

the Dynamic Router to perform a multilevel lookup to resolve the actor to receive a given message.

In *Enterprise Integration Patterns* [EIP], the decision was to create a last-registration-wins rule base. Stated another way, the rule is such that whichever interested party is the last one to register for a given message type, that interested party will receive all the messages for that type. In that example, the rule is simply the name of the message of interest, and a hash table stores the message type as the key and the receiver's queue name as the value. This means the most latent registrant's queue name will replace the value previously associated with the specific message type key.

This example uses a similar approach but registers actors rather than queue names. Also, if more than one actor registers for the same message type, this Dynamic Router holds it as a secondary receiver. It's not that the secondary receiver will be sent all the same messages as the primary registrant. That would be an implementation of Recipient List, which is considered a violation of Dynamic Router. Rather, the secondary receiver actor is held in case the primary actor decides it no longer has interest in the specific message type. When the primary actor deregisters, the secondary is swapped in to take its place.

Here's a look at the Dynamic Router control code, which creates actors and runs the example:

```
package co.vaughnvernon.reactiveenterprise.dynamicrouter

import reflect.runtime.currentMirror
import akka.actor._
import co.vaughnvernon.reactiveenterprise._

case class InterestedIn(messageType: String)
case class NoLongerInterestedIn(messageType: String)

case class TypeAMessage(description: String)
case class TypeBMessage(description: String)
case class TypeCMessage(description: String)
case class TypeDMessage(description: String)

object DynamicRouter extends CompletableApp(5) {
  val dunnoInterested =
        system.actorOf(
              Props[DunnoInterested],
              "dunnoInterested")

  val typedMessageInterestRouter =
        system.actorOf(
              Props(classOf[TypedMessageInterestRouter],
                dunnoInterested, 4, 1),
```

```
                      "typedMessageInterestRouter")

    val typeAInterest =
        system.actorOf(
            Props(classOf[TypeAInterested],
                typedMessageInterestRouter),
            "typeAInterest")

    val typeBInterest =
        system.actorOf(
            Props(classOf[TypeBInterested],
                typedMessageInterestRouter),
            "typeBInterest")

    val typeCInterest =
        system.actorOf(
            Props(classOf[TypeCInterested],
                typedMessageInterestRouter),
            "typeCInterest")

    val typeCAlsoInterested =
        system.actorOf(
            Props(classOf[TypeCAlsoInterested],
                typedMessageInterestRouter),
            "typeCAlsoInterested")

    awaitCanStartNow()

    typedMessageInterestRouter !
        TypeAMessage("Message of TypeA.")
    typedMessageInterestRouter !
        TypeBMessage("Message of TypeB.")
    typedMessageInterestRouter !
        TypeCMessage("Message of TypeC.")

    awaitCanCompleteNow()

    typedMessageInterestRouter !
        TypeCMessage("Another message of TypeC.")
    typedMessageInterestRouter !
        TypeDMessage("Message of TypeD.")

    awaitCompletion
    println("DynamicRouter: is completed.")
}
```

Notice a few extra await conditions here. These have been added for two reasons. The first one, `awaitCanStartNow()`, allows time for the interested actors to fully register before any messages will be dispatched through the Dynamic Router (`TypedMessageInterestRouter`). The second one, awaitCanCompleteNow(), allows the primary `TypeCInterested` to be replaced with the secondary `TypeCAlsoInterested` when `TypeCInterested` deregisters. As a result, the first `TypeCMessage` is sent to `TypeCInterested`. The second `TypeCMessage` is sent to `TypeCAlsoInterested`.

Don't fear that this approach is being promoted as a worthwhile solution for production code. In fact, it is not. In the following text I explain the reason for this code, which is primarily to simplify the example.

As part of the overview, here's the output of this process:

```
TypeAInterested: received: TypeAMessage(Message of TypeA.)
TypeBInterested: received: TypeBMessage(Message of TypeB.)
TypeCInterested: received: TypeCMessage(Message of TypeC.)
TypeCAlsoInterested: received: TypeCMessage(Another↵
 message of TypeC.)
DunnoInterest: received undeliverable message:↵
 TypeDMessage(Message of TypeD.)
DynamicRouter: is completed.
```

Note that the final message, `TypeDMessage`, is not delivered to an actor that specializes in receiving that type. Rather, the `DunnoInterest` actor receives it. This can be viewed as a *dead letter*, or catchall, actor.

```
class DunnoInterested extends Actor {
  def receive = {
    case message: Any =>
      println(s"DunnoInterest: received undeliverable↵
 message: $message")
      DynamicRouter.completedStep()
  }
}
```

Next up are the actors interested in the special types of messages, `TypeAMessage`, `TypeBMessage`, and `TypeCMessage`. Upon construction, each of the actors registers interest in a specific message type, which they can do because they are endowed [Actor-Endowment] with a reference to `TypedMessageInterestRouter`.

```
class TypeAInterested(interestRouter: ActorRef)
    extends Actor {
  interestRouter !
        InterestedIn(TypeAMessage.getClass.getName)

  def receive = {
    case message: TypeAMessage =>
```

```
      println(s"TypeAInterested: received: $message")
      DynamicRouter.completedStep()
    case message: Any =>
      println(s"TypeAInterested: unexpected: $message")
  }
}

class TypeBInterested(interestRouter: ActorRef)
    extends Actor {
  interestRouter !
        InterestedIn(TypeBMessage.getClass.getName)

  def receive = {
    case message: TypeBMessage =>
      println(s"TypeBInterested: received: $message")
      DynamicRouter.completedStep()
    case message: Any =>
      println(s"TypeBInterested: unexpected: $message")
  }
}

class TypeCInterested(interestRouter: ActorRef)
    extends Actor {
  interestRouter !
        InterestedIn(TypeCMessage.getClass.getName)

  def receive = {
    case message: TypeCMessage =>
      println(s"TypeCInterested: received: $message")

      interestRouter ! NoLongerInterestedIn(
                    TypeCMessage.getClass.getName)

      DynamicRouter.completedStep()

    case message: Any =>
      println(s"TypeCInterested: unexpected: $message")
  }
}

class TypeCAlsoInterested(interestRouter: ActorRef)
    extends Actor {
  interestRouter !
        InterestedIn(TypeCMessage.getClass.getName)

  def receive = {
    case message: TypeCMessage =>
      println(s"TypeCAlsoInterested: received: $message")

      interestRouter ! NoLongerInterestedIn(
                    TypeCMessage.getClass.getName)
```

```
        DynamicRouter.completedStep()
      case message: Any =>
        println(s"TypeCAlsoInterested: unexpected: $message")
  }
}
```

Of these four actors, the two that register interest in `TypeCMessage` are particularly noteworthy. One will register first and become the primary. The other will registered as the secondary. (It usually happens that `TypeCInterested` is the primary and `TypeCAlsoInterested` the secondary.) After one of the two receives the first `TypeCMessage`, that specific actor sends a `NoLongerInterestedIn` message to the `TypedMessageInterestRouter`. This causes the `TypedMessageInterestRouter` to deregister the primary and replace it with the secondary.

This leads me to show the linchpin of the example, the Dynamic Router:

```
import scala.collection.mutable.Map

class TypedMessageInterestRouter(
    dunnoInterested: ActorRef,
    canStartAfterRegistered: Int,
    canCompleteAfterUnregistered: Int) extends Actor {

  val interestRegistry =
        Map[String, ActorRef]()
  val secondaryInterestRegistry =
        Map[String, ActorRef]()

  def receive = {
    case interestedIn: InterestedIn =>
      registerInterest(interestedIn)
    case noLongerInterestedIn: NoLongerInterestedIn =>
      unregisterInterest(noLongerInterestedIn)
    case message: Any =>
      sendFor(message)
  }

  def registerInterest(interestedIn: InterestedIn) = {
    val messageType =
        typeOfMessage(interestedIn.messageType)
    if (!interestRegistry.contains(messageType)) {
      interestRegistry(messageType) = sender
    } else {
      secondaryInterestRegistry(messageType) = sender
    }

    if (interestRegistry.size +
```

```
                secondaryInterestRegistry.size
                >= canStartAfterRegistered) {
      DynamicRouter.canStartNow()
    }
  }

  def sendFor(message: Any) = {
    val messageType =
              typeOfMessage(
                  currentMirror
                    .reflect(message)
                    .symbol
                    .toString)

    if (interestRegistry.contains(messageType)) {
      interestRegistry(messageType) forward message
    } else {
      dunnoInterested ! message
    }
  }

  def typeOfMessage(rawMessageType: String): String = {
    rawMessageType
        .replace('$', ' ')
        .replace('.', ' ')
        .split(' ')
        .last
        .trim
  }

  var unregisterCount: Int = 0

  def unregisterInterest(
        noLongerInterestedIn: NoLongerInterestedIn) = {
    val messageType =
        typeOfMessage(noLongerInterestedIn.messageType)

    if (interestRegistry.contains(messageType)) {
      val wasInterested = interestRegistry(messageType)

      if (wasInterested.compareTo(sender) == 0) {
        if (secondaryInterestRegistry
              .contains(messageType)) {
          val nowInterested =
              secondaryInterestRegistry
                  .remove(messageType)

          interestRegistry(messageType) =
                  nowInterested.get
        } else {
          interestRegistry.remove(messageType)
        }
```

```
            unregisterCount = unregisterCount + 1;
            if (unregisterCount >=
                this.canCompleteAfterUnregistered) {
                    DynamicRouter.canCompleteNow()
            }
          }
        }
      }
  }
```

The implementation is fairly straightforward. For starters, `TypedMessage-InterestRouter` can handle an `InterestedIn` message and a `NoLonger-InterestedIn` message. These two allow interested parties to register and deregister themselves for interest in a given type of message.

The final message filter accepts any other message type but will forward a given message only if there is a registered interest in its specific type.

```
...
  case message: Any =>
    sendFor(message)
...
def sendFor(message: Any) = {
  val messageType =
          typeOfMessage(
            currentMirror
              .reflect(message)
              .symbol
              .toString)

  if (interestRegistry.contains(messageType)) {
    interestRegistry(messageType) forward message
  } else {
    dunnoInterested ! message
  }
}
```

All other messages—those without a type-specific registered interest—are instead sent to `DunnoInterested`.

This example does well in pointing out the trouble that can come from assuming message order, synchronization of actors, and other temporal dependencies. This example guarantees that the primary actor interested in `TypeC-Message` is replaced by the secondary by building in a synchronization point. To keep the example as simple as possible, this was done using `Dynamic-Router.canCompleteNow()`. However, that approach is a bad idea for an actual application. Instead, a primary actor would have to be prepared to accept any number of `TypeCMessage` instances even after it has sent `No-LongerInterestedIn` to the `TypedMessageInterestRouter`, allowing time for the secondary actor to be registered as the primary.

   Otherwise, you'd have to work out another protocol. One possibility is for the `TypeCInterested` and `TypeCAlsoInterested` actors to establish a protocol for swapping registrations, but this would probably work best if the `TypedMessageInterestRouter` managed the negotiation or was at least included in it.

Note

You may be thinking that since the `TypedMessageInterestRouter` receives only one message at a time, the secondary (for example, `TypeCAlsoInterested`) will replace the primary (for example, `TypeCInterested`) before `TypedMessageInterestRouter` can dispatch the next `TypeCMessage`. That is true only if no `TypeCMessage` instances precede the specific `NoLongerInterestedIn` in the `TypedMessageInterestRouter` mailbox. Relying on that or any similar assumption will no doubt result in problems.

Recipient List

A Recipient List is analogous to the To and Cc fields in an e-mail message, where you specify any number of intended recipients of the e-mail message. Thus, a Recipient List may be predetermined depending on the kind of message being sent. Yet, it is also possible for a Recipient List to take on the characteristics of a *Dynamic Router (237)* in that the recipients may be determined by some set of business rules (see Figure 7.4).

   The example provided here performs price quoting. When the `Mountain-eeringSuppliesOrderProcessor` receives a `RequestForQuotation` message, it calculates a Recipient List based on a set of business rules, which means it is a kind of *Dynamic Router (237)*.

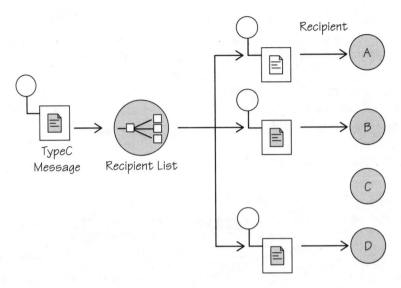

Figure 7.4 Use a Recipient List to distinguish which specific actors should receive a given *Message (130).*

The `MountaineeringSuppliesOrderProcessor` receives `PriceQuoteInterest` messages from any number of quoting services. The example includes the following quote engines, and each is an actor:

- `BudgetHikersPriceQuotes`

- `HighSierraPriceQuotes`

- `MountainAscentPriceQuotes`

- `PinnacleGearPriceQuotes`

- `RockBottomOuterwearPriceQuotes`

As each of these actors is created, it is given a reference to the `MountaineeringSuppliesOrderProcessor`. To the individual quote engine actor, the reference it receives is just an "interest registrar." The quote engine actor immediately sends a `PriceQuoteInterest` message to the registrar, indicating under what conditions it will accept `RequestPriceQuote` messages. Here's the `PriceQuoteInterest` message sent by Budget Hikers:

```
interestRegistrar ! PriceQuoteInterest(
        self.path.toString, self, 1.00, 1000.00)
```

This indicates that Budget Hikers wants to receive `RequestPriceQuote` messages for items that are part of orders with a total retail price of at least $1 and no more than $1,000. A higher-end retailer such as Pinnacle Gear specifies a different range.

```
interestRegistrar ! PriceQuoteInterest(
        self.path.toString, self, 250.00, 500000.00)
```

All retail orders that price out between $250 and $500,000 get the attention of Pinnacle Gear's pricing engine. (Everest expedition for ten, anyone?)

Here's the support message classes and the driver for the example:

```
package co.vaughnvernon.reactiveenterprise.recipientlist

import akka.actor._
import co.vaughnvernon.reactiveenterprise._

case class RequestForQuotation(
        rfqId: String,
        retailItems: Seq[RetailItem]) {
  val totalRetailPrice: Double =
        retailItems.map(retailItem =>
                retailItem.retailPrice).sum
}

case class RetailItem(
        itemId: String,
        retailPrice: Double)

case class PriceQuoteInterest(
        path: String,
        quoteProcessor: ActorRef,
        lowTotalRetail: Money,
        highTotalRetail: Money)

case class RequestPriceQuote(
        rfqId: String,
        itemId: String,
        retailPrice: Money,
        orderTotalRetailPrice: Money)

case class PriceQuote(
        rfqId: String,
        itemId: String,
        retailPrice: Money,
        discountPrice: Money)

object RecipientList extends CompletableApp(5) {
  val orderProcessor =
```

```
            system.actorOf(
                Props[MountaineeringSuppliesOrderProcessor],
                "orderProcessor")

    system.actorOf(
            Props(classOf[BudgetHikersPriceQuotes],
                orderProcessor),
            "budgetHikers")
    system.actorOf(
            Props(classOf[HighSierraPriceQuotes],
                orderProcessor),
            "highSierra")
    system.actorOf(
            Props(classOf[MountainAscentPriceQuotes],
                orderProcessor),
            "mountainAscent")
    system.actorOf(
            Props(classOf[PinnacleGearPriceQuotes],
                orderProcessor),
            "pinnacleGear")
    system.actorOf(
            Props(classOf[RockBottomOuterwearPriceQuotes],
                orderProcessor),
            "rockBottomOuterwear")

    orderProcessor ! RequestForQuotation("123",
        Vector(RetailItem("1", 29.95),
            RetailItem("2", 99.95),
            RetailItem("3", 14.95)))

    orderProcessor ! RequestForQuotation("125",
        Vector(RetailItem("4", 39.99),
            RetailItem("5", 199.95),
            RetailItem("6", 149.95),
            RetailItem("7", 724.99)))

    orderProcessor ! RequestForQuotation("129",
        Vector(RetailItem("8", 119.99),
            RetailItem("9", 499.95),
            RetailItem("10", 519.00),
            RetailItem("11", 209.50)))

    orderProcessor ! RequestForQuotation("135",
        Vector(RetailItem("12", 0.97),
            RetailItem("13", 9.50),
            RetailItem("14", 1.99)))

    orderProcessor ! RequestForQuotation("140",
        Vector(RetailItem("15", 107.50),
            RetailItem("16", 9.50),
            RetailItem("17", 599.99),
            RetailItem("18", 249.95),
```

```
              RetailItem("19", 789.99)))
}
```

As the `MountaineeringSuppliesOrderProcessor` receives each of the `RequestForQuotation` messages, it checks the business rules of every registered `PriceQuoteInterest`. If the `totalRetailPrice` of a given `RequestForQuotation` message falls between the low and high ranges for the interest, that interested price quote engine receives a `RequestPrice-Quote` message for each item in the order.

```
import scala.collection.mutable.Map

class MountaineeringSuppliesOrderProcessor

    extends Actor {
  val interestRegistry = Map[String, PriceQuoteInterest]()

  def calculateRecipientList(
      rfq: RequestForQuotation): Iterable[ActorRef] = {
    for {
      interest <- interestRegistry.values
      if (rfq.totalRetailPrice >= interest.lowTotalRetail)
      if (rfq.totalRetailPrice <= interest.highTotalRetail)
    } yield interest.quoteProcessor
  }

  def dispatchTo(
     rfq: RequestForQuotation,
     recipientList: Iterable[ActorRef]) = {
    recipientList.map { recipient =>
      rfq.retailItems.map { retailItem =>
        println("OrderProcessor: "
                + rfq.rfqId
                + " item: "
                + retailItem.itemId
                + " to: "
                + recipient.path.toString)
        recipient ! RequestPriceQuote(
                    rfq.rfqId,
                    retailItem.itemId,
                    retailItem.retailPrice,
                    rfq.totalRetailPrice)
      }
    }
  }

  def receive = {
    case interest: PriceQuoteInterest =>
      interestRegistry(interest.path) = interest
```

```
    case priceQuote: PriceQuote =>
      println(s"OrderProcessor: received: $priceQuote")
    case rfq: RequestForQuotation =>
      val recipientList = calculateRecipientList(rfq)
      dispatchTo(rfq, recipientList)
    case message: Any =>
      println(s"OrderProcessor: unexpected: $message")
  }
```

The MountaineeringSuppliesOrderProcessor method calculate-RecipientList() uses a Scala *for comprehension* to determine all the recipients based on the registered business rules. Given a Recipient List, the order processor then dispatches the items of a RequestForQuotation as Request-PriceQuote messages to each of the recipients.

Next are the individual pricing engines:

```
class BudgetHikersPriceQuotes(interestRegistrar: ActorRef)
        extends Actor {
  interestRegistrar ! PriceQuoteInterest(
                        self.path.toString,
                        self, 1.00, 1000.00)

  def receive = {
    case rpq: RequestPriceQuote =>
      val discount = discountPercentage(
                        rpq.orderTotalRetailPrice) *
                      rpq.retailPrice
      sender ! PriceQuote(rpq.rfqId, rpq.itemId,
                        rpq.retailPrice,
                        rpq.retailPrice - discount)

    case message: Any =>
      println(s"BudgetHikersPriceQuotes: unexpected:↵
$message")
  }

  def discountPercentage(
      orderTotalRetailPrice: Double) = {
    if (orderTotalRetailPrice <= 100.00) 0.02
    else if (orderTotalRetailPrice <= 399.99) 0.03
    else if (orderTotalRetailPrice <= 499.99) 0.05
    else if (orderTotalRetailPrice <= 799.99) 0.07
    else 0.075
  }
}

class HighSierraPriceQuotes(interestRegistrar: ActorRef)
        extends Actor {

  interestRegistrar ! PriceQuoteInterest(
```

```
                      self.path.toString, self,
                      100.00, 10000.00)

  def receive = {
    case rpq: RequestPriceQuote =>
     val discount = discountPercentage(
                     rpq.orderTotalRetailPrice) *
                     rpq.retailPrice
       sender ! PriceQuote(rpq.rfqId, rpq.itemId,
                     rpq.retailPrice,
                     rpq.retailPrice - discount)

    case message: Any =>
      println(s"HighSierraPriceQuotes: unexpected:↵
$message")
  }

  def discountPercentage(
      orderTotalRetailPrice: Double): Double = {
    if (orderTotalRetailPrice <= 150.00) 0.015
    else if (orderTotalRetailPrice <= 499.99) 0.02
    else if (orderTotalRetailPrice <= 999.99) 0.03
    else if (orderTotalRetailPrice <= 4999.99) 0.04
    else 0.05
  }
}

class MountainAscentPriceQuotes(interestRegistrar: ActorRef)
      extends Actor {

  interestRegistrar ! PriceQuoteInterest(
                      self.path.toString, self,
                      70.00, 5000.00)
  def receive = {
    case rpq: RequestPriceQuote =>
     val discount = discountPercentage(
                     rpq.orderTotalRetailPrice) *
                     rpq.retailPrice
       sender ! PriceQuote(rpq.rfqId, rpq.itemId,
                     rpq.retailPrice,
                     rpq.retailPrice - discount)

    case message: Any =>
      println(s"MountainAscentPriceQuotes: unexpected:↵
$message")
  }

  def discountPercentage(
      orderTotalRetailPrice: Double) = {
    if (orderTotalRetailPrice <= 99.99) 0.01
    else if (orderTotalRetailPrice <= 199.99) 0.02
    else if (orderTotalRetailPrice <= 499.99) 0.03
    else if (orderTotalRetailPrice <= 799.99) 0.04
```

```
        else if (orderTotalRetailPrice <= 999.99) 0.045
        else if (orderTotalRetailPrice <= 2999.99) 0.0475
        else 0.05
    }
}

class PinnacleGearPriceQuotes(interestRegistrar: ActorRef)
        extends Actor {
  interestRegistrar ! PriceQuoteInterest(
                            self.path.toString, self,
                            250.00, 500000.00)

  def receive = {
    case rpq: RequestPriceQuote =>
      val discount = discountPercentage(
                            rpq.orderTotalRetailPrice) *
                        rpq.retailPrice
      sender ! PriceQuote(rpq.rfqId, rpq.itemId,
                        rpq.retailPrice,
                        rpq.retailPrice - discount)

    case message: Any =>
      println(s"PinnacleGearPriceQuotes: unexpected:↵
$message")
  }

  def discountPercentage(
        orderTotalRetailPrice: Double) = {
    if (orderTotalRetailPrice <= 299.99) 0.015
    else if (orderTotalRetailPrice <= 399.99) 0.0175
    else if (orderTotalRetailPrice <= 499.99) 0.02
    else if (orderTotalRetailPrice <= 999.99) 0.03
    else if (orderTotalRetailPrice <= 1199.99) 0.035
    else if (orderTotalRetailPrice <= 4999.99) 0.04
    else if (orderTotalRetailPrice <= 7999.99) 0.05
    else 0.06
  }
}

class RockBottomOuterwearPriceQuotes(
        interestRegistrar: ActorRef)
      extends Actor {

  interestRegistrar ! PriceQuoteInterest(
                            self.path.toString, self,
                            0.50, 7500.00)

  def receive = {
    case rpq: RequestPriceQuote =>
      val discount = discountPercentage(
                            rpq.orderTotalRetailPrice) *
                        rpq.retailPrice
```

```
          sender ! PriceQuote(rpq.rfqId, rpq.itemId,
                              rpq.retailPrice,
                              rpq.retailPrice - discount)

      case message: Any =>
        println(s"RockBottomOuterwearPriceQuotes: ↵
unexpected: $message")
    }

  def discountPercentage(
        orderTotalRetailPrice: Double) = {
      if (orderTotalRetailPrice <= 100.00) 0.015
      else if (orderTotalRetailPrice <= 399.99) 0.02
      else if (orderTotalRetailPrice <= 499.99) 0.03
      else if (orderTotalRetailPrice <= 799.99) 0.04
      else if (orderTotalRetailPrice <= 999.99) 0.05
      else if (orderTotalRetailPrice <= 2999.99) 0.06
      else if (orderTotalRetailPrice <= 4999.99) 0.07
      else if (orderTotalRetailPrice <= 5999.99) 0.075
      else 0.08
    }
}
```

The basic difference between each of the pricing engines is the implementation of `discountPercentage()`. I purposely avoided inheritance (class extension) of an abstract base class with these actors. It is highly unlikely that the pricing engines for the disparate number of retailers will inherit from the same base class. Thus, the idea is to imply that there is an independent implementation of each engine, even though they are similar.

Here is an abbreviated portion of the plentiful output from the process:

```
OrderProcessor: 123 item: 1 to: akka://mtnSupplies↵
/user/rockBottomOuterwear
OrderProcessor: 123 item: 2 to: akka://mtnSupplies/↵
user/rockBottomOuterwear
OrderProcessor: 123 item: 3 to: akka://mtnSupplies/↵
user/rockBottomOuterwear
OrderProcessor: 123 item: 1 to: akka://mtnSupplies/↵
user/mountainAscent
...
OrderProcessor: 140 item: 19 to: akka://mtnSupplies/↵
user/highSierra
OrderProcessor: received: PriceQuote(123,1,29.95,29.351)
OrderProcessor: received: PriceQuote(123,2,99.95,↵
97.95100000000001)
OrderProcessor: received: PriceQuote(123,3,14.95,14.651)
OrderProcessor: received: PriceQuote(123,1,29.95,29.351)
OrderProcessor: received: PriceQuote(123,2,99.95,↵
97.95100000000001)
```

```
OrderProcessor: received: PriceQuote(123,3,14.95,14.651)
OrderProcessor: received: PriceQuote(123,1,29.95,29.0515)
OrderProcessor: received: PriceQuote(123,2,99.95,↵
96.95150000000001)
...
OrderProcessor: received: PriceQuote(140,19,789.99,758.3904)
```

You are no doubt wondering how the `MountaineeringSuppliesOrder-Processor` joins all the data from each of the quote engines back into a meaningful single quote for the buyer. That's the subject of the *Aggregator (257)*, which together with the Recipient List forms a kind of *Scatter-Gather (272)*.

Splitter

Use Splitter when a large composite message must be separated into its individual parts and sent as smaller messages. The Splitter might be considered similar to the *Content-Based Router (228)* because it is the part content of the message that determines how parts are routed. However, *Content-Based Router (228)* is primarily concerned with routing the whole message to a specific subsystem based on the overarching message type. On the other hand, with Splitter you are more concerned with routing individual parts of a single composite message to separate subsystems.

Here's an example of splitting an `OrderPlaced` message into separate `Type[?]ItemOrdered` messages:

```
package co.vaughnvernon.reactiveenterprise.splitter

import scala.collection.Map
import akka.actor._
import co.vaughnvernon.reactiveenterprise._

case class OrderItem(
    id: String,
    itemType: String,
    description: String,
    price: Money) {

  override def toString = {
    s"OrderItem($id, $itemType, '$description', $price)"
```

```scala
  }
}

case class Order(orderItems: Map[String, OrderItem]) {
  val grandTotal: Double =
        orderItems.values.map(_.price).sum

  override def toString = {
    s"Order(Order Items: $orderItems Totaling:↵
 $grandTotal)"
  }
}

case class OrderPlaced(order: Order)
case class TypeAItemOrdered(orderItem: OrderItem)
case class TypeBItemOrdered(orderItem: OrderItem)
case class TypeCItemOrdered(orderItem: OrderItem)

object Splitter extends CompletableApp(4) {
  val orderRouter =
        system.actorOf(
              Props[OrderRouter],
              "orderRouter")

  val orderItem1 = OrderItem("1", "TypeA",
                        "An item of type A.", 23.95)
  val orderItem2 = OrderItem("2", "TypeB",
                        "An item of type B.", 99.95)
  val orderItem3 = OrderItem("3", "TypeC",
                        "An item of type C.", 14.95)
  val orderItems = Map(
        orderItem1.itemType -> orderItem1,
        orderItem2.itemType -> orderItem2,
        orderItem3.itemType -> orderItem3)

  orderRouter ! OrderPlaced(Order(orderItems))

  awaitCompletion
  println("Splitter: is completed.")
}

class OrderRouter extends Actor {
  val orderItemTypeAProcessor = context.actorOf(
                Props[OrderItemTypeAProcessor],
                "orderItemTypeAProcessor")
  val orderItemTypeBProcessor = context.actorOf(
                Props[OrderItemTypeBProcessor],
                "orderItemTypeBProcessor")
  val orderItemTypeCProcessor = context.actorOf(
                Props[OrderItemTypeCProcessor],
                "orderItemTypeCProcessor")

  def receive = {
```

```scala
        case OrderPlaced(order) =>
          println(order)
          order.orderItems foreach {
            case (itemType, orderItem) => itemType match {
            case "TypeA" =>
              println(s"OrderRouter: routing $itemType")
              orderItemTypeAProcessor !
                        TypeAItemOrdered(orderItem)
            case "TypeB" =>
              println(s"OrderRouter: routing $itemType")
              orderItemTypeBProcessor !
                        TypeBItemOrdered(orderItem)
            case "TypeC" =>
              println(s"OrderRouter: routing $itemType")
              orderItemTypeCProcessor !
                        TypeCItemOrdered(orderItem)
          }}

          Splitter.completedStep()
        case _ =>
          println("OrderRouter: received unexpected message")
    }
}

class OrderItemTypeAProcessor extends Actor {
  def receive = {
    case TypeAItemOrdered(orderItem) =>
      println(s"OrderItemTypeAProcessor: handling↵
  $orderItem")
      Splitter.completedStep()
    case _ =>
      println("OrderItemTypeAProcessor: unexpected")
  }
}

class OrderItemTypeBProcessor extends Actor {
  def receive = {
    case TypeBItemOrdered(orderItem) =>
      println(s"OrderItemTypeBProcessor: handling↵
  $orderItem")
      Splitter.completedStep()
    case _ =>
      println("OrderItemTypeBProcessor: unexpected")
  }
}

class OrderItemTypeCProcessor extends Actor {
  def receive = {
    case TypeCItemOrdered(orderItem) =>
      println(s"OrderItemTypeCProcessor: handling↵
  $orderItem")
      Splitter.completedStep()
```

```
    case _ =>
      println("OrderItemTypeCProcessor: unexpected")
  }
}
```

The output from this process is as follows:

```
Order(Order Items: Map(TypeA -> OrderItem(1,↵
 TypeA, 'An item of type A.', 23.95), TypeB ->↵
 OrderItem(2, TypeB, 'An item of type B.', 99.95),↵
 TypeC -> OrderItem(3, TypeC, 'An item of type C.',↵
 14.95)) Totaling: 138.85)
OrderRouter: routing TypeA
OrderRouter: routing TypeB
OrderItemTypeAProcessor: handling OrderItem(1, TypeA,↵
 'An item of type A.', 23.95)
OrderRouter: routing TypeC
OrderItemTypeBProcessor: handling OrderItem(2, TypeB,↵
 'An item of type B.', 99.95)
OrderItemTypeCProcessor: handling OrderItem(3, TypeC,↵
 'An item of type C.', 14.95)
Splitter: is completed.
```

The sample `Order` has three `OrderItem` instances, each with a different type. When the `OrderRouter` receives an `OrderPlaced` message, it iterates over each of the `OrderItem` instances. Based on the `OrderItem`'s `itemType` value, the `OrderItem` is packaged into a new message and dispatched to the specific type processor.

Aggregator

The *Recipient List (245)* example doesn't demonstrate how the `PriceQuote` replies are assimilated by the `MountaineeringSuppliesOrderProcessor`. To correlate `PriceQuote` replies to the original `RequestForQuotation`, you need to use the unique `rfqId`—a *Correlation Identifier (215)*—that has been passed along with each message.

```
orderProcessor ! RequestForQuotation("123", ...)
...
recipient ! RequestPriceQuote(rfq.rfqId, ...)
...
sender ! PriceQuote(rpq.rfqId, ...)
```

The example from *Recipient List (245)* is extended here to include an *Aggregator*, which tracks the fulfillment of all requested price quotes. Here there are several `PriceQuoteFulfillment` *Event Messages (207)* that are aggregated into a single `QuotationFulfillment` *Document Message (204)*, which is depicted in Figure 7.5.

Looking at the *Aggregator* example, first note the new message types.

```
case class PriceQuoteFulfilled(priceQuote: PriceQuote)

case class RequiredPriceQuotesForFulfillment(
    rfqId: String,
    quotesRequested: Int)

case class QuotationFulfillment(
    rfqId: String,
    quotesRequested: Int,
    priceQuotes: Seq[PriceQuote],
    requester: ActorRef)
```

Next, the driver object creates a new actor, the `PriceQuoteAggregator`, and endows the `MountaineeringSuppliesOrderProcessor` with it.

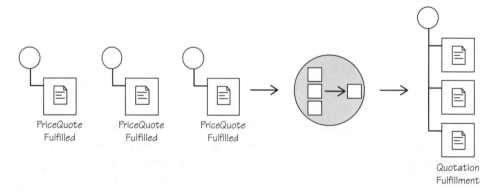

Figure 7.5 An *Aggregator* is used to place a number of individual fulfillment *Messages (130)* into a whole quotation.

```
object Aggregator extends CompletableApp(5) {
  val priceQuoteAggregator =
            system.actorOf(
                Props[PriceQuoteAggregator],
                "priceQuoteAggregator")

  val orderProcessor = system.actorOf(
      Props(classOf[MountaineeringSuppliesOrderProcessor],
                  priceQuoteAggregator),
            "orderProcessor")
...
```

Now when the `MountaineeringSuppliesOrderProcessor` dispatches
to a calculated *Recipient List (245)*, it asks the `PriceQuoteAggregator`
to track all `PriceQuote` instances to the point of fulfillment by sending it a
`RequiredPriceQuotesForFulfillment` message.

```
import scala.collection.mutable.Map

class MountaineeringSuppliesOrderProcessor(
        priceQuoteAggregator: ActorRef)
      extends Actor {
  val interestRegistry =
        Map[String, PriceQuoteInterest]()

  def calculateRecipientList(
        rfq: RequestForQuotation): Iterable[ActorRef] = {
    for {
      interest <- interestRegistry.values
      if (rfq.totalRetailPrice >= interest.lowTotalRetail)
      if (rfq.totalRetailPrice <= interest.highTotalRetail)
    } yield interest.quoteProcessor
  }

  def dispatchTo(
        rfq: RequestForQuotation,
        recipientList: Iterable[ActorRef]) = {
    var totalRequestedQuotes = 0
    recipientList.map { recipient =>
      rfq.retailItems.map { retailItem =>
        println("OrderProcessor: " + rfq.rfqId
            + " item: " + retailItem.itemId + " to: "
            + recipient.path.toString)
        recipient ! RequestPriceQuote(
              rfq.rfqId, retailItem.itemId,
              retailItem.retailPrice, rfq.totalRetailPrice)
      }
    }
  }
```

```scala
def receive = {
  case interest: PriceQuoteInterest =>
    interestRegistry(interest.quoterId) = interest
  case priceQuote: PriceQuote =>
    priceQuoteAggregator !
        PriceQuoteFulfilled(priceQuote)
    println(s"OrderProcessor: received: $priceQuote")
  case rfq: RequestForQuotation =>
    val recipientList = calculateRecipientList(rfq)
    priceQuoteAggregator !
        RequiredPriceQuotesForFulfillment(
            rfq.rfqId,
            recipientList.size
                * rfq.retailItems.size)
    dispatchTo(rfq, recipientList)
  case fulfillment: QuotationFulfillment =>
    println(s"OrderProcessor: received: $fulfillment")
    Aggregator.completedStep()
  case message: Any =>
    println(s"OrderProcessor: unexpected: $message")
  }
}
```

The PriceQuoteAggregator handles two kinds of messages, Required-
PriceQuotesForFulfillment and PriceQuoteFulfilled.

```scala
import scala.collection.mutable.Map

class PriceQuoteAggregator extends Actor {
  val fulfilledPriceQuotes =
        Map[String, QuotationFulfillment]()

  def receive = {
    case required: RequiredPriceQuotesForFulfillment =>
      fulfilledPriceQuotes(required.rfqId) =
            QuotationFulfillment(
                required.rfqId,
                required.quotesRequested,
                Vector(),
                sender)
    case priceQuoteFulfilled: PriceQuoteFulfilled =>
      val previousFulfillment =
            fulfilledPriceQuotes(
                priceQuoteFulfilled.priceQuote.rfqId)
      val currentPriceQuotes =
                previousFulfillment.priceQuotes :+
                        priceQuoteFulfilled.priceQuote
      val currentFulfillment =
        QuotationFulfillment(
            previousFulfillment.rfqId,
```

```
            previousFulfillment.quotesRequested,
            currentPriceQuotes,
            previousFulfillment.requester)

      if (currentPriceQuotes.size >=
           currentFulfillment.quotesRequested) {
        currentFulfillment.requester ! currentFulfillment
        fulfilledPriceQuotes.remove(
             priceQuoteFulfilled.priceQuote.rfqId)
      } else {
        fulfilledPriceQuotes(
             priceQuoteFulfilled.priceQuote.rfqId) =
                      currentFulfillment
      }

      println(s"PriceQuoteAggregator: fulfilled↵
 price quote: $priceQuoteFulfilled")
    case message: Any =>
      println(s"PriceQuoteAggregator: unexpected: $message")
  }
}
```

When `RequiredPriceQuotesForFulfillment` is received, the `PriceQuoteAggregator` establishes a new `QuotationFulfillment` entry in the `fulfilledPriceQuotes` map. Thereafter, as each `PriceQuoteFulfilled` is received, the `PriceQuoteAggregator` aggregates each `PriceQuote` (contained in the `PriceQuoteFulfilled` message) into a `QuotationFulfillment`. Once the `PriceQuoteAggregator` has received a `PriceQuote` for each one requested, it sends the completed `QuotationFulfillment` to the `OrderProcessor`.

```
      if (currentPriceQuotes.size >=
           currentFulfillment.quotesRequested) {
        currentFulfillment.requester ! currentFulfillment
        fulfilledPriceQuotes.remove(
             priceQuoteFulfilled.priceQuote.rfqId)
      } else {
        fulfilledPriceQuotes(
             priceQuoteFulfilled.priceQuote.rfqId) =
                      currentFulfillment
      }
```

Finally, the `MountaineeringSuppliesOrderProcessor` receives each `QuotationFulfillment`.

```
class MountaineeringSuppliesOrderProcessor(
```

```
          priceQuoteAggregator: ActorRef)
        extends Actor {
    ...
  def receive = {
    ...
    case fulfillment: QuotationFulfillment =>
      println(s"OrderProcessor: received: $fulfillment")
      Aggregator.completedStep()
    ...
  }
}
```

The following is the (partial) output from the process:

```
OrderProcessor: 123 item: 1 to: akka://default/↵
user/rockBottomOuterwear
OrderProcessor: 123 item: 2 to: akka://default/↵
user/rockBottomOuterwear
OrderProcessor: 123 item: 3 to: akka://default/↵
user/rockBottomOuterwear
OrderProcessor: 123 item: 1 to: akka://default/↵
user/mountainAscent
...
OrderProcessor: 140 item: 19 to: akka://default/↵
user/highSierra
OrderProcessor: received: PriceQuote(123,1,29.95,29.351)
PriceQuoteAggregator: fulfilled price quote:↵
 PriceQuoteFulfilled(PriceQuote(123,1,29.95,29.351))
OrderProcessor: received: PriceQuote(123,2,99.95,↵
97.95100000000001)
PriceQuoteAggregator: fulfilled price quote:↵
 PriceQuoteFulfilled(PriceQuote(123,2,99.95,↵
97.95100000000001))
OrderProcessor: received: PriceQuote(123,3,14.95,14.651)
OrderProcessor: received: PriceQuote(123,1,29.95,29.351)
PriceQuoteAggregator: fulfilled price quote:↵
 PriceQuoteFulfilled(PriceQuote(123,3,14.95,14.651))
...
PriceQuote(125,7,724.99,695.9904)),Actor[↵
akka://default/user/orderProcessor])
OrderProcessor: received: QuotationFulfillment(129,16,↵
Vector(PriceQuote(129,8,119.99,112.7906),↵
 PriceQuote(129,9,499.95,469.953), PriceQuote(129,10,↵
519.0,487.86), PriceQuote(129,11,209.5,196.93),↵
 PriceQuote(129,8,119.99,115.1904), PriceQuote(129,9,↵
499.95,479.952), PriceQuote(129,10,519.0,498.24),↵
 PriceQuote(129,11,209.5,201.12), PriceQuote(129,8,↵
119.99,114.290475), PriceQuote(129,9,499.95,↵
476.20237499999996), PriceQuote(129,10,519.0,494.3475),↵
 PriceQuote(129,11,209.5,199.54875), PriceQuote(129,↵
8,119.99,115.1904), PriceQuote(129,9,499.95,479.952),↵
 PriceQuote(129,10,519.0,498.24), PriceQuote(129,11,↵
```

```
209.5,201.12)), Actor[akka://default/user/orderProcessor])
OrderProcessor: received:↵
 QuotationFulfillment(135,6,Vector(PriceQuote(135,12,↵
0.97,0.95545), PriceQuote(135,13,9.5,9.3575),↵
 PriceQuote(135,14,1.99,1.96015), PriceQuote(135,↵
12,0.97,0.9506), PriceQuote(135,13,9.5,9.31),↵
 PriceQuote(135,14,1.99,1.9502)),Actor[akka://↵
default/user/orderProcessor])
OrderProcessor: received:
QuotationFulfillment(140,20,Vector(PriceQuote(↵
140,15,107.5,101.05), PriceQuote(140,16,9.5,8.93),↵
 PriceQuote(140,17,599.99,563.9906), PriceQuote(↵
140,18,249.95,234.953), PriceQuote(140,19,789.99,↵
742.5906), PriceQuote(140,15,107.5,103.2),↵
 PriceQuote(140,16,9.5,9.12), PriceQuote(140,17,↵
599.99,575.9904), PriceQuote(140,18,249.95,239.952),↵
 PriceQuote(140,19,789.99,758.3904), PriceQuote(140,↵
15,107.5,102.39375), PriceQuote(140,16,9.5,9.04875),↵
 PriceQuote(140,17,599.99,571.4904750000001), PriceQuote↵
(140,18,249.95,238.077375), PriceQuote(140,19,789.99,↵
752.465475), PriceQuote(140,15,107.5,103.2),↵
 PriceQuote(140,16,9.5,9.12), PriceQuote(140,17,↵
599.99,575.9904), PriceQuote(140,18,249.95,239.952),↵
PriceQuote(140,19,789.99,758.3904)),Actor[akka://↵
default/user/orderProcessor])
Aggregator: is completed.
```

An Aggregator can be designed with varying termination criteria:

- Wait for All

- Timeout

- First Best

- Timeout with Override

- External Event

This example uses the first, Wait for All.

Actually, the combination of *Recipient List (245)* and Aggregator demonstrated here is one way to implement the *Scatter-Gather (272)* pattern. Yet, a *Scatter-Gather (272)* can also be implemented using a *Publish-Subscribe Channel (154)* rather than a *Recipient List (245)*.

A *Recipient List (245)* and Aggregator—or when using a Publish-Subscribe Channel instead—comprises a larger pattern, the *Composed Message Processor (270)*. The advantage to viewing these as a *Composed Message Processor (270)* allows the combined components to more readily serve as a single filter in the *Pipes and Filters (135)* style.

Resequencer

At this point I've covered a number of Message Routers in addition to some less complex, but essential, messaging patterns. With regard to my discussion of *Request-Reply (209)*, you may be wondering about the order of message delivery and asking, "How do I handle message sequencing?"

With Akka and other Actor model systems, in general you do not need to worry about the sequence in which messages will be received by an actor as a result of direct message sends from another actor. As discussed in the Akka documentation [Akka-Message-Guarantees], direct messages from one actor to a second actor are always received in the order in which the first actor sent them. From the Akka documentation here, assume the following:

- Actor A1 sends messages M1, M2, and M3 to A2.

- Actor A3 sends messages M4, M5, and M6 to A2.

Based on these two scenarios, you arrive at these facts:

1. If M1 is delivered, it must be delivered before M2 and M3.

2. If M2 is delivered, it must be delivered before M3.

3. If M4 is delivered, it must be delivered before M5 and M6.

4. If M5 is delivered, it must be delivered before M6.

5. A2 can see messages from A1 interleaved with messages from A3.

6. Since there is no (default) guaranteed delivery, any of the messages may be dropped, that is, not arrive at A2.

The bottom line here is, don't be concerned about a sequence of basic messages sent directly from one actor to another being received out of order. It just won't happen.

Still, there are occasions in complex message routing scenarios when there are multiple sender actors, a sequence of messages could well be received out of order (see the previous #5 where messages from A1 and A3 are interleaved as they arrive at A2). This can happen, for example, when using a *Content-Based*

Router (228), such as a *Splitter (254)*. Imagine one large message being slit into several smaller messages and then routed based on the content of the smaller messages. The number of processes and the time required to process all the fine-grained messages could easily cause the results to be received out of order at their final destination.

In some cases, such as with our *Scatter-Gather (272)* example, this may not matter. Yet, in other cases the messages will need to be received according to an original sequence. When this is so, use a Resequencer, as illustrated in Figure 7.6.

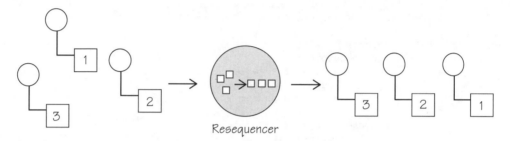

Resequencer

Figure 7.6 When it is not good enough to allow *Messages (130)* to arrive in an arbitrary order, use a Resequencer to arrange them into their required order.

A Resequencer is responsible for receiving a set of messages that are out of their original sequence and putting them back in to their required sequence before sending them on to a final destination. Here's an example, starting with the driver application:

```
package co.vaughnvernon.reactiveenterprise.resequencer

import java.util.concurrent.TimeUnit
import java.util.Date
import scala.concurrent._
import scala.concurrent.duration._
import scala.util._
import ExecutionContext.Implicits.global
import akka.actor._
import co.vaughnvernon.reactiveenterprise._

case class SequencedMessage(
    correlationId: String,
    index: Int,
    total: Int)
```

```scala
case class ResequencedMessages(
        dispatchableIndex: Int,
        sequencedMessages: Array[SequencedMessage]) {

  def advancedTo(dispatchableIndex: Int) = {
    ResequencedMessages(
          dispatchableIndex,
          sequencedMessages)
  }
}

object Resequencer extends CompletableApp(10) {
  val sequencedMessageConsumer = system.actorOf(
                Props[SequencedMessageConsumer],
                "sequencedMessageConsumer")

  val resequencerConsumer =
        system.actorOf(
            Props(classOf[ResequencerConsumer],
                sequencedMessageConsumer),
            "resequencerConsumer")

  val chaosRouter = system.actorOf(
            Props(classOf[ChaosRouter],
                resequencerConsumer),
            "chaosRouter")

  for (index <- 1 to 5)
        chaosRouter !
          SequencedMessage("ABC", index, 5)
  for (index <- 1 to 5)
        chaosRouter !
          SequencedMessage("XYZ", index, 5)

  awaitCompletion
  println("Resequencer: is completed.")
}
```

First you set up three actors: the ultimate `SequencedMessageConsumer` that requires messages to be delivered in the proper sequence, the `ResequencerConsumer` that receives messages out of sequence and then places them into proper sequence, and the `ChaosRouter` that receives messages in proper sequence but purposely forces them out of sequence.

The `SequencedMessage` contains a `correlationId`, an `index` of the given message sequence, and a `total` number of messages. The `correlationId` is explained in *Correlation Identifier (215)*.

The sample driver application first sends a number of `SequencedMessage` instances to the `ChaosRouter`. So, let's take a look there first:

```
class ChaosRouter(consumer: ActorRef) extends Actor {
  val random = new Random((new Date()).getTime)

  def receive = {
    case sequencedMessage: SequencedMessage =>
      val millis = random.nextInt(100) + 1
      println(s"ChaosRouter: delaying delivery↵
 of $sequencedMessage for $millis milliseconds")

      val duration =
          Duration.create(
              millis,
              TimeUnit.MILLISECONDS)

      context.system.scheduler.scheduleOnce(
              duration,
              consumer,
              sequencedMessage)

    case message: Any =>
      println(s"ChaosRouter: unexpected: $message")
  }
}
```

The `ChaosRouter` is endowed with an `ActorRef` for its direct consumer, which is the `ResequencerConsumer`. The basic responsibility of the `Chaos-Router` is to create havoc with message sequencing. It simply sets a timer for some random number of milliseconds between 1 and 100. Once the timer elapses, it will dispatch the associated `SequencedMessage` to its consumer, the `ResequencerConsumer`. Let's take a look there next:

```
class ResequencerConsumer(
        actualConsumer: ActorRef)
  extends Actor {
  val resequenced =
        scala.collection.mutable.Map[
                String,
                ResequencedMessages]()

  def dispatchAllSequenced(
        correlationId: String) = {
    val resequencedMessages = resequenced(correlationId)
    var dispatchableIndex =
        resequencedMessages.dispatchableIndex

    resequencedMessages.sequencedMessages.map {
            sequencedMessage =>
      if (sequencedMessage.index == dispatchableIndex) {
```

```scala
        actualConsumer ! sequencedMessage

        dispatchableIndex += 1
      }
    }

    resequenced(correlationId) =
      resequencedMessages.advancedTo(dispatchableIndex)
}

def dummySequencedMessages(
        count: Int): Seq[SequencedMessage] = {
  for {
    index <- 1 to count
  } yield {
    SequencedMessage("", -1, count)
  }
}

def receive = {
  case unsequencedMessage: SequencedMessage =>
    println(s"ResequencerConsumer: received:↵
$unsequencedMessage")
    resequence(unsequencedMessage)
    dispatchAllSequenced(unsequencedMessage.correlationId)
    removeCompleted(unsequencedMessage.correlationId)
  case message: Any =>
    println(s"ResequencerConsumer: unexpected: $message")
}

def removeCompleted(correlationId: String) = {
  val resequencedMessages = resequenced(correlationId)

  if (resequencedMessages.dispatchableIndex >
      resequencedMessages.sequencedMessages(0).total) {
    resequenced.remove(correlationId)
    println(s"ResequencerConsumer: removed completed:↵
$correlationId")
  }
}

def resequence(
        sequencedMessage: SequencedMessage) = {
  if (!resequenced.contains(
          sequencedMessage.correlationId)) {
    resequenced(sequencedMessage.correlationId) =
      ResequencedMessages(
              1,
              dummySequencedMessages(
                  sequencedMessage.total).toArray)
  }

  resequenced(sequencedMessage.correlationId)
```

```
      .sequencedMessages
      .update(sequencedMessage.index — 1,
              sequencedMessage)
  }
}
```

By `correlationId`, the `ResequencerConsumer` gradually places each `SequencedMessage` that it receives into the original, proper sequence. As soon as it has any number of `SequencedMessage` instances in the order in which they must be received by `SequencedMessageConsumer`, it dispatches them to it. Depending on the order in which the messages are received, this may happen in a single burst, a few bursts, or one at a time. For example, if messages are received with sequences 5, 4, 3, 2, and then 1, when method `dispatchAllSequenced()` sees the message with index 1, it will send a burst of messages 1–5 to its `actualConsumer`.

Finally, you can look at the `ResequencerConsumer` `actualConsumer`, which is the simple `SequencedMessageConsumer`. It only shows each `SequencedMessage` it receives, proving that they are received in proper sequential order.

```
class SequencedMessageConsumer extends Actor {
  def receive = {
    case sequencedMessage: SequencedMessage =>
      println(s"SequencedMessageConsumer: received:↵
$sequencedMessage")
      Resequencer.completedStep()
    case message: Any =>
      println(s"SequencedMessageConsumer: unexpected:↵
$message")
  }
}
```

Here's the (partial) output from one run of the process:

```
ChaosRouter: delaying delivery of SequencedMessage(↵
ABC,1,5) for 14 milliseconds
ChaosRouter: delaying delivery of SequencedMessage(↵
ABC,2,5) for 71 milliseconds
ChaosRouter: delaying delivery of SequencedMessage(↵
ABC,3,5) for 1 milliseconds
ChaosRouter: delaying delivery of SequencedMessage(↵
XYZ,5,5) for 63 milliseconds
...
ResequencerConsumer: received: SequencedMessage(XYZ,4,5)
ResequencerConsumer: received: SequencedMessage(ABC,3,5)
ResequencerConsumer: received: SequencedMessage(XYZ,5,5)
```

```
ResequencerConsumer: received: SequencedMessage(ABC,5,5)
ResequencerConsumer: received: SequencedMessage(XYZ,1,5)
ResequencerConsumer: received: SequencedMessage(ABC,2,5)
SequencedMessageConsumer: received: SequencedMessage(↵
XYZ,1,5)
ResequencerConsumer: received: SequencedMessage(XYZ,2,5)
ResequencerConsumer: received: SequencedMessage(ABC,1,5)
SequencedMessageConsumer: received: SequencedMessage(↵
XYZ,2,5)
SequencedMessageConsumer: received: SequencedMessage(↵
ABC,1,5)
SequencedMessageConsumer: received: SequencedMessage(↵
ABC,2,5)
SequencedMessageConsumer: received: SequencedMessage(↵
ABC,3,5)
ResequencerConsumer: received: SequencedMessage(XYZ,3,5)
ResequencerConsumer: removed completed: XYZ
SequencedMessageConsumer: received: SequencedMessage(↵
XYZ,3,5)
ResequencerConsumer: received: SequencedMessage(ABC,4,5)
SequencedMessageConsumer: received: SequencedMessage(↵
XYZ,4,5)
ResequencerConsumer: removed completed: ABC
SequencedMessageConsumer: received: SequencedMessage(↵
XYZ,5,5)
SequencedMessageConsumer: received: SequencedMessage(↵
ABC,4,5)
SequencedMessageConsumer: received: SequencedMessage(↵
ABC,5,5)
Resequencer: is completed.
```

Composed Message Processor

When a *Recipient List (245)* and *Aggregator (257)* are used together and when a *Content-Based Router (228)* and a *Splitter (254)* are used in conjunction, these comprise a larger pattern: the Composed Message Processor. The advantage to viewing these as a Composed Message Processor allows the combined components to more readily serve as a single filter in the *Pipes and Filters (135)* style.

For example, Figure 7.7 shows some of the detail that comprises a Composed Message Processor.

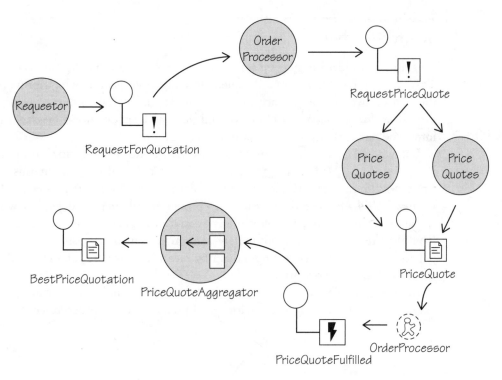

Figure 7.7 This Composed Message Processor is of the Scatter-Gather variety.

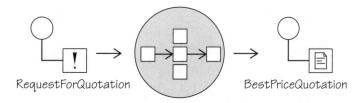

Figure 7.8 You can compose the Scatter-Gather processing into a single actor.

Composing this, the same processor can be abstracted and represented as a much simpler filter, as shown in Figure 7.8.

For an example of a Composed Message Processor, see *Scatter-Gather (272)*.

Scatter-Gather

You've actually already stepped through one implementation of Scatter-Gather. This was the combination of Recipient List and Aggregator, which provides the first of two Scatter-Gather variants. The second variant—that of using a *Publish-Subscribe Channel (154)* to send `RequestPriceQuote` messages to interested participants—is discussed here (see Figure 7.9).

But wait. The `MountaineeringSuppliesOrderProcessor` from the *Recipient List (245)* and *Aggregator (257)* samples already maintains an `interestRegistry`. While true, it's not the same as a *Publish-Subscribe Channel (154)*. Rather than arbitrarily providing all interested parties with requests for quotation, the `MountaineeringSuppliesOrderProcessor` from the previous examples ultimately determines which interests will participate in providing quotes. It filters them by means of business rules checked in `calculateRecipientList()`.

In this example, however, you will drop the prequalifying formality of examining each quoting engine for their preferred total order price range.

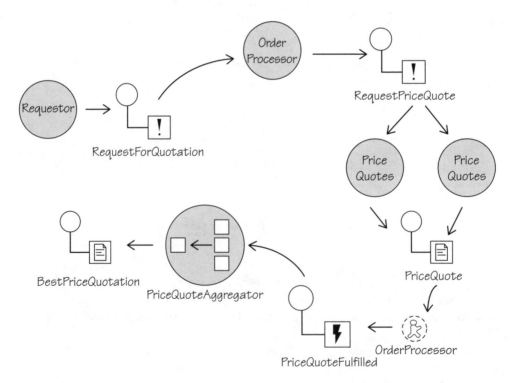

Figure 7.9 This Scatter-Gather processing is used to find a best price quotation.

Instead, you will just publish a `RequestPriceQuote` message to each registered interest subscriber and allow the interested quote engine to provide a quote if it chooses.

This, of course, forces `MountaineeringSuppliesOrderProcessor` to relinquish much of its control of the process. Still, it can control at least two aspects: time and best quote. In this example, the `Mountaineering-SuppliesOrderProcessor` will use a timeout to shut down quotations for a given order after a period of time. (Actually, it is the `PriceQuoteAggregator` that manages the timeout.) Additionally, the `PriceQuoteAggregator` will select the best quote—similar to accepting the best bid in an auction—to determine who wins the business.

The sample code starts out much like the *Recipient List (245)* and *Aggregator (257)* samples but with a few new or modified message types.

```scala
package co.vaughnvernon.reactiveenterprise.scattergather

import java.util.concurrent.TimeUnit
import scala.concurrent._
import scala.concurrent.duration._
import ExecutionContext.Implicits.global
import akka.actor._
import co.vaughnvernon.reactiveenterprise._

case class RequestForQuotation(
        rfqId: String,
        retailItems: Seq[RetailItem]) {
  val totalRetailPrice: Double =
        retailItems.map(retailItem =>
                retailItem.retailPrice).sum
}

case class RetailItem(
    itemId: String,
    retailPrice: Double)

case class RequestPriceQuote(
    rfqId: String,
    itemId: String,
    retailPrice: Money,
    orderTotalRetailPrice: Money)

case class PriceQuote(
    quoterId: String,
    rfqId: String,
    itemId: String,
    retailPrice: Money,
    discountPrice: Money)

case class PriceQuoteFulfilled(priceQuote: PriceQuote)
```

```scala
case class PriceQuoteTimedOut(rfqId: String)

case class RequiredPriceQuotesForFulfillment(
    rfqId: String,
    quotesRequested: Int)

case class QuotationFulfillment(
    rfqId: String,
    quotesRequested: Int,
    priceQuotes: Seq[PriceQuote],
    requester: ActorRef)

case class BestPriceQuotation(
    rfqId: String,
    priceQuotes: Seq[PriceQuote])

case class SubscribeToPriceQuoteRequests(
    quoterId: String,
    quoteProcessor: ActorRef)

object ScatterGather extends CompletableApp(5) {
  val priceQuoteAggregator =
      system.actorOf(
                Props[PriceQuoteAggregator],
                "priceQuoteAggregator")

  val orderProcessor =
      system.actorOf(
          Props(
           classOf[MountaineeringSuppliesOrderProcessor],
               priceQuoteAggregator),
           "orderProcessor")

  system.actorOf(
          Props(classOf[BudgetHikersPriceQuotes],
              orderProcessor),
          "budgetHikers")

  system.actorOf(
          Props(classOf[HighSierraPriceQuotes],
              orderProcessor),
          "highSierra")

  system.actorOf(
          Props(classOf[MountainAscentPriceQuotes],
               orderProcessor),
          "mountainAscent")

  system.actorOf(
          Props(classOf[PinnacleGearPriceQuotes],
               orderProcessor),
          "pinnacleGear")
```

```
system.actorOf(
        Props(classOf[RockBottomOuterwearPriceQuotes],
            orderProcessor),
        "rockBottomOuterwear")

orderProcessor ! RequestForQuotation("123",
    Vector(RetailItem("1", 29.95),
        RetailItem("2", 99.95),
        RetailItem("3", 14.95)))

orderProcessor ! RequestForQuotation("125",
    Vector(RetailItem("4", 39.99),
        RetailItem("5", 199.95),
        RetailItem("6", 149.95),
        RetailItem("7", 724.99)))

orderProcessor ! RequestForQuotation("129",
    Vector(RetailItem("8", 119.99),
        RetailItem("9", 499.95),
        RetailItem("10", 519.00),
        RetailItem("11", 209.50)))

orderProcessor ! RequestForQuotation("135",
    Vector(RetailItem("12", 0.97),
        RetailItem("13", 9.50),
        RetailItem("14", 1.99)))

orderProcessor ! RequestForQuotation("140",
    Vector(RetailItem("15", 1295.50),
        RetailItem("16", 9.50),
        RetailItem("17", 599.99),
        RetailItem("18", 249.95),
        RetailItem("19", 789.99)))

awaitCompletion
println("Scatter-Gather: is completed.")
}
```

Note the BestPriceQuotation message type, which is the final message sent to MountaineeringSuppliesOrderProcessor. After the processor receives five such messages, one for each RequestForQuotation it receives, the Scatter-Gather sample process completes.

The dispatch() for this version of the MountaineeringSupplies-OrderProcessor sends a RequestPriceQuote message to every subscriber rather than constraining the quote processors by some business rule.

```
import scala.collection.mutable.Map

class MountaineeringSuppliesOrderProcessor(
```

```
        priceQuoteAggregator: ActorRef)
  extends Actor {
 val subscribers =
        Map[String, SubscribeToPriceQuoteRequests]()

  def dispatch(rfq: RequestForQuotation) = {
    subscribers.values.map { subscriber =>
      val quoteProcessor = subscriber.quoteProcessor
      rfq.retailItems.map { retailItem =>
        println("OrderProcessor: "
                + rfq.rfqId
                + " item: "
                + retailItem.itemId
                + " to: "
                + subscriber.quoterId)
        quoteProcessor !
                RequestPriceQuote(
                    rfq.rfqId,
                    retailItem.itemId,
                    retailItem.retailPrice,
                    rfq.totalRetailPrice)
      }
    }
  }

  def receive = {
    case subscriber: SubscribeToPriceQuoteRequests =>
      subscribers(subscriber.path) = subscriber
    case priceQuote: PriceQuote =>
      priceQuoteAggregator !
            PriceQuoteFulfilled(priceQuote)
      println(s"OrderProcessor: received: $priceQuote")
    case rfq: RequestForQuotation =>
      priceQuoteAggregator !
            RequiredPriceQuotesForFulfillment(
                rfq.rfqId,
                subscribers.size * rfq.retailItems.size)
      dispatch(rfq)
    case bestPriceQuotation: BestPriceQuotation =>
      println(s"OrderProcessor: received:↵
$bestPriceQuotation")
      ScatterGather.completedStep()
    case message: Any =>
      println(s"OrderProcessor: unexpected: $message")
  }
}
```

As its name indicates, `BestPriceQuotation` contains an aggregated `Vector` of the best `PriceQuote` instances from any quotation engine. This brings us to the *Aggregator (257)*.

```scala
import scala.collection.mutable.Map

class PriceQuoteAggregator extends Actor {
  val fulfilledPriceQuotes =
          Map[String, QuotationFulfillment]()

  def bestPriceQuotationFrom(
          quotationFulfillment: QuotationFulfillment)
          : BestPriceQuotation = {
    val bestPrices = Map[String, PriceQuote]()

    quotationFulfillment.priceQuotes.map { priceQuote =>
      if (bestPrices.contains(priceQuote.itemId)) {
        if (bestPrices(priceQuote.itemId).discountPrice >
            priceQuote.discountPrice) {
          bestPrices(priceQuote.itemId) = priceQuote
        }
      } else {
        bestPrices(priceQuote.itemId) = priceQuote
      }
    }

    BestPriceQuotation(
        quotationFulfillment.rfqId,
        bestPrices.values.toVector)
  }

  def receive = {
    case required: RequiredPriceQuotesForFulfillment =>
      fulfilledPriceQuotes(required.rfqId) =
              QuotationFulfillment(
                  required.rfqId,
                  required.quotesRequested,
                  Vector(),
                  sender)

      val duration = Duration.create(2, TimeUnit.SECONDS)

      context.system.scheduler.scheduleOnce(
              duration, self,
              PriceQuoteTimedOut(required.rfqId))

    case priceQuoteFulfilled: PriceQuoteFulfilled =>
      priceQuoteRequestFulfilled(priceQuoteFulfilled)
      println(s"PriceQuoteAggregator: fulfilled price↵
quote: $PriceQuoteFulfilled")
    case priceQuoteTimedOut: PriceQuoteTimedOut =>
      priceQuoteRequestTimedOut(priceQuoteTimedOut.rfqId)

    case message: Any =>
      println(s"PriceQuoteAggregator: unexpected: $message")
```

```
    }

    def priceQuoteRequestFulfilled(
        priceQuoteFulfilled: PriceQuoteFulfilled) = {
      if (fulfilledPriceQuotes.contains(
            priceQuoteFulfilled.priceQuote.rfqId)) {
        val previousFulfillment =
                fulfilledPriceQuotes(
                    priceQuoteFulfilled.priceQuote.rfqId)
        val currentPriceQuotes =
                previousFulfillment.priceQuotes :+
                    priceQuoteFulfilled.priceQuote
        val currentFulfillment =
            QuotationFulfillment(
                previousFulfillment.rfqId,
                previousFulfillment.quotesRequested,
                currentPriceQuotes,
                previousFulfillment.requester)

        if (currentPriceQuotes.size >=
              currentFulfillment.quotesRequested) {
          quoteBestPrice(currentFulfillment)
        } else {
          fulfilledPriceQuotes(
              priceQuoteFulfilled.priceQuote.rfqId) =
              currentFulfillment
        }
      }
    }

    def priceQuoteRequestTimedOut(rfqId: String) = {
      if (fulfilledPriceQuotes.contains(rfqId)) {
        quoteBestPrice(fulfilledPriceQuotes(rfqId))
      }
    }

    def quoteBestPrice(
        quotationFulfillment: QuotationFulfillment) = {
      if (fulfilledPriceQuotes.contains(
            quotationFulfillment.rfqId)) {
        quotationFulfillment.requester !
            bestPriceQuotationFrom(quotationFulfillment)
        fulfilledPriceQuotes.remove(
            quotationFulfillment.rfqId)
      }
    }
  }
}
```

The `PriceQuoteAggregator` manages several important things. First notice that when reacting to the `RequiredPriceQuotesForFulfillment` message, a timeout is set in order to restrict the entire quote process for each

RequestForQuotation to a duration. The duration used in this example is two seconds, but it could be changed to any practical value as determined by the business. If a timeout occurs, the PriceQuoteTimedOut message is received by the PriceQuoteAggregator, and the process for the given RequestForQuotation terminates. Terminating the process doesn't spell failure. Rather, it serves to inform the PriceQuoteAggregator to provide a BestPriceQuotation message to the MountaineeringSuppliesOrderProcessor based on the number of PriceQuoteFulfilled messages that the PriceQuoteAggregator has already received.

That leads us to consider the quoteBestPrice() and bestPriceQuotationFrom() operations. It is method quoteBestPrice() that sends the BestPriceQuotation to the MountaineeringSuppliesOrderProcessor when the aggregation is completed. However, quoteBestPrice() uses method bestPriceQuotationFrom() to create the BestPriceQuotation by keeping only the PriceQuote instances with the lowest discountPrice.

Finally, let's look at the individual quote engines. These are mostly the same as before, but two of them have some slight differences. Both BudgetHikersPriceQuotes and RockBottomOuterwearPriceQuotes ignore quotes for orders that are more than $1,000 and $2,000, respecively. This causes the process for some quotes to time out since the expected number of PriceQuote messages will not be received by MountaineeringSuppliesOrderProcessor (and the corresponding number of PriceQuoteFulfilled messages by PriceQuoteAggregator) in all cases.

```
class BudgetHikersPriceQuotes(
      priceQuoteRequestPublisher: ActorRef)
  extends Actor {
  val quoterId = self.path.name

  priceQuoteRequestPublisher !
        SubscribeToPriceQuoteRequests(quoterId, self)

  def receive = {
    case rpq: RequestPriceQuote =>
      if (rpq.orderTotalRetailPrice < 1000.00) {
        val discount = discountPercentage(
                         rpq.orderTotalRetailPrice) *
                       rpq.retailPrice
        sender ! PriceQuote(
                     quoterId,
                     rpq.rfqId,
                     rpq.itemId,
                     rpq.retailPrice,
                     rpq.retailPrice - discount)
      } else {
```

```
                    println(s"BudgetHikersPriceQuotes: ignoring: $rpq")
            }

        case message: Any =>
            println(s"BudgetHikersPriceQuotes: unexpected:↵
$message")
     }

     def discountPercentage(
            orderTotalRetailPrice: Double) = {
        if (orderTotalRetailPrice <= 100.00) 0.02
        else if (orderTotalRetailPrice <= 399.99) 0.03
        else if (orderTotalRetailPrice <= 499.99) 0.05
        else if (orderTotalRetailPrice <= 799.99) 0.07
        else 0.075
     }
}

class HighSierraPriceQuotes(
            priceQuoteRequestPublisher: ActorRef)
    extends Actor {
    val quoterId = self.path.name

    priceQuoteRequestPublisher !
            SubscribeToPriceQuoteRequests(quoterId, self)

    def receive = {
        case rpq: RequestPriceQuote =>
            val discount = discountPercentage(
                             rpq.orderTotalRetailPrice) *
                          rpq.retailPrice
            sender ! PriceQuote(
                        quoterId,
                        rpq.rfqId,
                        rpq.itemId,
                        rpq.retailPrice,
                        rpq.retailPrice - discount)

        case message: Any =>
            println(s"HighSierraPriceQuotes: unexpected:↵
$message")
     }

     def discountPercentage(
            orderTotalRetailPrice: Double): Double = {
        if (orderTotalRetailPrice <= 150.00) 0.015
        else if (orderTotalRetailPrice <= 499.99) 0.02
        else if (orderTotalRetailPrice <= 999.99) 0.03
        else if (orderTotalRetailPrice <= 4999.99) 0.04
        else 0.05
     }
}
```

```scala
class MountainAscentPriceQuotes(
        priceQuoteRequestPublisher: ActorRef)
  extends Actor {
  val quoterId = self.path.name

  priceQuoteRequestPublisher !
        SubscribeToPriceQuoteRequests(quoterId, self)

  def receive = {
    case rpq: RequestPriceQuote =>
      val discount = discountPercentage(
                        rpq.orderTotalRetailPrice) *
                      rpq.retailPrice
      sender ! PriceQuote(
                      quoterId,
                      rpq.rfqId,
                      rpq.itemId,
                      rpq.retailPrice,
                      rpq.retailPrice - discount)

    case message: Any =>
      println(s"MountainAscentPriceQuotes: unexpected:↵
$message")
  }

  def discountPercentage(
        orderTotalRetailPrice: Double) = {
    if (orderTotalRetailPrice <= 99.99) 0.01
    else if (orderTotalRetailPrice <= 199.99) 0.02
    else if (orderTotalRetailPrice <= 499.99) 0.03
    else if (orderTotalRetailPrice <= 799.99) 0.04
    else if (orderTotalRetailPrice <= 999.99) 0.045
    else if (orderTotalRetailPrice <= 2999.99) 0.0475
    else 0.05
  }
}

class PinnacleGearPriceQuotes(
        priceQuoteRequestPublisher: ActorRef)
  extends Actor {
  val quoterId = self.path.name

  priceQuoteRequestPublisher !
        SubscribeToPriceQuoteRequests(quoterId, self)

  def receive = {
    case rpq: RequestPriceQuote =>
      val discount = discountPercentage(
                        rpq.orderTotalRetailPrice) *
                      rpq.retailPrice
      sender ! PriceQuote(
                      quoterId,
                      rpq.rfqId,
```

```
                        rpq.itemId,
                        rpq.retailPrice,
                        rpq.retailPrice - discount)

    case message: Any =>
      println(s"PinnacleGearPriceQuotes: unexpected:↵
$message")
 }

  def discountPercentage(
          orderTotalRetailPrice: Double) = {
    if (orderTotalRetailPrice <= 299.99) 0.015
    else if (orderTotalRetailPrice <= 399.99) 0.0175
    else if (orderTotalRetailPrice <= 499.99) 0.02
    else if (orderTotalRetailPrice <= 999.99) 0.03
    else if (orderTotalRetailPrice <= 1199.99) 0.035
    else if (orderTotalRetailPrice <= 4999.99) 0.04
    else if (orderTotalRetailPrice <= 7999.99) 0.05
    else 0.06
  }
}

class RockBottomOuterwearPriceQuotes(
          priceQuoteRequestPublisher: ActorRef)
  extends Actor {
  val quoterId = self.path.name

  priceQuoteRequestPublisher !
          SubscribeToPriceQuoteRequests(quoterId, self)

  def receive = {
    case rpq: RequestPriceQuote =>
      if (rpq.orderTotalRetailPrice < 2000.00) {
        val discount = discountPercentage(
                            rpq.orderTotalRetailPrice) *
                        rpq.retailPrice
        sender ! PriceQuote(
                        quoterId,
                        rpq.rfqId,
                        rpq.itemId,
                        rpq.retailPrice,
                        rpq.retailPrice - discount)
      } else {
        println(s"RockBottomOuterwearPriceQuotes:↵
ignoring: $rpq")
      }

    case message: Any =>
      println(s"RockBottomOuterwearPriceQuotes: unexpected:↵
$message")
 }

  def discountPercentage(
```

```
        orderTotalRetailPrice: Double) = {
    if (orderTotalRetailPrice <= 100.00) 0.015
    else if (orderTotalRetailPrice <= 399.99) 0.02
    else if (orderTotalRetailPrice <= 499.99) 0.03
    else if (orderTotalRetailPrice <= 799.99) 0.04
    else if (orderTotalRetailPrice <= 999.99) 0.05
    else if (orderTotalRetailPrice <= 2999.99) 0.06
    else if (orderTotalRetailPrice <= 4999.99) 0.07
    else if (orderTotalRetailPrice <= 5999.99) 0.075
    else 0.08
  }
}
```

The following output was produced by the sample process:

```
OrderProcessor: 123 item: 1 to: rockBottomOuterwear
OrderProcessor: 123 item: 2 to: rockBottomOuterwear
OrderProcessor: 123 item: 3 to: rockBottomOuterwear
OrderProcessor: 123 item: 1 to: highSierra
OrderProcessor: 123 item: 2 to: highSierra
OrderProcessor: 123 item: 3 to: highSierra
OrderProcessor: 123 item: 1 to: pinnacleGear
OrderProcessor: 123 item: 2 to: pinnacleGear
OrderProcessor: 123 item: 3 to: pinnacleGear
OrderProcessor: 123 item: 1 to: budgetHikers
OrderProcessor: 123 item: 2 to: budgetHikers
OrderProcessor: 123 item: 3 to: budgetHikers
OrderProcessor: 123 item: 1 to: mountainAscent
OrderProcessor: 123 item: 2 to: mountainAscent
OrderProcessor: 123 item: 3 to: mountainAscent
...
BudgetHikersPriceQuotes: ignoring: RequestPriceQuote(↵
125,4,39.99,1114.88)
OrderProcessor: 129 item: 11 to: mountainAscent
BudgetHikersPriceQuotes: ignoring: RequestPriceQuote(↵
125,5,199.95,1114.88)
OrderProcessor: 135 item: 12 to: rockBottomOuterwear
BudgetHikersPriceQuotes: ignoring: RequestPriceQuote(↵
125,6,149.95,1114.88)
OrderProcessor: 135 item: 13 to: rockBottomOuterwear
BudgetHikersPriceQuotes: ignoring: RequestPriceQuote(↵
125,7,724.99,1114.88)
OrderProcessor: 135 item: 14 to: rockBottomOuterwear
BudgetHikersPriceQuotes: ignoring: RequestPriceQuote(↵
129,8,119.99,1348.44)
OrderProcessor: 135 item: 12 to: highSierra
BudgetHikersPriceQuotes: ignoring: RequestPriceQuote(↵
129,9,499.95,1348.44)
OrderProcessor: 135 item: 13 to: highSierra
BudgetHikersPriceQuotes: ignoring: RequestPriceQuote(↵
129,10,519.0,1348.44)
```

```
OrderProcessor: 135 item: 14 to: highSierra
OrderProcessor: 135 item: 12 to: pinnacleGear
...
PriceQuoteAggregator: fulfilled price quote:↵
 PriceQuoteFulfilled
OrderProcessor: received: PriceQuote(highSierra,125,↵
4,39.99,38.3904)
OrderProcessor: received: PriceQuote(highSierra,125,↵
5,199.95,191.952)
OrderProcessor: received: PriceQuote(highSierra,125,↵
6,149.95,143.952)
...
OrderProcessor: received:↵
 BestPriceQuotation(140,Vector(PriceQuote(mountainAscent,↵
140,15,1295.5,1233.96375),↵
 PriceQuote(mountainAscent,140,18,249.95,238.077375),↵
 PriceQuote(mountainAscent,140,17,599.99,571.4904750000001),↵
 PriceQuote(mountainAscent,140,16,9.5,9.04875),↵
 PriceQuote(mountainAscent,140,19,789.99,752.465475)))
OrderProcessor: received:↵
 BestPriceQuotation(125,Vector(PriceQuote(rockBottomOuterwear,↵
125,5,199.95,187.953),↵
 PriceQuote(rockBottomOuterwear,125,7,724.99,681.4906),↵
 PriceQuote(rockBottomOuterwear,125,4,39.99,37.5906),↵
 PriceQuote(rockBottomOuterwear,125,6,149.95,140.953)))
OrderProcessor: received: BestPriceQuotation(129,↵
Vector(PriceQuote(rockBottomOuterwear,129,8,119.99,↵
112.7906), PriceQuote(rockBottomOuterwear,129,11,↵
209.5,196.93), PriceQuote(rockBottomOuterwear,129,↵
9,499.95,469.953), PriceQuote(rockBottomOuterwear,129,↵
10,519.0,487.86)))
Scatter-Gather: is completed.
```

BudgetHikersPriceQuotes and RockBottomOuterwearPrice-
Quotes split the winnings of most of the price quote bids with two each.
Yet, MountainAscentPriceQuotes is able to win one of the Request-
ForQuotation bids since BudgetHikersPriceQuotes and RockBottom-
OuterwearPriceQuotes refuse to bid on those greater than $1,000 and
$2,000, respectively, and RequestForQuotation #140 is more than $2,900.
By ignoring certain price quote opportunities, the sample process experiences
time-outs and spreads the deal making across sellers.

The Scatter-Gather pattern as a combination of *Recipient List (245)* and
Aggregator (257), or using a *Publish-Subscribe Channel (154)*, comprises a
larger pattern, the *Composed Message Processor (270)*. But why view the finer-
grained patterns as a larger one? When composing these into a larger pattern,
the *Composed Message Processor (270)* can more readily serve as a single filter
in the *Pipes and Filters (135)* style.

Routing Slip

Use a Routing Slip when a large business procedure logically does one thing but physically requires a series of processing steps. This achieves a service composition commonly recognized as SOA. In our Routing Slip process, each step is handled by an individual actor. The process of this example is customer registration, as described by *Enterprise Integration Patterns* [EIP], which includes the following steps:

1. Create a new customer.

2. Record the customer's contact information.

3. Request a service plan for the customer.

4. Run a credit check for the new customer.

First let's look at the top of `RoutingSlip.scala` and the Value Objects [IDDD] that comprise the data body of the registration message.

```
package co.vaughnvernon.reactiveenterprise.routingslip

import akka.actor._
import co.vaughnvernon.reactiveenterprise._

case class CustomerInformation(
    val name: String,
    val federalTaxId: String)

case class ContactInformation(
    val postalAddress: PostalAddress,
    val telephone: Telephone)

case class PostalAddress(
    val address1: String,
    val address2: String,
    val city: String,
    val state: String,
    val zipCode: String)

case class Telephone(val number: String)
```

```
case class ServiceOption(
    val id: String,
    val description: String)

case class RegistrationData(
    val customerInformation: CustomerInformation,
    val contactInformation: ContactInformation,
    val serviceOption: ServiceOption)
```

It's all composed into an immutable `RegistrationData` Value Object [IDDD]. Next is the Routing Slip implementation, namely, `Registration-Process`, which is composed of individual `ProcessStep` instances.

```
case class ProcessStep(
    val name: String,
    val processor: ActorRef)

case class RegistrationProcess(
    val processId: String,
    val processSteps: Seq[ProcessStep],
    val currentStep: Int) {

  def this(
      processId: String,
      processSteps: Seq[ProcessStep]) {
    this(processId, processSteps, 0)
  }

  def isCompleted: Boolean = {
    currentStep >= processSteps.size
  }

  def nextStep(): ProcessStep = {
    if (isCompleted) {
      throw new IllegalStateException(
          "Process had already completed.")
    }

    processSteps(currentStep)
  }

  def stepCompleted(): RegistrationProcess = {
    new RegistrationProcess(
        processId,
        processSteps,
        currentStep + 1)
  }
}
```

Each `ProcessStep` has a name and a reference to the actor that performs the step. The `RegistrationProcess` knows how to mark each step completed, determine whether the entire process is completed, and figure out how to retrieve the next step to be processed. The design is such that every actor in the process will receive the same message, `RegisterCustomer`.

```
case class RegisterCustomer(
    val registrationData: RegistrationData,
    val registrationProcess: RegistrationProcess) {

  def advance():Unit = {
    val advancedProcess =
          registrationProcess.stepCompleted
    if (!advancedProcess.isCompleted) {
      advancedProcess.nextStep().processor !
         RegisterCustomer(
               registrationData,
               advancedProcess)
    }
    RoutingSlip.completedStep()
  }
}
```

When an actor receives the `RegisterCustomer` message, it uses the parts of the `RegistrationData` that it needs to carry out its specific step in the process (see the previous list of steps). The second-to-last operation in the individual step is to advance the `RegistrationProcess` to the next step and dispatch to its actor. (The final operation is discussed in a moment.) Each actor does this using the `advance()` method on the received `RegisterCustomer` message.

```
        val registrationData =
              registerCustomer.registrationData
        ...
        registerCustomer.advance()
        ...
```

That makes the `RegisterCustomer` message a kind of *Envelope Wrapper (314)*. The `advance()` method creates a new immutable `RegisterCustomer` message but with the `currentStep` index incremented to point to the step beyond the one just executed.

The driver for the example, the `RoutingSlip` object, composes the `RegistrationProcess` with `ProcessStep` instances and initializes its `currentStep` to 0 (the first step).

```
object RoutingSlip extends CompletableApp(4) {
  val processId = java.util.UUID.randomUUID().toString

  val step1 = ProcessStep(
              "create_customer",
              ServiceRegistry.customerVault(
                        system,
                        processId))

  val step2 = ProcessStep(
              "set_up_contact_info",
              ServiceRegistry.contactKeeper(
                        system,
                        processId))

  val step3 = ProcessStep(
              "select_service_plan",
              ServiceRegistry.servicePlanner(
                        system,
                        processId))

  val step4 = ProcessStep(
              "check_credit",
              ServiceRegistry.creditChecker(
                        system,
                        processId))

  val registrationProcess =
      new RegistrationProcess(
                        processId,
                        Vector(
                            step1,
                            step2,
                            step3,
                            step4))

  val registrationData =
        new RegistrationData(
          CustomerInformation(
                "ABC, Inc.", "123-45-6789"),
          ContactInformation(
              PostalAddress(
                "123 Main Street", "Suite 100",
                "Boulder", "CO", "80301"),
              Telephone("303-555-1212")),
          ServiceOption(
                "99-1203",
                "A description of 99-1203."))

  val registerCustomer =
          RegisterCustomer(
```

```
                    registrationData,
                    registrationProcess)

    registrationProcess
            .nextStep
            .processor ! registerCustomer

    awaitCompletion
    println("RoutingSlip: is completed.")
}
```

To look up each of the processing step actors, `RoutingSlip` uses a `Service-Registry` object. As it turns out, the `ServiceRegistry` simply creates a new actor instance each time a specific one is requested. It could just as easily reuse the same actor instances (creating just one of each), but if new customers are seldom registered, this is unnecessary.

```scala
object ServiceRegistry {
  def contactKeeper(
        system: ActorSystem,
        id: String) = {
    system.actorOf(
          Props[ContactKeeper],
          "contactKeeper-" + id)
  }

  def creditChecker(
        system: ActorSystem,
        id: String) = {
    system.actorOf(Props[CreditChecker],
                "creditChecker-" + id)
  }

  def customerVault(
        system: ActorSystem,
        id: String) = {
    system.actorOf(Props[CustomerVault],
                "customerVault-" + id)
  }

  def servicePlanner(
        system: ActorSystem,
        id: String) = {
    system.actorOf(Props[ServicePlanner],
                "servicePlanner-" + id)
  }
}
```

Still the individual actors must be cleaned up, and this is a responsibility that each actor can easily take on.

```scala
class CreditChecker extends Actor {
  def receive = {
    case registerCustomer: RegisterCustomer =>
      val federalTaxId =
            registerCustomer.registrationData
                .customerInformation.federalTaxId

      println(s"CreditChecker: handling register↵
 customer to perform credit check: $federalTaxId")

      registerCustomer.advance()

      context.stop(self)
    case message: Any =>
      println(s"CreditChecker: unexpected: $message")
  }
}

class ContactKeeper extends Actor {
  def receive = {
    case registerCustomer: RegisterCustomer =>
      val contactInfo =
            registerCustomer.registrationData
                .contactInformation

      println(s"ContactKeeper: handling register↵
 customer to keep contact information: $contactInfo")

      registerCustomer.advance()

      context.stop(self)
    case message: Any =>
      println(s"ContactKeeper: unexpected: $message")
  }
}

class CustomerVault extends Actor {
  def receive = {
    case registerCustomer: RegisterCustomer =>
      val customerInformation =
            registerCustomer.registrationData
                .customerInformation

      println(s"CustomerVault: handling register↵
 customer to create a new customer: $customerInformation")

      registerCustomer.advance()

      context.stop(self)
```

```
      case message: Any =>
        println(s"CustomerVault: unexpected: $message")
    }
}

class ServicePlanner extends Actor {
  def receive = {
    case registerCustomer: RegisterCustomer =>
      val serviceOption =
            registerCustomer
                .registrationData.serviceOption

      println(s"ServicePlanner: handling register↵
 customer to plan a new customer service: $serviceOption")

      registerCustomer.advance()

      context.stop(self)
    case message: Any =>
      println(s"ServicePlanner: unexpected: $message")
  }
}
```

As soon as the actor finishes processing its specific business logic, the actor requests that the `RegisterCustomer` be advanced to any next step and then terminates itself.

```
      case registerCustomer: RegisterCustomer =>
        ...
        registerCustomer.advance()
        context.stop(self)
```

The process output follows:

```
CustomerVault: handling register customer to create↵
 a new custoner:
   CustomerInformation(ABC, Inc.,123-45-6789)
ContactKeeper: handling register customer to keep↵
 contact information:
   ContactInformation(
      PostalAddress(123 Main Street,Suite 100,Boulder, ↵
CO,80301),
      Telephone(303-555-1212))
ServicePlanner: handling register customer to plan a↵
 new customer service:
   ServiceOption(99-1203,A description of 99-1203.)
CreditChecker: handling register customer to perform↵
 credit check: 123-45-6789
RoutingSlip: is completed.
```

The way the `RoutingSlip` driver object assembles the `Registration-Process` could be changed, placing the sequence of steps in any logical order that would allow the overall process to succeed. What is more, steps could be added and even inserted between any of the currently existing steps. The Routing Slip implementation would continue to function properly since its step advancement is driven off of a Scala `Seq`, which in this example is implemented as a `Vector`.

Process Manager

Use a Process Manager to route a message through multiple processing steps, even when the required steps may not be known at design time and may not be sequential. A *Routing Slip (285)* is a kind of Process Manager but only for a series of fixed, linear processing steps. Choose the simpler *Routing Slip (285)* if there is no need for conditional branching or looping. Yet, those are the kinds of concerns that are dealt with by a full-blown Process Manager, as shown in Figure 7.10. Note that each processing step delegated to the banks is concurrent and is thus marketed by the same step number 2.

I think there are two primary ways to implement a Process Manager. One way is to create a domain-specific language (DSL) and interpreter. The DSL is itself the high-level programming language that allows you to describe the rules of various business processes. One such language is Business Process Execution Language (BPEL), and there are several tools available that read, interpret, and manage business processes that are defined with it. When using such an approach, the Process Manager itself cannot be a core part of your process definition because the interpreter must be able to manage a wide range of business processes. That kind of Process Manager is not specific to your business domain. In other words, the Process Manager itself is highly reusable, in a similar way as any high-level programming language compiler/interpreter.

I have not attempted to create such an interpretive Process Manager here. Instead, you will examine a Process Manager that follows what I consider to be the second of the two primary approaches. This is a Process Manager that is built specifically for the purpose of handling requests for bank loan quotes, so

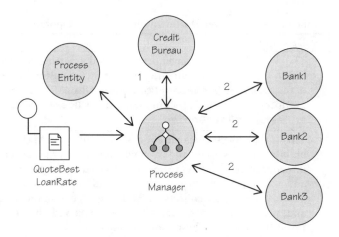

Figure 7.10 A Process Manager handles a multistep process where each step may not be known at design time and that may not be sequential. The parallel processing steps of each bank are shown as the same sequence number, 2.

it *is* domain-specific. The Process Manager must, from a single request, gather quotes from any participating number of banks and then provide the best loan rate quotation from among them. Flow control rules are coded directly into the specialized Process Manager, and it is assisted by a separate process instance entity that maintains the state of a process and, based on process state, gives transition direction to the overarching manager. Table 7.1 describes the actors used in the example. I think you will tend to model Process Managers like this one as you design your actor applications. This one models actors according to their primary roles, which is well suited to the Domain-Driven Design approach [IDDD].

Although I generally prefer to avoid all centralized points of control, a Process Manager tends to be just that. However, this doesn't mean that you can't decentralize. For example, by using the `DistributedPubSubMediator` described in *Publish-Subscribe Channel (154)*, you can implement a distributed Process Manager. In the following example, though, the design is based on a centralized actor.

To get started on the code review, first consider the driver application.

Table 7.1 The Components of the Process Manager Dealing with Loan Rate Quotations

Actor	Description
LoanBroker	This is the Process Manager, implemented as a *Message Broker (308)*. It receives an originating request for quotation by means of message type QuoteBestLoanRate. Ultimately the broker produces a resulting output message, either BestLoanRateQuoted or BestLoanRateDenied.
LoanRateQuote	This is the process instance entity that the Process Manager uses to maintain process state and from which it receives process transition direction. One entity is created per received QuoteBestLoanRate and is used from the beginning to the end of the loan quotation process. This entity collects all bank-provided loan rate quotes and, when all expected quotes have been received, informs the LoanBroker of the best quote among them.
CreditBureau	This provides a credit score for each party that requests a loan quote. This actor accepts a CheckCredit *Command Message (202)* and replies with a CreditChecked *Event Message (207)*.
Bank1, Bank2, Bank3	There is actually just one Bank actor type, but the driver application creates three total actor instances. Separate configurations and some random multipliers allow each bank to generally quote a different loan interest rate for each QuoteBestLoanRate request.

```
object ProcessManagerDriver extends CompletableApp(5) {
  val creditBureau =
          system.actorOf(
              Props[CreditBureau],
              "creditBureau")

    val bank1 =
          system.actorOf(
              Props(classOf[Bank], "bank1", 2.75, 0.30),
              "bank1")
    val bank2 =
          system.actorOf(
              Props(classOf[Bank], "bank2", 2.73, 0.31),
              "bank2")
    val bank3 =
          system.actorOf(
              Props(classOf[Bank], "bank3", 2.80, 0.29),
              "bank3")

    val loanBroker = system.actorOf(
        Props(classOf[LoanBroker],
            creditBureau,
            Vector(bank1, bank2, bank3)),
        "loanBroker")
```

```
loanBroker ! QuoteBestLoanRate("111-11-1111", 100000, 84)

    awaitCompletion
}
```

This `ProcessManagerDriver` application first creates the `Credit-Bureau` actor and then three `Bank` actors. Each of the `Bank` actors is given a different prime rate and premium, which are used when calculating each quoted interest rate. The final actor to be created is the Process Manager—the `LoanBroker`—and is given the actor reference for the `CreditBureau` and the ones for each `Bank`. The driver then sends the `QuoteBestLoanRate` message to the `LoanBroker`. This is considered the *triggering message* that causes a new complex process to start, one that manages what appears to the client to be a simple *Request-Reply (209)*.

The `LoanBroker` extends a special `ProcessManager` abstract base class. This base class itself extends `Actor` and also provides some basic reusable Process Manager behavior.

```
case class ProcessStarted(
    processId: String,
    process: ActorRef)

case class ProcessStopped(
    processId: String,
    process: ActorRef)

abstract class ProcessManager extends Actor {
  private var processes = Map[String, ActorRef]()
  val log: LoggingAdapter = Logging.getLogger(context.system, self)

  def processOf(processId: String): ActorRef = {
    if (processes.contains(processId)) {
      processes(processId)
    } else {
      null
    }
  }

  def startProcess(processId: String, process: ActorRef) = {
    if (!processes.contains(processId)) {
      processes = processes + (processId -> process)
      self ! ProcessStarted(processId, process)
    }
  }

  def stopProcess(processId: String) = {
    if (processes.contains(processId)) {
```

```
        val process = processes(processId)
        processes = processes - processId
        self ! ProcessStopped(processId, process)
    }
  }
}
```

The abstract base class is used to manage the life cycle of each process. When each new process is started, the concrete actor uses `startProcess()` to persist the new process instance entity by identity. In this implementation, the persistence is in-memory only but could be implemented to some form of database persistence. Function `startProcess()` responds by sending a `ProcessStarted` message to itself. When the concrete Process Manager actor needs to interact with the process entity actor, it asks for it by providing the entity's unique identity to `processOf()`. As each process reaches a completion state, the concrete actor uses `stopProcess()`, which causes the persisted state to be removed, and the `ProcessStopped` message is sent to itself. The two life-cycle messages allow the concrete Process Manager actor to do special processing, such as telling the actor to stop.

```
class LoanBroker(
    creditBureau: ActorRef,
    banks: Seq[ActorRef])
  extends ProcessManager {
  ...
    case message: ProcessStopped =>
      log.info(s"$message")

      context.stop(message.process)  ...
}
```

The `LoanBroker`, which serves as the Process Manager in this example, receives the life-cycle message `ProcessStopped` and arranges for the actor that implements the process instance entity to be stopped.

Let's look at the remainder of the `LoanBroker` implementation. First you see the message types of the external `LoanBroker` contract.

```
case class QuoteBestLoanRate(
    taxId: String,
    amount: Integer,
    termInMonths: Integer)

case class BestLoanRateQuoted(
```

```
    bankId: String,
    loanRateQuoteId: String,
    taxId: String,
    amount: Integer,
    termInMonths: Integer,
    creditScore: Integer,
    interestRate: Double)
case class BestLoanRateDenied(
    loanRateQuoteId: String,
    taxId: String,
    amount: Integer,
    termInMonths: Integer,
    creditScore: Integer)
```

Clients send the `LoanBroker` actor a `QuoteBestLoanRate` *Command Message (202)*, with the expectation of receiving in reply a `BestLoanRate-Quoted` *Event Message (207)*. There could be a problem, however, providing a loan quote. If the individual requesting the quotation has a credit score that is too low to be considered, the `LoanBroker` will reply with a `BestLoanRate-Denied` *Event Message (207)*.

Let's now see how `LoanBroker` handles the incoming `QuoteBestLoan-Rate` *Command Message (202)*.

```
class LoanBroker(
    creditBureau: ActorRef,
    banks: Seq[ActorRef])
  extends ProcessManager {
    ...
    case message: QuoteBestLoanRate =>
      val loanRateQuoteId = LoanRateQuote.id

      log.info(s"$message for: $loanRateQuoteId")

      val loanRateQuote =
          LoanRateQuote(
              context.system,
              loanRateQuoteId,
              message.taxId,
              message.amount,
              message.termInMonths,
              self)

      startProcess(loanRateQuoteId, loanRateQuote)
  }
  ...
}
```

Each new process begins by creating a new `LoanRateQuote` actor, which is the process instance entity that maintains the state of each request for quotation. Once created, the actor-based process is started. It may seem as if from here the process just falls off a cliff. However, you must look at the handler for `ProcessStarted` messages and the `LoanRateQuote` actor itself to see the collaboration that occurs between the Process Manager and a managed process.

```
class LoanBroker(
    creditBureau: ActorRef,
    banks: Seq[ActorRef])
  extends ProcessManager {
    ...
    case message: ProcessStarted =>
      log.info(s"$message")

      message.process ! StartLoanRateQuote(banks.size)
    ...
}
```

The `LoanBroker` uses the `ProcessStarted` life-cycle message as its cue to send the `LoanRateQuote` its first business process message, `StartLoanRateQuote`. This message contains the number of banks that are currently participating in interest rate quotations. The `LoanRateQuote` entity must know this because it acts as a message *Aggregator (257)*, collecting the full complement of quotes, one from each bank. You could pass in the number of participating banks as a constructor argument, as is done with other `LoanRateQuote` configurations. Yet, sending the number of banks with the `StartLoanRateQuote` message helps make the intention to aggregate the specific number of bank quotes more explicitly part of the process.

```
class LoanRateQuote(
    loanRateQuoteId: String,
    taxId: String,
    amount: Integer,
    termInMonths: Integer,
    loanBroker: ActorRef)
  extends Actor {

  var bankLoanRateQuotes = Vector[BankLoanRateQuote]()
  var creditRatingScore: Int = _
  var expectedLoanRateQuotes: Int = _

  def receive = {
    case message: StartLoanRateQuote =>
      expectedLoanRateQuotes =
```

```
        message.expectedLoanRateQuotes
      loanBroker !
        LoanRateQuoteStarted(
            loanRateQuoteId,
            taxId)
    ...
}
```

Once the `expectedLoanRateQuotes` value has been recorded in the `LoanRateQuote` entity, the entity sends a `LoanRateQuoteStarted` message to the `LoanBroker`. When receiving this message, the `LoanBroker` knows it can next request a credit score from the `CreditBureau` by sending a `CheckCredit` message. This sort of collaborative interaction continues through the entire life cycle of the process. To fully understand the process, you will need to trace the message sends between the `LoanBroker`, the `LoanRateQuote`, the `CreditBureau`, and the `Bank` instances. These activities are (mostly) illustrated in Figure 7.11.

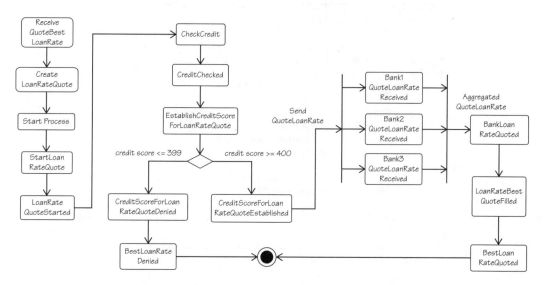

Figure 7.11 The activities of the Process Manager that supports loan rate quotations.

Next is the entirety of the `LoanBroker` implementation:

```
class LoanBroker(
    creditBureau: ActorRef,
    banks: Seq[ActorRef])
```

```
extends ProcessManager {

def receive = {
  case message: BankLoanRateQuoted =>
    log.info(s"$message")

    processOf(message.loadQuoteReferenceId) !
        RecordLoanRateQuote(
            message.bankId,
            message.bankLoanRateQuoteId,
            message.interestRate)

  case message: CreditChecked =>
    log.info(s"$message")

    processOf(message.creditProcessingReferenceId) !
        EstablishCreditScoreForLoanRateQuote(
            message.creditProcessingReferenceId,
            message.taxId,
            message.score)

  case message: CreditScoreForLoanRateQuoteDenied =>
    log.info(s"$message")

    processOf(message.loanRateQuoteId) !
            TerminateLoanRateQuote()

    ProcessManagerDriver.completeAll

    val denied =
        BestLoanRateDenied(
            message.loanRateQuoteId,
            message.taxId,
            message.amount,
            message.termInMonths,
            message.score)

    log.info(s"Would be sent to original requester: $denied")

  case message: CreditScoreForLoanRateQuoteEstablished =>
    log.info(s"$message")

    banks map { bank =>
      bank ! QuoteLoanRate(
        message.loanRateQuoteId,
        message.taxId,
        message.score,
        message.amount,
        message.termInMonths)
    }

    ProcessManagerDriver.completedStep
```

```
  case message: LoanRateBestQuoteFilled =>
    log.info(s"$message")

    ProcessManagerDriver.completedStep

    stopProcess(message.loanRateQuoteId)

    val best = BestLoanRateQuoted(
        message.bestBankLoanRateQuote.bankId,
        message.loanRateQuoteId,
        message.taxId,
        message.amount,
        message.termInMonths,
        message.creditScore,
        message.bestBankLoanRateQuote.interestRate)

    log.info(s"Would be sent to original requester:↵
$best")

  case message: LoanRateQuoteRecorded =>
    log.info(s"$message")

    ProcessManagerDriver.completedStep

  case message: LoanRateQuoteStarted =>
    log.info(s"$message")

    creditBureau ! CheckCredit(
        message.loanRateQuoteId,
        message.taxId)

  case message: LoanRateQuoteTerminated =>
    log.info(s"$message")

    stopProcess(message.loanRateQuoteId)

  case message: ProcessStarted =>
    log.info(s"$message")

    message.process ! StartLoanRateQuote(banks.size)

  case message: ProcessStopped =>
    log.info(s"$message")

    context.stop(message.process)

  case message: QuoteBestLoanRate =>
    val loanRateQuoteId = LoanRateQuote.id

    log.info(s"$message for: $loanRateQuoteId")

    val loanRateQuote =
```

```
                    LoanRateQuote(
                        context.system,
                        loanRateQuoteId,
                        message.taxId,
                        message.amount,
                        message.termInMonths,
                        self)

                startProcess(loanRateQuoteId, loanRateQuote)
        }
    }
```

Next is the source for the `LoanRateQuote` implementation, including the messages of its contract and its companion object:

```
case class StartLoanRateQuote(
    expectedLoanRateQuotes: Integer)

case class LoanRateQuoteStarted(
    loanRateQuoteId: String,
    taxId: String)

case class TerminateLoanRateQuote()

case class LoanRateQuoteTerminated(
    loanRateQuoteId: String,
    taxId: String)

case class EstablishCreditScoreForLoanRateQuote(
    loanRateQuoteId: String,
    taxId: String,
    score: Integer)

case class CreditScoreForLoanRateQuoteEstablished(
    loanRateQuoteId: String,
    taxId: String,
    score: Integer,
    amount: Integer,
    termInMonths: Integer)

case class CreditScoreForLoanRateQuoteDenied(
    loanRateQuoteId: String,
    taxId: String,
    amount: Integer,
    termInMonths: Integer,
    score: Integer)

case class RecordLoanRateQuote(
    bankId: String,
    bankLoanRateQuoteId: String,
    interestRate: Double)
```

```scala
case class LoanRateQuoteRecorded(
    loanRateQuoteId: String,
    taxId: String,
    bankLoanRateQuote: BankLoanRateQuote)

case class LoanRateBestQuoteFilled(
    loanRateQuoteId: String,
    taxId: String,
    amount: Integer,
    termInMonths: Integer,
    creditScore: Integer,
    bestBankLoanRateQuote: BankLoanRateQuote)

case class BankLoanRateQuote(
    bankId: String,
    bankLoanRateQuoteId: String,
    interestRate: Double)

object LoanRateQuote {
  val randomLoanRateQuoteId = new Random()

  def apply(
      system: ActorSystem,
      loanRateQuoteId: String,
      taxId: String,
      amount: Integer,
      termInMonths: Integer,
      loanBroker: ActorRef): ActorRef = {

       val loanRateQuote =
         system.actorOf(
           Props(
               classOf[LoanRateQuote],
                   loanRateQuoteId, taxId,
                   amount, termInMonths, loanBroker),
               "loanRateQuote-" + loanRateQuoteId)

    loanRateQuote
  }

  def id() = {
    randomLoanRateQuoteId.nextInt(1000).toString
  }
}

class LoanRateQuote(
    loanRateQuoteId: String,
    taxId: String,
    amount: Integer,
    termInMonths: Integer,
    loanBroker: ActorRef)
  extends Actor {
```

```scala
var bankLoanRateQuotes = Vector[BankLoanRateQuote]()
var creditRatingScore: Int = _
var expectedLoanRateQuotes: Int = _

private def bestBankLoanRateQuote() = {
  var best = bankLoanRateQuotes(0)

  bankLoanRateQuotes map { bankLoanRateQuote =>
    if (best.interestRate >
        bankLoanRateQuote.interestRate) {
      best = bankLoanRateQuote
    }
  }

  best
}

private def quotableCreditScore(
    score: Integer): Boolean = {
  score > 399
}

def receive = {
  case message: StartLoanRateQuote =>
    expectedLoanRateQuotes =
      message.expectedLoanRateQuotes
    loanBroker !
        LoanRateQuoteStarted(
            loanRateQuoteId,
            taxId)

  case message: EstablishCreditScoreForLoanRateQuote =>
    creditRatingScore = message.score
    if (quotableCreditScore(creditRatingScore))
     loanBroker !
        CreditScoreForLoanRateQuoteEstablished(
            loanRateQuoteId,
            taxId,
            creditRatingScore,
            amount,
            termInMonths)
    else
      loanBroker !
        CreditScoreForLoanRateQuoteDenied(
            loanRateQuoteId,
            taxId,
            amount,
            termInMonths,
            creditRatingScore)

  case message: RecordLoanRateQuote =>
    val bankLoanRateQuote =
      BankLoanRateQuote(
```

```
                    message.bankId,
                    message.bankLoanRateQuoteId,
                    message.interestRate)
            bankLoanRateQuotes =
              bankLoanRateQuotes :+ bankLoanRateQuote
            loanBroker !
                  LoanRateQuoteRecorded(
                      loanRateQuoteId,
                      taxId,
                      bankLoanRateQuote)

            if (bankLoanRateQuotes.size >=
                  expectedLoanRateQuotes)
              loanBroker !
                  LoanRateBestQuoteFilled(
                      loanRateQuoteId,
                      taxId,
                      amount,
                      termInMonths,
                      creditRatingScore,
                      bestBankLoanRateQuote)

        case message: TerminateLoanRateQuote =>
          loanBroker !
              LoanRateQuoteTerminated(
                  loanRateQuoteId,
                  taxId)
    }
}
```

Look at function `quotableCreditScore()`. There you can see the business rule that individuals must have a credit score higher than 399 to receive a quote. If their score is 399 or lower, the `LoanRateQuote` will send `CreditScoreForLoanRateQuoteDenied` to the `LoanBroker`, which in turn results in the `LoanBroker` sending `BestLoanRateDenied` to its client.

Here is the implementation of `CreditBureau`:

```
case class CheckCredit(
    creditProcessingReferenceId: String,
    taxId: String)

case class CreditChecked(
    creditProcessingReferenceId: String,
    taxId: String,
    score: Integer)

class CreditBureau extends Actor {
  val creditRanges = Vector(300, 400, 500, 600, 700)
  val randomCreditRangeGenerator = new Random()
```

```
    val randomCreditScoreGenerator = new Random()

    def receive = {
      case message: CheckCredit =>
        val range =
          creditRanges(
              randomCreditRangeGenerator.nextInt(5))
        val score =
          range
          + randomCreditScoreGenerator.nextInt(20)

        sender !
            CreditChecked(
                message.creditProcessingReferenceId,
                message.taxId,
                score)
    }
}
```

Finally, here is the implementation of `Bank`:

```
case class QuoteLoanRate(
    loadQuoteReferenceId: String,
    taxId: String,
    creditScore: Integer,
    amount: Integer,
    termInMonths: Integer)

case class BankLoanRateQuoted(
    bankId: String,
    bankLoanRateQuoteId: String,
    loadQuoteReferenceId: String,
    taxId: String,
    interestRate: Double)

class Bank(
    bankId: String,
    primeRate: Double,
    ratePremium: Double)
  extends Actor {

  val randomDiscount = new Random()
  val randomQuoteId = new Random()

  private def calculateInterestRate(
      amount: Double,
      months: Double,
      creditScore: Double): Double = {

    val creditScoreDiscount = creditScore / 100.0 / 10.0 -
```

```
            (randomDiscount.nextInt(5) * 0.05)

    primeRate + ratePremium + ((months / 12.0) / 10.0) -
        creditScoreDiscount
  }

  def receive = {
    case message: QuoteLoanRate =>
      val interestRate =
        calculateInterestRate(
            message.amount.toDouble,
            message.termInMonths.toDouble,
            message.creditScore.toDouble)

      sender ! BankLoanRateQuoted(
          bankId, randomQuoteId.nextInt(1000).toString,
          message.loadQuoteReferenceId, message.taxId, interestRate)
  }
}
```

Both the `CreditBureau` and the `Bank` are implemented to provide random results. The `Bank` uses the individual's credit score to determine a possible discount, with better credit scores yielding better discounts.

Here is output from running the process with a credit score that allows for a successful best rate loan quote:

```
QuoteBestLoanRate(111-11-1111,100000,84) for: 151
ProcessStarted(151,Actor[akka://reactiveenterprise/user/↵
loanRateQuote-151])
LoanRateQuoteStarted(151,111-11-1111)
CreditChecked(151,111-11-1111,610)
CreditScoreForLoanRateQuoteEstablished(151,111-11-1111,↵
610,100000,84)
BankLoanRateQuoted(bank2,853,151,111-11-1111,3.33)
BankLoanRateQuoted(bank3,911,151,111-11-1111,3.23)
BankLoanRateQuoted(bank1,292,151,111-11-1111,3.34)
LoanRateQuoteRecorded(151,111-11-1111,BankLoanRateQuote(↵
bank2,853,3.33))
LoanRateQuoteRecorded(151,111-11-1111,BankLoanRateQuote(↵
bank3,911,3.23))
LoanRateQuoteRecorded(151,111-11-1111,BankLoanRateQuote(↵
bank1,292,3.34))
LoanRateBestQuoteFilled(151,111-11-↵
1111,100000,84,610,BankLoanRateQuote(bank3,911,3.23))
Would be sent to original requester: BestLoanRateQuoted(↵
bank3,151,111-11-1111,100000,84,610,3.23)
ProcessStopped(151,Actor[akka://reactiveenterprise/user/↵
loanRateQuote-151])
```

Message Broker

Use a Message Broker to decouple the receiver of a message from the message sender while maintaining central control over the flow of messages. As is illustrated in Figure 7.12, a Message Broker is largely concerned with routing messages between disparate applications, but ones that must integrate. This diagram shows a Message Broker hierarchy, where there are "subnets" of applications that are under the control of a single Message Broker but where a Centralized Message Broker can be used to deliver any given message from an application in one subnet to an application in a different subnet.

A Message Broker is implemented using one or more other message routing patterns described in this chapter. As *Enterprise Integration Patterns* [EIP] points out, Message Broker is an architecture style, while the individual routing approaches are design patterns. Thus, you can use multiple design patterns within the overarching Message Broker style, depending on the kinds of routing that your broker needs to support.

A few fundamental problems with a Message Broker are the need for every message sent from one application to another to pass through the broker and the

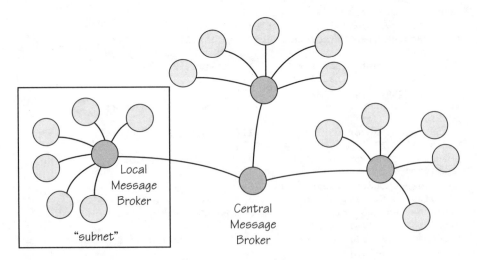

Figure 7.12 A central Message Broker with three subnets.

need for the broker to translate messages from one application format to another application format. Considering all the messages that must pass through the broker, it can become not only a routing bottleneck but also a message translation bottleneck. Add to these performance overheads the possible large number of data format translators that must be supported. In Figure 7.12 there are 16 different participant applications represented, which means there could be as many as 16^2 or 256 data format translators required since any one application could send a message to any other application.[1]

These are problems that many enterprise application integration (EAI) tools attempt to solve. Horizontally scaling the number of message receivers in the broker is one way to deal with the possibilities of a bottleneck caused by the sheer number of messages. An EAI tool will typically provide data format translators primarily for commercial applications whose formats can be obtained from known vendors. You can't expect an EAI tool to have a translator available for your internal enterprise applications, unless you pay for them to be custom developed after acquiring a license. Thus, the next chapter provides solutions for a number of Message Transformation patterns. These can be used to develop your own message data format translators, which may make more sense for your solutions given the trend toward rejecting EAI tools.

SOA is a set of architecture and design principles that are recommended guidance when implementing services. One such principle is *service autonomy*. An autonomous service is one that depends only on its own service input and output contract, its internal implementation, and its data. Because tool vendors are generally more interested in selling tools than in adhering to the actual principles of a given approach, the popularity of SOA became a magnet for EAI tools that claimed to support service-oriented development. But instead of supporting SOA principles, such as service autonomy, typically EAI tools cause the centralization of service control, with Message Broker playing the key role. For this reason, I don't emphasize the use of this pattern or provide a specific implementation example.

For those who want to study Message Brokers, I believe that this book's *Message Bus (192)* and *Process Manager (292)* provide decent samples. Although the trend is to move away from large, monolithic Message Brokers, *Message Buses (192)*, and *Process Managers (292)*, which are generally combined in a single tool, those found in this book are straightforward implementations. In particular, you will find that the *Process Manager (292)*

---

1. While it may seem unlikely that every application would actually need to integrate with every other application, the possibility exists. You cannot rule out the potential for this scenario to play out over years of business refinements.

implementation in this book is clearly focused on the concepts around requests for bank loan quotes. You will need to create *Process Managers (292)* like that one as you design your own process-based actor applications.

Consider the similarities between Message Broker and *Message Bus (192)*. A *Message Bus (192)* is considered to be a specialized *Message Channel (128)* because its focus is more on how a message sent on one channel will be switched onto another channel through which the message will be delivered. It is the job of a *Message Router (140)* to determine on which channel the message must be delivered. In other words, messages that are sent to the *Message Bus (192)* must be routed to actors that have registered interest with the bus for specific kinds of messages, which requires the *Message Bus (192)* to provide the means to maintain and execute the routing rules. Since both a *Message Bus (192)* and a Message Broker depend on the use of a *Canonical Message Model (333)*, it makes both of these patterns a kind of *Content-Based Router (228)*.

To deal with data format translations, a *Message Bus (192)* employs a Channel Adapter *(183)* to transform messages between the data formats of applications that use the bus. Again, this is a feature that is similar or identical to that required by the Message Broker to translate between application data formats.

There may be few differences between a *Message Bus (192)* and a Message Broker. One is that a Message Broker can be hierarchical. Even so, you could design a *Message Bus (192)* to route messages from one subnet to another by means of a separate, centralized *Message Bus (192)* trafficker.

With such few differences—and possibly reconcilable ones at that—between a bus and a broker, you may think of a bus just as negatively as a broker. Perhaps that is a fair assessment and one reason why the more recent trend is to move away from solutions that emphasize centralized control. Still, just because tool vendors have used Message Broker, *Message Bus (192)*, and *Process Manager (292)* patterns to create large, expensive, slow, and complex EAI tools, it doesn't mean that designing a Message Broker for your specific enterprise solutions should be viewed negatively. In fact, it could be just what is needed.

Summary

In this chapter you discovered a whole slew of reactive routers. You will tend to create these kinds of tools, especially some more than others, when you use a Domain-Driven Design [IDDD] approach to modeling actors. This will be true of your use of *Process Managers (292)*, *Aggregators (257)*, *Scatter-Gather (272)*, and *Routing Slip (285)*.

Don't overlook the other tools found in this chapter. *Message Filter (232)*, *Recipient List (245)*, *Splitter (254)*, and *Resequencer (264)* all have an important role to play both in application design and in integration efforts in your enterprise.

Chapter 8

Message Transformation

In Chapter 4, "Messaging with Actors," I discussed *Message Translator (143)* as a general topic. In this chapter, you will dig deeper into various kinds of transformations that messages may undergo in your applications and integrations.

- *Envelope Wrapper*: In typical middleware messaging systems there is a message header with distinct, standardized properties. The Actor model, and Akka specifically, doesn't support message headers. However, you may want to wrap some messages inside an envelope-type structure that might even mimic a message header. The *Envelope Wrapper (314)* may be called on to perform some specific application functionality, such as filling the role of *Channel Adapter (183)*, or as a sort of *Message Router (140)* used to dispatch a response in a *Request-Reply (209)* communication.

- *Content Enricher*: It may so happen that your actor system will need to send a message to an integrator, but your internal message type is not rich enough for the other systems that need to consume it. You can use a *Content Enricher (317)* to fortify any given *Message (130)* so it can be consumed by a specific *Datatype Channel (167)*.

- *Content Filter*: The opposite of a *Content Enricher (317)*, a *Content Filter (321)* removes certain information from a *Message (130)*. This is different from a *Message Filter (232)* that may dispose of entire *Messages (130)*. Rather, this kind of filter is responsible for removing content from a *Message (130)*, perhaps because it is too sensitive to expose to the outside.

- *Claim Check*: You can use a *Claim Check (325)* when you must break up a composite message into smaller parts but must also provide access to any of the parts on demand.

- *Normalizer*: A *Normalizer (332)* is a no-holds-barred transformer. It is used when your system receives messages that are of types that are not supported, and you need to transform the messages into ones that are supported.

- *Canonical Message Model*: Make use of this pattern when several applications in your enterprise integrate with each other. For example, if you

313

have five to seven, or even more, applications that must all send messages to each other, use *Canonical Message Model (333)* pattern to make a common set of messages for all the applications to share.

Although some of these patterns may not seem at first to deal with message transformations, they really do. It's just that each of these explores the variants of the vanilla *Message Translator (143)*.

Envelope Wrapper

I've discussed a few ways to use *Return Address (211)* with the Actor model, which allows a message-receiving actor to reply to an actor other than the direct sender or forwarder of the message. Sometimes, however, it might work out for the best if your messages themselves support the means to dispatch to a reply-to actor. This can be accomplished if a message has an Envelope Wrapper.

Oftentimes an Envelope Wrapper is used when there are multiple transport layers or when a message must be tunneled through to a network other than the one on which it originated. Generally speaking, a message that is produced by an actor system such as Akka will not need an envelope for those reasons, or the actor system itself may provide the needed transport-specific envelope. Yet, there may be other reasons for actors in a given system to use an envelope, as is indicated in Figure 8.1.

Consider, for example, that an original message enters the system, but the base message type is not natively supported by any one actor. It's possible to wrap such an incompatible message in an envelope. What could be accomplished by doing so?

- The envelope can be used as an Adapter [GoF] from the original message to the actor-supported message type when the Envelope Wrapper supports/extends the protocol of the message type that the actor system understands.

- Since the message may have originated from a remote system, if the Envelope Wrapper provides the means to reply to the originating "actor," the reply can be made in a convenient way. Actually the "actor" in the

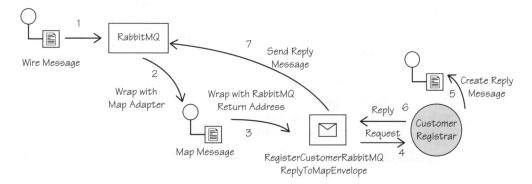

Figure 8.1 Use an Envelope Wrapper when you need to maintain the reply-to address needed by a middleware messaging system.

message-originating system may not be at all like the actors in the local system (for example, not Akka actors). Thus, replying to the originating "actor" may be quite involved, perhaps using Transmission Control Protocol/ Internet Protocol (TCP/IP) or some other transport and network protocol, such as via some message-oriented middleware. By supporting the means to reply, the envelope greatly reduces the complexity of a local system actor interacting with the "actor" in the originating system.

Perhaps the originating system sends a message as a map of key-value pairs, which may even contain metadata about how to reply, such as a *Return Address (211)*. As soon as the message arrives in the local actor-based system, it is wrapped in an envelope message and then sent to a native actor. Notice the use of *Return Address (211)* in this solution, but this time it's providing a way to reply to an external system via RabbitMQ.

```scala
trait ReplyToSupport {
  def reply(message: Any) = { }
  def setUpReplyToSupport(returnAddress: String) = { }
}

trait RabbitMQReplyToSupport extends ReplyToSupport {
  override def reply(message: Any) = {
    ...
  }

  override def setUpReplyToSupport(returnAddress: String) = {
    ...
```

```
  }
}

trait RegisterCustomer {
  ...
}

case class RegisterCustomerRabbitMQReplyToMapEnvelope(
        mapMessage: Map[String, String])
      extends RegisterCustomer with RabbitMQReplyToSupport {

  this.setUpReplyToSupport(mapMessage("returnAddress"))
}
...

val mapMessage = receivedMessageAsMap(wireMessage)

val registerCustomer =
      RegisterCustomerRabbitMQReplyToMapEnvelope(mapMessage)

customerRegistrar ! registerCustomer
```

The `ReplyToSupport` abstract trait behavior must be overridden in an extending concrete class, as is the case with `RabbitMQReplyToSupport`. The Envelope Wrapper is utilized when extended by `RegisterCustomerRabbitMQReplyToMapEnvelope`. The concrete envelope uses `setUpReplyToSupport()` during construction to ensure that subsequent use of `reply()` can succeed. You give the `setUpReplyToSupport()` the originator-supplied *Return Address (211)* metadata from the incoming mapped message.

When the `CustomerRegistrar` needs to reply to the originating "actor," it simply requests that the envelope reply.

```
class CustomerRegistrar extends Actor {
  def receive = {
    case registerCustomer: RegisterCustomer =>
      ...
      registerCustomer.reply(CustomerRegistered(...))
    case _ =>
      ...
  }
}
```

This is not the only use of an Envelope Wrapper, but it's one way to ease the tension between disparate systems and messages of varying types.

Content Enricher

With the *Envelope Wrapper (314)*, an incompatible message from an external system is made compatible with the actor system. Yet, the opposite situation may be true; a message that the local actor system needs to send is not compatible with an external system because the external system needs more content than the local system stores. What is more, the external system cannot or should not retrieve the extra information it requires. This situation can be resolved by using a Content Enricher.

The basic solution put forth by *Enterprise Integration Patterns* [EIP] uses another component—in our case, an actor—to enrich the content of the message before it is sent on to the external system, such that the message will contain all the content needed by that system once it is delivered, as shown in Figure 8.2.

Using the same example provided by *Enterprise Integration Patterns* [EIP], you enrich messages sent by a scheduler system with all the information required by the final consumer, the accounting system.

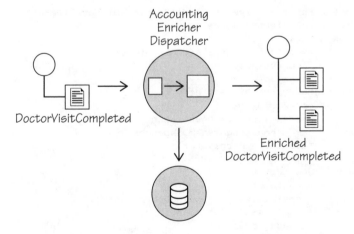

Figure 8.2 Here a Content Enricher adds more information to the `DoctorVisitCompleted` message. The extra data is retrieved from a database.

```scala
package co.vaughnvernon.reactiveenterprise.contentenricher

import akka.actor._
import co.vaughnvernon.reactiveenterprise._
import java.util.Date

case class DoctorVisitCompleted(
    val patientId: String,
    val firstName: String,
    val date: Date,
    val patientDetails: PatientDetails) {
  def this(patientId: String,
           firstName: String,
           date: Date) = {
    this(patientId, firstName, date,
        PatientDetails(null, null, null))
  }

  def carrier = patientDetails.carrier
  def lastName = patientDetails.lastName
  def socialSecurityNumber = patientDetails.socialSecurityNumber
}

case class PatientDetails(
    val lastName: String,
    val socialSecurityNumber: String,
    val carrier: String)

case class VisitCompleted(dispatcher: ActorRef)

object ContentEnricherDriver extends CompletableApp(3) {
  val accountingSystemDispatcher =
          system.actorOf(
              Props[AccountingSystemDispatcher],
              "accountingSystem")

  val accountingEnricherDispatcher =
          system.actorOf(
              Props(classOf[AccountingEnricherDispatcher],
                  accountingSystemDispatcher),
              "accountingDispatcher")

  val scheduledDoctorVisit =
          system.actorOf(
              Props(classOf[ScheduledDoctorVisit],
                  "123456789", "John"),
              "scheduledVisit")

  scheduledDoctorVisit !
      VisitCompleted(accountingEnricherDispatcher)
```

```
    awaitCompletion
    println("ContentEnricher: is completed.")
}

class AccountingEnricherDispatcher(
    val accountingSystemDispatcher: ActorRef)
  extends Actor {
  def receive = {
    case doctorVisitCompleted: DoctorVisitCompleted =>
      println("AccountingEnricherDispatcher: "
              + "querying and forwarding.")
      // query the enriching patient information...
      // ...
      val lastName = "Doe"
      val carrier = "Kaiser"
      val socialSecurityNumber = "111-22-3333"
      val enrichedDoctorVisitCompleted =
          DoctorVisitCompleted(
              doctorVisitCompleted.patientId,
              doctorVisitCompleted.firstName,
              doctorVisitCompleted.date,
              PatientDetails(
                  lastName,
                  socialSecurityNumber,
                  carrier))
      accountingSystemDispatcher forward
          enrichedDoctorVisitCompleted
      ContentEnricher.completedStep
    case _ =>
      println("AccountingEnricherDispatcher: unexpected")
  }
}

class AccountingSystemDispatcher extends Actor {
  def receive = {
    case doctorVisitCompleted: DoctorVisitCompleted =>
      println("AccountingSystemDispatcher: "
              + "sending to Accounting System...")
      ContentEnricher.completedStep
    case _ =>
      println("AccountingSystemDispatcher: unexpected")
  }
}

class ScheduledDoctorVisit(
    val patientId: String, val firstName: String)
  extends Actor {

  var completedOn: Date = _

  def receive = {
```

```
    case visitCompleted: VisitCompleted =>
      println("ScheduledDoctorVisit: completing visit.")
      completedOn = new Date()
      visitCompleted.dispatcher !
          new DoctorVisitCompleted(
                  patientId,
                  firstName,
                  completedOn)
      ContentEnricher.completedStep
    case _ =>
      println("ScheduledDoctorVisit: unexpected")
  }
}
```

This process produces the following output:

```
ScheduledDoctorVisit: completing visit.
AccountingEnricherDispatcher: querying and forwarding.
AccountingSystemDispatcher: sending to Accounting System...
ContentEnricher: is completed.
```

The `ScheduledDoctorVisit` is provided a *Return Address (211)*, that is, the actor that dispatches the `DoctorVisitCompleted` message. If this message did not require enrichment, the dispatcher could be the `Accounting-SystemDispatcher`. However, since this message must be enriched prior to being sent to the accounting system, the `CompleteVisit` message instead contains the `ActorRef` for the `AccountingEnricherDispatcher`.

It could be appropriate for the `AccountingEnricherDispatcher` to send `DoctorVisitCompleted` directly to the accounting system. Yet, it makes sense to place this responsibility only on the `AccountingSystemDispatcher`. Thus, the `AccountingEnricherDispatcher` is constructed so it will forward the `DoctorVisitCompleted` message to the `AccountingSystemDispatcher`.

Immutable DoctorVisitCompleted

It's a good idea to design `DoctorVisitCompleted` as immutable. A Domain Event [IDDD] should be immutable, and `DoctorVisitCompleted` is an *Event Message (207)*. The `DoctorVisitCompleted` is designed with two constructors, one that takes only the local attributes and the other that also accepts complete `PatientDetails`.

This allows the `ScheduledDoctorVisit` to dispatch the final message type, but with only the minimal locally available information. When the `AccountingEnricherDispatcher` retrieves the additional patient details, it creates the final instance of `DoctorVisitCompleted`.

Should the AccountingEnricherDispatcher Be Local?

So, should the `AccountingEnricherDispatcher` be deployed in the scheduler system? This may be a matter of taste. Apparently *Enterprise Integration Patterns* [EIP] intends for this actor to reside outside the scheduler system since they argue that the scheduler system should not depend on the customer care system. Thus, the `AccountingEnricherDispatcher` could be a remote actor. On the other hand, you might consider the `AccountingEnricherDispatcher` to be a self-contained actor that could be deployed on any practical system. Consider the competing forces. The final decision may be mostly influenced by the ability to deploy actors, or lack thereof, in any given system.

Still, there may be another factor. If the kind of integration required between the scheduler system and the customer care system is complex, and the scheduler system cannot support such a heavyweight integration, you will have to move it outside the Scheduler Bounded Context [IDDD]. Yet, if there is some way for the customer care system to lower the barrier by making the integration easier, it could go a long way in simplifying things. Many times making a simple RESTful resource available through a link (URI) will produce just the ease of use you seek.

Content Filter

With *Envelope Wrapper (314)*, you already dealt with the situation where an external message is incompatible with your local actor system. You used the envelope to both adapt the external message to one locally acceptable, and you also designed the envelope to reply to the originating external system. This made dealing with the external messaging system, and the message itself, seamless. Further, you used a *Content Enricher (317)* to augment your local message with more information needed by an external system before the message is sent to it.

There are times, however, when a message could contain too much information or for other reasons be difficult to consume. Consider some cases:

- Data may be easily obtained from a database when local application-specific queries are employed. Yet, the rich amount of data may be too sensitive to send to outside systems.

- The local application data that is queried may also be too large to be practical to send over the network, and most of it may not be necessary for most consumers, even local actors.

- Not only the amount of data but also its structure may be too complex for it to be practical to consume by some local actors or remote systems.

For these situations, use a Content Filter. It might be enough to use a single filter to reduce the size and complexity of the information passed in a given message. On the other hand, it may be necessary to design a *Splitter (254)* to break one large data structure into several smaller message types.

Note that the motivation of a Content Filter is different from the *Envelope Wrapper (314)*. You don't only want to adapt a large, complex data structure to a format with which a consumer is compatible. You want to reduce its content to the subset that consumers are authorized to receive, reduce its overall size to only that which is necessary, or make accessing the reduced amount of information easier for authorized consumers.

Filters and Pipes and Filters

A Content Filter is not necessarily the same as a filter in the *Pipes and Filters (135)* architecture. When defining a filter for the *Pipes and Filters (135)* style, the filter may simply be a processor that in no way alters the message content. Yet, it may be a *Content Enricher (317)* or possibly a Content Filter. As usual, it depends.

Of course a Content Filter may reside on either side of a system boundary, that is, in the sending system and/or in the receiving system. If the concern is primarily a matter of authority, the filter should reside on the sender system. Authorization notwithstanding, if the data structure is potentially large, the sending system should also be concerned with network optimizations.

However, when dealing with a complex third-party—even publicly accessible—integration, it's quite possible that the producing system will be less concerned with network optimization than with providing all the data possible in order to eliminate the special needs of the plethora of consumers with one-off requirements. In such cases the Content Filter would be placed in the consumer system.

If you've already studied the *Content Enricher (317)*, looking at an example for a Content Filter may seem less interesting. The way to employ an actor-based filter is much like how you'd employ a *Content Enricher (317)*, but with the opposite motivation. Still, the filter example can be interesting, although for different reasons. Since the example of the enricher deals with outgoing messages, let's consider filtering incoming messages and use a different approach for dispatching to the ultimate message consumers.

```scala
package co.vaughnvernon.reactiveenterprise.contentfilter

import akka.actor._
import co.vaughnvernon.reactiveenterprise.CompletableApp

case class FilteredMessage(
    light: String,
    and: String,
    fluffy: String,
    message: String) {
  override def toString = {
    s"FilteredMessage(" + light + " " + and + " "
                        + fluffy + " " + message + ")"
  }
}

case class UnfilteredPayload(largePayload: String)

object ContentFilter extends CompletableApp(3) {
  val messageExchangeDispatcher =
          system.actorOf(
              Props[MessageExchangeDispatcher],
              "messageExchangeDispatcher")

  messageExchangeDispatcher !
          UnfilteredPayload(
              "A very large message with complex↵
 structure...")

  awaitCompletion
  println("RequestReply: is completed.")
}

class MessageExchangeDispatcher extends Actor {

  val messageContentFilter =
          context.actorOf(
              Props[MessageContentFilter],
              "messageContentFilter")

  def receive = {
    case message: UnfilteredPayload =>
      println("MessageExchangeDispatcher: "
              + "received unfiltered message: "
              + message.largePayload)
      messageContentFilter ! message
      ContentFilter.completedStep
    case message: FilteredMessage =>
      println("MessageExchangeDispatcher: dispatching: "
              + message)
      ContentFilter.completedStep
    case _ =>
      println("MessageExchangeDispatcher: unexpected")
```

```
    }
}

class MessageContentFilter extends Actor {
  def receive = {
    case message: UnfilteredPayload =>
      println("MessageContentFilter: "
              + "received unfiltered message: "
              + message.largePayload)
      // filtering occurs...
      sender ! FilteredMessage(
                "this", "feels", "so", "right")
      ContentFilter.completedStep
    case _ =>
      println("MessageContentFilter: unexpected")
  }
}
```

The process produces the following output:

```
MessageExchangeDispatcher: received unfiltered message:↵
 A very large message with complex structure...
MessageContentFilter: received unfiltered message: A very↵
 large message with complex structure...
MessageExchangeDispatcher: dispatching: FilteredMessage(↵
this feels so right)
RequestReply: is completed.
```

It is appropriate here to consider the rules of the Object-Capability model of security [OCM]. Possibly the strongest form of security is found in rule #2, Parenthood. When a parent actor creates a child actor, at the moment of creation the parent holds the only reference to the child. This fact ensures that the parent can completely isolate all messaging to the child, which makes the child as secure as its tests prove it is. No other actors can send it messages unless the child is designed to itself create children or to receive messages from or send messages to additional actors, which would lead to the other rules of the Object-Capability model.

For instance, the *Content Enricher (317)* example also adheres to the Object-Capability model but uses a combination of rules #3 and #4. The Accounting-EnricherDispatcher is *endowed* (#3) with an AccountingSystem-Dispatcher, and the ScheduledDoctorVisit is *introduced* (#4) to an AccountingEnricherDispatcher. However, this Content Filter example uses possibly the strongest guarantee that the MessageContentFilter will not transform/process a rouge message on behalf of a rouge actor.

Possible Actor Selection Caveat

Note that perhaps the greatest potential for hazardous use of the Actor model is when an actor can look up another actor by name and send it a message. Using this approach breaks the intent of the Object-Capability model, unless the actor performing the lookup is the parent of the sought-after actor.

Why wouldn't the parent just hold an `ActorRef` for each child that it needs to interact with, rather than using a lookup? Perhaps there are too many children to track in that way, and a well-placed look up will help conserve system memory or reduce the complexity of managing the children individually by reference.

Claim Check

When you need to break up a composite message into smaller parts but provide access to any of the parts on demand, use a Claim Check.

Consider the Claim Check a unique identifier used to store and access a *checked item*. You pass as part of a processing message the identity of the specific checked item, which is its Claim Check. Each step in the process can use the Claim Check to retrieve all or part of the composite message content as needed.

The Claim Check pattern can be used with a *Content Enricher (317)* to reconstitute the message in full, to get only a particular part, or to do something in between. However, the important thing is that any given step in the message-based process can retrieve one or more parts of the original message content on demand. In fact, the example presented here does not use the Claim Check to enrich messages. It uses the Claim Check to get specific parts of the original message but just the part needed for a given processing step (see Figure 8.3).

Here are the message types and the driver application object of a Claim Check sample:

```
package co.vaughnvernon.reactiveenterprise.claimcheck

import akka.actor._
import co.vaughnvernon.reactiveenterprise._
import java.util.UUID
```

```scala
case class Part(name: String)

case class CompositeMessage(
    id: String,
    part1: Part,
    part2: Part,
    part3: Part)

case class ProcessStep(
    id: String,
    claimCheck: ClaimCheck)

case class StepCompleted(
    id: String,
    claimCheck: ClaimCheck,
    stepName: String)

object ClaimCheckDriver extends CompletableApp(3) {
  val itemChecker = new ItemChecker()

  val step1 =
        system.actorOf(
            Props(classOf[Step1], itemChecker),
            "step1")
  val step2 =
        system.actorOf(
            Props(classOf[Step2], itemChecker),
            "step2")
  val step3 =
        system.actorOf(
            Props(classOf[Step3], itemChecker),
            "step3")

  val process =
        system.actorOf(
            Props(classOf[Process],
                (Vector(step1, step2, step3),
                itemChecker)),
            "process")

  process ! CompositeMessage(
                "ABC",
                Part("partA1"),
                Part("partB2"),
                Part("partC3"))

  awaitCompletion
  println("ClaimCheck: is completed.")
}
```

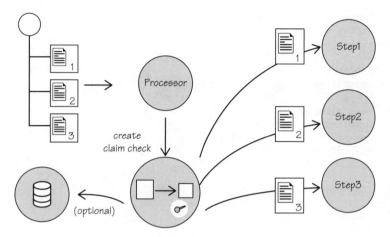

Figure 8.3 The Claim Check is used to get specific parts of the original message, but just the part needed for a given processing step.

The `ItemChecker` is a simple data store used to persist a checked item that is referenced by the Claim Check. The `ItemChecker` is not implemented as an actor, but it could be. And the `ItemChecker` could have backing database, but in this case persistence is in-memory only.

Each of the steps in the process is an individual actor. The controlling `Process` is also an actor, and all of the steps are given it in a `Vector`.

Here is the `ItemChecker` and the `ClaimCheck`, `CheckedItem`, and `CheckedPart` types:

```scala
import scala.collection.mutable.Map

case class ClaimCheck() {
  val number = UUID.randomUUID().toString

  override def toString = {
    "ClaimCheck(" + number + ")"
  }
}

case class CheckedItem(
    claimCheck: ClaimCheck,
    businessId: String,
    parts: Map[String, Any])

case class CheckedPart(
```

```
        claimCheck: ClaimCheck,
        partName: String,
        part: Any)

class ItemChecker {
  val checkedItems = Map[ClaimCheck, CheckedItem]()

  def checkedItemFor(
      businessId: String,
      parts: Map[String, Any]) = {
    CheckedItem(ClaimCheck(), businessId, parts)
  }

  def checkItem(item: CheckedItem) = {
    checkedItems.update(item.claimCheck, item)
  }

  def claimItem(claimCheck: ClaimCheck): CheckedItem = {
    checkedItems(claimCheck)
  }

  def claimPart(
      claimCheck: ClaimCheck,
      partName: String): CheckedPart = {
    val checkedItem = checkedItems(claimCheck)

    CheckedPart(
        claimCheck,
        partName,
        checkedItem.parts(partName))
  }

  def removeItem(claimCheck: ClaimCheck) = {
    if (checkedItems.contains(claimCheck)) {
      checkedItems.remove(claimCheck)
    }
  }
}
```

The ItemChecker stores whole CheckedItem instances. Clients can query for a whole CheckedItem or a minimal CheckedPart. This specific ItemChecker component understands the fact that CheckedItem instances have CheckedPart instances. Thus, the ItemChecker provides aggregate navigation and queries. If there is an underlying data store, it is quite likely that the ItemChecker is built on top of that store, allowing it to provide domain-specific queries to the Process and its individual steps.

After a Process has completed all its assigned steps, its CheckedItem is removed from the ItemChecker. Let's take a look at the Process:

```
class Process(
    steps: Vector[ActorRef],
    itemChecker: ItemChecker)
  extends Actor {

  var stepIndex = 0

  def receive = {
    case message: CompositeMessage =>
      val parts =
        Map(
            message.part1.name -> message.part1,
            message.part2.name -> message.part2,
            message.part3.name -> message.part3)

      val checkedItem =
            itemChecker
              .checkedItemFor(message.id, parts)

      itemChecker.checkItem(checkedItem)

      steps(stepIndex) !
          ProcessStep(
            message.id,
            checkedItem.claimCheck)

    case message: StepCompleted =>
      stepIndex += 1

      if (stepIndex < steps.size) {
        steps(stepIndex) !
            ProcessStep(
                message.id,
                message.claimCheck)
      } else {
        itemChecker.removeItem(message.claimCheck)
      }

      ClaimCheckApp.completedStep

    case message: Any =>
      println(s"Process: unexpected: $message")
  }
}
```

The `Process` is endowed with a `Vector` of `ActorRef` instances, each of which carry out one step in the overall process. The `Process` is also given a reference to the `ItemChecker`. Using its `ItemChecker` the `Process` stores a `CheckedItem` based on the contents of the received `CompositeMessage`.

Then each of the processing steps is executed by sending a `ProcessStep` message. As each step receives the `ProcessStep` message, it obtains the `Checked-Part` needed for its specific step from the `ItemChecker`. Once a processing step has been completed, it sends a StepCompleted *Event Message (207)* to the sender of the `ProcessStep` message that it is currently handling.

The sender of every `ProcessStep` message is the `Process` actor, which means it receives every `StepCompleted` *Event Message (207)*. As each `Step-Completed` is received, the `Process` dispatches to the next step, continuing until all steps are completed.

Here are the three actors that each perform an individual step in the `Process`:

```scala
class Step1(itemChecker: ItemChecker) extends Actor {
  def receive = {
    case processStep: ProcessStep =>
      val claimedPart =
            itemChecker.claimPart(
                processStep.claimCheck,
                "partA1")

      println(s"Step1: processing $processStep\n
  with $claimedPart")

        sender !
          StepCompleted(
              processStep.id,
              processStep.claimCheck,
              "step1")

    case message: Any =>
      println(s"Step1: unexpected: $message")
  }
}

class Step2(itemChecker: ItemChecker) extends Actor {
  def receive = {
    case processStep: ProcessStep =>
      val claimedPart =
            itemChecker
                .claimPart(
                    processStep.claimCheck,
                    "partB2")

      println(s"Step2: processing $processStep\n
  with $claimedPart")

        sender !
          StepCompleted(
```

```
                processStep.id,
                processStep.claimCheck,
                "step2")

      case message: Any =>
        println(s"Step2: unexpected: $message")
    }
}

class Step3(itemChecker: ItemChecker) extends Actor {
  def receive = {
    case processStep: ProcessStep =>
      val claimedPart =
            itemChecker.claimPart(
                processStep.claimCheck,
                "partC3")

      println(s"Step3: processing $processStep\n↵
 with $claimedPart")

      sender !
          StepCompleted(
              processStep.id,
              processStep.claimCheck,
              "step3")

      case message: Any =>
        println(s"Step3: unexpected: $message")
    }
}
```

As shown by the output, each of the process steps claims a different part of the original message. Each part corresponds to that which is needed by the specific step.

```
Step1: processing ProcessStep(ABC,ClaimCheck(7b5d2d71↵
-fcc1-4e94-8801-1f70397e0834))
 with CheckedPart(ClaimCheck(7b5d2d71-fcc1-4e94-8801↵
-1f70397e0834),Part(partA1))
Step2: processing ProcessStep(ABC,ClaimCheck(7b5d2d71↵
-fcc1-4e94-8801-1f70397e0834))
 with CheckedPart(ClaimCheck(7b5d2d71-fcc1-4e94-8801↵
-1f70397e0834),Part(partB2))
Step3: processing ProcessStep(ABC,ClaimCheck(7b5d2d71↵
-fcc1-4e94-8801-1f70397e0834))
 with CheckedPart(ClaimCheck(7b5d2d71-fcc1-4e94-8801↵
-1f70397e0834),Part(partC3))
ClaimCheck: is completed.
```

Certainly each of the processing steps could use a *Content Enricher (317)* to reconstitute some greater portion of the original message. It all depends on the amount of data required by a given step. If employing a *Content Enricher (317)*, the enricher would be responsible for directly using the `ItemChecker` to get the whole `CheckedItem` or any number of `CheckedPart` instances.

But why is it that the `ItemChecker` is not an actor? It could well be. Yet, in this case, a fully synchronous approach has been chosen. This allows each step to immediately react to its received `ProcessStep` message. There could be advantages to implementing the `ItemChecker` as an actor, which would make retrieving a `CheckedItem` or `CheckedPart` an asynchronous request. For sure, a remote actor implementation of `ItemChecker` would allow almost any process step anywhere to request and receive a `CheckedItem` or `Checked-Part`. This is considered an important requisite of the Claim Check implementation when actors almost anywhere can participate in the process.

Normalizer

Use a Normalizer when your system receives messages that are of types that are not supported and you need to transform the messages into ones that are supported. Sometimes you must support integrations with external systems that cannot, or whose teams will not, adhere to your supported message data formats. Under such circumstances, you will have to translate unsupported incoming messages to message types that are supported internally. The same/similar topic is discussed in *Implementing Domain-Driven Design* [IDDD] concerning the use of Anti-Corruption Layers (see Figure 8.4).

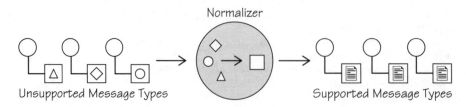

Figure 8.4 This Normalizer translates unsupported incoming messages to message types that are supported internally.

Obviously, when there are many integrators and few or none are willing to send supported messages, you will need to support a large number of *Message Translators (143)*. As the Normalizer receives each message, it uses a *Message Router (140)* to route each unsupported message to the appropriate *Message Translator (143)*. A big challenge can occur when either the incoming message formats or the internal formats change often. Also, the really sticky problem here arises when the incoming message formats are not readily distinguished by their content. Thus, the *Message Router (140)* can itself require complex code to detect incoming message types even before the messages can be routed to the appropriate translator. Any way you slice it, this requires a *Content-Based Router (228)*, but the router may not have a simple message type or *Format Indicator (222)* to keep its work on the lighter side.

Translating message formats may be the kind of job that you want to outsource, especially when there is a lot of it to do and it represents an ongoing workload. Although it is essential for the ultimately processed messages to support your system's standard formats, performing the wide range of incoming message type detections and translations can become a huge gruntwork effort. Since the routing and translation code almost certainly does not represent an investment in your core business software models, you probably don't want to continually commit the efforts of your valuable developer staff in this kind of sinkhole. After the first few router and translator challenges are tackled by your team, forming a well-understood approach, delegating the ongoing routing and translation work as a necessary evil can be a big benefit to your internal teams.

Canonical Message Model

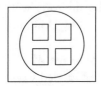

Typically a Canonical Data Model [EIP] is used when you need to integrate several or many applications, and you want to reduce the dependencies of each application on the others' types. Consider the six applications in the diagram in Figure 8.5. One of the main reasons you would choose to use this pattern is if each of the six applications integrates with every other application. Developing a common set of message types could greatly reduce the number and complexity of translating or mapping all the necessary messages.

Using the diagrammed applications and assuming that each application has a distinct model, you would need 6 × 5, or 30, such translators (one for the

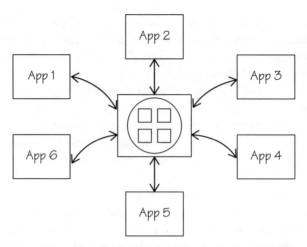

Figure 8.5 Use a Canonical Message Model when applications integrate with each other. Here six applications use a select set of messages.

received messages and one for the sent messages). However, when employing a Canonical Message Model and assuming that each application has a distinct model, you would need only 12 translators.

However, in practice, supporting a cross-application model in the manner that the Canonical Data Model prescribes often proves to be a futile effort. For one thing, it's nearly impossible to get every stakeholder representing the number of applications (for example, the six in Figure 8.5) to agree on a minimal model that can support everyone. So, the Canonical Data Model usually ends up with a superset of all the objects and properties that all the stakeholders imagine they might need at some point in time. The model becomes unwieldy from the start and ends up not serving any single one of the interests well [Tilkov-CDM]. This is far from the sensible approach emphasized by Domain-Driven Design's *Bounded Context* and how they are integrated [IDDD].

Consider an alternative approach that I call *Canonical Message Model (333)*. Using this approach, you allow each of the applications (Bounded Contexts) to determine their own *Command Messages (202)* for actions, *Event Messages (207)* for past happenings, and *Document Messages (204)* for query results, that the team is comfortable in providing. Document these to a reasonable degree as a *Published Language* [IDDD] and allow each team to make progress on its own terms [Tilkov-CDM]. Thus, view the model represented at the center of Figure 8.5 as a conglomeration of that which is approved by each application (for example, Bounded Context) team.

This is a much more natural way to think of such an information exchange model because you can actually reduce much of your *Canonical Message Model*

(333) to the *Command Messages (202)*, *Event Messages (207)*, and *Document Messages (204)* that are needed by any given application. Design *commands* support the actions that each application can perform. Design *events* are properly named and have enough data to accurately inform dependent applications that are interested in knowing about the range of occurrences in your applications. Design *documents* that provide query results, such as when using Command Query Responsibility Segregation (CQRS). That is, if your *Event Messages (207)* lack some richness that certain consuming applications would like to have, provide the desired informational richness in *Document Messages (204)* that are the result of querying when a given austere *Event Message (207)* is received.

These topics are treated exhaustively in *Implementing Domain-Driven Design* [IDDD] under "Architecture," "Domain Events," and "Integrating Bounded Contexts," as well as in other chapters.

Actor Systems Require a Canon

When using the Actor model, it is necessary to make actors depend on the messages of other actors. It is, therefore, quite explicitly required to think carefully about how you will exchanges messages and which actors within any one or various applications will be dependent on any others' messages. Hence, using this approach you may very well avoid message translations altogether because actors may instead depend only on externally shared message types.

Message (130) discusses a supporting approach, which is demonstrated in *Message Bus (192)*. To summarize, place all common messages of your Canonical Message Model in a single Scala source file, allowing the message types to be easily deployed on various dependent systems. For example, the following are a set of *Command Messages (202)* and *Event Messages (207)* used in the sample Trading Bus and placed in a common source file:

```
// Command Messages
case class ExecuteBuyOrder(portfolioId: String,
    symbol: Symbol, quantity: Int, price: Money)
case class ExecuteSellOrder(portfolioId: String,
    symbol: Symbol, quantity: Int, price: Money)
...
// Event Messages
case class BuyOrderExecuted(portfolioId: String,
    symbol: Symbol, quantity: Int, price: Money)
case class SellOrderExecuted(portfolioId: String,
    symbol: Symbol, quantity: Int, price: Money)
...
```

Since each of these message types would have to be sent by at least one actor and received by at least one other actor, placing them in a common source file for messages can make dependencies easier to support. See *Message (130)* for a discussion of the advantages and disadvantages of following this approach.

Summary

In this chapter, you drilled deeper into various kinds of transformations that messages may undergo in your applications and integrations. Each of the patterns expanded on the *Message Translator (143)*, providing specialty transformations based on specific application needs: wrapping, enriching, filtering, tracking, normalizing, and commonizing.

Chapter 9

Message Endpoints

In Chapter 4, "Messaging with Actors," you were introduced to *Message End-points (145)* as actors in the Actor model. In this chapter, you will see the diverse kinds of endpoints.

- *Messaging Gateway*: An Akka actor system and its actors form a natural *Messaging Gateway (338)*. The code required to interact with the messaging system, where one actor sends a message to another, is simple.

- *Messaging Mapper*: Use a *Messaging Mapper (344)* to map parts of one or more domain objects to a message.

- *Transactional Client/Actor*: This pattern, as used with Akka actors, is about transactions both for client/sender actors and for receiver actors.

- *Polling Consumer*: Polling involves a consumer that requests information from a given resource, which requires the consumer to block until the resource information can be provided. It doesn't work that way with the Actor model. You will see how to use *Request-Reply (209)* to roughly mimic polling. You will also see how to make an Akka actor carefully poll a hardware resource with minimal or no blocking.

- *Event-Driven Consumer*: This pattern is not about sending an *Event Message (207)*, but it includes this. An *Event-Driven Consumer (371)* is one that is reactive to any messages sent to it.

- *Competing Consumers*: *Competing Consumers (371)*, as a specialty group, react to multiple messages simultaneously. Depending on the implementation of *Polling Consumer (362)* and *Message Dispatcher (374)*, these can be natural *Competing Consumers (371)*.

- *Message Dispatcher*: The *Message Dispatcher (374)* is comparable to the *Content-Based Router (228)*. It is possible for a *Message Dispatcher (374)* to look at the content of a message, such as a message type, and then dispatch the message to actors corresponding to each type of messages. The difference between the two is that a *Message Dispatcher (374)* is generally interested in workload, dispatching messages only to actors who can react promptly.

- *Selective Consumer*: A *Selective Consumer (377)* is a kind of *Message Filter (232)*. If your actor receives messages of various types but can process only some of the message types, it can discard those that it is not designed to handle.

- *Durable Subscriber*: Use a *Durable Subscriber (379)* when you need to ensure that the message handler will not miss messages that are sent while the handler is not actively listening.

- *Idempotent Receiver*: Design an actor to be an *Idempotent Receiver (382)* when there is the possibility for it to receive a given message multiple times and processing that message each time would cause problems. Since the standard message delivery contract for the Actor model is "at most once," it may seem like this could never be a problem. The problem can arise, however, when you use the `AtLeastOnceDelivery` mix-in.

- *Service Activator*: Use a *Service Activator (390)* when you have an internal service that may be requested using one or more externally available access resources. All actors that receive messages at the outer edge of the application and dispatch inward to service or domain model actors are *Service Activators (390)*.

You may have to combine patterns found in this chapter to achieve a reactive design goal. As shown in *Polling Consumer (362)*, the solution's work consumer actually uses both *Competing Consumer (371)* and *Polling Consumer (362)*. In the same solution, the work provider is a *Message Dispatcher (374)*, which is concerned about workload and responsiveness and will dispatch only the number of items that the work consumer says it can handle. Depending on the kind of work that the work consumer does, it may need to be a *Transactional Actor (354)*, which aligns with the Aggregate pattern [IDDD].

Messaging Gateway

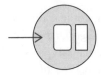

An Akka actor system and its actors form a natural Messaging Gateway. Akka makes message sending between actors simple. In most cases, there is no need to create another abstraction layer overtop Akka or its actors to simplify access to its messaging. Whether actors are sending messages to other actors that are within the same JVM or remote actors in another JVM, the interface is equally simplistic to use.

```
riskAssessment ! AttachDocument("This is a HIGH risk...")
```

Is the actor referenced by `riskAssessment` local or remote? Part of the natural Message Gateway provided by Akka that makes sending *Messages (130)* between local and remote actors includes the abstractions provided by `ActorRef` and `RemoteActorRef`. An actor in one Java virtual machine (JVM) need not have any knowledge that the actor to which it is sending a *Message (130)* is either local or remote. So, to some extent, you don't know whether `riskAssessment` is local or remote, and under normal circumstances you needn't care.

One reason you may choose to use an additional Messaging Gateway abstraction is if you want Akka to do something that it doesn't normally do straight "out of the box." One such situation is when you want an actor with Entity or Aggregate characteristics [IDDD] to have transient behavior, where the actor can be loaded and unloaded dynamically based on criteria such as usage patterns. In this case, the actor has a unique identity and the potential for mutable state and may be currently cached in memory or have its state persisted to disk. If a client sends this actor a message and it is already cached in memory, the message would need to be received by the actor in a nearly direct way. When a client sends a message to such an actor that is not currently cached, the system must arrange for the actor to be reconstituted from disk and loaded into cache before the message can be received.

What follows is a simple example of such a system of transient actors. The basic idea is to implement a domain model with actors implemented as Aggregates [IDDD]. Here is the `DomainModel` class and companion object:

```scala
object DomainModel {
  def apply(name: String): DomainModel = {
    new DomainModel(name)
  }
}

class DomainModel(name: String) {
  val aggregateTypeRegistry =
    scala.collection.mutable.Map[String, AggregateType]()
  val system = ActorSystem(name)

  def aggregateOf(typeName: String, id: String): AggregateRef = {
    if (aggregateTypeRegistry.contains(typeName)) {
      val aggregateType = aggregateTypeRegistry(typeName)
```

```
        aggregateType.cacheActor ! RegisterAggregateId(id)
        AggregateRef(id, aggregateType.cacheActor)
    } else {
      throw new IllegalStateException(
          "DomainModel type registry does not have a $typeName")
    }
  }

  def registerAggregateType(typeName: String): Unit = {
    if (!aggregateTypeRegistry.contains(typeName)) {
      val actorRef = system.actorOf(
            Props(classOf[AggregateCache],typeName), typeName)
      aggregateTypeRegistry(typeName) = AggregateType(actorRef)
    }
  }

  def shutdown() = {
    system.shutdown()
  }
}
...
case class AggregateType(cacheActor: ActorRef)
```

The `DomainModel` is a basic abstraction that allows you to manage a cache of Aggregate types. In fact, in this example each Aggregate type comprises one cache. You can see this in the first half of the `DomainModelDriver` application.

```
object DomainModelDriver extends CompletableApp(1) {

  val orderType = "co.vaughnvernon.reactiveenterprise.domainmodel.↵
Order"

  val model = DomainModel("OrderProcessing")

  model.registerAggregateType(orderType)

  val order = model.aggregateOf(orderType, "123")

  ...
}
```

After creating the `DomainModel` instance, the `Order` type is registered with the `DomainModel` as an Aggregate type. Next, you can ask the `DomainModel` to provide an Aggregate actor instance according to the newly registered `Order` type. The `DomainModel` then yields a new `Order` actor reference instance, which is assigned the Entity global unique identity "123".

This is the simple `Order` Aggregate actor, which really does nothing much of significance other than provide an actor to ultimately receive messages.

```
case class InitializeOrder(amount: Double)
case class ProcessOrder()

class Order extends Actor {
  var amount: Double = _

  def receive = {
    case init: InitializeOrder =>
      println(s"Initializing Order with $init")
      this.amount = init.amount
    case processOrder: ProcessOrder =>
      println(s"Processing Order is $processOrder")
      DomainModelPrototype.completedStep
  }
}
```

Notice, however, that the `Order` actor reference returned by the `Domain-Model` `aggregateOf()` function is not the familiar `ActorRef`. Instead, it is a special type `AggregateRef`. This `AggregateRef`, which is used much like the `ActorRef`, serves as the linchpin for the Messaging Gateway abstraction that allows you to implement the transient Aggregate actors.

Looking again at the `DomainModelDriver` application, once an `Order` is provided by the `DomainModel`, you can send the `Order` messages via the `AggregateRef`.

```
object DomainModelDriver extends CompletableApp(1) {

  val orderType = "co.vaughnvernon.reactiveenterprise.domainmodel.↵
Order"
  val model = DomainModel("OrderProcessing")

  model.registerAggregateType(orderType)

  val order = model.aggregateOf(orderType, "123")
  order ! InitializeOrder(249.95)
  order ! ProcessOrder()

  awaitCompletion
  model.shutdown()

  println("DomainModelDriver: is completed.")
}
```

Yet, the messages are not sent directly to the `Order` in the same manner that they would be when using an `ActorRef`. They must first pass through the Messaging Gateway that is abstracted away by the `AggregateRef`.

```scala
case class AggregateRef(id: String, cache: ActorRef) {
  def tell(message: Any)(implicit sender: ActorRef = null): Unit = {
    cache ! CacheMessage(id, message, sender)
  }

  def !(message: Any)(implicit sender: ActorRef = null): Unit = {
    cache ! CacheMessage(id, message, sender)
  }
}
```

Every Aggregate actor is managed by a special cache actor, an instance of `AggregateCache`. When the `DomainModel` creates a new Aggregate actor, it ensures that it will be managed by the appropriate type-based `Aggregate-Cache`. Thus, all messages sent to the Aggregate actor, such as an `Order`, will first be sent to the managing cache.

```scala
case class CacheMessage(
      id: String,
      actualMessage: Any,
      sender: ActorRef)

case class RegisterAggregateId(id: String)

class AggregateCache(typeName: String) extends Actor {
  val aggregateClass: Class[Actor] =
        Class
            .forName(typeName)
          .asInstanceOf[Class[Actor]]
  val aggregateIds =
        scala.collection.mutable.Set[String]()

  def receive = {
    case message: CacheMessage =>
      val anId = message.id
      val aggregate = context.child(anId).getOrElse {
        if (!aggregateIds.contains(anId)) {
          throw new IllegalStateException(
            s"No aggregate of type $typeName and id $anId")
        } else {
          context.actorOf(Props(aggregateClass), anId)

          // reconstitute aggregate state
```

```
                // here if pre-existing
            }
        }
        aggregate.tell(message.actualMessage, message.sender)

      case register: RegisterAggregateId =>
        this.aggregateIds.add(register.id)
  }
}
```

The `AggregateCache` is responsible for handing two messages, the `Cache-Message` and the `RegisterAggregateId`. The `RegisterAggregateId` is processed first when a new Aggregate actor is created by the `DomainModel`.

```
class DomainModel(name: String) {
  ...
  def aggregateOf(
      typeName: String, id: String):
  AggregateRef = {
    if (aggregateTypeRegistry.contains(typeName)) {
      val aggregateType = aggregateTypeRegistry(typeName)
      aggregateType.cacheActor ! RegisterAggregateId(id)
      AggregateRef(id, aggregateType.cacheActor)
    } else {
      throw new IllegalStateException(
       s"DomainModel registry doesn't have $typeName")
    }
  }
  ...
}
```

When the `RegisterAggregateId` is received by the `AggregateCache`, it stores the newly allocated unique identity. In this simple implementation, all Aggregate unique identities are held by an in-memory `Set` that is managed by the `AggregateCache`. This could be improved by storing all or some of the identities on disk, perhaps keeping only the `Set` of most recently used identities in memory. Ultimately, you would want all such identities stored on disk in case one of the `AggregateCache` actors crashed. That way you'd never lose track of an Aggregate actor and wrongly create a duplicate because the `Aggregate-Cache` thinks it doesn't exist.

The more interesting `AggregateCache` behavior comes when it receives a `CacheMessage`. A `CacheMessage` is sent by the `AggregateRef` to the `AggregateCache`. The original message being sent to the Aggregate actor, such as `InitializeOrder` and `ProcessMessage`, is wrapped by the

`CacheMessage`. After the `AggregateCache` successfully looks up the cached Aggregate actor, creates it for the first time, or reconstitutes it from disk and caches it, the original message is finally dispatched to the Aggregate actor.

```
aggregate.tell(message.actualMessage, message.sender)
```

In this way, the receiving Aggregate actor receives the message in such a way that it thinks it received the message from the original sender, rather than from the `AggregateCache` by way of the `AggregateRef`. So, this Messaging Gateway is not meant to simplify the already simple Akka message-sending semantics. Rather, it is used to implement a transient actor cache that is not otherwise supported by Akka's core features.

See *Guaranteed Delivery (175)* for ways to ensure that actors, such as Aggregates, that must absolutely receive a sent message will always receive them.

Messaging Mapper

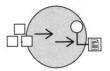

Use a Messaging Mapper to map parts of one or more domain objects, such as Aggregates [IDDD], to a message. Depending on how you use Akka, it is possible that your Aggregates are themselves actors and may map a subset of their own state to an *Event Message (207)*, a *Command Message (202)*, or a *Document Message (204)*. This example shows how an *Event Message (207)* is mapped from Aggregate actor state and sent to a `TradingBus`:

```
...
val event =
    SellOrderExecuted(
        portfolioId,
        symbol,
        quantity,
        price)

tradingBus ! TradingNotification(
            "SellOrderExecuted", event)
```

This constitutes the `Order` Aggregate actor itself a Messaging Mapper. The subset of the state of the `Order` actor is mapped to the `SellOrderExecuted`, which is an *Event Message (207)*. This is a simple and straightforward mapping and actually just the way it should be done in most cases. *Event Messages (207)* shouldn't have many fields/attributes but should have as few values as absolutely necessary in order to communicate what happened to the `Order`. The same goes for *Command Messages (202)* in that they must have only enough data to communicate what must happen to the model.

Sometimes, though, when you think of any kind of mapper, you think of handling a complex mapping effort. For example, you probably think of taking parts of several Aggregates and mapping them into a large *Document Message (204)*. While this may be the case, you should avoid it whenever possible.

Still, it's possible that a *Document Message (204)* being mapped in response to a Command Query Responsibility Segregation (CQRS) [IDDD] query may need to build up a rather large payload. When that is so, you may have to use a more sophisticated mapper utility. Unfortunately, most mapper utilities that run on the JVM will support the JavaBeans specification. This means your Scala-based message objects will need to provide public getters and setters, or the mapper utility will need to support field-level reflection, especially if your messages are declared as case classes.

One way to get around this problem is to design your *Document Messages (204)* to have a single `String`-based field, such as `messageBody`. You can then set this single field to a JavaScript Object Notation (JSON), or possibly Extensible Markup Language (XML), payload, which can then be read by an appropriate parser on the consumer side. The *Implementing Domain-Driven Design* [IDDD] chapter "Integrating Bounded Contexts" discusses in detail the way to generate messages that are compatible with any kind of system platform by way of the Google GSON parser, which uses field-level introspection and reflection. Field-level access supports any kind of Java/Scala object, even those that don't support the JavaBean specification. In fact, your messaging mapper can even be considered a serializer.

The following source code contains both a Java-based `AbstractSerializer` and a concrete `MessageSerializer` that can serve as a way to map Scala case classes, or any kind of Scala object, to JSON. These use the Google GSON parser.

```
public abstract class AbstractSerializer {

  protected class CustomAdapter {
    private Object adapter;
    private Type type;

    CustomAdapter(Type aType, Object anAdapter) {
      this.type = aType;
```

```
      this.adapter = anAdapter;
    }

    protected Object adapter() {
      return this.adapter;
    }

    protected Type type() {
      return this.type;
    }
  }

  private Gson gson;

  protected AbstractSerializer(boolean isCompact) {
    this(false, isCompact);
  }

  protected AbstractSerializer(
      boolean isPretty,
      boolean isCompact) {
    super();

    if (isPretty && isCompact) {
      this.buildForPrettyCompact();
    } else if (isCompact) {
      this.buildForCompact();
    } else {
      this.build();
    }
  }

  protected abstract Collection<CustomAdapter>
      customAdapters();

  protected Gson gson() {
    return this.gson;
  }

  private void build() {
    this.gson =
      this
        .builderWithAdapters()
        .serializeNulls()
        .create();
  }

  private void buildForCompact() {
    this.gson = this.builderWithAdapters().create();
  }

  private void buildForPrettyCompact() {
```

```java
    this.gson =
      this
        .builderWithAdapters()
        .setPrettyPrinting()
        .create();
  }

  private class DateSerializer
      implements JsonSerializer<Date> {
    public JsonElement serialize(
            Date source,
            Type typeOfSource,
            JsonSerializationContext context) {
      return new JsonPrimitive(
                  Long.toString(source.getTime()));
    }
  }

  private class DateDeserializer
      implements JsonDeserializer<Date> {
    public Date deserialize(
            JsonElement json,
            Type typeOfTarget,
            JsonDeserializationContext context)
      throws JsonParseException {
      String nr = json.getAsJsonPrimitive().getAsString();
      long time = Long.parseLong(nr);
      return new Date(time);
    }
  }

  private GsonBuilder builderWithAdapters() {
    GsonBuilder builder = new GsonBuilder();

    builder.registerTypeAdapter(
            Date.class,
            new DateSerializer());
    builder.registerTypeAdapter(
            Date.class,
            new DateDeserializer());

    for (CustomAdapter adapter : this.customAdapters()) {
      builder
          .registerTypeAdapter(
              adapter.type(),
              adapter.adapter());
    }

    return builder;
  }
}
```

```java
public class MessageSerializer extends AbstractSerializer {

  public interface AggregateRefProvider {
    public AggregateRef fromTypeNameWithId(
        String typeName,
        String id);
  }

  private static MessageSerializer serializer;

  public static MessageSerializer instance() {
    if (serializer == null) {
      throw new IllegalStateException(
        "Must first use newInstance(...) before using↵
instance().");
    }
    return serializer;
  }

  public static synchronized MessageSerializer newInstance(
        AggregateRefProvider anAggregateRefProvider) {

    if (MessageSerializer.serializer == null) {
      MessageSerializer.serializer =
            new MessageSerializer(anAggregateRefProvider);
    }

    return MessageSerializer.serializer;
  }

  private AggregateRefProvider aggregateRefProvider;

  public String serialize(Object aMessage) {
    String serialization = this.gson().toJson(aMessage);

    return serialization;
  }

  public <T extends Object> T deserialize(
        String aSerialization, final Class<T> aType) {
    T message = this.gson().fromJson(aSerialization, aType);

    return message;
  }

  public <T extends Object> T deserializeOriginalMessage(
        String aSerialization, final Class<T> aType) {
    T message = this.gson().fromJson(aSerialization, aType);

    return message;
  }

  @SuppressWarnings("unchecked")
```

```java
public Class<Message> messageClassFrom(String aMessageType) {
  Class<Message> messageClass = null;

  try {
    messageClass =
        (Class<Message>) Class.forName(aMessageType);
  } catch (Exception e) {
    throw new IllegalArgumentException(
        "Cannot get class for message of type: "
        + aMessageType, e);
  }

  return messageClass;
}

@Override
protected Collection<CustomAdapter> customAdapters() {
  List<CustomAdapter> customAdapters =
        new ArrayList<CustomAdapter>();

  customAdapters.add(
        new CustomAdapter(
            AggregateRef.class,
            new AggregateRefSerializer()));
  customAdapters.add(
        new CustomAdapter(
            AggregateRef.class,
            new AggregateRefDeserializer()));

  return customAdapters;
}

private MessageSerializer(boolean isCompact) {
  this(false, isCompact);
}

private MessageSerializer(
    boolean isPretty,
    boolean isCompact) {
  super(isPretty, isCompact);
}

private MessageSerializer(
    AggregateRefProvider anAggregateRefProvider) {
  this(false, false);

  this.aggregateRefProvider = anAggregateRefProvider;
}

private class AggregateRefSerializer
    implements JsonSerializer<AggregateRef> {

  public JsonElement serialize(
```

```
                AggregateRef source,
                Type typeOfSource,
                JsonSerializationContext context) {
            String cacheType = source.cache().path().name();
            String aggregateId = source.id();
            return new JsonPrimitive(
                        cacheType + " " + aggregateId);
        }
    }

    private class AggregateRefDeserializer
        implements JsonDeserializer<AggregateRef> {

      public AggregateRef deserialize(
            JsonElement json,
            Type typeOfTarget,
            JsonDeserializationContext context)
        throws JsonParseException {
          String refParts =
                    json.getAsJsonPrimitive().getAsString();
          int separator = refParts.indexOf(' ');
          if (separator == -1) {
            throw new IllegalStateException(
              "The AggregateRef parts are incorrectly↵
      formatted: " + refParts);
          }

          return aggregateRefProvider.fromTypeNameWithId(
            refParts.substring(0, separator),
                refParts.substring(separator+1));
      }
    }
}
```

The `MessageSerializer` has the ability to serialize and deserialize messages, or any Scala objects in general, that include `java.util.Date` and even `AggregateRef` values. You can read about the use of `AggregateRef` in *Messaging Gateway (338)*.

This serializer also allows a large *Document Message (204)* to be assembled by building a JSON payload that gets set on the `String`-based `messageBody` field.

```
case class ReallyBigQueryResult(messageBody: String)

class OrderQueryService extends Actor {
  val serializer = MessageSerializer.instance()
  ...
  def receive = {
```

```
    ...
    case query: QueryMonthlyOrdersFor =>
      val queryResult = monthlyOrdersFor(query.customerId)

      val messageBody = serializer.serialize(queryResult)

      sender ! ReallyBigQueryResult(messageBody)
    ...
  }
}
```

Now the original sender of `QueryMonthlyOrdersFor` need only understand how to consume the JSON-based `messageBody` of the `ReallyBig-QueryResult` *Document Message (204)*. This is a matter of the message-originating team crafting a *Published Language* [IDDD], as is described in regard to *Format Indicator (222)*, and the receiver designing an Anti-Corruption Layer [IDDD], as described in regard to *Message Translator (143)*, so that consumers of `ReallyBigQueryResult` and other similar result messages can read the payload.

Transactional Client/Actor

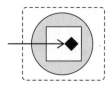

The Transactional Client pattern, as used with Akka actors, is about transactions both for client actors and for receiver actors. Appropriately, for the purposes of use with the Actor model, this pattern has been named Transactional Client/Actor. *Enterprise Integration Patterns* [EIP] discusses four characteristic ways to apply Transactional Client when using a typical messaging middleware tool.

- *Send-Receive Message Pairs*: Start a transaction, receive and process the first (received) message, create and send a second message, and then commit.

- *Message Groups*: Start a transaction, send or receive all of the messages in the group, and then commit.

- *Message/Database Coordination*: Start a transaction, receive a message, update the database, and then commit. Or, update the database and send a message to report the update to others and then commit.

- *Message/Flow Coordination*: Use a pair of *Request-Reply (209)* messages to perform a work item. Start a transaction, acquire a work item, send the request message, and then commit. Or, start another transaction, receive the reply message, complete or abort the work item, and then commit.

Using transactions to guarantee Akka message sends, message receipts, and the persistence of actor state transition *semantically* takes in all of these use cases.

Consider these necessary transactional steps: (A) To guarantee that any given actor can send a message to another actor and that it will be received, you need to use a transaction. (B) To guarantee the message receiving actor will receive the message and then confirm its receipt, you need to use a transaction. (C) To guarantee the message receiving actor will receive the message that causes any state transitions and then persists the new state, you need to use a transaction. Generally transaction step A will be in its own transaction, while steps B and C will be in a separate single transaction, as shown in Figure 9.1.

The state transaction persisted in step C (depicted by the dotted line in Figure 9.1) may be achieved by producing one or more outgoing *Event Messages (207)*. In that case, the *Event Messages (207)* produced by the actor may also be sent to other actors, resulting in use cases 3 and 4.

There are a few different approaches to make message sends and receipts transactional, along with state transitions. These are discussed when covering

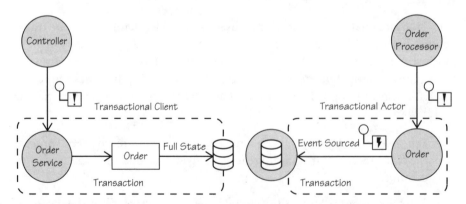

Figure 9.1 The two approaches: Transactional Client and Transactional Actor. While accomplishing the same things, the Transactional Actor is the best approach for the Actor model.

Guaranteed Delivery (175), *Durable Subscriber (379)*, and *Message Journal/ Store (402)*. Also, since steps A, B, and C all use the at-least-once delivery, you will also need to understand how to design an *Idempotent Receiver (382)*.

Transactional Client

You may decide to manage message sending, receipt, and transactional state transitions from a client perspective. When using a Service Layer [Fowler EAA] approach, you could find it more advantageous to stick with Akka's default at-most-once delivery rather than implementing an enhanced at-least-once delivery approach (steps A and B) but at the same time manage the persistence of system state transitions by means of transactions (step C). In such a case you need to decide where your transactional boundary begins and ends.

Using the Service Layer [Fowler EAA] approach, manage the transaction inside an actor that implements an Application Service [IDDD]. This actor, when receiving a certain message, will start a database transaction. The actor-based Application Service will then directly interact with the nonactor domain model. Following this, the Application Service will commit or roll back the transaction.

```
class OrderService extends TransactionalActor {
  def receive = {
    ...
    case processOrder: ProcessOrder =>
      startTransactionFor(processOrder.orderId)
      val order = findOrder(processOrder.orderId)
      try {
        order.process(processOrder) // not an actor
        commitFor(processOrder.orderId)
      } catch {
        case _ =>
          rollbackFor(processOrder.orderId)
      }
    ...
  }
}
```

The base class `TransactionalActor` provides the typical transactional behaviors, `startTransactionFor()`, `commitFor()`, and `rollback-For()`. These functions must each be supplied some sort of unique transaction ID, and for this you can use the unique identity of the `Order`. When receiving `ProcessOrder`, the transaction is started. If the `Order` successfully performs `processOrder()`, the transaction is committed. Otherwise, the transaction is rolled back. Using the `orderId` as the transaction ID allows each `TransactionalActor` to manage potentially many simultaneous transactions.

Given that this `OrderService` works as intended, a Transactional Client could cause any number of state transitions in the nonactor domain model. Be aware, though, that the more domain objects modified within a single transaction, the higher the probability of concurrency conflicts because of multiple simultaneous modifications of the same domain objects. See *Aggregates* [IDDD] for the best approaches to optimal transactional designs.

One practice that can help with this kind of situation is to use *eventual consistency* (see the "Eventual Consistency" section for more), which can be supported by the direct asynchronous messaging of the Actor model. Each Application Service participating in this sort of *long-running transaction* would receive an *Event Message (207)* indicating what had previously happened (such as `OrderProcessed`), which will tell the receiver what it must do to support the eventual consistency process.

This Transactional Client approach does not really follow the spirit of the Actor model, which is to be highly concurrent and treat "everything" as an actor. It will likely not perform as well as it could if making full use of actors. You could find the actors that do exist contending for database resources. It would be much better to design each of the actors in the domain model as a well-behaved citizen of the Actor model. This leads to the second approach, which is to design each actor in your domain model to manage the transaction on its own.

Transactional Actor

When Alan Kay, the pioneer of object orientation and codesigner of Smalltalk, said "The Actor model retained more of what I thought were the good features of the object idea," he was referring, at least in part, to the ability to isolate state management entirely within the actor and that collaboration among actors be possible only through messaging contracts. This alludes to a natural transactional boundary around each actor.

This doesn't mean that every actor is always transactional in the sense that a persistence transaction is at play during each received message. That just isn't the case. Yet, every received message can be viewed as a solitary, atomic reaction to the given message's stimulus. If you happen to manage a persistence transaction around that solitary, atomic reaction, then the actor itself is truly transactional. In the latter case, the actor makes a natural Aggregate [IDDD], which is the topic now under discussion.

To facilitate this, Akka provides a persistence add-on, namely, Akka Persistence. To get Akka Persistence working in your project, just reference the following JAR files from the akka/lib directory:

- *akka-persistence_x.y.z.jar*: Akka Persistence add-on. At the time of writing, this was still in an experimental stage, with the JAR file named akka-persistence-experimental_2.10-2.3.2.jar.

- *leveldb-x.y.jar*: LevelDB functionality.

- *leveldb-api-x.y.jar*: LevelDB application programming interface (API).

- *leveldbjni-all-x.y.jar*: LevelDB Java Native Interface (JNI) links.

- *protobuf-java-x.y.z.jar*: Google's ProtoBuf library for Java.

These filenames each have an *x.y.z* notation, which is a placeholder for its release version. Although LevelDB is the default journal, there is no need to use it as your production *Message Store (402)*. There are also various third-party replacements that support other data stores. Still, the previous JAR files will get you up and running quickly as you try Akka Persistence.

Persistent Actors

An actor that uses Akka for persistence extends the `PersistentActor` trait. Doing so enables the actor to persist its internal state as a stream of Domain Events, an approach called Event Sourcing [IDDD]. Event Sourcing emphasizes defining each saved event as a record only of what changed, not the whole actor state. Using Event Sourcing enables an actor that was stopped for any reason—such as by a supervisor or when being rebalanced to a new cluster shard location—to be reconstituted entirely from its most recently saved event stream. Here is how a `PersistentActor` works:

```
class Order(orderId: String) extends PersistentActor {

  override def persistenceId = orderId
  var open = false
  var lineItems = Vector[LineItem]()

  override def receiveCommand: Receive = {
    case cmd: StartOrder =>
      persist(OrderStarted(orderId, ...)) { event =>
        updateWith(event)
      }
    case cmd: AddOrderLineItem =>
      if (open) {
```

```
            val orderLineItemAdded =
              OrderLineItemAdded(orderId, ...)
            persist(orderLineItemAdded) { event =>
              updateWith(event)
            }
          }
        case cmd: PlaceOrder =>
          persist(OrderPlaced(orderId, ...)) { event =>
            updateWith(event)
          }
      }

      override def receiveRecover: Receive = {
        case event: OrderStarted =>
          updateWith(event)
        case event: OrderLineItemAdded =>
          updateWith(event)
        case event: OrderPlaced =>
          updateWith(event)
        case RecoveryCompleted =>
      }

      def updateWith(event: OrderStarted) = {
        open = true
      }

      def updateWith(event: OrderLineItemAdded) = {
        lineItems = lineItems :+ event.lineItem
      }

      def updateWith(event: OrderPlaced) = {
        open = false
      }
    }
```

Each `PersistentActor` must be uniquely identified by its `persistence-Id`. In this example, you use the unique `orderId` that is provided as a constructor parameter.

The `Order` is a `PersistentActor` that receives *Command Messages (202)* through its `receiveCommand` handler block. Upon receiving a `StartOrder` command, it persists an `OrderStarted` *Event Message (207)*. Once the `persist()` is successful, the state of the actor is updated using the `OrderStarted` event. At this point, the `Order` is marked as `open`. Subsequent commands are either `AddOrderLineItem` or `PlaceOrder`. As each `AddOrderLineItem` is received, assuming the `Order` is still marked `open`, the state of the actor is updated to hold the new `LineItem` that is contained in the persisted `OrderLineItemAdded` event. Finally, when the `PlaceOrder` command is received, the `OrderPlaced` event is persisted and then used to close the `Order`.

Should the `Order` actor be stopped and then restarted for any reason, the `PersistentActor` trait causes the `Order` to be reconstituted from its event stream. Each *Event Message (207)* is received by the `receiveRecover` handler block, which in turn delegates to one of the three `updateWith()` methods to apply the event to the state of the `Order`. Once the `Order` is completely recovered to the state of the last *Event Message (207)* in its event stream, `receive-Recover` receives the standard `RecoveryCompleted` event. This standard event allows you to perform any additional special initialization that must follow full recovery but must precede the receipt of any new *Command Messages (202)*.

Encouragingly, it really is simple to implement a `PersistentActor`. Yet, you may still benefit from a bit more explanation about Event Sourcing, including how to use snapshots.

Using Event Sourcing   Event Sourcing is a pattern where the state of some object or record is comprised of the past events that have occurred to that object or record. As the diagram in Figure 9.2 depicts, an `Order` actor has had four events occur, and its state is based on the interpretation of what those events mean to the actor.

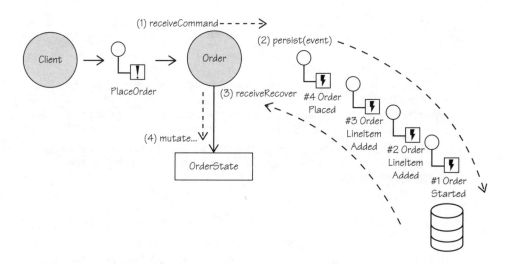

Figure 9.2 A Transactional Actor receives *Command Messages (202)* and persists its new state (steps 1 and 2). During state recovery mode, the previously persisted Domain Events are read to recover state (steps 3 and 4).

Each *Event Message (207)* persisted by the `Order` has been caused by a corresponding *Command Message (202)*, as shown in Figure 9.2.

1. After the actor is created and started, it receives a `StartOrder` command, which causes an `OrderStarted` event.

2. The user selects an item to be purchased through the `Order`, and an `AddOrderLineItem` command is sent that causes a `OrderLineItemAdded` event.

3. The user selects another item to be purchased, and another `AddOrderLineItem` command causes another `OrderLineItemAdded` event.

4. Finally, the user completes and places the order, which causes a `PlaceOrder` command to be sent to the `Order` actor. This command causes `OrderPlaced`.

Persisting the *Event Messages (207)* isn't all that's necessary. The `Order` actor must also react to each of those events so it can know how to transition its state, event by event. Each *Event Message (207)* must be received in the sequence in which it occurred, from 1 to 4, and so on.

Receiving events in this fashion works not only for ongoing state transitions. It also enables the actor's state to be fully reconstituted from persisted events if the actor must be stopped and restarted.

NOTE

It is not necessary to have a separate `OrderState` object held by the `Order` actor, but using such could help separate the details of actor state from *Command Message (202)* and *Event Message (207)* processing. If you were to choose not to use such an `OrderState` object, then any `val` and `var` referenced instances that would be held by it would have to be managed directly on the `Order` actor, which is the case in the previous code sample.

Additionally, using a separate `OrderState` will also make it easier to save a snapshot of the current actor state. The reasons to use a snapshot and how it is performed are discussed next.

Snapshots   When some large number of *Event Messages (207)* have been persisted for a given actor, reconstituting its state—from the first event that ever occurred to the last event that has occurred—can become a slow operation. The use of actor state snapshots can greatly reduce the time required to recover the actor's state from its *Message Store (402)*.

NOTE

It is not always necessary for actors that use Event Sourcing to support snapshots. For example, if an Order tends to have relatively few OrderLines and the total number of *Event Messages (207)* persisted by the Order may be in the range of, say, 200 or less, it may be unnecessary to save a snapshot of OrderState. On the other hand, if your Order instances tend to have several hundred or even thousands of OrderLines, then no doubt producing snapshots of OrderState will greatly reduce Order load times.

There is no one-size-fits-all guidance. Each Event Sourcing actor type must be analyzed to determine whether snapshots should be used at all and, if so, how often a snapshot must be persisted.

When a PersistentActor uses snapshots, it must indicate when each snapshot will be persisted. It can do so during the handling of a given *Command Message (202)*, or it can send itself a *Message (130)* that indicates that it is time to save a snapshot.

```scala
class Order(orderId: String) extends PersistentActor {

  override def persistenceId = orderId
  var orderState: OrderState(orderId)

  override def receiveCommand: Receive = {
    ...
    case cmd: AddOrderLineItem =>
      if (orderState.open) {
        val orderLineItemAdded =
          OrderLineItemAdded(orderId, ...)
        persist(orderLineItemAdded) { event =>
          updateWith(event)
        }

        if ((orderState.totalLineItems % 250) == 0) {
          self ! SaveOrderSnapshot()
        }
      }

    case SaveOrderSnapshot =>
      deleteSnapshot(SnapshotSelectionCriteria.Latest)
      saveSnapshot(orderState)
    ...
  }

  override def receiveRecover: Receive = {
    case SnapshotOffer(metadata, offeredSnapshot) =>
      orderState = offeredSnapshot
```

```
      case event: OrderStarted =>
        updateWith(event)
      case event: OrderLineItemAdded =>
        updateWith(event)
      case event: OrderPlaced =>
        updateWith(event)
      case RecoveryCompleted =>
    }
  ...
}
```

Here you can see the few steps that are needed to manage snapshots. Note that this time you have designed with an `OrderState` object, which can make it easier to deal with snapshots.

First, the `Order` determines that every 250th `LineItem` (that is, 250, then 500, then 750, ...) will cause a snapshot to be saved. The `Order` will send a `SaveOrderSnapshot` message to itself requesting a snapshot. When the `SaveOrderSnapshot` *Command Message (202)* is received, the `Order` both deletes the previously saved snapshot (if any) and then saves a new one.

Finally, during `Order` recovery, if there is a saved snapshot, the `Persistent-Actor` offers it as a means to recover the state of the `Order` to that point. Next, only *Event Messages (207)* that are younger than the snapshot will be delivered to `receiveRecover` and applied to the `orderState`.

Eventual Consistency

There's another important aspect to address for your actor-based domain model. When you make a state modification on one actor-based Aggregate [IDDD], there could be other actor-based Aggregates that have dependencies on that modification. Since each `PersistentActor` manages its own trans-action, it is actually impossible for dependent actors to simultaneously update their own state as a reaction. That's actually a good thing because it will help your domain model succeed with better transactional results.

Even so, any actors that are dependent on the modifications to a given actor must be updated within some specific time. For this use Eventual Consistency. How so? As the modified actor is completing the handling of a given *Command Message (202)*, it should produce an *Event Message (207)* that defines what happened to it (for example, `OrderPlaced`). That *Event Message (207)* can be sent to one or more dependent actors, and they will react to it by modifying their own state accordingly. If the extent of dependencies and necessary reactions are minimal, sending a few key *Event Messages (207)* may be all that is needed. However, when managing this sort of *long-running process* becomes more complex, you will likely want employ a *Process Manager (292)*.

In fact, when using Domain-Driven Design [IDDD] with the Actor model, you will probably make use of *Process Managers (292)* liberally in order to explicitly model your business processes with fine-grained control.

Persistent Views

At the time of writing, Akka Persistence supports a `PersistentView`, which is a means to denormalize the state of a `PersistentActor` to make it easier to use by your application's view logic. However, the `PersistentView` is not to be long-lived and is to be replaced by a solution that uses Akka Streams. At this time, the Akka Streams solution has not been started, and there is currently no definite schedule for when it will be completed. I have decided that I will, rather than wait on this to happen, complete the book. As a way to make up for this once the Akka Streams solution is in place, I intend to blog about it in order to augment the book.

At this point, I will provide only cursory coverage of `PersistentView`, and you will find additional uses when I discuss *Durable Subscriber (379)*. So, here's how a `PersistentView` works:

```
class OrderView(orderId: String) extends PersistentView {

  override def persistenceId = orderId
  override def viewId = orderId + "-view"
  var viewState = OrderViewState()

  override def receive: Receive = {
    case event: OrderStarted =>
      viewState = viewState.startedWith(event)
    case event: OrderLineItemAdded =>
      viewState = viewState.addedTo(event)
      if ((viewState.totalLineItems % 250) == 0) {
        self ! SaveOrderViewSnapshot()
      }
    case event: OrderPlaced =>
      viewState = viewState.placedWith(event)
    case QueryOrderViewState =>
      sender ! viewState
    case SaveOrderSnapshot =>
      deleteSnapshot(SnapshotSelectionCriteria.Latest)
      saveSnapshot(viewState)
  }

  override def receiveRecover: Receive = {
    case SnapshotOffer(metadata, offeredSnapshot) =>
      viewState = offeredSnapshot
    case event: OrderStarted =>
      viewState = viewState.startedWith(event)
```

```
    case event: OrderLineItemAdded =>
      viewState = viewState.addedTo(event)
    case event: OrderPlaced =>
      viewState = viewState.placedWith(event)
    case RecoveryCompleted =>
    }
  }
}
```

Your `PersistentView` must have the same `persistenceId` as the corresponding `PersistentActor`, which will be used to read its event stream from its journal. The `viewId` should be different from the `persistenceId` and can be formed by concatenating the text `"-view"` to the end of the text of the `persistenceId`, for example.

In the `receive` handler block you react to each *Event Message (207)* that has been saved by the corresponding `PersistentActor`. You will likely want to maintain a denormalized data structure, as is represented here by `Order-ViewState`. As was the case with `Order`, the `OrderView` will save a snapshot of its state at every 250th line item. Additionally, the `OrderView` allows its view state to be queried by sending it a `QueryOrderViewState` message. In response, it replies to the sender with its immutable `OrderViewState` instance.

For recovery, you again see a `receiveRecover` in the `PersistentView`. Here you must react to a `SnapshotOffer`, as well as to each of the three possible events: `OrderStarted`, `OrderLineItemAdded`, and `OrderPlaced`.

You are probably wondering how often a `PersistentView` is refreshed with newly persisted events. This happens according to the following standard configuration, which indicates every five seconds:

```
akka.persistence.view.auto-update-interval = 5s
```

This configuration can be changed by an individual `PersistentView` by overriding the `autoUpdateInterval()` method, returning a custom interval.

Polling Consumer

Polling involves a consumer that requests information from a given resource, which requires the consumer to block until the resource information can be provided. Contrary to this, when using the Actor model, there is no way for one actor to poll another actor for information because actor-to-actor collaborations don't block. The only way for actors to get information from other actors is by means of *Request-Reply (209)*. That said, how could you use *Request-Reply (209)* to effectively mimic a Polling Consumer? Further, how can an actor itself be used to poll some resource (for example, device) that is not event-driven but requires consumers to poll the resource for information?

In a typical procedural polling environment, a Work Consumer would request Work Items from a Work Items Provider. The Work Consumer would block until the requested Work Items could be allocated by the Work Item Provider and then returned to the Work Consumer. This simply can't happen with the Actor model. With actors, as soon as the Work Consumer tells the Work Item Provider that it wants to Allocate Work Items, the Work Consumer will continue operation on its own thread, and the request sent to the Work Item Provider will not actually be received for some period of time (however lengthy or brief). The blocking required (with a procedural polling approach) to allocate and reply with the requested Work Items, regardless of the actual time required to receive and process the request, cannot be achieved.

Still, you can accomplish similar results using *Request-Reply (209)*, as shown in Figure 9.3. What you want to do is design the Work Consumer to request Work Items from the Work Items Provider and to obtain them.

Here's how this can be achieved:

```
package co.vaughnvernon.reactiveenterprise.pollingconsumer

import scala.collection.immutable.List
import akka.actor._
import co.vaughnvernon.reactiveenterprise._

object PollingConsumerDriver extends CompletableApp(1) {
  val workItemsProvider =
          system.actorOf(
              Props[WorkItemsProvider],
              "workItemsProvider")
  val workConsumer =
          system.actorOf(
              Props(classOf[WorkConsumer],
                  workItemsProvider),
              "workConsumer")

  workConsumer ! WorkNeeded()

  awaitCompletion
}
```

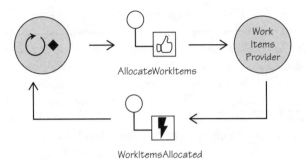

Figure 9.3 A Work Consumer actor requests Work Items from a Work Items Provider actor. The Work Items Provider actor replies with allocated Work Items.

The `PollingConsumerDriver` creates the `WorkItemsProvider` and `WorkConsumer` actors. It then starts the process of consuming and performing work by telling the `WorkConsumer` that it needs work to do. This is done by sending it the `WorkNeeded` message.

The `WorkConsumer` declares two messages for its own contract: `WorkNeeded` and `WorkOnItem`. The `WorkNeeded` message can be sent by a client to kick off the initial processing, and it will also be sent by the `WorkConsumer` itself to indicate when more work is needed. The `WorkOnItem` message is sent only internally by the `WorkConsumer` itself. It's a message that indicates an individual `WorkItem` that must be performed.

```
case class WorkNeeded()
case class WorkOnItem(workItem: WorkItem)

class WorkConsumer(workItemsProvider: ActorRef)
  extends Actor {
  var totalItemsWorkedOn = 0

  def performWorkOn(workItem: WorkItem) = {
    totalItemsWorkedOn = totalItemsWorkedOn + 1
    if (totalItemsWorkedOn >= 15) {
      context.stop(self)
      PollingConsumerDriver.completeAll
    }
  }

  override def postStop() = {
    context.stop(workItemsProvider)
  }

  def receive = {
```

```
      case allocated: WorkItemsAllocated =>
        println("WorkItemsAllocated...")
        allocated.workItems map { workItem =>
          self ! WorkOnItem(workItem)
        }
        self ! WorkNeeded()
      case workNeeded: WorkNeeded =>
        println("WorkNeeded...")
        workItemsProvider ! AllocateWorkItems(5)
      case workOnItem: WorkOnItem =>
        println(s"Performed work on:↵
  ${workOnItem.workItem.name}")
        performWorkOn(workOnItem.workItem)
    }
}
```

When the `WorkConsumer` receives a `WorkNeeded` message, it uses the `WorkItemsProvider` that it received during initialization to request a number of work items to be allocated. To do this, it sends the `AllocateWorkItems` message. When received by the `WorkItemsProvider`, it allocates the requested number of `WorkItem` instances. When the `WorkItem` instances have been allocated, they are sent to the requester via the `WorkItemsAllocated` *Event Message (207)*.

```
case class AllocateWorkItems(numberOfItems: Int)
case class WorkItemsAllocated(workItems: List[WorkItem])
case class WorkItem(name: String)

class WorkItemsProvider extends Actor {
  var workItemsNamed: Int = 0

  def allocateWorkItems(
        numberOfItems: Int): List[WorkItem] = {
    var allocatedWorkItems = List[WorkItem]()
    for (itemCount <- 1 to numberOfItems) {
      val nameIndex = workItemsNamed + itemCount
      allocatedWorkItems =
              allocatedWorkItems :+
                  WorkItem("WorkItem" + nameIndex)
    }
    workItemsNamed = workItemsNamed + numberOfItems
    allocatedWorkItems
  }

  def receive = {
    case request: AllocateWorkItems =>
      sender !
        WorkItemsAllocated(
```

```
            allocateWorkItems(
                request.numberOfItems))
    }
}
```

Now looking back at the `WorkConsumer`, when the `WorkItemsAllo-cated` message is received, the consumer divides up the work into individual `WorkOnItem` tasks by sending itself one such message for each `WorkItem`. Then, to complete its reaction to `WorkItemsAllocated`, it sends itself a fresh `WorkNeeded` message. This `WorkNeeded` message is received at the point where there are no more `WorkOnItem` tasks remaining. Here is the output of the polling-like process:

```
WorkNeeded...
WorkItemsAllocated...
Performed work on: WorkItem1
Performed work on: WorkItem2
Performed work on: WorkItem3
Performed work on: WorkItem4
Performed work on: WorkItem5
WorkNeeded...
WorkItemsAllocated...
Performed work on: WorkItem6
Performed work on: WorkItem7
Performed work on: WorkItem8
Performed work on: WorkItem9
Performed work on: WorkItem10
WorkNeeded...
WorkItemsAllocated...
Performed work on: WorkItem11
Performed work on: WorkItem12
Performed work on: WorkItem13
Performed work on: WorkItem14
Performed work on: WorkItem15
```

When 15 `WorkItem` tasks have been performed, the `WorkConsumer` is stopped. Finally, in the `WorkConsumer` `postStop()` function, the `Work-ItemsProvider` is also stopped.

This example creates only a single instance of `WorkConsumer`. You can imagine, however, creating possibly one `WorkConsumer` for the number of cores on the host computer. This would allow all of the `WorkConsumer` actors to be handling work simultaneously.

This actually provides a volunteering style of the *Message Dispatcher (374)*. Each `WorkConsumer` actor must inform the `WorkItemsProvider` when it needs more work. It does require the worker to know about the distributor. It

also requires more message sending than, say, using the Akka standard `Bal-
ancingDispatcher` because workers must send `AllocateWorkItems` mes-
sages to their `WorkItemsProvider`. However, this approach removes the
overhead of the checks required to use one or more of the Akka standard tools
discussed in *Message Dispatcher (374)*. This volunteering style also requires no
knowledge of Akka internals.

Resource Polling

You have just seen how to approximate an actor-to-actor Polling Consumer.
Now, though, you want to consider the design of an actor-based Polling Consumer that must poll some nonactor resource for information. This could be an
especially sticky situation because, unless the access is carefully designed, the
polling actor's thread could block for a long time on the desired resource, even
causing system unresponsiveness.

In this example, you will be monitoring a special "device," the `Even-
NumberDevice`. It is a "device" that provides even numbers when they are
available.

```
class EvenNumberDevice() {
  val random = new Random(99999)

  def nextEvenNumber(waitFor: Int): Option[Int] = {
    val timeout = new Timeout(waitFor)
    var nextEvenNumber: Option[Int] = None

    while (!timeout.isTimedOut && nextEvenNumber.isEmpty) {
      Thread.sleep(waitFor / 2)

      val number = random.nextInt(100000)

      if (number % 2 == 0) nextEvenNumber = Option(number)
    }

    nextEvenNumber
  }

  def nextEvenNumber(): Option[Int] = {
    nextEvenNumber(-1)
  }
}
```

As you probably expected, this device generates random numbers and
returns the first one that is even, if one is available. There are two overloaded
API functions. One of the functions never times out, while the other times

Chapter 9 Message Endpoints

out within some specific number of milliseconds. If an even number cannot be read within the timeout period, a `None Option` is returned. Obviously, if you use the nontimeout version of the `nextEvenNumber()` function, the calling actor's thread will block until an even number is available. The length of time required for the operation is undefined. You definitely don't want to cause that situation, so the actor must always call the `nextEvenNumber(waitFor: Int)` version of the function.

Here's the simple `Timeout` utility used by the `EvenNumberDevice`:

```scala
class Timeout(withinMillis: Int) {
  val mark = currentTime

  def isTimedOut(): Boolean = {
    if (withinMillis == -1) false
    else currentTime - mark >= withinMillis
  }

  private def currentTime(): Long = {
    (new Date()).getTime
  }
}
```

Now for the driver application that sets everything in motion, which awaits the `EvenNumberMonitor` to complete ten successful reads of the `Even-NumberDevice`. The `EvenNumberMonitor` is set in motion when the driver tells it to `Monitor`.

```scala
object DevicePollingConsumerDriver
    extends CompletableApp(10) {
  val evenNumberDevice = new EvenNumberDevice()

  val monitor = system.actorOf(
          Props(classOf[EvenNumberMonitor],
              evenNumberDevice),
          "evenNumberMonitor")

  monitor ! Monitor()

  awaitCompletion
}
```

Finally, here is the `EvenNumberMonitor` actor implementation:

```scala
case class Monitor()
```

```
class EvenNumberMonitor(
        evenNumberDevice: EvenNumberDevice)
    extends Actor {
    val scheduler =
                new CappedBackOffScheduler(
                        500,
                        15000,
                        context.system,
                        self,
                        Monitor())

    def monitor = {
      val evenNumber = evenNumberDevice.nextEvenNumber(3)
      if (evenNumber.isDefined) {
        println(s"EVEN: ${evenNumber.get}")
        scheduler.reset
        DevicePollingConsumerDriver.completedStep
      } else {
        println(s"MISS")
        scheduler.backOff
      }
    }

    def receive = {
      case request: Monitor =>
        monitor
    }
}
```

This monitor actor creates, as part of its construction, an instance of
`CappedBackOffScheduler`. This scheduler is used to send `Monitor` messages to the monitor actor on intervals. The interval starts out at a minimal
500 milliseconds. On any given probe of the device that results in a successful read of an even number, the following interval will be 500 milliseconds.
Otherwise, each successive unsuccessful read doubles the next interval. Here is
the `CappedBackOffScheduler` implementation:

```
class CappedBackOffScheduler(
    minimumInterval: Int,
    maximumInterval: Int,
    system: ActorSystem,
    receiver: ActorRef,
    message: Any) {

  var interval = minimumInterval

  def backOff = {
```

```
        interval = interval * 2
        if (interval > maximumInterval)
            interval = maximumInterval
        schedule
    }

    def reset = {
        interval = minimumInterval
        schedule
    }

    private def schedule = {
        val duration =
            Duration.create(
                interval,
                TimeUnit.MILLISECONDS)

        system
            .scheduler
            .scheduleOnce(
                duration,
                receiver,
                message)
    }
}
```

Each time the scheduler is told to backOff, it calculates a new interval, at least until it reaches 15 seconds. When the scheduler is told to reset following each successful even-number read, the interval is set to half a second. Either way, the interval is used to schedule a new Monitor message. The Monitor message will be sent to the EvenNumberMonitor once the interval expires.

Here is sample output from the EvenNumberMonitor:

```
EVEN: 65290
EVEN: 67208
EVEN: 53130
MISS
MISS
EVEN: 63720
EVEN: 1810
EVEN: 25708
MISS
EVEN: 38840
EVEN: 92860
EVEN: 78328
EVEN: 87076
```

Event-Driven Consumer

The actors in an Actor model are naturally Event-Driven Consumers and implement a *Point-to-Point Channel (151)*. Since actors use direct asynchronous messaging, each actor that is sent a message by another actor consumes the message asynchronously (see Figure 9.4).

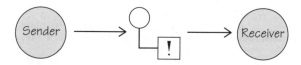

Figure 9.4 The Actor model forms a natural system of Event-Driven Consumers.

It's not that the message is of necessity an *Event Message (207)* that makes it an Event-Driven Consumer. It could well be a *Command Message (202)* or a *Document Message (204)* instead. Rather, it's the fact that an actor is reactive when it receives any kind of message that makes it an Event-Driven Consumer. Thus, the term *event-driven* in this case is used in contrast with *polling* to describe the kind of message the consumer is receiving.

Competing Consumers

Competing Consumers, as a specialty group, react to multiple messages simultaneously. Depending on the implementation of *Polling Consumer (362)* and *Message Dispatcher (374)*, these can be natural Competing Consumers.

Consider a *Message Dispatcher (374)* that implements a work dispatcher, as shown in Figure 9.5. The work dispatcher has a number of work performers

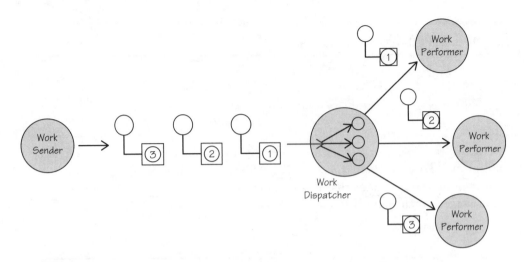

Figure 9.5 Competing Consumers receive new work based on how few *Messages (130)* are in their mailboxes.

as Competing Consumers (three are shown in the diagram). As the dispatcher receives a message indicating that some work must be done, it dispatches the actual work task to one of the work performers. But, which one of the work performers does it dispatch to? All of the workers are competing for work, and it should be the one that is currently least under load that is chosen. In fact, if there was a way to determine one out of all of the workers that is completely idle, that would be the best one to give the work.

One of Akka's standard routers supports Competing Consumer especially well. It's the `SmallestMailboxPool`. It is a router that can be configured to have a set number or resizing number of pooled routees (in other words, work performers) and that attempts to send messages to nonsuspended routees with the fewest number of messages in their own mailbox. This implies that all routee actors have their own mailbox. The pool of routees may be both local and remote, but a remote actor routee has a disadvantage because the router can't see its mailbox size. Understandable, routing to a remote actor is chosen by the router as the last and least desired routing option.

Here's an example of using the `SmallestMailboxPool`:

```
object CompetingConsumerDriver
    extends CompletableApp(100) {
  val workItemsProvider =
      system.actorOf(
```

```
                Props[WorkConsumer]
                    .withRouter(
                        SmallestMailboxPool(
                            nrOfInstances = 5)))

    for (itemCount <- 1 to 100) {
        workItemsProvider ! WorkItem("WorkItem" + itemCount)
    }

    awaitCompletion
}

case class WorkItem(name: String)

class WorkConsumer extends Actor {
    def receive = {
        case workItem: WorkItem =>
            println(s"${self.path.name} for: ${workItem.name}")

            CompetingConsumerDriver.completedStep
    }
}
```

As the actor referenced by `workItemsProvider` receives each message, it dispatches the work to one of the five `WorkConsumer` instances. The rule for choosing the dispatched-to actor is the one with the smallest mailbox, that is, the actor with the mailbox containing the least number of messages.

The partial output for this example follows:

```
$a for: WorkItem1
$c for: WorkItem3
$a for: WorkItem6
$d for: WorkItem4
$a for: WorkItem11
$d for: WorkItem9
$a for: WorkItem16
$d for: WorkItem14
$a for: WorkItem21
$d for: WorkItem19
$d for: WorkItem24
$b for: WorkItem2
$c for: WorkItem8
...
$b for: WorkItem98
$c for: WorkItem99
$d for: WorkItem100
$e for: WorkItem91
$a for: WorkItem90
```

Message Dispatcher

The Message Dispatcher is comparable to the *Content-Based Router (228)*. It is possible for a Message Dispatcher to look at the content of a message, such as a message type, and then dispatch the message to actors corresponding to each type of messages. However, a *Content-Based Router (228)* is not necessarily concerned with workload, while that is often the primary concern of a Message Dispatcher. Also, a *Content-Based Router (228)* will likely distribute messages across process boundaries, but a Message Dispatcher prefers to dispatch work tasks within the same process. Even if a Message Dispatcher checks some message content, such as a message type, before dispatching the message to a type-specific worker, it will also likely consider the workload already placed on its pool of—most likely in-process—workers and dispatch to the worker that has the least work to do. Figure 9.6 depicts the dispatching.

Akka supports a variety of Message Dispatchers, and actually some routers too, that can be employed in use cases that may benefit from the Message Dispatcher pattern. The reason why there are both standard dispatchers and standard routers that both apply is historical. Before there were routers, there

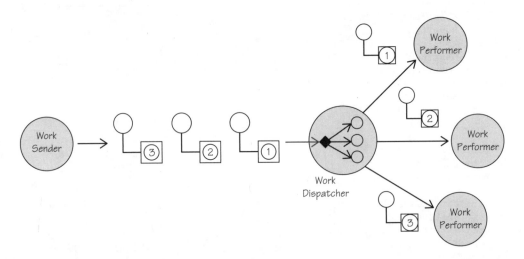

Figure 9.6 The Work Dispatcher is a Message Dispatcher.

was the `BalancingDispatcher`. However, the `BalancingDispatcher` was a bit troublesome, so the Akka team decided to provide routers instead. Some believe that if the decision was made today, there would never have been a `BalancingDispatcher`.

Here are some of the Akka standard dispatchers:

- `Dispatcher`: The default dispatcher, which associates a set of actors to a thread pool. You may choose a different dispatcher for any given actor.

- `PinnedDispatcher`: A dispatcher that pins a unique thread to each actor. Actually, the actor using this kind of dispatcher still has a thread pool but with just one actor allocated to it.

- `BalancingDispatcher`: This dispatcher attempts to distribute messages to actors that are the least tasked, which is true when the actor is completely idle. All the actors managed by this dispatcher share the same mailbox, and must all be of the same type. (Use is now discouraged.)

Here is how to create a `BalancingDispatcher` that has five `WorkConsumer` actors and then to dispatch 100 messages across them:

```
val workConsumers: List[ActorRef] =
  for (otherWorks <- (1 to 5).toList) yield {
    system.actorOf(Props[WorkConsumer]
        .withDispatcher("workconsumer-dispatcher"))
  }

val bestWorkConsumer = workConsumers(0)

for (itemCount <- 1 to 100) {
  bestWorkConsumer ! WorkItem("WorkItem" + itemCount)
}
```

Although you can use any of the five `WorkConsumer` reference instances, you need a reference to only one. That's because all of the five `WorkConsumer` instances share the same mailbox. When you send a message to `bestWorkConsumer`, the message will be delivered to any one of the five, depending on one that is idle. The `workconsumer-dispatcher` must exist in your Akka configuration:

```
workconsumer-dispatcher {
  type = BalancingDispatcher
}
```

Although you may use the `BalancingDispatcher`, it is discouraged. Instead, if you choose to use any of the Akka standard tools, you should favor one of the routers instead. The following are Akka standard routers. Called routers by name, they make great Message Dispatchers.

- `RoundRobinRouter`: A router that can be configured to have a set number or resizing number of routees and that sends messages to each of the routees in round-robin order. Implied is that this router makes no effort to determine the workload of any routee.

- `SmallestMailboxRouter`: A router that can be configured to have a set number or resizing number of routees and that attempts to send messages to nonsuspended routees with the fewest number of messages in their own mailbox. This implies that all routee actors have their own mailbox. The routees may be both local and remote, but a remote actor routee has a disadvantage because the router can't see its mailbox size. Understandably, routing to a remote actor is chosen as the last option. (This is possibly the best `BalancingDispatcher` replacement. You can find a usage example when I discuss *Competing Consumer (371)*.)

Here is how to create a `RoundRobinRouter` that has five `WorkConsumer` routees:

```
val workItemsProvider = system.actorOf(
        Props(classOf[WorkConsumer], workItemsProvider)
            .withRouter(
                RoundRobinRouter(
                    nrOfInstances = 5)))

workItemsProvider ! WorkItem("WorkItem1")
workItemsProvider ! WorkItem("WorkItem2")
workItemsProvider ! WorkItem("WorkItem3")
workItemsProvider ! WorkItem("WorkItem4")
workItemsProvider ! WorkItem("WorkItem5")
```

Each of the previous `WorkItem` messages will be delivered to a different `WorkConsumer`. See *Competing Consumer (371)* for an example of using `SmallestMailboxRouter`.

As an alternative to using an Akka standard dispatcher or router, you should also consider the volunteering style of work provider discussed in *Polling Consumer (362)*. The volunteering style allows each worker actor to inform the work provider when it needs more work. This requires the worker to know about the distributor. It also requires more message sending because workers must send "work needed" messages to their distributor. However, the volunteering style removes the overhead of the checks required to use one or more of the Akka standard tools. It also requires no knowledge of Akka internals to implement.

Selective Consumer

Use a Selective Consumer if your actor may receive messages of various types but can process only some of the message types. In this case, the Selective Consumer is a kind of *Message Filter (232)*, allowing only supported messages to be consumed by the system. You'll find an example of this slant on Selective Consumer in the discussion of *Message Filter (232)*.

You may also design a Selective Consumer to accept various types of messages on behalf of datatype consumers, where the Selective Consumer actor routes the various types of messages into *Datatype Channels (167)*. This approach is demonstrated by *Dynamic Router (237)*, but another example lacking dynamic routing rules is provided here.

The `SelectiveConsumerDriver` creates the three actors that are each consumers of specific message types, making them internal *Datatype Channels (167)*.

```
object SelectiveConsumerDriver
    extends CompletableApp(3) {
  val consumerOfA =
    system.actorOf(
        Props[ConsumerOfMessageTypeA],
        "consumerOfA")

  val consumerOfB =
    system.actorOf(
        Props[ConsumerOfMessageTypeB],
        "consumerOfB")

  val consumerOfC =
    system.actorOf(
        Props[ConsumerOfMessageTypeC],
        "consumerOfC")

  val selectiveConsumer =
```

```
    system.actorOf(
        Props(classOf[SelectiveConsumer],
            consumerOfA, consumerOfB, consumerOfC),
        "selectiveConsumer")

  selectiveConsumer ! MessageTypeA()
  selectiveConsumer ! MessageTypeB()
  selectiveConsumer ! MessageTypeC()

  awaitCompletion
}
```

Once the three message type consumers are created, the driver creates the SelectiveConsumer and sends three messages, one each of Message-TypeA, MessageTypeB, and MessageTypeC. These are then received by the SelectiveConsumer and then dispatched to the *Datatype Channels (167)*.

```
case class MessageTypeA()
case class MessageTypeB()
case class MessageTypeC()

class SelectiveConsumer(
    consumerOfA: ActorRef,
    consumerOfB: ActorRef,
    consumerOfC: ActorRef) extends Actor {

  def receive = {
    case message: MessageTypeA =>
      consumerOfA forward message
    case message: MessageTypeB =>
      consumerOfB forward message
    case message: MessageTypeC =>
      consumerOfC forward message
  }
}
```

Finally, here are the three specific message-type consumers:

```
class ConsumerOfMessageTypeA extends Actor {
  def receive = {
    case message: MessageTypeA =>
      println(s"ConsumerOfMessageTypeA: $message")
      SelectiveConsumerDriver.completedStep
  }
}

class ConsumerOfMessageTypeB extends Actor {
```

```
  def receive = {
    case message: MessageTypeB =>
      println(s"ConsumerOfMessageTypeB: $message")
      SelectiveConsumerDriver.completedStep
  }
}

class ConsumerOfMessageTypeC extends Actor {
  def receive = {
    case message: MessageTypeC =>
      println(s"ConsumerOfMessageTypeC: $message")
      SelectiveConsumerDriver.completedStep
  }
}
```

This is sample output from running the driver:

```
ConsumerOfMessageTypeA: MessageTypeA()
ConsumerOfMessageTypeC: MessageTypeC()
ConsumerOfMessageTypeB: MessageTypeB()
```

Durable Subscriber

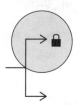

Use a Durable Subscriber when you need to ensure that the receiving actor will not miss messages that are sent while it is not actively running. The Akka toolkit does not, at the time of writing, provide support explicit for Durable Subscriber. However, if you need this sort of functionality, then with some imagination and ingenuity it is not out of your grasp. And, although Enterprise Integration Patterns [EIP] names this pattern for use with *Publish-Subscribe Channel (154)* only, you can make use of it actually with any kind of actor *Message Channel (128)*.

Akka Persistence has support for what is called a `PersistentView`. A `PersistentView` is one way that Akka supports the CQRS pattern [CQRS], where a `PersistentActor` can have its state projected into a customized view. You can use the same mechanisms to create a Durable Subscriber.

The first part of this solution is to create a `PersistentActor` that is used to represent the special *Message Channel (128)* through which *Messages (130)* will be published or enqueued. You can think of this `PersistentActor` as the named topic/queue to which *Messages (130)* are published/sent. The name is provided by the actor's `persistenceId`. As each *Message (130)* is received by this named topic/queue `PersistentActor`, all that the actor does is persist them to its own journal.

```
class PublishedTopic extends PersistentActor {

  override def persistenceId = "my-topic-name"

  override def receiveCommand: Receive = {
    case message: Any =>
      persistAsync(message)
  }
}
```

In this case, you can use a special form of `persist()`, which is `persist-Async()`. There is no need to wait for successful persistence before accepting the next message, so you can use the most optimal persistence operation available to the `PersistentActor`.

The second part of the solution is to create one `PersistentView` instance for each subscriber. If you want to treat this as a named queue, then you would have only one `PersistentView` as the queue consumer. In any case, each `PersistentView` instance that is to receive *Messages (130)* from the topic/queue would set its `persistenceId` to that of the `PersistentActor`. It will then receive every *Message (130)* that is persisted to the named topic/queue.

```
class TopicSubscriber extends PersistentView {

  override def persistenceId = "my-topic-name"
  override def viewId = "my-topic-name-subscriber-1"
  var dummyState = 0

  def handleMessage(message: Any) = {
    ...
  }

  override def receive: Receive = {
    case message: Any =>
      handleMessage(message)
      deleteSnapshots(SnapshotSelectionCriteria.Latest)
      saveSnapshot(dummyState)
```

```
  }

  override def receiveRecover: Receive = {
    case SnapshotOffer(metadata, snapshot) =>
      dummyState = snapshot // can actually toss out
    case RecoveryCompleted =>
  }
}
```

> **NOTE**
>
> At the time of writing, the `PersistentView` is to be replaced by an Akka
> Streams solution. I have been assured that the Akka Streams solution will work
> as well as the `PersistentView` approach and be intuitively similar enough
> that it will not be difficult to change this code to use it.

There is one additional requirement for the `TopicSubscriber`. It must keep track of which *Messages (130)* it has already received. It can do this by producing a new snapshot as it receives messages, as is shown in the previous example. This way when the `TopicSubscriber` is stopped and restarted, it will not reprocess previously received *Messages (130)*, only those that it has not yet received.

With this setup, the `TopicSubscriber` will never miss a *Message (130)* sent to the `PublishedTopic`, even when the `TopicSubscriber` is not running for some time. When the `TopicSubscriber` starts up again, it will receive any previously unreceived *Messages (130)*.

A possible downside to this approach is that currently there is no removal of *Messages (130)* from the journal of the `PersistentActor` (for example, `PublishedTopic`). If need be, you can periodically delete *Messages (130)* from the journal once you know it is safe to remove them.

```
class PublishedTopic extends PersistentActor {

  override def persistenceId = "my-topic-name"

  override def receiveCommand: Receive = {
    case cg: CollectGarbage =>
        deleteMessages(cg.maximumSequenceNr)
    case message: Any =>
      persist(message)
  }
}
```

This will permanently delete from the journal all messages with a sequence number less than or equal to the value of `maximumSequenceNr`. (Permanent deletion is, however, supported only if the underlying journal implementation provides this feature.) Figuring out how to safely delete a range of messages is a problem for you to work out. You might use some approach based on subscriber confirmations, for example. However, you may not know how many subscribers you have, so this may not be practical. You might instead do something based on a safe date and time solution, where essentially you determine the maximum durability of each message. Of course, this is an easy problem to solve if you have only one listener or a clear set number of them. Still, in the end, this approach will work best if you don't have to worry very much about message cleanup.

One entirely different option would be to create a solution around Apache Kafka [Kafka], which was originally developed to be used as a high-throughput *Publish-Subscribe (154)* mechanism. It's a more elaborate solution to the one provided here but has all the *Publish-Subscribe (154)* features, including maximum message retention, built in.

Perhaps the Akka team or some other contributor will work out a more explicit Durable Subscriber solution, but until then, the solution provided herein has the correct semantics with no overhead. Should you desire that the programming interface be more like *Publish-Subscribe Channel (154)*, you can encapsulate the `PersistentActor` and `PersistentView` with traits that use the correct terminology.

Idempotent Receiver

Design an actor to be an Idempotent Receiver when there is the possibility for it to receive a given message multiple times and processing that message each time would cause problems. Since the standard message delivery contract for the Actor model is "at most once," it may seem like this could never be a problem. The problem still arises under this basic condition:

> A message sender expects an acknowledgment, and if acknowledgment is not received, it will resend the same message. The receiver does process the message, but its acknowledgment is not delivered to the sender. If the receiver is not

designed idempotent, the redelivery of the already processed message could cause problems to the state of the actor and any other actors that process resulting messages from the receiver.

In fact, in this case, not only would one or a few actors have invalid state. The state of a major part of the system could be compromised. This is true whether *Guaranteed Delivery (175)* or *Durable Subscriber (379)* is at play because at-most-once delivery has been replaced with at-least-once delivery.

There are a few ways to prevent this kind of compromised state condition and design actors to be *idempotent*. Essentially, being idempotent means that when the same message is received multiple times, there is no change to the actor's state. Here are some approaches:

- De-duplicate incoming messages by recognizing duplicate messages by identity.

- Design state transitioning messages to cause the same impact each time they are received.

- Allow the state transition to render harmless the receipt of duplicate messages.

Message De-duplication

The de-duplication approach is discussed at length in *Enterprise Integration Patterns* [EIP]. Implementing this requires the message receiver to track the messages it has already received and ignore the ones that are redelivered. It's possible to maintain an in-memory or database-persisted collection of received message identities. That means that each message that is de-duplicated must be assigned a unique identity. And *Enterprise Integration Patterns* [EIP] rightly warns against using a unique business identity for this since the same business identity could accompany multiple unique messages.

The other challenge to the de-duplication approach is determining how long to track the unique identities of messages already received. *Enterprise Integration Patterns* [EIP] suggests using the Transmission Control Protocol/Internet Protocol (TCP/IP) approach of de-duplication by using a window size. This can be achieved by indicating that only 100 or 1,000 message identities will be tracked, and when that window size is exceeded, the oldest message identities are dropped. Of course, you risk the potential that your window size is too small. Design this support carefully. Perhaps a time-based window is better than a capped collection.

Design Messages with Identical Impact

As suggested in *Enterprise Integration Patterns* [EIP], you can design your messages such that each time they are processed, they will have the same impact on the actor's state. Reusing the example from *Enterprise Integration Patterns* [EIP], compare these two message types and their usage:

```
case class Deposit(amount: Money)
...
account ! Deposit(Money(10))
...
case class SetBalance(amount: Money)
...
account ! SetBalance(currentBalance + Money(10))
```

The first message, `Deposit`, must be de-duplicated in some way. Otherwise, if it is received twice, it will cause the account to have an incorrect balance. The second message type, `SetBalance`, need not be de-duplicated because it simply sets a given state.

I really dislike this approach, especially with this specific example. In any messaging environment, assuming that the state of a receiver will be the stable between your query of current state and receiving your *Command Message (202)* to set its next state is highly unlikely. It's not that no message type can ever be designed this way, but I think it is obvious that the example from *Enterprise Integration Patterns* [EIP] never would. Thus, the previous example would be best designed as follows:

```
case class Deposit(
    transactionId: TransactionId,
    amount: Money)
...
account ! Deposit(TransactionId(), Money(10))
```

Oddly enough, to complete this example, you are led to the third approach.

State Transition Renders Duplicates Harmless

Continuing the previous example, you will now use a `TransactionId` to render harmless the receipt of duplicate `Deposit` messages. Must you de-duplicate based on `TransactionId`? Possibly, but the solution may be as simple as this:

```scala
case class AccountBalance(
    accountId: AccountId,
    amount: Money)

case class Deposit(
    transactionId: TransactionId,
    amount: Money)

case class QueryBalance()

case class Withdraw(
    transactionId: TransactionId,
    amount: Money)

class Account(accountId: AccountId) extends Actor {
  val transactions = Map.empty[TransactionId, Transaction]

  def receive = {
    case deposit: Deposit =>
      val transaction =
          Transaction(
              deposit.transactionId,
              deposit.amount)
      println(s"Deposit: $transaction")
      transactions += (deposit.transactionId -> transaction)
      AccountDriver.completedStep
    case withdraw: Withdraw =>
      val transaction =
          Transaction(
              withdraw.transactionId,
              withdraw.amount.negative)
      println(s"Withdraw: $transaction")
      transactions +=
          (withdraw.transactionId -> transaction)
      AccountDriver.completedStep
    case query: QueryBalance =>
      sender ! calculateBalance()
      AccountDriver.completedStep
  }

  def calculateBalance(): AccountBalance = {
    var amount = Money(0)

    transactions.values map { transaction =>
      amount = amount + transaction.amount
    }

    println(s"Balance: $amount")

    AccountBalance(accountId, amount)
  }
}
```

Because the `Map` of `transactions` will have just one entry for each `TransactionId`, receiving the same `Deposit` multiple times will have no impact on the balance of the `Account`. In this case, it works because this particular `Map` operation itself is idempotent. And calculating the balance is as easy as adding all `Deposit` messages and subtracting all `Withdraw` messages.

Here is the driver and the output:

```
object AccountDriver extends CompletableApp(17) {
  val account =
      system.actorOf(
          Props(classOf[Account], AccountId()),
          "account")

  val deposit1 = Deposit(TransactionId(), Money(100))
  account ! deposit1
  account ! QueryBalance()
  account ! deposit1
  account ! Deposit(TransactionId(), Money(20))
  account ! QueryBalance()
  account ! deposit1
  account ! Withdraw(TransactionId(), Money(50))
  account ! QueryBalance()
  account ! deposit1
  account ! Deposit(TransactionId(), Money(70))
  account ! QueryBalance()
  account ! deposit1
  account ! Withdraw(TransactionId(), Money(100))
  account ! QueryBalance()
  account ! deposit1
  account ! Deposit(TransactionId(), Money(10))
  account ! QueryBalance()

  awaitCompletion
}
```

```
Deposit: Transaction(TransactionId(1),Money(100.0))
Balance: Money(100.0)
Deposit: Transaction(TransactionId(1),Money(100.0))
Deposit: Transaction(TransactionId(2),Money(20.0))
Balance: Money(120.0)
Deposit: Transaction(TransactionId(1),Money(100.0))
Withdraw: Transaction(TransactionId(3),Money(-50.0))
Balance: Money(70.0)
Deposit: Transaction(TransactionId(1),Money(100.0))
Deposit: Transaction(TransactionId(4),Money(70.0))
Balance: Money(140.0)
Deposit: Transaction(TransactionId(1),Money(100.0))
Withdraw: Transaction(TransactionId(5),Money(-100.0))
Balance: Money(40.0)
Deposit: Transaction(TransactionId(1),Money(100.0))
```

```
Deposit: Transaction(TransactionId(6),Money(10.0))
Balance: Money(50.0)
```

Although the first `Deposit` is sent six different times, only the first receipt is actually kept as a `Transaction`.

Another way to make an actor idempotent is to maintain a status that allows or disallows a specific transition. The `Map` of transactions used previously could serve as a status or flag indicating whether a specific action could occur.

```
class Account(accountId: AccountId) extends Actor {
  val transactions = Map.empty[TransactionId, Transaction]

  def receive = {
    case deposit: Deposit
        if (!transactions.contains(
              deposit.transactionId)) =>
      val transaction =
        Transaction(deposit.transactionId, deposit.amount)
      println(s"Deposit: $transaction")
      transactions += (deposit.transactionId -> transaction)
      AccountDriver.completedStep
    ...
```

With this conditional expression as part of the `Deposit` matching, the case will not be matched at all if the `TransactionId` is already in the `Map`. You can think of many other ways in which a variable (mutable) status can transition from one state to another and how those various statuses can be used to represent that the actor has already received one or more messages. Otherwise, if the variable is in a given state, you know that one or more messages have already been processed.

```
case attachment: AttachDocument
        if (document.isNotAttached) =>
  ...
```

There is yet another way to make an actor's state safe from the receipt of duplicate messages. This way is also based on state but takes a different slant. It's called *become*, and you are going to use this built-in Akka actor feature to manage risk assessment classification.

```
case class AttachDocument(documentText: String)
case class ClassifyRisk()
case class RiskClassified(classification: String)
```

```
case class Document(documentText: Option[String]) {
  if (documentText.isDefined) {
    val text = documentText.get
    if (text == null || text.trim.isEmpty) {
      throw new IllegalStateException(
          "Document must have text.")
    }
  }

  def determineClassification = {
    val text = documentText.get.toLowerCase

    if (text.contains("low")) "Low"
    else if (text.contains("medium")) "Medium"
    else if (text.contains("high")) "High"
    else "Unknown"
  }

  def isNotAttached = documentText.isEmpty
  def isAttached = documentText.isDefined
}

class RiskAssessment extends Actor {
  var document = Document(None)

  def documented: Receive = {
    case attachment: AttachDocument =>
      // already received; ignore

    case classify: ClassifyRisk =>
      sender ! RiskClassified(
                    document.determineClassification)
  }

  def undocumented: Receive = {
    case attachment: AttachDocument =>
      document = Document(Some(attachment.documentText))
      context.become(documented)
    case classify: ClassifyRisk =>
      sender ! RiskClassified("Unknown")
  }

  def receive = undocumented
}
```

Take a look at the two partial functions, documented and undocumented. These represent the possible message receive blocks for a Risk-
Assessment. The receive block is initially set to undocumented. When
the AttachDocument message is received by the undocumented block, the
Document is created and set as state on the RiskAssessment. At the same
time, the RiskAssessment is told to become documented.

```
case attachment: AttachDocument =>
  document = Document(Some(attachment.documentText))
  context.become(documented)
```

Note also that when the receive block is undocumented, all attempts to ask for a risk classification will result in an answer of Risk-Classified-("Unknown").

When the RiskAssessment becomes documented, you are aware that the state has already transitioned because of receiving an AttachDocument message, so the actor's documented block can now safely ignore future AttachDocument messages. Further, it is only when the actor has become documented that when asking ClassifyRisk, the actor can determine an actual risk classification. The actual risk classification takes a simpleton approach and is assessed only by checking the document text for the words *low*, *medium*, and *high*.

First take a look at the following driver application, which uses Akka Future to obtain answers to its questions:

```
object RiskAssessmentDriver extends CompletableApp(2) {
  implicit val timeout = Timeout(5 seconds)

  val riskAssessment =
        system.actorOf(
            Props[RiskAssessment],
            "riskAssessment")

  val futureAssessment1 = riskAssessment ? ClassifyRisk()
  printRisk(futureAssessment1)

  riskAssessment ! AttachDocument("This is a HIGH risk.")

  val futureAssessment2 = riskAssessment ? ClassifyRisk()
  printRisk(futureAssessment2)

  awaitCompletion

  def printRisk(futureAssessment: Future[Any]): Unit = {
    val classification =
      Await.result(futureAssessment, timeout.duration)
          .asInstanceOf[RiskClassified]
    println(s"$classification")

    completedStep
  }
}
```

Now, note the output from asking for risk assessment classifications.

```
RiskClassified(Unknown)
RiskClassified(High)
```

You have now successfully made **RiskAssessment** an Idempotent Receiver based on the use of Akka's *become* support.

Service Activator

Use a Service Activator when you have an internal service that may be requested using one or more externally available access resources. For example, a client may make a request via an actor, a middleware messaging system, a RESTful resource, or a remote procedure call (RPC). No matter how the request is made, the request receiver delegates to an internal Application Service [IDDD]. Figure 9.7 shows how this works.

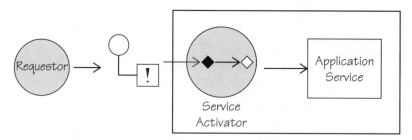

Figure 9.7 A Service Activator dispatches to an Application Service.

This follows the Hexagonal *or* Ports and Adapters architecture defined in *Implementing Domain-Driven Design* [IDDD] (see Figure 9.8). The client application interacts only with the outside adapters of the receiving application, and the outside adapters delegate to the inside application components, which are Application Services.

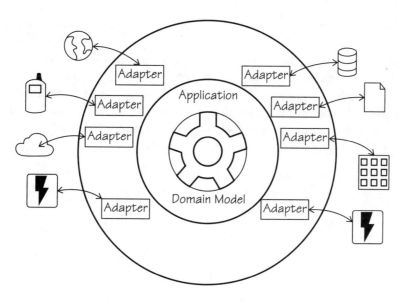

Figure 9.8 A Ports and Adapters architecture

This allows for any number of Service Activator types to be provided at the outside part of the architecture, while supporting a common, reusable Application Service layer on the inside. In Figure 9.8, all incoming Adapter types (outside left) are Service Activators. Each set of types adapt input parameters—*Message (130)* properties—to parameters that can be passed to the API implemented by the Application Services on the inside. Of course, the Application Services could be implemented as actors should the application use the reactive style throughout.

Summary

This chapter provided detailed treatment of a dozen kinds of *Message Endpoints (145)*, including two ways for actors to support transactions. You saw how the Actor model provides a natural *Messaging Gateway (338)* and how you can implement a *Messaging Mapper (344)*. You also learned how you can support Aggregates [IDDD] through a *Transactional Actor (354)* that uses Event Sourcing.

You saw how to create a nonblocking *Polling Consumer (362)*, how actors are by definition *Event-Driven Consumers (369)*, and how you can leverage Akka's standard routers to create *Competing Consumers (371)*. You saw the importance of supporting workload trafficking through *Message Dispatchers (374)*. I also discussed how actors can be *Selective Consumers (377)*, reacting to only certain kinds of *Messages (130)*.You discovered a way to support *Durable Subscribers (379)* using Akka Persistence. You found out that when using *Guaranteed Delivery (175)*, it is important for actors to be designed as *Idempotent Receivers (382)*. Finally, you learned that all actors that receive messages at the outer edge of the application and dispatch inward to service or domain model actors are *Service Activators (390)*.

Chapter 10

System Management and Infrastructure

Unlike the previous pattern chapters, this chapter is not an exploration of one of the top-level messaging patterns from Chapter 4, "Messaging with Actors." Rather, this chapter presents additional patterns that provide advanced application, infrastructural, and debugging tools.

- *Control Bus*: Use a *Control Bus (394)* as a central location to monitor and manage both development and production messaging.

- *Detour*: Toggle on a *Detour (395)* to route any *Message (130)* through a set of special components for logging, validation, testing, and debugging features, as it travels on its way to its ultimate destination. Different from a *Wire Tap (397)*, a *Detour (395)* can at times be used to modify *Message (130)* content before forwarding it.

- *Wire Tap*: A *Wire Tap (397)* is used to inspect *Messages (130)* that are sent from actor to actor.

- *Message Metadata/History*: Attach metadata to a *Message (130)* to indicate who has done what with the *Message (130)*.

- *Message Journal/Store*: Use a *Message Journal (402)* as a means to support *Guaranteed Delivery (175)* and possibly *Durable Subscribers (379)*.

- *Smart Proxy*: Sometimes you will need to design a *Wire Tap (397)* that knows how to handle a full *Request-Reply (209)* using the *Return Address (211)* of the original sender. That's the job of a *Smart Proxy (406)*.

- *Test Message*: Send a *Test Message (411)* to an actor when you need to determine whether *Messages (130)* are being received properly.

- *Channel Purger*: A *Channel Purger (414)* is used to delete some set of *Messages (130)* from the *Message Store (402)* before testing or before continuing with production.

You will tend to use *Message Metadata (398)* and *Message Journal (402)* with most of your reactive enterprise applications. The other patterns will definitely come in handy at different stages of development, test, and production, and they can be mixed and matched as needed.

Control Bus

Use a Control Bus to monitor and manage the actor systems and actors within. There was previously a Control Bus prebuilt for Akka, called the Typesafe Console. The Typesafe Console supported the monitoring and control of several parts of the Typesafe Platform, including Akka nodes, actor systems, and the actors that run inside. This tool has been deprecated in favor of third-party tools and the possibility that a future version of the Typesafe Activator may support some of the vital monitoring features.

Here are some of the things[1] that a Control Bus for Akka should be able to help you observe and manage, during development, in test, and in production:

- Nodes, actor systems, dispatchers, actors, and deviations

- Message rates and peaks

- Individual trace events linked as trace trees or spans

- Latency between predefined or user defined points

- Latency distributions

- Actor supervisor hierarchies

- Actor mailbox queue size and delays

- Actor message dispatcher status

- Status of remote messaging and system errors

- Java virtual machine (JVM) and operating system health

Monitored data should be scoped by node, groups of actors, or individual actors, which are defined as follows:

---

1.   Some of this content was provided by the official Typesafe Console documentation.

- *Nodes*: A node corresponds to a JVM, and there may be several nodes running on a single physical or virtual server. Of all managed nodes, you should be able to select a single node in order to view the details.

- *Node overview*: Within a single node you should be able to view the numbers of Actor Systems running on it and the details within a single actor system.

- *Actor systems*: View any individual actor system running on a given node. Inside the actor system you should be able to view the number of message dispatchers, the number of actors, and the number of deviations, as well as the health of each.

- *Dispatchers*: A given actor system will have one or more dispatchers. Each dispatcher services a number of actors and a number of deviations. By viewing dispatcher details you should be able to see details about throughput, number of threads, executors, thread pools, mailbox size, message counts, and deviations.

- *Actors*: You should be able to view the actors that are running within a given actor system.

- *Deviations*: On a given actor system, you must be able to view the errors, warnings, dead letters, deadlocks, and unhandled messages.

Detour

You can send an actor-to-actor *Message (130)* on a Detour by contextually routing it through a set of special components as it travels on its way to its ultimate destination. Using Detour, you can design in the ability to turn on the special contextual routing and turn it off, even on demand. A Detour can be used to add logging, validation, testing, and debugging features to your actor systems, in a seamless way.

A Detour is different from a *Wire Tap (397)*, in that a Detour may choose to inspect or modify the *Message (130)*, while a Wire Tap can be used only to inspect. A Detour is often associated with a *Control Bus (394)* because the *Control Bus (394)* needs a way to examine various aspects of the system, including performance and errors.

When you consider the basic ideas behind Detour, it becomes clear that it is a form of *Pipes and Filters (135)* architecture. Using *Pipes and Filters (135)* is an especially effective way to implement a Detour in the Actor model. In fact, as demonstrated when discussing *Pipes and Filters (135)*, one of the easiest ways to create a Detour through one or more specialty components is to wire filter actors into each sending actor.

```
object DetourDriver extends CompletableApp(5) {
  ...

  val orderProcessor = system.actorOf(
        Props[OrderProcessor],
        "orderProcessor")

  val debugger = system.actorOf(
        Props(classOf[MessageDebugger],orderProcessor),
        "debugger")

  val tester = system.actorOf(
        Props(classOf[MessageTester],debugger),
        "tester")

  val validator = system.actorOf(
        Props(classOf[MessageValidator],tester),
        "validator")

  val logger = system.actorOf(
        Props(classOf[MessageLogger],validator),
        "logger")

  val orderProcessorDetour = logger

  orderProcessorDetour ! ProcessOrder(order)

  awaitCompletion()

  println("DetourDriver: is completed.")
}
```

This Detour marches the `ProcessOrder` *Message (130)* from the `MessageLogger` to the `MessageValidator`, then to the `MessageTester`, then to the `MessageDebugger`, and finally to the `OrderProcessor`. If you wanted to turn off the Detour, you could do so like this:

```
object DetourDriver extends CompletableApp(5) {
  ...
  val orderProcessor = system.actorOf(
```

```
          Props[OrderProcessor],
          "orderProcessor")
    ...

    val orderProcessorDetour = orderProcessor

    orderProcessorDetour ! ProcessOrder(order)

    awaitCompletion()

    println("DetourDriver: is completed.")
}
```

This causes the `ProcessOrder` *Message (130)* to be sent directly to the `OrderProcessor`.

Wire Tap

You can use a Wire Tap to inspect *Messages (130)* that are sent from actor to actor. There are several similarities between Wire Tap and *Detour (395)*. One of the main differences is that a Wire Tap can only inspect *Messages (130)*, while a *Detour (395)* can both inspect and modify *Message (130)* content.

Another difference is that the Wire Tap tends to be a single filter component, while a Detour may tend to have multiple filtering steps. At the point of the Wire Tap, the *Message (130)* is sent both to its final destination and to an inspecting actor component, that is, if the tap itself does not perform the inspection step.

This is an example of a Wire Tap that is used to perform message logging:

```
object WireTapDriver extends CompletableApp(2) {
  ...
  val orderProcessor = system.actorOf(
            Props[OrderProcessor],
            "orderProcessor")

  val logger = system.actorOf(
            Props(classOf[MessageLogger],orderProcessor),
            "logger")
```

```
    val orderProcessorWireTap = logger

    orderProcessorWireTap ! ProcessOrder(order)

    awaitCompletion()

    println("WireTapDriver: is completed.")
}
```

The MessageLogger will log each message sent to the OrderProcessor and then forward the message on to OrderProcessor. In this case, the Message-Logger is both the Wire Tap and the filtering component that logs messages.

Message Metadata/History

Attach Message Metadata to a *Message (130)* to associate a list of all users and actors that have sent and received it and what activities have been performed using it. *Enterprise Integration Patterns* [EIP] discusses Message History as a debugging and analysis tool. Here I generalize this pattern even more as Message Metadata because the metadata that you may choose to associate with any given *Message (130)* could be used in any number of ways. You can even use metadata to resolve concurrent business operations that may conflict with one another, which can provide a means for error recovery. Use the Message Metadata to your advantage, whatever advantages it may provide.

Here is a general-purpose facility that can be used to attach metadata to a given *Message (130)*:

```
object Metadata {
  def apply() = new Metadata()

  case class Who(name: String)
  case class What(happened: String)
  case class Where(actorType: String, actorName: String)
  case class Why(explanation: String)

  case class Entry(who: Who, what: What, where: Where,
                   when: Date, why: Why) {
```

```
      def this(who: Who, what: What, where: Where, why: Why) =
        this(who, what, where, new Date(), why)

      def this(who: String, what: String, actorType: String,
               actorName: String, why: String) =
        this(Who(who), What(what), Where(actorType, actorName),
               new Date(), Why(why))

      def asMetadata = (new Metadata()).including(this)
  }
}

import Metadata._

case class Metadata(entries: List[Entry]) {
  def this() = this(List.empty[Entry])
  def this(entry: Entry) = this(List[Entry](entry))

  def including(entry: Entry): Metadata = {
    Metadata(entries :+ entry)
  }
}
```

This `Metadata` facility comes with both a companion object and a case class. The `Metadata` container is composed of a `List` of `Entry` elements. Each `Entry` contains a full description of who, what, where, when, and why notations. To create a new, empty `Metadata` instance, you can define an `Entry` and ask the `Entry` for itself as metadata using the `asMetadata()` method.

```
val entry = Entry(
    Who("user"),
    What("Did something"),
    Where(this.getClass.getSimpleName, "component1"),
    new Date(),
    Why("Because..."))

val metadata = entry.asMetadata
```

Now consider one message type that carries metadata:

```
case class SomeMessage(
    payload: String,
    metadata: Metadata = new Metadata()) {

  def including(entry: Entry): SomeMessage = {
```

```
            SomeMessage(payload, metadata.including(entry))
     }
}
```

The message type `SomeMessage` has a simple `String`-based data `pay-`
`load` value and an instance of `Metadata`, which may be defaulted with an
empty list of `entries`. Given an instance of `SomeMessage`, you can ask it
for a copy of the same `SomeMessage`, but with a new `Entry` included in its
`Metadata`. So, you get a new instance of `SomeMessage` with the same `pay-`
`load` but with a new `Metadata` that has an additional `Entry`.

Here's how a `Metadata`-enriched *Message (130)* can be used as it is sent
from actor to actor. You start with the `MessageMetadataDriver`.

```
object MessageMetadataDriver extends CompletableApp(3) {
  import Metadata._

  val processor3 = system.actorOf(
          Props(classOf[Processor],None),
          "processor3")
  val processor2 = system.actorOf(
          Props(classOf[Processor],Some(processor3)),
          "processor2")
  val processor1 = system.actorOf(
          Props(classOf[Processor],Some(processor2)),
          "processor1")

  val entry = Entry(
      Who("driver"),
      What("Started"),
      Where(this.getClass.getSimpleName, "driver"),
      new Date(),
      Why("Running processors"))

  processor1 ! SomeMessage("Data...", entry.asMetadata)

  awaitCompletion
}
```

The driver creates three instances of the `Processor` actor, each with a
unique name. The processors are chained together, allowing `processor1` to
send to `processor2` and allowing `processor2` to send to `processor3`.
Next an `Entry` is created with its who, what, where, when, and why notations, and the `Entry` is then converted to a `Metadata` that is used to create an
instance of `SomeMessage`. The message is then sent to `processor1`.

Here is the `Processor` actor:

```
class Processor(next: Option[ActorRef]) extends Actor {
  import Metadata._

  val random = new Random()

  def receive = {
    case message: SomeMessage =>
      report(message)

      val nextMessage = message.including(entry)

      if (next.isDefined) {
        next.get ! nextMessage
      } else {
        report(nextMessage, "complete")
      }

      MessageMetadataDriver.completedStep
  }

  def because = s"Because: ${random.nextInt(10)}"

  def entry =
    Entry(Who(user),
          What(wasProcessed),
          Where(this.getClass.getSimpleName,
                self.path.name),
          new Date(),
          Why(because))

  def report(message: SomeMessage,
             heading: String = "received") =
    println(s"${self.path.name} $heading: $message")

  def user = s"user${random.nextInt(100)}"

  def wasProcessed = s"Processed: ${random.nextInt(5)}"
}
```

When `SomeMessage` is received by the particular processor, it reports the received message and then creates a new instance of `SomeMessage` with its processing details `Entry` appended. Then, if the processor is assigned a next processor, it sends the new `SomeMessage` to that processor. If, however, `processor3` has been reached, the new instance of `SomeMessage` is reported as the completion step.

Here is the output from running the driver (with formatting to fit the page):

```
processor1 received: SomeMessage(Data...,↵
Metadata(List(Entry(Who(driver),What(Started),↵
```

```
Where(MessageMetadataDriver$,driver),Wed Apr 30 15:57:41 MDT↵
 2014,Why(Running processors)))))
processor2 received: SomeMessage(Data...,↵
Metadata(List(Entry(Who(driver),What(Started),↵
Where(MessageMetadataDriver$,driver),Wed Apr 30 15:57:41 MDT↵
 2014,Why(Running processors)), Entry(Who(user50),↵
What(Processed: 4),Where(Processor,processor1),Wed Apr 30↵
 15:57:41 MDT 2014,Why(Because: 0)))))
processor3 received: SomeMessage(Data...,↵
Metadata(List(Entry(Who(driver),What(Started),↵
Where(MessageMetadataDriver$,driver),Wed Apr 30 15:57:41 MDT↵
 2014,Why(Running processors)), Entry(Who(user50),↵
What(Processed: 4),Where(Processor,processor1),↵
Wed Apr 30 15:57:41 MDT 2014,Why(Because: 0)),↵
 Entry(Who(user80),What(Processed: 4),Where(Processor,↵
processor2),Wed Apr 30 15:57:41 MDT 2014,Why(Because: 1)))))
processor3 complete: SomeMessage(Data...,↵
Metadata(List(Entry(Who(driver),What(Started),↵
Where(MessageMetadataDriver$,driver),Wed Apr 30 15:57:41↵
 MDT 2014,Why(Running processors)), Entry(Who(user50),↵
What(Processed: 4),Where(Processor,processor1),Wed Apr ↵
30 15:57:41 MDT 2014,Why(Because: 0)), Entry(Who(user80),↵
What(Processed: 4),Where(Processor,processor2),Wed Apr 30↵
 15:57:41 MDT 2014,Why(Because: 1)), Entry(Who(user71),↵
What(Processed: 2),Where(Processor,processor3),Wed Apr↵
 30 15:57:41 MDT 2014,Why(Because: 3)))))
```

As shown in the output, a new `Entry` is included in each successive message through every step of the processing.

While not discussed in detail here, Message Metadata can be used to achieve *causal consistency* [AMC-Causal Consistency] among *Messages (130)* that must be replicated across a network with full ordering preserved [Bolt-on Causal Consistency].

Message Journal/Store

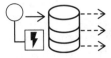

Use a Message Journal as a means to support *Guaranteed Delivery (175)* and *Durable Subscribers (379)*. A *Message (130)* that is written to a journal may represent the state transition of some actor at a certain point in its life cycle and can also be used to subsequently deliver to a receiving actor.

You can use a Message Store as a permanent location to keep *Messages (130)* that have already been delivered. The emphasis on a Message Store is that it can more readily be used for later analysis of previously sent and delivered *Messages (130)*. Although you could design a strong schema for the Message Store that would make it easy to query, many times it works out best to use a weak schema and deal with *Messages (130)* only in their original form. You can reconstitute the stored *Messages (130)* from the store and stream over them as you examine them by their object properties. If you do desire to use a strong(er) schema, this could be accomplished using a relational database or one that supports querying JavaScript Object Notation (JSON) or Extensible Markup Language (XML). For example, PostgreSQL supports saving JSON and querying on JSON attributes.

Actually the Message Journal and the Message Store may be implemented by the same mechanism. The Akka Persistence can purge each *Message (130)* from the Message Journal after it has been delivered. However, if you will potentially use the *Messages (130)* again in the future, you can keep them in the Message Journal, which will then also be considered a Message Store. Otherwise, you could also use an Akka Persistence View to create a separate Message Store, as depicted in Figure 10.1.

In this case, the original `Sender` sends a *Command Message (202)* to a `Processor`. Once the `Processor` completes, it produces an *Event Message (207)*. That event is appended to the journal before it is delivered to the `View`. Once the `View` receives the *Event Message (207)*, it may append it to a separate *Message Store (402)*. Although this may seem like an inappropriate use of a Akka Persistence View, this is not actually so. A View doesn't always have to be used to produce a Command and Query Responsibility Segregation (CQRS) type of user interface view or some kind of report. You could also accomplish something similar to this using a *Wire Tap (397)*.

In general, you can think of a Message Journal and Message Store as having the logical format found in Figure 10.2.

Figure 10.1 An *Event Message (207)* starts out being written to a Message Journal but is later also written to a Message Store.

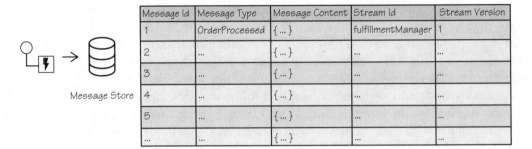

Message Id	Message Type	Message Content	Stream Id	Stream Version
1	OrderProcessed	{ ... }	fulfillmentManager	1
2	...	{ ... }	...	...
3	...	{ ... }	...	...
4	...	{ ... }	...	...
5	...	{ ... }	...	...
...	...	{ ... }	...	...

Message Store

Figure 10.2 The optional and required columns/segments of a Message Journal

Since Akka Persistence leaves the actual journal/store schema to its implementers, it could well be that a given store produces this example schema. Here are the descriptions of the value "columns" or "segments":

- *Message Id*: Each Message may have a unique identity, which is generated sequentially. This allows for each persisted *Message (130)* to be uniquely identified and uniquely ordered within a single journal/store. However, it also represents a potential bottleneck since the allocation of each ascending Message Id is not a scalable operation. Thus, this is an optional "column" or "segment" that may very likely not be implemented in any given Message Journal.

- *Message Type*: The store must maintain the type of the message in order to reconstitute it from its serialized form.

- *Message Content*: This is the serialized form of the actual message, which could be some binary format, or text such as JSON or XML.

- *Stream Id*: This is the unique identity of the actor (for example, `Processor` with its `processorId`) that was the receiver of this persisted *Message (130)*. In other words, each actor has its own message stream, and this is the primary identity of that actor.

- *Stream Version*: This is the index—starting from 1 and incrementing by 1 for each message—that describes the order in which the message was received by the actor. The combination of Stream Id:Stream Version describes the order of a given message. Stream Id:1 – Stream Id:N describes the entire message stream of the actor.

If a given actor (for example, `fulfillmentManager`) has received 100 messages, its *message stream* is comprised of `StreamId:1` through `Stream-Id:100` and is sorted in ascending order according to Stream Version. Thus, if a `PersistentActor` named `fulfillmentManager` needs to reconstitute its state from stored messages, it does so by recovering from messages `StreamId:1` through `StreamId:100`, in that order.

The default Akka Persistence journal, which uses Level DB, does not actually use the previous schema. It's schema is more like that in Figure 10.3.

This has the advantage that appending to the journal/store is extremely fast. Each `PersistentActor` maintains its own Stream Version—called a `sequenceNr`—and increments it as each *Event Message (207)* is persisted. And since there is no separate sequential Message Id, there is no bottleneck when inserting.

The disadvantage here is that each persisted *Message (130)* is not uniquely identified nor uniquely ordered within a single journal/store. This means that replaying all *Messages (130)* in the journal/store from the beginning to the end is not as straightforward as reading from Message Id 1 to Message Id N. Even so, a technique called *causal consistency* [AMC-Causal Consistency] can be used to achieve the same.

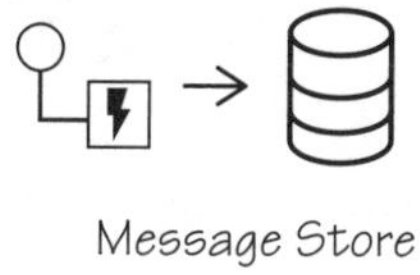

Stream Id	Stream Version	Message Type	Message Content
fulfillmentManager	1	OrderProcessed	{ ... }
fulfillmentManager	2	OrderProcessed	{ ... }
...	N	...	{ ... }
...	N	...	{ ... }
...	N	...	{ ... }
...	N	...	{ ... }

Message Store

Figure 10.3 The logical schema used by the default Akka Persistence journal implemented to use LevelDB

Smart Proxy

Use a Smart Proxy when you need to design a *Wire Tap (397)* that knows how to handle a full *Request-Reply (209)* using the *Return Address (211)* of the original sender. In some cases, a *Wire Tap (397)* need only analyze something about the incoming request *Message (130)*, and then it can simply send the request to the intended destination actor. Yet, in other situations the *Wire Tap (397)* may need to take responsibility for receiving the reply *Message (130)* as well, analyze it, and then send the reply to the original sender.

Figure 10.4 shows an example of such a Smart Proxy, with the overall process captured in the diagram.

I start off by showing you the `ServiceProvider` actor that will eventually receive all incoming requests.

```
class ServiceProvider extends Actor {
  def receive = {
    case one: ServiceRequestOne =>
      sender ! ServiceReplyOne(one.requestId)
    case two: ServiceRequestTwo =>
      sender ! ServiceReplyTwo(two.requestId)
    case three: ServiceRequestThree =>
      sender ! ServiceReplyThree(three.requestId)
  }
}
```

This `ServiceProvider` doesn't do much, but you can imagine there being a healthy amount of work to be done for any number of incoming requests to be fulfilled. The point is, however, that when the `ServiceProvider` receives

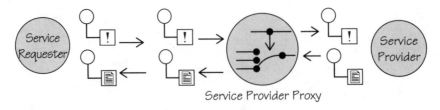

Figure 10.4 The process common to Smart Proxy

a request, it must send a reply *Message (130)* to the requester. When a reply *Message (130)* is created, it must be given the `requestId` of the incoming request, which provides the means for the proxy to correlate outgoing messages with the original request sender.

Here are the request messages and reply messages that the service must support, which use Scala traits and its *Uniform Access Principle*[2] [Meyer-OOSC] to provide common `ServiceRequest` and `ServiceResponse` types across concrete messages.

```scala
trait ServiceRequest {
  def requestId: String
}

case class ServiceRequestOne(requestId: String) extends ServiceRequest
case class ServiceRequestTwo(requestId: String) extends ServiceRequest
case class ServiceRequestThree(requestId: String) extends↵
 ServiceRequest

trait ServiceReply {
  def replyId: String
}

case class ServiceReplyOne(replyId: String) extends ServiceReply
case class ServiceReplyTwo(replyId: String) extends ServiceReply
case class ServiceReplyThree(replyId: String) extends ServiceReply
```

A requester may make requests by sending one of three messages: `Service-RequestOne`, `ServiceRequestTwo`, and `ServiceRequestThree`. When the `ServiceProvider` replies, it must do so by sending one of the three corresponding messages: `ServiceReplyOne`, `ServiceReplyTwo`, and `Service-ReplyThree`. The common theme among the messages is that they must all carry a `requestId` or `replyId`, and, as you will see, this is key to properly implementing a Smart Proxy.

Next let's look at the actor that requests services from the `ServiceProvider`, the `ServiceRequester`:

```scala
case class RequestService(service: ServiceRequest)

class ServiceRequester(serviceProvider: ActorRef) extends Actor {
```

---

2. "All services offered by a module should be available through a uniform notation, which does not betray whether they are implemented through storage or through computation." In this example, you can't distinguish whether `requestId` and `replyId` are attributes or functions or where they are declared and defined.

```
  def receive = {
    case request: RequestService =>
      println(s"ServiceRequester: ${self.path.name}: $request")
      serviceProvider ! request.service
      SmartProxyDriver.completedStep
    case reply: Any =>
      println(s"ServiceRequester: ${self.path.name}: $reply")
      SmartProxyDriver.completedStep
  }
}
```

The `ServiceRequester` will receive `RequestService` messages indicating that it should request a service of the `ServiceProvider`. In this example, the `RequestService` message contains the concrete `ServiceRequest` message that should be requested and that will be sent to the `ServiceProvider`.

The missing actor in the middle is the Smart Proxy implementation, which in this example is the `ServiceProviderProxy`:

```
class ServiceProviderProxy(serviceProvider: ActorRef) extends Actor {
  val requesters = scala.collection.mutable.Map[String, ActorRef]()

  def receive = {
    case request: ServiceRequest =>
      requesters(request.requestId) = sender
      serviceProvider ! request
      analyzeRequest(request)
    case reply: ServiceReply =>
      val sender = requesters.remove(reply.replyId)
      if (sender.isDefined) {
       analyzeReply(reply)
        sender.get ! reply
      }
  }

  def analyzeReply(reply: ServiceReply) = {
    println(s"Reply analyzed: $reply")
  }

  def analyzeRequest(request: ServiceRequest) = {
    println(s"Request analyzed: $request")
  }
}
```

One job of the `ServiceProviderProxy` is to take all incoming `ServiceRequest` messages, analyze them, and then send them on to the `ServiceProvider`. Its other job is to take all incoming `ServiceReply` messages, analyze them, and then send them on to the original requester, the

ServiceRequester. To close the loop, the Smart Proxy must establish a *Correlation Identifier (215)* and associate it with the `ActorRef` of the original `ServiceRequester` sender. The identifier that is used for this is already attached to the incoming `ServiceRequest` message. In this case, you can rely on this identifier to be unique because that simple application driver arranges for that to be so. In your applications you may need to design the Smart Proxy implementation to generate a unique *Correlation Identifier (215)*. This can be accomplished using `java.util.UUID`.

```
val requestId = UUID.randomUUID.toString
val request = ServiceRequestOne(requestId)
```

The obvious problem with this is that the Smart Proxy will have to know how to individually re-create every incoming request by adding in a *Correlation Identifier (215)*, or it will need to put all concrete `ServiceRequest` messages in an *Envelope Wrapper (314)*.

```
class ServiceProviderProxy(serviceProvider: ActorRef) extends Actor {
  val requesters = scala.collection.mutable.Map[String, ActorRef]()

  def receive = {
    case request: ServiceRequest =>
      requesters(request.requesterIdentity) = sender
      val requestId = UUID.randomUUID.toString
      val envelope = ServiceRequestEnvelope(requestId, request)
      serviceProvider ! envelope
      analyzeRequest(request)
    ...
  }
}
```

Doing so, however, means extra work in the `ServiceProvider` to unwrap the service message. Perhaps the worst of all is that it requires the `ServiceProvider` to acknowledge the existence of the Smart Proxy and that there is a *Wire Tap (397)*. It would be best if any service requester could be trusted to supply a unique identity that can be reused as a *Correlation Identifier (215)*. If for some reason this cannot be done, you will have to take the rougher road.

Now take a look at the `SmartProxyDriver`:

```
object SmartProxyDriver extends CompletableApp(6) {
  val serviceProvider = system.actorOf(
```

```
        Props[ServiceProvider],
        "serviceProvider")

   val proxy = system.actorOf(
        Props(classOf[ServiceProviderProxy],serviceProvider),
        "proxy")

   val requester1 = system.actorOf(
        Props(classOf[ServiceRequester],proxy),
        "requester1")

   val requester2 = system.actorOf(
        Props(classOf[ServiceRequester],proxy),
        "requester2")

   val requester3 = system.actorOf(
        Props(classOf[ServiceRequester],proxy),
        "requester3")

   requester1 ! RequestService(ServiceRequestOne("1"))
   requester2 ! RequestService(ServiceRequestTwo("2"))
   requester3 ! RequestService(ServiceRequestThree("3"))

   awaitCompletion
}
```

The driver first creates the ultimate `ServiceProvider`, followed by the `ServiceProviderProxy`. The proxy actor is given a reference to the ultimate `ServiceProvider`. Then three instances of the `ServiceRequester` are created, each being given a reference to the `ServiceProviderProxy`. Finally, each of the requester actors is told to request a specific server. Here is the output of the process:

```
ServiceRequester: requester1:↵
 RequestService(ServiceRequestOne(1))
ServiceRequester: requester2:↵
 RequestService(ServiceRequestTwo(2))
ServiceRequester: requester3:↵
 RequestService(ServiceRequestThree(3))
Request analyzed: ServiceRequestOne(1)
Request analyzed: ServiceRequestTwo(2)
Request analyzed: ServiceRequestThree(3)
Reply analyzed: ServiceReplyOne(1)
ServiceRequester: requester1: ServiceReplyOne(1)
Reply analyzed: ServiceReplyTwo(2)
ServiceRequester: requester2: ServiceReplyTwo(2)
Reply analyzed: ServiceReplyThree(3)
ServiceRequester: requester3: ServiceReplyThree(3)
```

A Smart Proxy as a *Wire Tap (397)* like this one could be used to perform some special analysis—perhaps something very application specific—on messages that the Akka *Control Bus (394)* doesn't provide.

Test Message

Send a Test Message to an actor when you need to determine whether *Messages (130)* are being received properly. Proper receipt of a message is not only a matter that it arrives but also that all the data it should carry arrives as expected.

Since by default Akka provides an `UnboundedMailbox` for each actor, it is possible for a JVM to run out of memory when many actors are receiving many messages. With other mailbox implementations, such as `Bounded-Mailbox`, it is possible for some messages to be dropped when the mailbox is full. When sending messages to a remote actor, it's possible for the network transport to break or become unreliable, which could cause messages to be completely lost or arrive with garbled data. Thus, there are various reasons why you could benefit by setting up a means to send Test Messages to various actors in your systems.You can create Test Messages in two basic ways. You can create a *Message (130)* that has the appearance of an actual, valid *Message (130)*, but that contains only test data. This *Message (130)* would need to have a *Format Indicator (222)* of sorts to identify the payload as being for test purposes only. In other words, you don't want to process a Test Message as if it were a real, production *Message (130)*. This approach can be somewhat troublesome because you need the ability to create correctly formatted messages, which means producing realistic test data. Sometimes it's just plain difficult to come up with test data or to come up with enough unique test data that the system can function in a normal fashion. Perhaps the easiest way to do this is to replicate production messages into a Test Message that has a *Format Indicator (222)* that marks it as test. Once you determine how to appropriately implement this approach, then there is the need to properly place branching logic in your receiving actor so that test data isn't processed as production and production data is not lost in test code. Don't take this step for granted.

```
trait Testable {
  def isTest(): Boolean
}

case class ProcessOrder(..., forTest: Boolean) extends Testable {
  def this(...) = { this(..., false) } // default construction
  override def isTest(): Boolean = { forTest }
  ...
}

class OrderProcessor extends Actor {
  case processOrder: ProcessOrder if (processOrder.isTest) =>
    // test this message here
  case processOrder: ProcessOrder =>
    // production processing here
  ...
}
```

A second way to create a Test Message is to design an independent *Message (130)* that can carry test data or even a copy of an actual production *Message (130)*. This can work out well because it allows you to deal with Test Messages using completely different case matching.

```
case class TestMessage(actualMessage: Any)

class OrderProcessor extends Actor {
  case processOrder: ProcessOrder =>
    // production processing here
  case testMessage: TestMessage =>
    // test this message here
  ...
}
```

This is probably the safest way to support Test Messages because the following potential problems are eliminated:

- You mark a production message, such as `ProcessOrder`, as testable.

- You mark a test message, such as `ProcessOrder`, as not testable.

- Your actor case matching does not branch properly.

- Your message format changes, and the receiving actor mistakenly processes the newer message as if an older message.

Enterprise Integration Patterns [EIP] specifies a number of components that can be used to help implement full support for Test Message. Here's a list:

- *Test Data Generator*: This actor would create Test Messages in one of the previous two ways. This may imply some sort of user interface that allows you to generate specific kinds of Test Messages based on the kinds of *Messages (130)* the actor supports.

- *Test Message Injector*: This actually performs the sending operation to the target actors. This may imply some sort of user interface that allows you to look up actors dynamically by actor system and then choose from among its supported *Message (130)* types the ones to be sent. Such a user interface could also allow you to select the total number of such messages to send, the frequency of sends, and so on.

- *Test Message Separator (or Test Output Processor)*: If you are performing some form of analytical functions on the Test Messages that are processed by target actors, those actors should send output to this component. Itself an actor, this "separator" is responsible for taking test output and using it in whatever way is appropriate for your system. This component is named "separator" because in an environment such as *Enterprise Integration Patterns* [EIP] discusses, it would function as a *Content-Based Router (228)*, sending production output on one *Message Channel (128)* and test output on another. However, since in the case of using the Actor model the *Message Channel (128)* is the actor's mailbox, any production output would naturally be sent to a production actor, and the test output would be sent to this "separator" actor. In this case, consider naming this component Test Output Processor.

- *Test Data Verifier*: This is one of the analytical functions performed as a result of sending output through the Test Output Processor as the verification of test data. The verification may be both for the incoming Test Messages and for outgoing result *Messages (130)*. The Test Output Processor may act as the supervisor of several analytical steps, passing *Messages (130)* requiring the verification step to the Test Data Verifier.

See *Enterprise Integration Patterns* [EIP] for more details on how to leverage these components, but be prepared to mentally map these to actor-based implementations.

Channel Purger

Use a Channel Purger when your actors support *Guaranteed Delivery (175)* but you must delete some set of *Messages (130)* from the *Message Store (402)* before testing or continuing with production. It may also be necessary to purge the mailbox of certain actors even when they don't use *Guaranteed Delivery (175)*, but the *Messages (130)* in the live system may for some reason need to be scrapped rather than processed.

Actor systems that don't use *Guaranteed Delivery (175)* automatically purge the mailboxes when test runners terminate because actors stop and all mailbox memory is freed upon termination. However, both *Guaranteed Delivery (175)* systems and actors that support only at-most-once message delivery via basic mailboxes may need to support purging.

If *Guaranteed Delivery (175)* and a *Message Store (402)* are in use, it can be relatively easy to create an actor or other component that implements the *Channel Purger (414)* pattern. The purger would go directly to the *Message Store (402)* and delete some or all *Messages (130)*. The purger can be designed to filter *Messages (130)* to be deleted by the identity of the sending actor, the intended receiver actor, or both.

On the other hand, if you intend to support only a normal at-most-once delivery mailbox, it may actually be a bit more challenging to purge any given actor's mailbox. This is because the default `UnboundedMailbox` automatically assigned to actors is a first-in, first-out (FIFO) queue, and the actor's receive block is subject to receiving just one message at a time in the order it was received. Thus, if you attempt to send such an actor a message that indicates its mailbox should be cleared, the actor won't receive that message until all other messages have been received. That being the case, perhaps the easiest way to purge an actor's mailbox is to stop the actor and then restart it.

```
system.stop(actorRef)

// or...

context.stop(childRef)
```

Stopping an actor causes it to complete the processing of its current message; then all messages left in the mailbox will be purged, and the actor will be stopped. Note that the use of the `PoisonPill` message will not cause near-immediate termination of the actor as does `stop()`. Instead, the `PoisonPill` message will enter the actor's mailbox in normal order—FIFO by default—and be processed in that order. Thus, under FIFO mailbox conditions, all messages prior to the `PoisonPill` will be processed. The `Kill` message is processed in the same order as `PoisonPill`, but when `Kill` is received, it causes the `ActorKilledException` to be thrown. When the killed actor's supervisor receives the exception, it can make the determination to restart it. Still, the point here is that to truly purge an actor's mailbox immediately using out-of-the-box features, you stop it with `stop()`.

As an alternative to stopping an actor and then restarting it, you could use a priority queue mailbox (for example, `PriorityBlockingQueue`), allowing you to send a high-priority "purge" message to the actor. When the actor receives this "purge" message, it can *become* a purging, blackhole actor and throw away all messages.

```
class OrderProcessor extends Actor {
  ...
  def normal: Receive = {
    case processOrder: ProcessOrder =>
      ...
    case purge: PurgeNow =>
      context.become(purger)
  }

  def purger: Receive = {
    case noPurge: StopPurge =>
      context.become(normal)
    case ignore: Any =>
  }

  def receive = normal
}
```

Of course, you would have to send this actor a low-priority message that tells it to stop purging so it can once again safely consume messages. Otherwise, the `OrderProcessor` would never *become* a `normal` processor again.

Summary

In this chapter, you toured various tools that can be used in the development, test, and production environments of actor systems. Most prominent among these tools are *Message Metadata (398)* and *Message Journal (402)*, which you will likely tend to use in most actor-based applications. Still, you will occasionally find that *Detour (395)*, *Wire Tap (397)*, *Smart Proxy (406)*, *Test Message (411)*, and *Channel Purger (414)* are good tools to include on your workbench.

Appendix A

Dotsero: An Akka-like Toolkit for .NET

This appendix introduces you to Dotsero [Dotsero Toolkit], a simple yet powerful toolkit for developing with the Actor model on the .NET platform. It also introduces you to the basics of actors using the C# programming language. This should be a welcome sight to those less accustomed to the Java or Scala programming language. By examining the basic actor messaging style using *Request-Reply (209)*, you will remove from your mind any lingering mystery about actors.

Dotsero Actor System

Dotsero supports most of the basic features of the Akka toolkit and at least those that are expected for similar use. Figure A.1 illustrates the big items available with Dotsero.

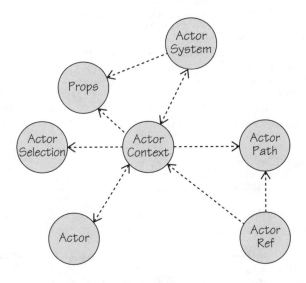

Figure A.1 The basic elements of an actor system that are supported by Dotsero

As shown in Figure A.1, Dotsero supports all the primary concepts of Akka including an `ActorSystem`, `Props`, `Actor`, `ActorRef`, `ActorContext`, `ActorSelection`, and `ActorPath`. This implies support for a significant set of features through the methods available on each object. Since these are all used in the same way as Akka for Scala, I won't spend a lot of time explaining them here. Yet, to confirm that they are used in the same way, I do provide some simple code snippets.

This test block shows how you create and shut down an `ActorSystem`:

```
ActorSystem system =
    ActorSystem.Create("ActorSystemTests");
Assert.AreEqual("ActorSystemTests", system.Name);
system.Shutdown();
```

In this test, you also assert that the name of the `ActorSystem` is the one it was created with. You can even ask the `ActorSystem` for its uptime, or the amount of time it has been running.

```
Assert.IsTrue(system.UpTime.Ticks > 100);
```

The `ActorSystem` has two primary paths from the root: the user guardian and the system guardian (`sys`).

```
Assert.AreEqual("/user", system.Context.Path.Value);
Assert.IsFalse(system.Context.Path.IsRoot());
Assert.AreEqual("/sys", system.SystemContext.Path.Value);
Assert.IsFalse(system.Context.Path.IsRoot());
Assert.AreEqual(ActorPath.RootName,
                system.Context.Parent.Path.Value);
Assert.IsTrue(system.Context.Parent.Path.IsRoot());
```

The `ActorSystem` also comes with a `DeadLetters` pseudo-actor, which supports the *Dead Letter Channel (172)* pattern.

```
Assert.AreEqual("deadLetters",
                system.DeadLetters.Path.Name);
```

If you try to send a message to a nonexistent actor, it actually goes to `DeadLetters`.

```
ActorSelection selection =
    system.ActorSelection("/user/NonExistingActor42");
selection.Tell("TESTING DEAD LETTERS");
```

The previous code shows that `ActorSelection` is also supported, which will find an actor under the user guardian. You can also use `ActorSelection` from an `ActorContext` (from inside an actor), which will find an actor under a given hierarchical context if it exists. This test sends messages to a hierarchy of actors from the user guardian, downward:

```
system.ActorSelection("/user/sel1").Tell("TEST");
system.ActorSelection("/user/sel1/sel2").Tell("TEST");
system.ActorSelection("/user/sel1/sel2/sel3").Tell("TEST");
```

The first message is sent to `sel1`, which is just under the user guardian. The second message is sent to `sel2`, which is a child of `sel1`. The third message is sent to `sel3`, which is a child of `sel2`.

As indicated in Figure A.2, Dotsero also supports actor supervision, allowing a parent actor to watch after the life cycle of its children.

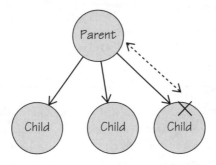

Figure A.2 Dotsero support supervision of child hierarchies

If a parent actor wants to detect when one of its child actors crashes via an exception, it must register a supervision strategy.

```
public class EscalateSupervisorStrategy : SupervisorStrategy
{
    public EscalateSupervisorStrategy()
        : base(SupervisorStrategy.StrategyType.OneForOne)
    {
    }

    public override Directive Decide(Exception e)
    {
        return SupervisorStrategy.Directive.Escalate;
```

```
        }
    }

public class Level1 : Actor
{
    ...
}

public class Level2 : Actor
{
    public Level2()
    {
        SupervisorStrategy =
            new EscalateSupervisorStrategy();
    }
    ...
}

public class Level3 : Actor
{
    ...
    public void OnReceive(string message)
    {
        throw new InvalidOperationException(
                "TEST ESCALATE");
    }
}
```

In this example, there are three levels of actors. There is a `Level1` grandparent, a `Level2` child, and a `Level3` grandchild. In this particular example, a special supervision strategy is registered at the `Level2` actor and instructs that when a child actor—the `Level3`—crashes, it should escalate to the parent of `Level2`, which is `Level1`. So, the grandchild, `Level3`, throws the `InvalidOperationException`, which is initially handled by its parent, `Level2`. Yet, the `Level2` decider says to escalate up to the parent of `Level2`, which is `Level1`. At the point where `Level1` gains control of the supervision, it uses the default strategy (no other strategy is set by its constructor), which is to stop and restart the `Level2` child, which in turn will cause a restart of `Level3`.

Actors Using C# and .NET

Now with a background in using the basic Dotsero system support, let's look at how actors work. This example uses a `Manager` actor and a `Worker` actor, where the two actors perform some basic *Request-Reply (209)* interaction. First let's look at the `Manager` actor.

```
public class Manager : Actor
{
    private EventWaitHandle helloBackEvent;
    private ActorRef worker;

    public Manager(
        ActorRef worker,
        EventWaitHandle helloBackEvent)
    : base()
    {
        this.worker = worker;
        this.helloBackEvent = helloBackEvent;
    }

    public void OnReceive(string message)
    {
        switch (message)
        {
            case "start":
                worker.Tell("hello", Self);
                break;

            case "hello, back":
                helloBackEvent.Set();
                break;

            default:
                Assert.Fail("Invalid message type.");
                break;
        }
    }
}
```

The Manager extends the Actor base class, so you can assume that there is a basic protocol that actors must implement. You will soon examine some of the details of the Actor base type, but for now you can just focus on the things that a Manager does.

This Manager is created with a few parameters. The first parameter is a reference to another actor, actually the worker, that it will collaborate with. Interestingly, the Manager doesn't need to know the concrete type of the worker actor. It just needs to know that it has an ActorRef to which it can send messages about the work that it needs to have done. It is the direct client or parent of the Manager that is responsible for endowing the Manager with an ActorRef to the actor that can do the work. The second parameter is a EventWaitHandle, which is a nonactor, yet reactive means to communicate to the outside that the Manager has completed its job. The Manager holds a reference to the `ActorRef` in its `worker` instance, and the `EventWait-Handle` parameter is held in `helloBackEvent`.

Now that a `Manager` exists and is initialized, it can't do anything at all until it is told to do something. Sure, that's like a normal object. However, unlike an object, you can't actually invoke some behavioral method on the `Manager`. Instead, you tell the `Manager` actor to do something by sending it a message.

```
Manager manager = new Manager(worker, doneEvent);

manager.Tell("start");
```

The `Tell()` isn't just some gimmick that makes doing things cooler because of the decoupled approach. It is the messaging mechanism behind `Tell()` that makes the `Manager` reactive and work in an environment that is more scalable and easier to reason about when designing for concurrency. In fact, if it weren't for those benefits, many C# and Java programmers would likely conclude that it makes programming far less convenient than just invoking behavioral methods directly on an object. So, you can tell the `Manager` to `"start"`. Look back to the `Manager` implementation for the method `OnReceive()`. It gives the actor a way to handle the messages that are sent to it. The messages you send to actors need not be of type `string` only. You can send messages of `int` or `double` type, and so on, or any type of `object` for that matter. All you need to do is create an overloaded `OnReceive()` method for each message type. Whatever type you send as a message, it should be immutable. That helps you uphold the *share nothing* characteristic of the Actor model.

When the `OnReceive()` method of the `Manager` is invoked with the `"start"` message, the `Manager` reacts by telling its `worker` `"hello"`. Along with the `"hello"` message, the `Manager` also tells the `worker` that it is the sender by passing its `Self` reference. Curious, but you'll see in a moment why that's important.

```
...
public void OnReceive(string message)
{
   switch (message)
   {
      case "start":
         worker.Tell("hello", Self);
         break;
      ...
   }
}
```

In fact, now is about as good a time as any to show the `Worker` actor implementation:

```csharp
public class Worker : Actor
{
    public Worker()
    {
    }

    public void OnReceive(string message)
    {
        Assert.AreEqual("hello", message);

        if (this.CanReply)
        {
            Sender.Tell("hello, back", Self);
        }
        else
        {
            Assert.Fail("Worker: no reply-to available...");
        }
    }
}
```

All that the `Worker` does when it receives the `"hello"` message is tell the `Sender` actor `"hello, back"`. That's why the `Self` parameter accompanies the message object when invoking `Tell()`. It allows the receiver actor to reply to the actor that sent the request. The `Self` parameter—the `ActorRef` instance of the sender—is available as the `Sender` property in the receiving actor's `OnReceive()`.

This looks like a game of ping-pong. A lot of actor-based programming, but not all of it, is just like that. So, you'll find this basic *Request-Reply (209)* code in a lot of use cases.

Also, it's not that you'd normally implement an `Actor` with only a default constructor (zero parameters). Unless you pass parameters in the actor creation `Props`, however, there's no reason for the actor's constructor to accept parameters. You can compare the `Worker` constructor to the `Manager` constructor, which does accept parameters.

Looking back at the `Manager` now, when it receives the `"hello, back"` message, it completes by firing the `helloBackEvent`. This leads to where you can consider the test case.

```csharp
namespace DotseroTest
{
```

```csharp
using Dotsero.Actor;
using Microsoft.VisualStudio.TestTools.UnitTesting;
using System.Threading;

[TestClass]
public class ActorManagerWorkerTests
{
    [TestMethod]
    public void ManagerUsesWorker()
    {
        ActorSystem system =
            ActorSystem.Create("ActorSystemTests");

        ActorRef worker =
            system.ActorOf(
                typeof(Worker),
                Props.None,
                "worker");

        AutoResetEvent helloBackEvent =
            new AutoResetEvent(false);

        AutoResetEvent specificEvent =
            new AutoResetEvent(false);

        ActorRef manager =
            system.ActorOf(
                typeof(Manager),
                Props.With(worker, helloBackEvent),
                "manager");

        manager.Tell("start");

        var helloBackDone =
            helloBackEvent.WaitOne(1000, false);

        system.Stop(worker);

        system.Stop(manager);

        system.Shutdown();

        Assert.IsTrue(helloBackDone);
    }
}
```

Since class `ActorManagerWorkerTests` is not an `Actor`, the test method `ManagerUsesWorker()` can't tell the `Manager` actor that `ActorManager-WorkerTests` is the message sender. In other words, the overloaded `Tell()` takes the `"start"` message only because the test can't pass a reference to the sending `ActorRef` as the second parameter. That's fine for the test and the reason why you create and use the `helloBackDone` as a means to assert that the *Request-Reply (209)* messaging worked. If the `Manager` doesn't receive a `"hello, back"` message, the `helloBackDone.Set()` won't fire, and the test method's assertion will fail.

Dotsero Implementation

Under the hood the Dotsero implementation uses the open source Retlang library [Retlang]. This is Mark Rettig's implementation of some lower-level abstractions that allows programmers to do things with C# on .NET that one might do using Erlang. The Retlang project claims to implement the Actor model, but in actuality it is much more a low-level thread-based messaging application programming interface (API). So, it's not really that much like Erlang, and that's why I put a simple actor abstraction around it, because using Retlang alone is far from simple (well, at least it's not simple in comparison to using a real the Actor model toolkit like Dotsero).

> **More on Retlang, Compared with Akka**
>
> One caveat that Mark Rettig provides regarding the Retlang implementation is that it is nowhere as scalable as Erlang's actor systems, or Akka's for that matter. Rettig suggests that creating thousands of channel-fiber pairs that would be needed to support thousands of actors, will "hurt performance" [Retlang-CTX]. Of course, his statement is made in comparison to direct object method invocations, which are always fastest, even if a message uses minimal indirection. Yet, I've already discussed the vast number of advantages to actor system designs when it comes to overall application performance. Performance because of concurrency with parallelism is far different from the performance of direct object method invocations, not to mention the additional scalability and other positive consequences that accompany actor-based applications.
>
> Anyway, you can achieve some degree of multithreaded performance and scale improvements if you decide to limit your system to a few hundred or a thousand actors. Perhaps the hybrid Object model with the Actor model blend could prove to be a secret weapon, using the Actor model only to more comfortably deal with the absolutely critical hotspots of your application.
>
> However, you may find that using many more Retlang-based actors could prove to have a much more favorable outcome, such as is commonly experienced with the Actor model. It ultimately depends on Retlang's design.
>
> Akka, on the other hand, is designed to scale to several million actors in a single Java virtual machine (JVM). Even with millions of actors, you can confidently assert that the application will not experience associated performance degradation. There's no guesswork required.

Dotsero internally creates an `IChannel` and an `IFiber`, where the `IChannel` instance is created from the default `Channel` class and the `IFiber` instance is created as a `PoolFiber`. To avoid going deep into the Retlang implementation, for now just understand that the `IChannel` is the way that messages are sent, and the `IFiber` is how the messages are delivered. The important detail to understand about `BaseActor` is that the `IFiber` is thread-pool based. When a message is sent through the `IChannel`, the `IFiber` implementation will deliver the message to an actor by using a thread from a .NET system `IThreadPool` when a thread is available.

Internally when an `ActorRef` receives a `Tell()` invocation, it enqueues at `Delivery` instance.

```
public class ActorRef
{
    ...
    public void Tell(object message, ActorRef sender)
    {
        if (!Context.Terminated)
        {
            Context.Enqueue(new Delivery(message, sender));
        }
        else
        {
            Context
                .System
                .DeadLetters.Tell(message, sender);
        }
    }
}
```

Thus, each `Actor` extender, such as `Manager` and `Worker`, are capable of receiving messages of any type. All you have to do is create a different `OnReceive()` method for each message type that your actor supports. Here I've added a new `OnReceive()` for Manager to receive messages of type `SpecificMessage`:

```
public class Manager : Actor
{
    ...
    public void OnReceive(SpecificMessage specificMessage)
    {
        ...
    }
}
```

```
public sealed class SpecificMessage
{
    public static SpecificMessage Create(string message)
    {
        return new SpecificMessage(message);
    }

    public SpecificMessage(string payload)
    {
        this.Payload = payload;
    }

    public string Payload { get; private set; }

    public override string ToString()
    {
        return "SpecificMessage: " + Payload;
    }
}
```

This enables `Manager` to receive messages of type `SpecificMessage`. Note that the `SpecificMessage` is declared as a sealed class to ensure its immutability. This is also ensured by the fact that its `Payload` property has a public getter but only a private setter.

Of course, no `Actor` will receive messages until a client, such as another actor, tells your `Actor` something using one of the two overloaded `Tell()` methods. If the sender is itself an `Actor`, it should use the two-parameter `Tell()` and pass its `Self` value as a parameter. Other non-`Actor` senders can use the single-parameter `Tell()`.

Summary

Ideally you C# developers now feel a bit more welcomed to the Actor model. I don't provide extensive examples using C# in this book, but you can certainly see the possibilities of using the Actor model on the .NET platform. The Dotsero Github project [Dotsero Toolkit] contains a number of tests that show you how to use the various facilities provided by the toolkit. You can use Dotsero to try the book's samples in your familiar C# language.

Bibliography

[2,400-Node Cluster] http://typesafe.com/blog
/running-a-2400-akka-nodes-cluster-on-google-compute-engine

[ACM-Amazon] http://queue.acm.org/detail.cfm?id=1142065

[Actor Model] http://en.wikipedia.org/wiki/Actor_model

[Actor-Endowment] http://en.wikipedia.org/wiki/Object-capability_model

[Actors-Controversy] http://en.wikipedia.org/wiki
/Actor_model#Unbounded_nondeterminism_controversy

[Actors-Nondeterministic] http://pchiusano.blogspot.com/2013/09
/actors-are-overly-nondeterminstic.html

[Agha, Gul] Agha, Gul. *Actors: A Model of Concurrent Computation in
Distributed Systems.* Cambridge, MA: MIT Press, 1986.

[Akka-Google] http://typesafe.com/blog
/running-a-2400-akka-nodes-cluster-on-google-compute-engine

[Akka-Message-Guarantees] http://doc.akka.io/docs/akka/snapshot/general
/message-delivery-guarantees.html

[Ambysoft] www.ambysoft.com/surveys/success2013.html

[AMC-Causal Consistency] http://queue.acm.org/detail.cfm?id=2610533

[Amdahl's law] http://en.wikipedia.org/wiki/Amdahl's_law

[Atomic-Scala] Eckel, Bruce, and Marsh, Dianne. *Atomic Scala: Learn Programming in a Language of the Future.* Crested Butte, CO: Mindview LLC, 2013.

[Bolt-on Causal Consistency] www.bailis.org/papers/bolton-sigmod2013.pdf

[Brewer-Inktomi] https://www.usenix.org/legacy/publications/library
/proceedings/ana97/summaries/brewer.html

[CAP] http://en.wikipedia.org/wiki/CAP_theorem

[Chaos Report] http://blog.standishgroup.com/post/18

[Coursera] www.coursera.org

[CQRS] http://martinfowler.com/bliki/CQRS.html

[CQS] http://en.wikipedia.org/wiki/Command%E2%80%93query_separation

[Cray-CDC] http://en.wikipedia.org/wiki/CDC_1604

[DDD] Evans, Eric. *Domain-Driven Design: Tackling Complexity in the
Heart of Software.* Boston: Addison-Wesley, 2004.

[DDJ] www.drdobbs.com/architecture-and-design
/2010-it-project-success-rates/226500046

[Dotsero Toolkit] https://github.com/VaughnVernon/Dotsero

[EDA-Verification] http://eprints.cs.univie.ac.at/3723/1/4.pdf

[EIP] Hohpe, Gregor, and Woolf, Bobby. *Enterprise Integration Patterns:
Designing, Building, and Deploying Messaging Solutions.* Boston:
Addison-Wesley, 2004.

[False-Sharing] http://psy-lob-saw.blogspot.com/2014/06
/notes-on-false-sharing.html

[Fowler EAA] Fowler, Martin. *Patterns of Enterprise Application Architecture.* Boston: Addison-Wesley, 2003.

[GoF] Gamma, Erich et al. *Design Patterns: Elements of Reusable
Object-Oriented Software.* Boston: Addison-Wesley, 1995.

[Google-Architecture] http://infolab.stanford.edu/~backrub/google.html

[Google-Owies] http://aphyr.com/posts/288-the-network-is-reliable

[Google-Platform] http://en.wikipedia.org/wiki/Google_platform

[Gossip Protocol] http://en.wikipedia.org/wiki/Gossip_protocol

[Herb Sutter] www.gotw.ca/publications/concurrency-ddj.htm

[Hewitt-ActorComp] http://arxiv.org/ftp/arxiv/papers/1008/1008.1459.pdf

[Horstmann] www.horstmann.com/scala/index.htm

[IBM-History] http://en.wikipedia.org/wiki/IBM_7090

[IBM-zEC12] http://en.wikipedia.org/wiki/IBM_zEC12_(microprocessor)

[IDDD] Vernon, Vaughn. *Implementing Domain-Driven Design.* Boston:
Addison-Wesley, 2013.

[Inktomi-Architecture] www.thefreelibrary.com/Inktomi+Unveils+Third
+Generation+Search+Architecture%3B+Inktomi...-a061423190

[Intel-FalseSharing] https://software.intel.com/en-us/articles
/avoiding-and-identifying-false-sharing-among-threads

[Kafka] http://kafka.apache.org

[Kay-DDJ] www.drdobbs.com/architecture-and-design
/interview-with-alan-kay/240003442?pgno=3

[Kay-Squeak] http://lists.squeakfoundation.org/pipermail
/squeak-dev/1998-October/017019.html

[Kryo] https://github.com/EsotericSoftware/kryo

[Mackay] www.doc.ic.ac.uk/~nd/surprise_97/journal/vol2/pjm2/

[Mechanical-Sympathy] http://mechanical-sympathy.blogspot.com/2011/08
/false-sharing-java-7.html

[Meyer-OOSC] Meyer, Bertrand. *Object-Oriented Software Construction, Second Edition.* Upper Saddle River, NJ: Prentice Hall, 1997.

[Moore's Law] http://en.wikipedia.org/wiki/Moore's_law

[Network-Partition] http://en.wikipedia.org/wiki/Network_partition

[Nitsan Wakart] http://psy-lob-saw.blogspot.com/2014/06
/notes-on-false-sharing.html

[OCM] http://en.wikipedia.org/wiki/Object-capability_model

[POSA1] Buschmann, Frank et al. *Pattern-Oriented Software Architecture Volume 1: A System of Patterns.* Hoboken, NJ: Wiley, 1996.

[ProtoBuf] https://github.com/google/protobuf/

[Reactive Manifesto] www.reactivemanifesto.org/

[Read-Write] readwrite.com/2014/07/10
/akka-jonas-boner-concurrency-distributed-computing-internet-of-things

[Retlang] https://code.google.com/p/retlang/

[Retlang-CTX] http://www.jroller.com/mrettig/entry
/lightweight_concurrency_in_net_similar

[Roestenburg] http://doc.akka.io/docs/akka/snapshot/scala/testkit-example.html

[sbt-Suereth] Suereth, Josh and Farwell, Matthew. *SBT in Action: The simple Scala build tool.* Shelter Island, NY: Manning Publications, 2015.

[ScalaTest] www.scalatest.org/

[SIS] http://en.wikipedia.org/wiki/Strategic_information_system

[Split-Brain] https://en.wikipedia.org/wiki/Split-brain_(computing)

[SRP] http://en.wikipedia.org/wiki/Single_responsibility_principle

[Suereth] Suereth, Joshua. *Scala in Depth.* Shelter Island, NY: Manning Publications, 2012.

[Tilkov-CDM] https://www.innoq.com/en/blog
/thoughts-on-a-canonical-data-model/

[Transistor Count] http://en.m.wikipedia.org/wiki/Transistor_count

[Transistor] http://en.wikipedia.org/wiki/History_of_the_transistor

[Triode] http://en.wikipedia.org/wiki/Triode

[Typesafe] http://typesafe.com

[Vogels-AsyncArch] www.webperformancematters.com/journal/2007/8/21/asynchronous-architectures-4.html

[Vogels-Scalability] www.allthingsdistributed.com/2006/03/a_word_on_scalability.html

[Westheide] www.parleys.com/play/53a7d2c6e4b0543940d9e54d

[WhitePages] http://downloads.typesafe.com/website/casestudies/Whitepages-Final.pdf?_ga=1.150961718.1894161222.1397685553

Index

Symbols

! (exclamation character), symbols as method names in tell() method, 47

Numbers

32-bit processors, 111
64-bit processors, 111

A

Actor base class
  Dotsero, 421
  Implementing Actors, 50
Actor model, introduction to, 4
  actions actors perform, 13
  characteristics of actors and actor systems, 13–15
  concurrency and parallelism in, 16–17
  contrasted with general messaging systems, 18–19
  controversy regarding unbounded nondeterminism, 21
  explicit nature of, 22–23
  extensions available with Akka, 15
  as finite state machines, 18
  managing nondeterministic systems, 19–21
  Object-Capability model (OCM), 21–22
  origin of actors, 11–13
  overview of, 10–11
  performance benefits of, 122–124
  performance benefits of being lock-free, 16
  Request-Reply pattern, 17–18
  using EIP patterns with, xv–xvi
Actor system (ActorSystem)
  canon required by, 335–336
  characteristics of actors, 13–15
  creating multiple instances, 45
  default actors, 45–47
  Dotsero actor system, 417–420
  finding actors, 48–50
  implementing actors, 50
  managing with Control Bus, 395
  methods, 50–52
  overview of, 44–45
  remote access between, 59–63
  shutting down Dotsero actor system, 418
  supervision of, 55–59
  TaskManager in implementation of actors, 52–54
  top-level supervisors, 47–48

ActorContext, implementing actors, 52–55
actorof() method, 47
ActorRef
  ActorSelection compared with, 68–70
  finding actors, 48–50
  Return Address pattern and, 212–213, 215
  as value holder, 47
Actors. *See also* Transactional Clients/Actors
  actions performed by, 13
  behavioral testing, 101–102
  C# and .NET, 420–425
  characteristics of, 13–15
  implementing, 50–55
  life-cycle methods, 51
  managing with Control Bus, 395
  Object-Capability model (OCM) and, 21–22
  origin of, 11–13
  persistent, 355–357
  transactional, 354–355
  transient behavior, 339–344
  UnboundedMailbox for, 411
  unit testing, 99–101
ActorScript, types of actor programming languages, 25
ActorSelection
  ActorRef compared with, 68–70
  Dotsero support for, 419
  finding actors, 48–50
  obstacle to use of Object-Capability model, 22
  remote lookup and, 68
Adapters [GoF]
  Envelope Wrapper and, 314
  Service Activators as, 391
advance() method, in Routing Slip example, 287
Aggregates (IDDD)
  Aggregate domain model, 13
  mapping to messages. *See* Messaging Mappers
  natural aggregates, 354
  in transactional design, 354
  transient behavior and, 339–344
Aggregators
  combined with Recipient List to create Composed Message Processor, 270, 284

433

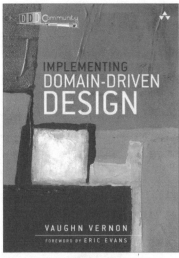